"For those unfamiliar with Asian Christianity, this collection of essays serves as an excellent introduction. It covers a range of topics, from an overview of the history of Christianity in Asia to specific contextual issues such as ecumenism and migration. The essays are judiciously chosen; some offer a bird's-eye view, while others give us a real feel of life on the ground. Overall, Sunquist makes the reader acutely aware of the complexity of Asian Christianity and the challenges it poses. It's a must-read for Christians aspiring to enter the borderlands of mission in Asia."

Simon Chan, Trinity Theological College, Singapore

"In this scholarly contribution to studies of church history, Professor Sunquist provides rich intellectual fare. He is a mature scholar with a comprehensive scope of vision that is evident all the way through this book. He has become one of the giants in the transition from a focus on Western missionaries to world Christianity."

Daniel H. Bays, professor emeritus, Spoelhof Endowed Chair, Calvin College

"*Explorations in Asian Christianity* cements Scott Sunquist's reputation as one of the most reliable and insightful storytellers of the many dimensions of Christianity in Asia. From first page to last, he brings into relief the reality that Christian history cannot be divorced from the study of mission, and that both the study of Scripture and Christian history as a whole are the story of Jesus-followers finding their identity in mission. Writing history in Sunquist's hands becomes profoundly theological. There is nothing like it to reveal to readers the depth and breadth of Asian Christianity and the way in which Asians have made it a vital Asian religion with many faces, not a remnant of Western colonialism. Of special value is the nuanced way in which Sunquist takes account of Catholic, classic Protestant, evangelical, and Pentecostal strands, and the ways in which they develop differently in different contexts."

William R. Burrows, managing editor emeritus, Orbis Books, research professor of missiology, New York Theological Seminary

"In these wide-ranging essays on the history, theory, and practice of Christian mission in Asia, Scott Sunquist challenges historians to take more seriously the normative theological commitments of the individuals, institutions, and movements they seek to represent. Attending to the cruciform shape of the apostolic witness, Sunquist combines a close reading of sources with careful reflection and insightful commentary. A must-read for all students of mission and world Christianity."

Thomas John Hastings, executive director, OMSC, editor, *International Bulletin of Mission Research*

EXPLORATIONS IN ASIAN CHRISTIANITY

History, Theology, and Mission

SCOTT W. SUNQUIST

An imprint of InterVarsity Press
Downers Grove, Illinois

InterVarsity Press
P.O. Box 1400, Downers Grove, IL 60515-1426
ivpress.com
email@ivpress.com

©2017 by Scott W. Sunquist

All rights reserved. No part of this book may be reproduced in any form without written permission from InterVarsity Press.

InterVarsity Press® is the book-publishing division of InterVarsity Christian Fellowship/USA®, a movement of students and faculty active on campus at hundreds of universities, colleges, and schools of nursing in the United States of America, and a member movement of the International Fellowship of Evangelical Students. For information about local and regional activities, visit intervarsity.org.

Scripture quotations, unless otherwise noted, are from the New Revised Standard Version of the Bible, copyright 1989 by the Division of Christian Education of the National Council of the Churches of Christ in the USA. Used by permission. All rights reserved.

Cover design: David Fassett
Interior design: Beth McGill
Images: The Raising of Lazarus, Watanabe, Sadao / Private Collection / Photo © Boltin Picture Library / Bridgeman Images

ISBN 978-0-8308-5100-3 (print)
ISBN 978-0-8308-9085-9 (digital)

Library of Congress Cataloging-in-Publication Data
Names: Sunquist, Scott W. (Scott William), 1953- author.
Title: Explorations in Asian Christianity : history, theology, and mission / Scott W. Sunquist.
Description: Downers Grove, IL : InterVarsity Press, 2017. | Series: Missiological engagements | Includes bibliographical references and index.
Identifiers: LCCN 2017000169 (print) | LCCN 2017000762 (ebook) | ISBN 9780830851003 (pbk.) | ISBN 9780830890859 (eBook)
Subjects: LCSH: Asia--Church history. | Missions--Asia. | Christian education--Asia.
Classification: LCC BR1065 .S86 2017 (print) | LCC BR1065 (ebook) | DDC 275--dc23
LC record available at https://lccn.loc.gov/2017000169

| P | 23 | 22 | 21 | 20 | 19 | 18 | 17 | 16 | 15 | 14 | 13 | 12 | 11 | 10 | 9 | 8 | 7 | 6 | 5 | 4 | 3 | 2 | 1 |
| Y | 37 | 36 | 35 | 34 | 33 | 32 | 31 | 30 | 29 | 28 | 27 | 26 | 25 | 24 | 23 | 22 | 21 | 20 | 19 | 18 | 17 | | |

These essays are dedicated to the students, faculty, and institutions who heard much of this material over the past fifteen years. I am grateful for the opportunities I have had to learn from all of you, and to know of the great work these schools continue to do in building up the Asian church.

Trinity Theological College, Republic of Singapore
TCA College, Republic of Singapore
Sabah Theological Seminary, Kota Kinabalu, Sabah, Malaysia
Presbyterian University and Theological Seminary, Seoul, South Korea
Yonsei University, Seoul, South Korea
McGilvery Faculty of Theology at Payap University, Chiang Mai, Thailand
Nanjing Union Theological Seminary, Nanjing, China
Shandong Theological Seminary, Jinan, China
Colombo Theological Seminary, Colombo, Sri Lanka
Myanmar Institute of Theology, Insein, Yangon, Myanmar

Contents

Acknowledgments	ix
INTRODUCTION	1
PART I: ASIA	
1 Christianity in Asia	11
2 Ancient Christianity in Asia	27
3 Ecumenism in Asia: Movements of Christian Unity	41
4 Evangelicalism in Asia	53
PART II: HISTORY	
5 *Missio Dei*: Christian History Envisioned as Cruciform Apostolicity	89
6 The Century That Changed the Religious Map: 1910–2010	107
7 Time, Lectures, and Redemption: The Princeton Student Mission Lectures	127
8 World Christianity: Transforming Church History and Theology	143
PART III: MISSIOLOGY	
9 Underwood, Moffett, and Korean Liberation: Making Sense of Early Korean Protestantism	167
10 The Importance of Shandong: A Missiological Evaluation of *Place*	179
11 Four Theorists, Three Selfs, Two Countries, One Goal: Missionary Practice in China and Korea	203
12 Mission and Migration: An Introductory Theology	225

Part IV: Education

  13 Moffett, Mateer, and McClure: Three Models,
     Two Continents, One Mission   249

  14 American Theological Education and Mission:
     Henry W. Luce, William R. Harper, and the
     Secularization of Christian Higher Education   263

  15 Asian Theological Education: Earliest Trajectories,
     Contemporary Concerns   281

Bibliography   303

Author Index   313

Subject Index   315

Acknowledgments

This volume is a product of communities of Christian scholars, and I wish to give many of the people in those communities credit for directing and redirecting my thinking about Christian mission, Christian development, and more specifically about Asian Christianity. The communities have included conferences, seminars, projects, and informal gatherings. I have been greatly helped by these people, some of whom I would like to mention here as a way of thanking them for aiding my vision by turning my head to movements, people, and themes I had not thought of.

First, the community that gathered around the development of *History of the World Christian Movement* project was a remarkable and talented group. Most important in challenging my thinking were Dale Irvin and Bill Burrows. I owe Dale and Bill not only for challenging my thinking at many levels, but possibly more importantly for introducing me to other wonderful Christian scholars who became my friends and my critics. Among the most influential have been Peter Phan, Ana María Bidegain, Charles Amjad-Ali, Akintunde E. Akinade, Klaus Koschorke, Peter Tze Ming Ng, Pablo Deiros, Steven Bevans, Roger Schroeder, Andrew Walls, Paul Kollman, David Daniels, and my most helpful African scholar, Ogbu Kalu (d. 2009). Many others were involved over the course of a decade in special conferences and group editing. It was a most remarkable moveable feast of global historical scholarship. Not all will agree with the direction I headed from that formative community, but many will hear some familiar tunes between these covers.

An earlier community that provided guidance in my thinking about Christianity in Asia was the faculty of Trinity Theological College in Singapore, an international and very ecumenical faculty devoted to equipping Christian leaders from over fifteen Asian nations. I learned much from our gatherings, both formal and informal. Most influential for me were Anglican archbishop John Chew, Choong Chee Pang, Methodist bishop Robert Solomon,[1] Simon Chan, David Wu, Walter Hansen, Lau Jen Sin, Lee Chong Kau, and the many students from Southeast and eastern Asia who wrote their church or national church histories for my Asian church history class. Many of my ideas and sensitivities came from reading these student papers.

During my time in Singapore I began work on an eleven-year project that became *A Dictionary of Asian Christianity*. Thus my third community is an intimate gathering of about 485 scholars, mostly from Asia. The idea for the project came from the lack of interest that Asian students had in Asian Christianity. So I began, with the help of John Chew and David Wu, to collect terms for the dictionary by traveling to thirteen countries and meeting with local Christian scholars, mostly historians. The project was not completed until I returned to the States to teach. However, after eleven years of reading articles about Christianity in Asia, I gained a new and more intimate appreciation of the unique history of Asian Christianity. The names of the people in this community are found in the front of the *Dictionary*.

Other communities where I have learned have been (generally) two- to three-hour sessions at professional societies. I have sought out panel discussions or spoken on Asian panel discussions at meetings of the American Society of Church History, the American Society of Missiology, and the American Academy of Religion. Each session has been for me a community of learning, before, during, and after the panel or presentation.

Finally, I have benefited greatly from my students: first my students for seventeen years at Pittsburgh Theological Seminary and now my PhD students at Fuller Theological Seminary during the past four years. All of my students have been from Asia. Reading the tutorial papers and theses has greatly enhanced my understanding of the love and care of these Asian scholars for the churches in their homelands. So I am indebted to my students: Lu Shi Min, Jong Jin Park (Barak), Kim Son Nguyen, Yukikazu Obata, Joenita Paulrajan, Jimmy Tan, and Kwon Hanjun.

Books like this do not get written and edited without two important real-

---

[1]Both Archbishop Chew and Bishop Solomon became bishops after teaching at TTC.

ities: a seminary administration that values deans keeping up their scholarship and an understanding and supportive wife. I am blessed with both. So I thank President Mark Labberton, former Provost Doug McConnell, School of Intercultural Studies staff, Wendy Walker, and Silvia Gutierrez. Once again, I thank my wife, Nancy, for her support and encouragement in another project. I have been very blessed.

This book, as the fifth book in the Missiological Engagements series, owes much to a great collegial relationship with Amos Yong. Thank you, Amos, for your steady editorial eye and encouragement in all things missiological.

Finally, I have been helped greatly in thinking about this volume and in its early editing by my thoughtful, careful, and kind son-in-law, Timothy J. Becker. I could not have pulled this together without his attention to detail and helpful suggestions. Dr. Becker made this book possible. Thank you, Tim.

Original Presentations of the Chapters

Most of the essays in this volume began as lectures, chapters in books, or journal articles. I am thankful for the many opportunities to reflect on Asian Christianity, missiology, and historiography (and their various nexus) at conferences and in journals. All of these essays have been sharpened through the academic discourse at conferences like those mentioned above, as well as the Bicentennial Celebration of Robert Morrison and the Centennial lecture series for the Presbyterian College in Seoul.

"Christianity in Asia" was first published in *Christianity: The Complete Guide*, edited by John Bowden. London: Continuum Publishing, 2005. Used by permission of Bloomsbury Publishing Plc.

"Ancient Christianity in Asia" was first published in *Blackwell Companion to World Christianity*, edited by Lamin Sanneh and Michael McClymond. Malden, MA: Wiley Blackwell, 2016. © 2016 John Wiley & Sons Ltd.

"Evangelicalism in Asia" was first published in *Global Evangelicalism: Theology, History and Culture in Regional Perspective*, edited by Donald M. Lewis and Richard V. Pierard, 197-231. Downers Grove, IL: IVP Academic, 2014.

"Evangelicalism in Asia" was first published in *Global Evangelicalism: Theology, History and Culture in Regional Perspective*, edited by Ogbu Kalu, Mark A. Noll, René Padilla, Scott Sunquist, Sarah Williams, et al., 197-231. Downers Grove, IL: IVP Academic, 2014.

"*Missio Dei*: Christian History Envisioned as Cruciform Apostolicity" was a lecture first delivered at the American Society of Missiology in 2008 and then published in *Missiology*, January 2009.

"The Century That Changed the Religious Map: 1910–2010" was a lecture delivered to church leaders in Port Elizabeth, South Africa, in 2010.

"Time, Lectures, and Redemption: The Princeton Student Mission Lectures" was one of the lectures delivered at Princeton Theological Seminary for the Student Mission Lectures series in October 2009.

"World Christianity: Transforming Church History and Theology" was a chapter written for the festschrift for Peter Phan and is published in the volume *World Christianity: Perspectives and Insights*, edited by Jonathan Y. Tan and Anh Q. Tran. Maryknoll, NY: Orbis, 2016.

"Underwood, Moffett, and Korean Liberation: Making Sense of Early Korean Protestantism" was a talk delivered at the American Society of Church History in 2002 and published in the volume *A Graced Horizon: Essays in Gospel, Culture and Church in Honour of the Rev. Dr. Choong Chee Pang*, edited by Roland Chia and Mark Chan, 178-85. Singapore: Genesis Books, 2005.

"The Importance of Shandong: A Missiological Evaluation of *Place*" was a lecture first delivered in Hong Kong at the bicentennial celebration of Robert Morrison's arrival in China. It was later published in *Ching Feng: A Journal on Christianity and Chinese Religion and Culture* 8, nos. 1–2 (2007): 131-52.

"Four Theorists, Three Selfs, Two Countries, One Goal: Missionary Practice in China and Korea" was a lecture delivered for graduate students at Nanjing Union Theological Seminary in 2006. It was translated by Zhao Hongiun and published in Chinese as 四个理论家,三自,两个国家,一个目标——中国和韩国的宣教实践, *Nanjing Theological Journal* 4 (2015).

"Mission and Migration: An Introductory Theology" was part of a lecture delivered at a mission conference at Sabah Theological Seminary and was later published in the festschrift for Dr. Thu En Yu, principal of STS: *Cross-Cultural Affection: Festschrift in Honour of Dr. Thu En Yu*. Kota Kinabalu: Sabah Theological Seminary, 2014.

"Moffett, Mateer, and McClure: Three Models, Two Continents, One Mission" was first published in *Pittsburgh Theological Seminary Journal*, Spring 2010. Used with permission of *Pittsburgh Theological Seminary Journal*.

"American Theological Education and Mission: Henry W. Luce, William R. Harper, and the Secularization of Christian Higher Education" was a lecture delivered at the sixth international conference of the North East Asia Council of Studies of History of Christianity in August 2007 in Seoul, South Korea, and later published in *Christian Mission and Education in Modern China, Japan and Korea: Historical Studies*, edited by Jan A. B. Jongeneel, Peter Tze Ming Ng, Chong Ku Paek, Scott W. Sunquist, and Yuko Watanabe. Frankfurt am Main: Peter Lang, 2009.

"Asian Theological Education: Earliest Trajectories, Contemporary Concerns" was published in a longer form as "Asian Theological Education: The Long View" in *A Cultured Faith: Essays in Honour of Prof. G. P. V. Somaratna on His Seventieth Birthday*, edited by Prabo Mihindukulasuriya, Ivor Poobalan, and Ravin Caldera, 197-224. Colombo: CTS Publishing, 2011.

Introduction

ASIAN CHRISTIANITY AND THE WORLD

Christianity began in Asia, but Asia has been the least hospitable region for Jesus and his followers. In the earliest centuries Christianity spread as rapidly east as it did to the west, and in some regions it was received much more pleasantly than among European communities. But, as we all know, that was the exception and not the rule. Jesus was born near the eastern edge of the Roman Empire, where one of the most precious of provinces was fought over again and again: Syria. To control Syria was to have access to Asian travel routes that brought in goods from Central Asia, India, and beyond. However, the Persian Empire under the Parthians was not easily defeated.

In contrast to the Romans, whose pluralism was anchored in the emperor cult, the Parthians were true pluralists, and so Christianity flourished in a truly pluralist society.[1] Although the Parthians converted to the Zoroastrian faith, Parthians as well as their rulers were a tolerant lot, studying the stars to determine the time and meaning of events, but also maintaining sacred fires in each district. Zoroastrianism in the early Christian centuries was an overlay to a myriad of local beliefs. "A Parthian Peace" is something Christians cherished, but seldom would this type of tolerance be experienced again in Asia. For ancient and even medieval cultures, a "people" or nation had a religion, and a king (or empress) enforced and guided the common faith for all the subjects: *cuius regio, eius religio* is the expression that was used for this arrangement in Christendom Europe. In Europe, Christians were fortunate enough to live where many of the rulers became Christian and enforced

---

[1] See, for example, *The Gospel and Pluralism Today: Reassessing Lesslie Newbigin in the 21st Century*, ed. Scott W. Sunquist and Amos Yong (Grand Rapids: Baker Academic, 2015). Newbigin, in his 1989 volume *The Gospel in a Pluralist Society* (Grand Rapids: Eerdmans), was one of the first to make a sustained argument for the value of a pluralist society for the Christian church.

Christian belief. Thus Christianity thrived as a royal religion. Asia was different. Asia has always been different in its expression of Christianity. In every other continent, even in the islands of the Pacific, Christianity has grown in large part by the support or protection of rulers. This was not the experience of Asian Christians.[2] I don't think we can emphasize this too much.

Upon the rise of the Sasanian Empire in Persia in the early third century, a purified or fundamentalist form of Zoroastrianism prevailed. This was followed by Arab invasions—ironically they were monotheists, but not Christians—so the Persian Christian community took two blows and never fully recovered. Christianity in Persia, as well as in India, turned into struggling *millet* or ghetto communities that were cut off from broader participation (and evangelization) in society. With the rise of Islam in the Middle East, Asia, and North Africa, the Christian West was cut off from social intercourse with Asian Christian communities east of Palestine. The ecumenical support of Persian Christianity and its church-planting efforts in China—something of vital importance for Christianity anywhere—was also lost. By the time European Christians regained contact with Persian and Indian communities, fellowship was strained or, even worse, completely broken. Christianity did not seem to find a home in Asia, or so it seemed.

Four Themes, One Interest

Over the past few decades I have been writing, reading, and speaking about the history of Christianity as a worldwide movement and about how we now must study Christianity in a postcolonial context. In this endeavor I have been helped by some of the premier Christian historians from Africa, Latin America, and Asia. Many of their names are mentioned in the acknowledgments. The volume you hold is focused on Asia; we have one interest, and that is to better understand Asian Christianity from many perspectives. This is a mosaic of essays, lectures, chapters, and articles that I have written related to Asian Christianity, but more specifically about the surprising and unique themes of Asian Christianity that have shaped and been shaped by world Christianity. I focus on four themes that I trust will draw the reader in to think more carefully about the uniqueness of Asian Christianity and the ways

---

[2]The few exceptions are notable because they are exceptions: Armenia, prefectures in Japan for a century, and the Philippines.

Introduction 3

we can approach our subject. The four themes are Asian surveys, historiography, missiology, and education. The one concern is Asian Christianity.

ASIAN SURVEYS

I have had the opportunity to study and envision Asian Christianity from many angles; four are mentioned in this first section. The first essay has a rather bland title but interesting story: "Christianity in Asia." This essay looks at some of the unique features of Christianity in Asia and traces the various developments and periods of decline. It lays the groundwork for the rest of the book. This essay should be read first, as a type of overview of all that follows. The second survey focuses just on the first eight centuries of Christianity as Jesus struggled to find a home from Jerusalem in the West to Xian in the East. It is a unique story in the history of Christianity because the earliest conversions of rulers were in Asia, but then there was a slow decline in the midst of creative and persistent missionary outreach.

The third essay, "Ecumenism in Asia," skips to the modern period of the nineteenth and twentieth centuries and reveals a checkered history of Christian unity and division in Asia. Many external forces were acting on Asian leaders and their churches. Much can be learned about unity today from this chapter, but we also learn about the uniqueness of the Asian ecumenical experience, guided by Christians' minority status, colonialism, communism, and Japanese imperialism. The final chapter (4) in part one focuses on another large slice of the Christian church in Asia, and that is evangelicalism. I use the term *evangelicalism* because it is a helpful summary of the mission churches that were energized by revivals and renewals in the West. They were "evangelical," which meant focusing on conversion, teaching the Bible in local languages, activism in local cultures, and the clear preaching of the cross.[3]

Protestant mission to Asia, the third of four waves of Christianity to Asia,[4] was more extensive, varied, and "democratic" than earlier forms of Christianity, and its impact on societies has been greater than its numbers. The vast majority, but not all, of these Protestant missions were evangelical.

---

[3]See David Bebbington, *Evangelicalism in Modern Britain: A History from the 1730s to the 1980s* (London: Unwin Hyman, 1989), 2-17.

[4]The first wave was the Syrian and Persian wave, the second was the Roman Catholic (during the age of exploration and reformation), the third was Protestant, and the final wave is the Asian evangelization of other Asian countries. See chapter one in this volume for more details.

Protestant missions were a very diverse lot. The more evangelical London Missionary Society was different from the Church Mission Society or the Society for the Propagation of the Gospel in Foreign Parts. The Mennonite Central Committee was different from the China Inland Mission (now the Overseas Missionary Fellowship). Reading chapters three and four in one sitting helps to see some of the Christian streams together that have been flowing throughout Asia.

History

Part two of this volume steps back and looks at how we study history and how we can or should view Christianity as a global movement. Along with the friends mentioned in the acknowledgments section, I have been involved in rethinking how we study, envision, and write about Christianity as a worldwide Christian movement. In part two I look at this type of historiography, more focused on "development" than "growth," more attuned to "movement" than "institutions," more sensitive to cultural or contextual matters than in the past, and always looking to Asia. The first essay in part two (chapter five), "*Missio Dei:* Christian History Envisioned as Cruciform Apostolicity," has one of the worst titles, but I think one of the more provocative themes. I posit that Christianity, its development through the ages, must be understood as a record of the mission of God in cruciformity. Asia, the continent with the greatest persecutions of Christians, illustrates this perspective well. Cruciformity is in stark contrast to earlier progressive models such as the work of most historicists.

Let me explain. As much as I have benefited from the great and expansive writing of Kenneth Scott Latourette[5] through the years, this essay (chapter five) and others in this section break away from Latourette's historiography and its periodic cycles of advance and recession. The second essay in this section (chapter six) explains some of the reasons for the shift. I am writing in the twenty-first century, and Latourette and others were writing in the middle of the twentieth century. What happened at the end of the twentieth

---

[5]Latourette's knowledge of mission was both expansive and detailed. I have heard from a reliable source (from a former editor, in fact) that when Stephen Neill was lecturing at Union Theological Seminary in Richmond, Virginia, in about 1964, he made the side comment that he had sent his manuscript of *A History of Christian Missions* to Latourette for comments. Latourette's response was positive but brief: "It is an excellent volume. I have only found two factual errors."

century globally was completely unpredicted and unprecedented.[6] For the first time Christianity began to develop uniquely Asian clothes and habits. Chapter six outlines some of these changes, which were as great as in any of the previous nineteen centuries. Actually most of the dramatic changes took place only after 1950, or even 1960. The other two chapters in part two elaborate further the shifts in historical thinking that are required in light of the experience of the twentieth century, and also in light of newer reflections on Scripture born of our experiences in the twentieth century.

Chapter seven develops an important theme for Asian Christianity: a unique feature of Christianity that challenges most Asian religious cosmologies. Most religions and cultures throughout time (ironically) have a cyclical view of time. Christianity challenges these basic assumptions and gives hope through the teaching of a God who created, redeems, and brings all things to perfection. Time as moving toward a goal and consummation transforms cultures. It is this concept that is explored using the missiology lectures and Asian Christianity as the backdrop. Chapter eight, the final chapter in part two, looks at how the recent shift from the study of "church history" to world Christianity has transformed not only how we view Christianity but also how we study theology and ethics.

Missiology

As it should become clear from reading part two, I do not believe the writing of Christian history should be divorced from missiology or the study of the mission of God. Just as there is a missional trajectory to all of the Bible, in a similar manner Christian history also has a missional trajectory. Although it is possible (and common) to study Christian history without the lens of missiology, it is a little misleading. I suggest that the trajectory of the church given to us from the life of Jesus, through the Acts of the Apostles and the New Testament letters (and even Revelation), shows that the nations and a "kingdom" are in view; the cross is the foundation. Thus, in part three I build on part two (history) and look at some historical vignettes in Asia through the lens of mission encounters.

---

[6]For a fuller explanation of this unpredicted, unprecedented, and unexpected history, see my volume *The Unexpected Christian Century: The Reversal and Transformation of Global Christianity, 1900–2000* (Grand Rapids: Baker Academic, 2015).

The first essay (chapter nine) attempts to answer the question, "How could a conservative Christian church, started by fairly conservative Presbyterian missionaries, develop almost liberationist perspectives on society and politics?" The answer involves politics, theology, and particular actors in Korea. To this day a fairly conservative church (theologically speaking) has a strong political life of resistance. The second article (chapter ten) is a missiological experiment that can be carried out in other important regions in Asia. I develop a "missiology of place" for a province in China, Shandong. Although Hong Kong and Beijing (and even Guandong and Shanghai) have been important for Christian development in China, I make the argument that the province of Shandong, for reasons of geography, topography, history, and religion, is the most significant location, missiologically, for China. It would be interesting and even enlightening to do the same for Singapore or for the Korean peninsula.

Chapter eleven is a missiological comparison of four mission theorists who served in two countries (China and Korea). How did the same general theory (three-self principle) work out so very differently in two countries that are so close that their histories are intertwined? The unique perspective of a Korean missionary sent to analyze what was going on in China sheds light on this anomaly. Chapter twelve focuses on another important and newer theme in mission studies: migration. Asia as much as any place in the world has seen migration as a central theme for the development of Christianity. This essay is a type of primer for thinking about the history, theology, and meaning of migration and Christian mission. In some ways the tables have been turned, missiologically speaking. Instead of Jesus saying "Go" to Christians, he is saying "Go" to the nations. With over 240 million people living outside their country of birth (Asia has 30 percent of those migrants), it is clear that the study of migration and mission will continue to be vital for the study of missiology. This essay shows the common theme of migration from Genesis 3 to the present and points to how Christian mission needs to frame how we think about migration theologically.

EDUCATION

Part four focuses on one of the key elements of Christian life and one of the most important tools in the toolbox of missionary work: education. These three articles are disparate but are held together by the important question: What is appropriate and effective Christian education for Asia? The first essay (chapter thirteen) is a comparative article, looking at three missionaries who worked in three different countries in two continents over the course of a century. There are some great differences, but also some common and very interesting similarities. I do not pretend to be objective and detached about this or the other two chapters in this section on education. I have invested my career in theological education, and I believe we have much to learn from those who have gone before us. One of the great lessons of history is that humanity does not just keep getting smarter and better: we forget a lot, and in these essays I suggest we would serve the church much better if we remembered some of these earlier lessons about education.

The second essay in this section (chapter fourteen) was originally a lecture given at the Sixth International Conference of the North East Asia Council of Studies of History of Christianity (NEACSHC), held in Seoul in 2007. I was given the task of giving an overview of Christian higher education in East Asia. The topic was much too large, so when I began to focus it became clear that one of the most important themes that dramatically changed higher education was the broader Western and now global phenomenon of secularization. This raises many questions regarding contextualization and social change, as well as cultural power and cultural imperialism. The final essay (chapter fifteen) returns us to the beginning of the book and a discussion of earliest Asian Christianity. In this case the question I look at is this: What was the earliest Christian education like in Asia (mostly in Persia), and in what way was it shaped by larger cultural and social factors? Not until I re-edited this chapter did I realize that, both in twentieth-century China and in sixth-century Persia, Christian education was influenced by "the West." It is just another reminder that culturally narrow Christian development is an anomaly. Christianity is always growing, developing, and moving in the folds of overlapping cultures. Negotiating these borderlands in light of the gospel and Christian tradition is much of what Asian Christianity is about. In fact this dynamic is what makes Christian mission and history fascinating and important, but also vital for human societies.

PART I

Asia

1

Christianity in Asia

PREFACE

Asia is both the birthplace of Christianity and the continent where the followers of Jesus are most persecuted. With only about 8 or 9 percent of the continent Christian, it is the least Christianized region of the world. And yet because Asia has such a huge population, this 8 percent amounts to over 315 million Christians, and the numbers are growing. It is important to remember that, unlike Europe, the Americas, the Pacific, and many countries of Africa, there is only one nation in Asia that can be considered a Christian nation: the Philippines. The diversity of Christianity in Asia is a product of the size of the continent (over 45 million square kilometers compared to 30 million square kilometers for Africa), the diversity of languages (31 percent of the world's languages), varied geography, and ancient religions and kingdoms. All of the major "world religions" originated in Asia, and most of the world's ancient empires have been found in Asia. Christianity is at home in Asia, but it has always been a home as a nomadic or refugee existence rather than as in a palace or among royalty. A sign of this nomadic Christian existence in Asia can be seen in the shifting centers of Christianity: from Jerusalem to Antioch to Edessa to Selucia-Ctesiphon to Malabar and today to places such as Seoul, Singapore, Sabah, and Xiamen. Christianity is a guest in Asia and often an unwelcome or misunderstood guest. History reveals for us something of why Christianity is still such a minority faith but also why it is more "Asian" today than it has ever been.

EARLIEST HISTORY

Before the massive persecutions under the great empires of the Romans, Persians, and Arabs, Christianity was spreading at a very rapid rate in west and central Asia. Although early evangelization in Asia outside the Roman

Empire is shrouded in myth and mystery, it is clear that the smaller kingdoms of Armenia, Adiabene, and Osrhoene were evangelized in the first century, and all became Christian by the beginning of the third century. These were smaller kingdoms, however, that were dominated by the larger empires of Persia and Rome, and later by the Arabs and Ottoman Turks. Persia, until about 225 CE, was controlled by the Parthians, a tolerant people who were mostly Zoroastrian. Thus, there was a greater acceptance of Christianity in Persia under this "Parthian Peace" than in the Roman Empire under the "Pax Romana." Parthians were, however, powerful people who prevented the spread of Roman rule to the east and who ruled from Syria to India and as far north as present-day Afghanistan. Both land and sea trade routes were open to the east, and so Christians spread the new faith as they traveled.

Parthians, and then after 225, the Sasanians, who next ruled Persia, were Zoroastrians. Christian monks and priests, often converts from Zoroastrianism, were trained at first in Edessa and Nisibis, and later in many monastic schools throughout Mesopotamia. Education was in Syriac and followed the liturgical calendar. Unlike the Hellenistic and Latin forms of theology that developed in the Roman Empire, early Asian theology and preaching was more "Semitic" and poetic. Theological development differed as a result of language and cultural surroundings. The Asian church also inherited and embraced many of the divisions of the Western church, and so two main streams—an east Syrian or "Nestorian" stream, and a west Syrian or "Jacobite" church—flourished in the Parthian and early Sasanian periods. In spite of the terrible persecutions of the fourth century, the Persian church sent out missionaries, or wandering monks, who traveled across the rooftop of Asia to the Middle Kingdom: China. The first of these east Syrian monks arrived in the Chinese Tang capital of Xian (Sian-fu) in the year 635, and soon thereafter it is likely that Christians from Persia reached the Pacific Ocean. Thus, Christian missionaries were officially received in China nearly 350 years before they would be received in Scandinavia.

The early spread of Christianity to India is generally related to the legend of St. Thomas. This legend comes down to us in at least three traditions, but all record the doubting disciple of Jesus as having gone, or been sent, to the East. Whether Thomas actually planted the St. Thomas Church in southeast India (south of Madras) and was martyred by angry Hindus in the late first century is debatable. What is not debatable is that Christianity has been present in south India from at least the second century CE, because third-century records describe this story. These records would not have been preserved if Christian communities had not been present in India as proof of the histories. Thus, Indian Christianity is among the oldest continuing lines of Christianity, preserving much of the second-century liturgy in the Syriac language.

In these early centuries Christianity also spread to the south: Arabia. In this region there were trade routes that passed from the eastern Mediterranean south to Yemen and across the Red Sea to the kingdom of Ethiopia. By the fifth century an internecine struggle was taking place in Arabia between the Christianity of Constantinople (Orthodox) and the two streams from Persia: west Syrian and east Syrian. In the midst of these struggles a new monotheism, Islam, developed, making these tragic Christian arguments irrelevant.

CHRISTIANITY, MISSION, AND THE RISE OF ISLAM (627–1400)

The history of Christianity in Asia is a long, difficult history of advance, suppression, compromise, new advance, more suppression, and sudden development. In Persia, the very age of the missionary expansion coincided with the age of Arab-Muslim conquest. Even as Zoroastrianism was in decline and Christianity was growing, the Persians were conquered by the sudden advance of Arabs from the south and west. At first this seemed to be a moment of liberation for Persian Christians, for their enemy had been conquered, and Christians (understood by the Arabs as monotheistic allies) were valued both as "People of the Book" and as responsible civil servants: jailers, accountants, and scribes. Over the course of the next five hundred years, Islam would slowly grow, both in land area and in local influence. Christianity was slowly but firmly isolated into ghetto or *millet* (*dhimmi*) communities, which cut them off from both social influence and Christian witness. Non-Muslims paid double taxes and were restricted in their movements and in building religious buildings. This has been the history of Christian communities in much of west Asia (Syria, Iran, Iraq, Pakistan) up to the present. The pattern was set in the seventh century. As a result of this restricting influence on Christianity in Arabia and Persia, the followers of Jesus survived, but only as isolated and restricted communities.

While the missionary bases in centers such as Nisibis, Kirkuk, Mosel, Arbela, and environs were succumbing to Arab Islamic restrictions, the missionary activity of these Asian churches was waxing strong. Bishoprics were established throughout central Asia, from Nishapur in northern Persia, across Sogdia in Bokhara, Samarkand, and Tashkent, to the western regions of present-day China. These early Chinese Christian communities began translating Christian writings, explaining Christian teachings in the form of sutras, and building monasteries in many if not all provinces of the Middle Kingdom. Evidence of seventh- through tenth-century Christianity in China is still being discovered along the "Old Silk Road" as well as in major cities like Xian. Best known among the artifacts of this early spread of Christianity in east Asia is the "Nestorian Monument," which records the arrival of Christianity from the West by a Syrian monk named Alopen in 635. The large public monument (over three meters tall) also gives an outline of Christian teachings, a history of the spread of Christianity in China, praise for the Tang rulers, and then a brief apologetic explaining that Christianity is good for the empire: "If there is only a Way [Tao] and no Sage, it [the Tao] will not expand. If there is a Sage and no Way, nothing great will result. When a Way and Sage are found together, then the whole Empire is cultured and enlightened." The Emperor Tai Tsung, the monument announces, was such a sage, and so the whole country benefited from the teaching of the Christian way (Tao). However, Christianity did not prosper for long. Whereas the west Asian Islamic restrictions on Christianity in Asia were passive, persistent, and pervasive, the Buddhist persecution against all other religions in China was sudden and strong. The tolerant and supportive Tang Dynasty collapsed in 907, and in its wake the violent era of the Ten Kingdoms and Five Dynasties arrived. Virtually no Christian presence among the Han Chinese survived. Once again, Christianity had a start in an Asian empire, but the reversal of imperial favor initiated a sudden decline.

By the beginning of the second millennium Christianity seemed to be limited in Asia to small pockets of communities surrounded by Muslim, Hindu, or Buddhist national religions. Armenia continued to be Christian, but it, along with the rapidly declining Christian center of Constantinople, was the sole exception as a Christian empire. All other Christian centers were island communities. Although the Han Chinese had officially rejected the

"Luminous Religion," some of the smaller east Asian nations continued to have fairly large east Syrian Christian communities. As the Mongol Empire was expanding it absorbed some of these groups, most notably the Kereits. Many of these Kereit Christians rose to leadership in the religiously tolerant Mongol Empire. But when the *Ilkhan* of Persia, Ghazan, rejected religious toleration (1295) for the one religion of Islam, Christian hopes faded. By the fourteenth century the Mongol toleration was replaced by the Turkic-Muslim fanaticism and violence of Tamerlane (Timur: 1363–1405). Thus, on the eve of Spanish and Portuguese exploration and colonization, Christianity in Asia was probably at its weakest point since the second century.

It is interesting to note that during the first twelve hundred years of Christian history in Asia, the Asian churches had virtually no contact with European Christians. Contact was greatly restricted by the imperial divisions (Roman versus Persian empires) and later by both politics and theology (most of the Asian churches followed minority christological formulas rejected in the West). One exception to this generalization was the restrained attempt of the papacy to contact, encourage, and build the Christian communities in central Asia from 1245 until 1346. Ten separate missions of mostly Franciscan friars were sent out during this time to the court of the Yuan (Mongol) emperors (Khans). These embassies are something of a historian's curiosity, but their impact was very small, being limited to the minority people (mostly Mongols) who were overthrown in 1368.

History During European and Asian Colonialisms

It was contact with the global Christian community that marked a whole new chapter of Christianity in Asia. This new contact was a mixed blessing. On one hand, the arrival of the Portuguese was an encouragement to the struggling Christian communities in south India. On the other hand, the Portuguese and later the Spanish in east Asia brought a militant and domineering form of Christianity that was new to Asia. Asian Christians had always been minority communities, dominated by militant Zoroastrian, Hindu, Buddhist, or Muslim cultures. The Portuguese came as militant Christian sailors. The goals of the Portuguese, however, were not always the same as the local Christians. Indian Christians found the Portuguese helpful in defending the Christian communities against Muslim rulers, but rather a nuisance in their desire to make them European Christians, subservient to the pope. Elsewhere, in Ceylon (Sri Lanka), Malacca, Siam (Thailand), Japan, and over to Macao, the Portuguese established their "shoestring empire" for trade and profit. Missionary work was of little interest to the captains and sailors. Religious orders, however, were quick to see the opportunities for missionary outreach. At first congregations such as the Augustinians, Franciscans, and Dominicans found their way on the Portuguese schooners, but the most innovative and newest order, the Society of Jesus (Jesuits, 1540), was the fastest growing and had the greatest impact on the way missionary work would be done in Asia.

A pattern of contextualization, pioneered by the early Jesuit father Francis Xavier (1506–1552), meant that missionary work would look different in different contexts. What this meant for Japan—bringing expensive gifts and wearing silk, rather than cotton, robes—was quite different from what it meant in India as carried out by Roberto de Nobili (1577–1656). Jesuits, like the later Protestants in Asia, pressed beyond the safe regions of the European colonies. Matteo Ricci (1552–1610) studied the Confucian classics and earned the respect of royalty and literati alike, carrying out Christian witness in the shadow of the emperor. His literary works were published in Peking, and in time Korean Confucianists, making their pilgrimages to the Chinese capital, discovered some of these Confucian-Christian writings and brought them back to Seoul. Thus, the earliest known Christian movement in Korea was spread from Peking, through Chinese works written by an Italian who studied missionary theory in India.

Another Jesuit, Alexandre de Rhodes (1592?–1660), presented the Christian faith in Vietnam, devising a script and a new catechism that spoke to the Vietnamese situation. Vietnam had some of the most rapid growth of Christianity in all of Asia up to the modern period. In many countries of Asia the Jesuit approach of accommodation came in conflict with the classic approach, especially of the Dominicans and Franciscans. By the early decades of the seventeenth century, Christianity was having the greatest impact ever on east and southeast Asia. This time the sudden decline in Christianity in areas such as Japan and China was not only the result of foreign governments or religious persecution; it was also the result of intrachurch conflict. The papacy ruled that the Jesuit contextual approach allowed for too much accommodation, and so their approach was no longer approved. Christianity went on a rapid decline in China, as the only form of Christianity that was acceptable to the empire was not approved by the papacy, and the only form approved by the papacy (Dominican) was not approved by the Chinese emperor. In Japan the new Tokugawa Shogunate unified the empire and persecuted Christianity (beginning 1614). All foreign priests were deported, the Christians went "underground" ("hidden Christians"), and Christianity has never fully recovered in Japan.

Elsewhere in Asia small communities of Christians were started in Southeast Asia, generally in close proximity to Portuguese trading ports and later Dutch centers (Java, Moluccas). In the Moluccas, Christianity struggled against the violence of the Portuguese and the militancy of the Muslim sultans. Christianity came to the Philippines from the east rather than from the west. Ferdinand Magellan first arrived in 1521, but major conversions did not begin to take place until the arrival of Miguel Lopez de Legaspi (1565), who was sent from Mexico both to develop the spice trade and to evangelize the people of the Philippines. Thus, the development of Christianity, spread by *conquistadores* and monks, followed more of the pattern of South and Central America than of the rest of Asia. Once again, resistance to Christianity was felt from the Muslim sultans, who, at the same time, were moving north from the "Dutch Indies." The Philippines became a Christian country by means of Spanish arms and preaching friars. West Asia during this same period came under the domination of the Ottoman Turks, and thus the churches of the region, including the Christian center of Constantinople, were marginalized. In western Asia, Christianity continued in a survival mode as a *dhimmi* community. Thus, by the beginning of the eighteenth century Christianity was growing as never before in south and east Asia, but in west Asia Christians labored under Turkish Muslim rule.

Protestant work in Asia came very late, most of the early work being done by chaplains attached to British, Danish, or Dutch communities. The work of the chaplains was mostly for the "expat" communities of Europeans, but many outstanding chaplains understood their calling to include local indigenous communities. Henry Martyn's (1781–1812) work, through the British East India Company in south and west Asia, resulted in the translation of the New Testament into Urdu and Persian. This marks a new approach to mission based not only on the acquisition of local languages, but also the translation of Scriptures into those languages; this became a Protestant priority. During the nineteenth century alone, Protestant missionaries and national church leaders translated the New Testament (or the whole Bible) into fifty-nine Asian languages. During the first eighteen centuries of Christianity in Asia, the Bible had only been translated into Syriac, Armenian, Georgian, Arabic, Malay (1733), and Tamil (1727).

The first Protestants to work in Asia not as chaplains but as missionaries were not English speaking. Often William Carey (1761–1834) is considered the "father of Protestant missions," but in fact the earliest Protestant missionaries were German Pietists working in Danish territories and supported by the Danish king and British evangelicals. Bartholomew Ziegenbalg (1683–1717) pioneered this work, arriving with his friend Henry Plutschau (1677–1752) in 1706. As Roman Catholic work was conflicted by the struggles between the Jesuits and the papacy, Protestants were just beginning the greatest Protestant advance ever. Protestant missionary societies grew rapidly beginning the last decade of the eighteenth century, both denominational and ecumenical (nondenominational) societies looking to the vast continent of Asia. Many of the trading companies and their colonial governments were not receptive of missionary work in their overseas lands. Missionaries learned the local languages, taught literacy, and baptized the local people. These were the same people the trading companies needed to exploit in order to increase their profit margin. In time, uneasy alliances were built as missionaries helped with translations and educating a civil service sector, and European colonialists provided transportation and social order. The alliance was never simple or static.

Although all regions of Asia were of concern for Protestant missionaries, there was a certain mystique around and concern for reaching the Chinese. The London Missionary Society developed a strategy to reach "closed" China by establishing churches around China that would train overseas Chinese to reach their "homeland." This "ring of light" approach was abandoned when Europeans forced China to open for trade through the "unequal treaties" of the 1840s. Missionaries who had been working with overseas Chinese pulled up stakes from Malaya, Singapore, and the East Indies and moved to one of the treaty ports of China. This early work was confused by the twin European concerns for selling opium and preaching Jesus. In addition, the often-violent reactions against foreigners and foreign religion made the work especially difficult. And yet, the Protestant work in China exploded unlike any other field: medical work, educational work, agricultural work, publishing work. As with the Roman Catholic mission work in China, the Protestants also had many theories about how to reach this largest and neediest of nations. Should an approach of social uplift through the best of Western science and education be used, or should missionaries identify with the local farmers and people in the villages, preaching a Jesus of the poor and needy? Both approaches were used, and the results were also mixed.

By the beginning of the twentieth century churches were established in most regions of Asia, if not among all the language groups. One of the last nations to be open to missionary work was Korea, but as with the first Roman Catholics, Protestantism also first came to Korea through Koreans leaving (this time for Manchuria) for China and coming back with Christian literature. This time the literature was the Gospels translated into Korean. Thus, Protestant Christian communities began in Korea before there was a resident missionary. The very time Protestant missionaries were arriving (1884), Japanese influence was spreading, displacing the Chinese in the imperial court. The Protestant approach in Korea was adopted from the strategy of John L. Nevius, Presbyterian missionary to China. This method strongly emphasized training local leaders to lead self-supporting, self-governing, and self-propagating churches. As a result, Christian leaders and Christian churches were closely identified with the local people and culture. The foreign oppressors, Japanese, insisted on a foreign religion (Shintoism) and a foreign language (Japanese). Christians were among the most culturally Korean, the best educated, and also the most nationalistic. Protestants working in British India (from present-day Pakistan to Myanmar) had similar debates regarding the approach to take in a highly stratified country. Even those who tried to reach the upper castes in India ended up having a much greater impact on the lower castes and the Dalits (outcasts). In many regions of India, beginning in the early nineteenth century mass movements of people came to faith, creating problems of leadership training. As in other areas of Asia, medical work took off with the discovery of bacteria, the use of sterilization, and vaccines. Thus, Christianity became identified with schools and hospitals by the end of the century.

By the beginning of the twentieth century three new trends were observable in Asia. First was the growth of newer faith missions such as the

China Inland Mission (1865, now Overseas Missionary Fellowship). Second, at the turn of the century the first Pentecostal groups began work in Asia. By the 1920s Asian Pentecostal evangelists (especially Chinese, Indian, and Ceylonese) began to have a continent-wide impact. Finally, movements multiplied that worked to nationalize and unite churches and missions. The formation of the Church of Christ in Thailand (1934), for example, came from both Baptist and Presbyterian polities, and the Church of South India (1947) came from Anglican, Methodist, and Reformed confessions. The Philippine Independent Church was founded in 1902 in part as an expression of Philippine independence and control over the church. This uniting and nationalizing of churches initiated a rapid growth of indigenous church leaders. National leaders such as Bishop Azariah of Dornakal pioneered both in new church and mission structures (India Missions Association, 1903), and in developing Asian theologies. Social transformations in Asia—both the resistance to foreign (European and Japanese) domination and the influence of communist and democratic ideals—had a tremendous impact on the development of Christianity in Asia. In these shadows one of the greatest evangelists of the twentieth century, John Sung, developed an extensive evangelistic ministry not only in China but among Chinese throughout east Asia. It wasn't until after the end of the Second World War, however, that the impact of these early national Christian leaders and other indigenizing trends had their full impact.

History After the Fall of Japanese and European Imperialism

With the collapse of the Japanese Empire came also the collapse of the various European empires. Great Britain, France, the Netherlands, and Portugal quickly scaled back or abandoned their Asian empires after the Pacific War. Suddenly, empires that had been neutral or partially supportive of Christian ministry were replaced by Buddhist-leaning governments (Sri Lanka, Burma, Laos, Cambodia), Hindu-dominated governments (Nepal, India), or Muslim governments (most of the Middle East, Indonesia, Bangladesh, Pakistan). Other countries—in central Asia—came under the sway of Soviet Russia; the spread of Marxist materialism in China, Vietnam, and other states of east Asia led to the rejection of Christianity as well as all other religions. It appeared that only liberated Japan would be a fertile mission field. In fact, it is only Japan (an imperial power) and Thailand (a noncolonized country) where Christian growth has been nearly imperceptible. With the exodus of foreign powers came severe restrictions on, or even expulsions of, foreign missionaries. The result was that the national churches in places such as India, Pakistan, Burma, Vietnam, Iran, Indonesia, and China had to stand on their own. Within a generation or less (from 1945 to 1968) Christian churches had to accept and express Christian faith in their own contexts. In many countries this meant that the schools and hospitals were "lost," being closed or nationalized. In Myanmar, for example, the newly formed independent government declared Buddhism the state religion in 1960, and then in 1962 all schools and hospitals were nationalized, and all missionaries were removed. Consequently, overnight leadership in health care, education, and the church was lost, and the churches were forced on their own resources.

In Southeast Asia the spread of communism was a major concern after the Pacific War. With North Korea, China, and Vietnam becoming communist, and communist agents, often Chinese, spreading their teachings overseas, the governments of Malaysia and Indonesia responded. These responses often aided in the growth of Christianity. In Indonesia the government insisted that all citizens declare a religion as a way of excluding communist sympathizers. Many declared themselves Christian and then later learned about what they had decided. The spread of communism in Vietnam, first in the north and then in the south, meant great restrictions on and persecution of Christians.

As East Asian nations moved into the global economy, greater openness to ecumenical contacts was a side benefit. As a rule of thumb, the years of restriction and persecution (in China from 1948 until about 1980) shattered the institutional structures of the churches but have fanned the flames of Christian identity and courage. When global Christian contacts have returned they have come as "light support" but weighty encouragement to Christians in places such as Vietnam, Cambodia, Myanmar, and China. Christians in China have chosen different paths of faithfulness to the gospel. Some have chosen to work in harmony with the government. Leaders such as Y. T. Wu in the China Christian Council and the Three Self-Patriotic Movement exemplify this approach. Others, such as Wang Mingdao, opposed the government and chose to accept long-term imprisonment as punishment. The church in China continues with these two approaches, one working officially, legally, and publicly; the other (not trusting the government) chooses to meet in unregistered house churches. Both streams are growing at one of the fastest rates ever in the history of Christianity.

In South Asia, Christianity has also grown significantly under local leadership, although mostly among the lower castes and classes. Mass movements of Dalits in India have occurred, in part in defiance of the oppressive nature of Hinduism for those not in a scheduled caste. Dalits who become Christian are able to break out of the cycle of poverty, attend school, and become a teacher, pastor, or doctor. In Pakistan, Christians also tend to be from lower-class families, and a conversion is seen as a step down, socially. Nepal was a closed Hindu kingdom from 1769 until it slowly began to open to the outside world beginning in the 1950s. With most of the missionary work being done by Indians, the church today is growing rapidly. In fact in all of South Asia thousands of full-time Asian crosscultural missionaries are working, mostly within their own political borders.

Some of the largest churches in the world today are in South Korea. Before the partition of Korea, the strongest churches were in the northern regions. With the Korean War came terrible persecutions of church leaders and a massive exodus to the south. Today Korea is one of the largest mission-sending nations in the world. As with all nations in Asia today, Christianity in Korea has been shaped by the local culture. One of the characteristics of Korean Christianity is daybreak prayer meetings. Most churches have prayer meetings, well attended, seven days a week at dawn. The influence of Christianity on modern Korea can be seen symbolically by the number of crosses seen across the skyline of Seoul at night.

Minority Status of Christian Communities

With all of the growth and indigenization of Christianity in Asia, it continues to be a minority religion with little support or protection by the national governments. This has been the case since the first century. What is different today is that these Christian communities are now more widely spread, they are in contact with one another, and church leaders often have a place at the table in social intercourse. As a minority faith, Christians are in daily contact with people of other faiths. Thus, interreligious relationships are very important for Christians in every country of Asia. In general we can speak of four patterns of Christian relationships with people of other faiths in Asia. First there are those countries that are more secular, or more concerned with international trade, who foster a pluralistic acceptance of religions. We might call this the new Parthian Peace—a toleration of beliefs as the best way to encourage stability and trade. Often, because there is no real threat from other religions, these Christian communities have very little contact with people of other religions. The Republic of Singapore, Taiwan, Thailand, and South Korea would fit in this first category. Second are those countries where tolerance is a government requirement, but in fact Christianity is perceived as a threat or enemy of people at the local level. Even though Christianity has few if any restrictions in these countries, there will be intermittent persecution that at times becomes fairly severe. In this category would be Turkey, Indonesia, India, and Pakistan. In these countries there are often places of interreligious dialogue and cooperation that make possible the healing of wounds and the reconciliation of estranged parties. The third pattern of Christian relationships with other religions are those countries where Christian activity is curtailed by the government. The restrictions placed by the government may be for religious reasons (as in Malaysia or Bangladesh) or secular reasons (as in China or Vietnam). The result is that Christian communities live a type of *millet* existence once again. Examples of restrictions that governments place on these communities vary greatly. In Malaysia, the name Allah can not be used for the Christian God, making all Indonesian-published Bibles officially illegal. In many countries each church must register and have approval for new buildings, and these legal requirements may be difficult or impossible to meet. When the governments are so restrictive, the persecution comes less from laypeople in other religions. In fact this type of governmental persecution often drives people of other faiths closer together. The fourth pattern of interreligious relationships is found mostly in Islamic republics such as Yemen, Saudi Arabia, and Iran. In these countries limited, if any, Christian practice is allowed except by foreigners. Non-Islamic practice in these Muslim lands is seen as an affront to the Muslim kingdom. Until 1990 Nepal was the only Hindu kingdom in the world, and although Christian foreign workers were allowed in the country to help with social, agricultural, and technical programs, no Christian witness was permitted. Now, however, the extreme forms of restriction placed on Christians exist only in Muslim states, in Laos, and in Bhutan (a Buddhist country). In these countries interreligious relationships are almost impossible.

Another way at looking at the Christian existence as a minority community in Asian countries is to see how individuals and communities creatively adapt to their contexts. In China, Communist Party members are not allowed to be Christian, and yet there are Party members and eager young intellectuals who are interested in the life of Jesus. Many attempt to follow Jesus but refuse to be baptized. These "culture Christians" often meet together to study the Bible and even pray, but they generally do not participate in normal church activities. In India, the dominance of Hindu culture and the closely knit ties in families around the Hindu faith and practices cause many Christians to refuse baptism. Baptism will cut them off from their families, but also from the possibility of Christian witness. These "unbaptized believers," as they are called, try to be faithful to their religion with the one exception of baptism. In some Muslim villages in South Asia where a *mullah* may become converted, leading those at his *masjid* or mosque to follow Christ, all of the external practices of the Muslim culture are retained. Only the beliefs change. Thus, in these villages worship is held on Friday, and prayers are said with men and women separated, in the name of Jesus the Messiah. Even with relaxed restrictions in most communist countries of Asia, there are millions of Christians who meet in house churches, whether in villages or in large urban areas. In all of these communities mentioned above, the two threads that link them together with the large fifty-thousand-member church in Seoul or the Christian ashram in India are the study of the Bible and the present reality of Jesus alive and active today.

ASIAN CHRISTIANITY TODAY

Christianity in Asia, by the beginning of the twenty-first century, had become a more vital religious force than in Europe. In all of Asia, between 7 and 8 percent of the population is Christian, but unlike Europe, nearly all of these Christians are active, attending weekly worship and concerned with Christian witness to non-Christians. The comparison with Europe is helpful in assessing both Christian presence and vitality in Asia today. In most countries of Europe today, less than 5 percent of the population attends church on a given Sunday. In many Buddhist, Muslim, Hindu, and communist countries in Asia, more than 5 percent of the population attends church, and the percentage is going up in these countries. The vitality of a religion can be measured a number of ways; here we will look at a few. In terms of numbers of adherents, in most countries of Asia the numbers and percentage of Christians are increasing. Two of the most rapidly growing Christian populations in the world are in Asia: Nepal and China. In terms of actual numerical growth, the Christian population in the People's Republic of China has grown faster than any church or empire ever in a single generation. Similar growth patterns are evident in other communist East Asian countries (e.g., Cambodia, Vietnam), but the absolute numbers are far greater in China. With over 68 million Bibles published and distributed in China in less than fifteen years, we get some clue as to the growth of Christianity. In addition, the Christian population in a number of countries is growing over 1.5 percent faster than the population: Bangladesh, Cambodia, China, Indonesia, North Korea, Laos, Mongolia, Myanmar (Burma), Nepal, Pakistan, Thailand, and Turkey. In Europe, virtually every country is declining in Christian population.

Another measure of Christian vitality is the number of new institutions and organizations that are started. It is very difficult to keep up with the new churches, denominations, Bible schools, and mission societies that are developing in Asia. Independent churches-cum-denominations such as the Church of Bangkok, Jesus Is the Lord Fellowship (Philippines), and True Jesus Church (Chinese), as well as the over one hundred Presbyterian denominations in South Korea, are signs of Christian vitality. Christian Bible schools and training centers continue to proliferate, not only in countries that are becoming more open to Christian witness, but in almost all Asian countries. Even in countries that have a declining Christian population—mostly Muslim countries (Azerbaijan, Iraq, Kazakhastan, Kyrgyzstan, Tajikistan, Turkmenistan, and Uzbekistan)—the decline is merely hiding another form of vitality. In most of these countries the decline is related to the Orthodox Russian exodus, but at the same time a smaller, but very diverse, growth of Protestant groups has begun. Other institutions such as missionary organizations are also growing rapidly in Asia. India, for example, now has over 130 indigenous missionary societies affiliated with just one Protestant umbrella organization: the India Missions Association. The number of societies and their members continue to grow.

Another measure of Christian vitality is the number of indigenous or local patterns that develop in each region. This is a sign that Christianity is not merely a foreign expression in Asian soil. Not only are there many newer Asian Roman Catholic orders, but we see patterns such as the Korean predawn prayer meetings, and the Chinese businessmen who plant churches, also as Asian patterns of Christian vitality. Asian Christian art and music continues to develop at a very rapid pace. Chinese Christian hymns and songs are being penned and published in China as well as Taiwan and among Chinese Christian communities throughout East Asia. In India and Sri Lanka, Christian ashrams have developed as a uniquely South Asian structure for spiritual retreat and pilgrimage. Other pilgrimage sites, in the Roman Catholic tradition, have developed in Asia, including Maryamabad in Pakistan, various sites of the apostle Thomas in Madras (Mylapore region), and other ancient Christian sites in south India. With all of these signs of Christian vitality, Christianity still lives a fragile and tentative existence in Asia, the continent of its birth.

2

Ancient Christianity in Asia

Earliest Christianity developed at the intersection of three continents, caught between two major empires, centered on the teachings of one Asian peasant. The early followers of Jesus spread in all directions from the eastern Mediterranean world of the Roman Empire, especially to the East, across the Persian Empire. By the end of the first century, Christians speaking Aramaic, Syriac, Latin, and Greek were found not only in the Roman regions of Asia, but also deep in the Persian (Parthian) Empire. In Roman Asia, Christians were persecuted because of their uncompromising monotheism and therefore their unwillingness to honor the *genius* of the emperor. By contrast, as Christianity spread into Parthian Asia, Christians had greater freedom. Parthia, even though Zoroastrianism was the dominant religion, had developed a peace based on tolerance of other religions: it became known later as a "Parthian Peace." This tolerance allowed for Christianity to develop, for Christian refugees from the Roman Empire to find a home, and for other religious people to prosper.

The centers of earliest Asian Christianity that we are aware of were major trading centers along the Silk Road and client kingdoms of Rome and Persia, as well as other political centers: Antioch, Aleppo, Edessa (Urfa), Nisibis, Kirkuk, Arbela, Seleucia-Ctesiphon, and by the seventh century, Kashgar, Samarqand, Almalik, and even Chang'an (Xian) in China. Thus, by the time Christianity had spread to Scandinavia (less than two thousand miles) it had already spread to the heart of China (over four thousand miles), had grown, developed, been persecuted, and declined. In fact there were bishops across central Asia before the czar of Russia sent his delegation to learn about Christianity in Constantinople. Asia had priority in the spread of Christianity in its first millennium.

However, the history of the very earliest communities outside the Roman Empire is shrouded in mystery and filled with half-converted saints and zealous ascetics. Asian Christianity did not develop a unified ecclesial order until the early fifth century. The vast territory, severe persecutions beginning in the third century, and the influx of refugees and Roman "heretics" gave a unique diversity to Asian Christianity that was not known in the West. It would be the waves of persecution—from Indian, Chinese, Persian, and Arab rulers—more than the theological diversity that prevented Asian Christianity from having a major influence in Asia until recent times. There has been a pattern to the development of Asian Christianity: ascetic missionaries move into new territories; growth under tolerant rulers; and then sudden changes in fortune under a new regime or dynasty. This pattern was first seen in Persia and India in the early centuries of Asian Christianity, and it has been true through the twentieth century up to the present day.

EARLIEST ASIAN CHRISTIANITY

The earliest followers of Jesus in non-Roman Asia were mostly Semitic peoples who spread the faith through both migration (trade) and intentional apostolic activity. Although no records remain, it is likely that some of the earliest Asian missionaries of Jesus were in Jerusalem at the time of Pentecost and the origin of the Jewish church. Of the Asian pilgrims mentioned in Acts 2, three groups would be considered Iranian: those from Parthia (which would probably be northeast Iran today), the Elamites, and the Medes. Mesopotamia, or present-day Iraq and Syria, is also mentioned, so it is likely that some of these earliest converts would have brought the new faith back to their villages. What evidence we do have of early Asian Christianity is sparse. The Odes of Solomon may be the earliest Asian Christian worship book, with hymns, small sermons, and liturgies. However, it is not clear whether all of the Odes were written in Syriac (the language of early Asian Christianity), Greek, or both languages. Neither is it clear whether the Odes came from western Syria (Antioch) or eastern Syria in a location such as Edessa. What the Odes do reveal is an early tradition of a Semitic theological style. Most of the hymns and sermons in Syriac were written in parallelism like the book of Psalms in the Bible. Their Christology is not orthodox as would be defined in the fourth century, but it expresses an emerging acceptance of the divinity of Jesus and a primitive trinitarian formula. The following, from Ode 7, is a christological hymn, which shows the poetic style of early Asian Christian literature, both liturgical and homiletic.

> He became like me, that I might receive Him.
> In form He was considered like me, that I might put Him on.
>
> And I trembled not when I saw Him,
> Because He was gracious to me.
>
> Like my nature He became, that I might understand Him.
> And like my form, that I might not turn away from Him.
>
> The Father of knowledge is the Word of knowledge.
>
> He who created wisdom is wiser than His works.[1]

Other evidence of early Asian Christianity includes the record of Asian rulers confessing the faith, the earliest record of a church building, and later records of bishoprics that indicate extensive missionary activity during the first three centuries. We will look at each one of these.

According to the late fourth-century Syriac work The Doctrine of Addai,[2] and confirmed by semiconverted court official Bardaisan in *The Book of the Laws of Countries*,[3] King Abgar V of Osrhoene (capital city, Edessa) came to faith soon after the death and resurrection of Jesus Christ. The Doctrine of Addai claims that King Abgar sent a delegation to bring the miracle worker Jesus of Nazareth to Edessa to cure him of his leprosy. A letter dictated by Jesus is recorded stating that Jesus was very busy, but after he returns to his Father, he will send a disciple to bring healing. Such an early royal conversion, plus the remarkable claims that Jesus sent a letter to the king and that the emissary Hanan drew a picture of Jesus and brought it back to Abgar, are unlikely. What is much more likely, or even certain, is that the later Abgar VIII (177–212), who ruled during the time of Bardaisan (154–222), came to faith and led his nation to follow Jesus of Nazareth. It is recorded in the Chronicles of Edessa that the church of the Christians was destroyed by

---

[1] James Hamilton Charlesworth, trans., *The Odes of Solomon: The Syriac Texts* (Chico, CA: Scholars Press, 1977), 35.
[2] Daniel Deleanu, trans., *The Doctrine of Addai the Apostle* (Toronto: LogoStar, 2012).
[3] H. J. W. Drijvers, ed., *The Book of the Laws of Countries: Dialogue on Fate of Bardaisan of Edessa* (Assen: Van Gorcum, 1965).

a huge flood in 201.[4] Christians were thus worshiping publicly, in all likelihood with the support of the government since Bardaisan was a court official and his *Book of the Laws of Countries* was a type of apologetic for the faith as he understood it.

Bardaisan's theology as expressed in the *The Book of the Laws of Countries* is a unique insight into how early "royal theology" was developing in Asia and, at the same time, it is a window into cultural practices of second-century western Asia and eastern Europe. Clearly with little outside guidance, Bardaisan seemed to be giving an apologetic for the Christian faith that seemed reasonable to him, while comparing Christian belief and practice with other cultural practices. Expressed as a dialogue, Bardaisan answers questions from his interlocutor, Avida, about God and the practices of various cultures; then, in the middle of the dialogue, there is a fascinating paragraph on what Christians do and what they believe. Positively speaking, Christians in all cultures ("nations") worship on the first day of the week, fast, attend to the reading of sacred texts, and are called by the name of their sovereign: *Christ*ians. Negatively speaking, "we" Christians do not follow many of the customs of the cultures in which we live.

> The brethren who are in Gaul do not take males *for wives*, nor those who are in Parthia two wives; nor do those who are in Judæa circumcise themselves; nor do our sisters who are among the Geli consort with strangers; nor do those brethren who are in Persia take their daughters for wives; nor do those who are in Media abandon their dead, or bury them alive, or give them as food to the dogs; nor do those who are in Edessa kill their wives or their sisters when they commit impurity, but they withdraw from them, and give them over to the judgment of God; nor do those who are in Hatra stone thieves to death; but, wherever they are, and in whatever place they are found, the laws of the several countries do not hinder them from obeying the law of their Sovereign, Christ; nor does the Fate of the celestial Governors compel them to make use of things which they regard as impure.[5]

Fate, a very strong Asian astrological concept, still had power for Bardaisan, but not final authority in a person's life. This was a theology not concerned

---

[4] Samuel Hugh Moffett, *A History of Christianity in Asia*, vol. 1, *Beginnings to 1500* (San Francisco: Harper, 1992), 58.
[5] Drijvers, *Book of the Laws of Countries*, 61.

with christological or trinitarian formulations, but with defending the universality and missionary nature of this new Asian religion.

Another small kingdom on the border between the Roman and Persian empires that accepted the faith of Christians was Armenia. Tradition has it that the missionary Addai, mentioned above, traveled in the region as the first to bring the teachings of Christ to villages in Armenia. By the time of the national conversion under the King Tiridates III circa 310, many of the villages were following Christian teachings with Syriac texts from Syrian regions of the Roman Empire. Credit for the conversion of the king and the nation usually is given to Gregory the Illuminator (ca. 240–332). The Armenian culture was soon transformed by the immediate translation of biblical and extrabiblical texts into Armenian. Armenian culture adopted Christian teachings and worship thoroughly and unlike any other Asian culture to the present day.

A third nation that received Christianity as its national religion in Asia in this early period was Georgia. Although tradition awards Georgia as the missionary field of the apostle Andrew, there is no direct evidence that he established churches by the early second century. However, Christian communities were common by the third century in eastern Georgia;[6] through the work of Georgian apostolic monks the faith spread, and in 337 King Mirian III (aka Mihran; 284–361) came to faith. Georgian Christianity, like Armenian, quickly became part of the fabric of the culture through the development of a Georgian script and the translation of the Bible and other sacred texts within the first century of the king's conversion. Not until the tenth century did theological and ecclesial uniformity develop in Georgia; diversity of beliefs and practices built around the Georgian Bible marked the first half-millennium of Georgian Christianity.

Although the earliest Asian Christianity outside the Roman Empire was diverse in language and cultural expressions, it was led by the Syrian forms and teachings and by the Syriac language.[7] Thus, most of the early Asian Christian writings were more biblical and allegorical and less philosophical

---

[6]Stephen H. Rapp Jr., "Georgian Christianity," in *The Blackwell Companion to Eastern Christianity*, ed. Kenneth Parry (Malden, MA: Blackwell, 2010), 138.
[7]Arthus Vööbus, *History of Asceticism in the Syrian Orient* (Louvain: Secrétariat du CorpusSCO), 1:iv–ix.

than what developed in the Hellenistic world. Syrian Christianity was also ascetic and monastic in expression, more than in other regions. This asceticism, however, shaped the Asian church to be strongly missionary and, ironically, to engage social issues and eventually to become the seedbed of both ecclesial and social leaders. Syrian missionary monasticism left its formative character on the church in Armenia, Georgia, Osrhoene, central Asia, India, and even to China. Monastic life was both missionary and scholarly, leaving behind a great treasure trove of early Asian Christian literature: biblical, spiritual, allegorical, and poetic.[8]

INDIA

Although there is no definitive proof of when Christianity first arrived in India, it is accepted among most Indian Christians that the apostle Thomas first brought Christianity at the end of the first or beginning of the second century. This is not impossible, because we know that trade, by both land and sea, was common between the West and south Asia in the early centuries of the Common Era. However, there is no reliable documentary evidence for the arrival of the first Christians or the first Christian missionaries in India. The apocryphal Acts of Judas Thomas, written in Syriac and dated to the early third century, tells how the apostles, after Jesus' ascension, divided up the world to evangelize all the nations, and Thomas was awarded India.[9] Unwilling to go, he was sold as a slave to a merchant going to India, whereupon he worked for King Gundaphar (Gundaphorus). In India, Thomas led people to faith and he cared for the poor; according to this account, he performed miracles of healing, raising from the dead, and exorcism, and he preached to bring about conversion. The form of Christian life Thomas endorses in this book is very ascetic or world denying. It reflects more from the Syrian Christian communities than the teachings of the apostles found in Scripture. However, there may very well be elements of truth at the core, for there was a King Gundaphar in India (in the north, however, not along the southern coast), and the type of resistance to Thomas does reflect the forms of persecution that Christians encountered from Hindus in India.

---

[8]Robert Murray, *Symbols of Church and Kingdom: A Study in Early Tradition* (Cambridge: Cambridge University Press, 1975).
[9]Moffett, *History of Christianity in Asia*, 1:24-44.

According to the historian Eusebius, it was not Thomas, but another apostle, Bartholomew, who first came to India. Eusebius, as well as Jerome, refers to the story told by the Egyptian theologian Pantaenus when he returned from a visit to India in the second century. Pantaenus went to help the persecuted Indian Christians after an Indian delegation came to Alexandria. His visit was sometime in the last two decades of the second century. This story, which has much more history to it than the Thomas legend, reveals that a robust witnessing community existed in south India by the 170s. How they got there, and whether Thomas or Bartholomew was the evangelist, we may never know. We do know that these Christian communities, mostly along the southern coasts (both the southeast and southwest coasts), have existed since the second century, and they suffered persecution from Hindus in the early centuries. All traditions (Greek and Syriac, as well as Indian) agree with this.

Early Theologies and Theologians in Asia

As we noted above, the earliest Christian theological writings were translations of Scripture (in Syriac, Armenian, and Georgian), and early liturgical writings such as the Odes of Solomon. Bardaisan represents the earliest attempts at a royal apologetic, with all the mixed motives and understandings involved in such an enterprise. The earliest Asian Christian literature and the richest literature for the first thousand years was in Syriac, and it was written between Antioch in the west and Persia and India to the east. The first major theologians from Persia would have to be Tatian (110–180), Aphrahat the Sage (writing 325–345), and Ephrem the Syrian (ca. 306–373). In the life and thought of Tatian, we see the cultural theological trends from Asia and from the Mediterranean. Tatian came from Mesopotamia but studied in Athens and traveled to Rome and even met Justin Martyr. What Tatian experienced in the ancient scholarly tradition in the Hellenistic world was far beyond what he had seen in Persia. It is likely that he was converted during his travels (probably in his study under Justin in Rome), and then he returned to Persia to establish a school of his own. The school that he established was very ascetic in its Christian life, highly critical of Western religion (as seen in his *Oration to the Greeks*), and focused on the life of Jesus as viewed through a single Gospel narrative: the *Diatessaron*. The *Diatessaron*, probably composed by Tatian in Syriac (and immediately translated into Greek, or vice versa) became the standard life of Jesus for over two centuries in the Syriac-speaking world. Later, Ephrem of Edessa would write a commentary on the *Diatessaron*. Tatian, the first real Asian theologian, was proud of his Asian heritage, although his scholarly abilities all came from his academic sojourn in the West.

Unlike Tatian, Aphrahat remained in Persian territory. Aphrahat, "the Persian Sage," is known solely for his *Demonstrations*, written between 336 and 345, a series of twenty-three short writings that give us one of the only windows into early fourth-century Persian Christianity. Little is known of Aphrahat's life except that he was most likely a member of the Sons of the Covenant, a basic monastic form of Asian Christianity. The first ten demonstrations or treatises prescribe for the reader how to live the Christian (not just ascetic) life. It is like a guidebook for the Christian life. Other treatises are actually letters, including a letter to a synod of bishops, and the final nine deal with relations with Jews. Aphrahat's context was very different from those of the Christians in the Roman Empire. His theological concerns were to promote a spiritual and practical theology that would help Christians to live faithfully and would, at the same time, correct the teachings of the Jews. His was an independent Christian tradition, with no knowledge of the christological or trinitarian controversies of the West. Persian Christianity, we see with Aphrahat, was an independent and vital tradition of Asian Christianity.

Ephrem, "the Harp of the Holy Spirit," is the best known of all Syriac-writing theologians. He is recognized as a saint by both the Roman Catholic and Orthodox Churches for his holy writings and life. His writings more than any other in Asia shaped the theology, structure, liturgy, even hymnody of the Persian church. Orthodoxy was established as much by Ephrem as any other single author in Persian Christianity. His influence was great because of both the variety and the extent of his writings. Ordained only as a deacon, Ephrem was possibly a member of the Sons of the Covenant, like Aphrahat, which gave a sense of community Christian life to his writings. Born in Nisibis to a Christian family, Ephrem's writings reflect the culturally and religiously pluralistic world of land between empires. His early writings were from Nisibis, where his teaching is identified as the founding of its famous school. Caught in the political events of his time, some of Ephrem's writings come out of the period when Nisibis was under siege by the Persian emperor, Shapur II. Nisibis had been under the influence of Constantine's

Roman Empire, but by 337, the year of Constantine's death, Shapur began to extend his borders to the west. At the same time, the persecution of Christians increased, including the requirement of paying a double tax. Bishops and priests were killed as Nisibis was under siege three times. Ephrem, in his *Carmina Nisibena*, reflects on this history with theological adroitness. History, theology, poetry, and biblical symbolism coalesce in these writings.

Eventually Nisibis fell to the Persian emperor, but unlike earlier victories for Shapur, in this case he allowed the Christians to flee to the "Christian" West. Previously, he had executed most of the citizens and allowed others to be displaced deep into the Persian Empire. Ephrem's last ten years were devoted to writing hymns and theology against the heresies of Manichaeism, the mixed theological teachings of Bardaisan, and against local deities (of which there were many). Cosmopolitan Edessa was given theological leadership under Ephrem. To battle many of the heresies, Ephrem gathered female choirs and wrote for the choirs to sing of the divinity of Jesus, the joys of chastity, and the truth of the Trinity. Consistent with his theology and life, Saint Ephrem died caring for the sick during a period of plague in 373.

Christianity was less ordered and more diverse in Asia outside the Roman Empire. Christological controversies in the West were settled within the context of a Christian empire that provided the structure (if not pressure) for the church to find its own unity regarding wording (theology) and bishoprics (order). The Asian church did not have this pressure, but it did have another type, the growing and changing persecution from nonsympathetic rulers. Asian Christianity collected the rejected theologies and theologians from the West and (after the rise of the Sasanians) it also struggled for its very existence under Sasanian and later Arab rulers. The early controversies in the West (mostly Arianism) were of no consequence in the East, but when Nestorius and his theology were condemned by the Council of Ephesus (431), many of his followers fled to the East, eventually becoming a mainstream of east Syrian orthodoxy, centered in the capital city of Selucia-Ctesiphon (later Baghdad). After the Miaphysite (Monophysite) controversy led to the Council of Chalcedon in 451, those who held on to the belief in the single nature in Christ (*mono-physis*) were exiled and became the west Syrian theological tradition. It was the west Syrian tradition that most identified with Egypt and Ethiopia. The east

Syrian, Diophysite theology became the theology of Asia that spread to the East. They held their own councils, beginning with the Synod of Isaac in 410. Most of these early Asian councils were called to reorganize the church after persecution; little theological discussion ensued. The second synod, in 420, also was called to bring about greater order and prevent schism, but the third synod in 424 is more memorable because it made a clear break with the church in the West. This Synod of Dadyeshu (424) claimed that the patriarch in Seleucia-Ctesiphon was equal to any patriarch in the West, giving the Asian church a de jure independence it had exhibited de facto for most of its life. From this point on, bishops in central Asia, India, and even China would be commissioned from the Persian capital.

Religious Pressures and Persecutions: Zoroastrian and Muslim

The advent of the Sasanian Dynasty in Persia around 225 brought with it a revival of the sixth-century BCE religion of Zoroastrianism. A dualistic faith with two creator gods—Ahura-Mazda, who creates what is good, and Ahriman, who creates a parallel evil creation—Zoroastrian life and worldview was closer to Judaism and Christianity than any of the local fertility or astrological faiths of Persia. The first ruler of the Sasanian Dynasty, Ardashir I (r. 225–240), appointed a religious adviser or *mobed* (magi) named Tansar, who revived the practice of regional sacred fires and purity laws. Purity, or separation from what is profane or polluted (created by Ahriman), is integral to the Zoroastrian faith. This is where major cultural conflicts occurred. Asian Christianity tended to be ascetic, but Zoroastrianism viewed "bounty" (many children, crops, and cattle) as a sign of sacredness. Ahura-Mazda's blessing was understood to be in a land that produced bounty. When Christians refused to marry or to have children, or when Christians buried their dead in the ground (polluting the land), they were unwittingly taking the side of the evil god, Ahriman. Later *mobeds* counseled the shahs to give stronger adherence to Zoroastrian teaching, and this inevitably brought greater persecution on the Christians.

Beginning 339, soon after the death of Constantine, persecution of Christians became extreme. Christians were to pay a double tax and were not allowed to build churches or to repair their existing ones. They were not allowed to evangelize or marry outside their community, effectively establishing Christians as a *millet*, or isolated ghetto community. The vitality of Christianity, its missionary outreach, was cut off. Many bishops and patriarchs, up to the time of the Arab invasions, were killed. For example, in 344 Bishop Simon (Bar-Sabbaʾe) of Seleucia-Ctesiphon, who refused to collect the double tax and then refused a bribe from the shah, was killed, but only after watching five other of his bishops and one hundred priests beheaded. This was his last sight before he himself was beheaded.

This persecution was precipitated because of the close cooperation between shah and *mobed*, but other persecution was more internal to the church. We mentioned above divisions in the church caused by Western controversies. Deep in Persia, another theological controversy began as a mixture of Jewish and Christian along with Zoroastrian teachings, with some additional elements of Hindu and Buddhist teachings. Founded by the prophet Mani, Manichaeism was a dualistic religion. What Manichaeism inherited most from Christianity was its missionary zeal and global vision. It was first established in India and then spread back to Mani's homeland of Persia, and eventually with missionary enthusiasm spread within the ranks of the Roman army and to the east along the Silk Road to the Pacific. Manichaean writings are often hard to distinguish from Christian writings because of the allegorical images of light and dark and their missionary themes. Mani claimed to be a disciple of Jesus and of Paul, but his religion was much more dualistic, denigrating the physical world and seeking through ascetic discipline to subdue the flesh, so that the inner divine light could break free. Many Christians were entrapped in Manichaean-believing communities, not knowing the difference between this and the faith of Jesus.

The last religious encounter of Asian Christians was the one that prevented a possible revival of Christianity during a period when the Sasanian Empire was in decline in the seventh century. Arab Muslim invasions swept through a weak Persian Empire and by 637 had conquered Seleucia-Ctesiphon. The fall of the enemy of the Christians was seen to be a Christian victory, and for a season this was the case. The Arab caliphs needed help in ruling this new Persian Empire, and they found the Christians the best-educated and most trusted citizens. Christians were hopeful that Muslims would become more centered on Christ. Muslims were hopeful that Christians would follow their lead in renewing monotheistic life. Both were disappointed. In the early years Persian Christians served as accountants, managers, and jailers, and, for their part, they were pleased to help fellow monotheists who had crushed their persecutors. Under the second caliph, 'Umar I (r. 634–644), other religious minorities were protected, but at the same time this protection had its price. Non-Muslims were consigned to a *dhimmi*, which was patterned after the *millet* communities of the Persians. In the seventh century, *dhimmi* existence had very few limitations for the Christian communities. However, by the first decades of the eighth century, Christians were socially ostracized by their prescribed dress, mode of transportation (they were required to ride side-saddle on horses), paying increased land and personal taxes, and by restrictions placed on church repairs. Most of the persecution under Arab rule up to the end of the first millennium was social, financial, and psychological. There were not the massive killings as under the Zoroastrian rulers. However, slowly Persian Christianity decayed from within. Patriarchs were chosen or approved by caliphs, and often bribery secured ecclesiastical positions. With contact outside the Christian *dhimmi* so tightly controlled, the Christian community atrophied; it decayed from within more than being crushed from without. The Asian church under Islamic rulers only survived in ancient forms, worshiping in an ancient language. One of the great tragedies of the decline of Persian Christianity was that it also meant the loss of a base for ongoing missionary work to the East.

Earliest Chinese Christianity

Persian monks who arrived in the Chinese capital of Xian (Chang-an) in 635 explained to Emperor Tai Zong that they had come to propagate the "Luminous Religion," or the religion of light. In these early years of the Tang Dynasty, emperors were open to new knowledge and to trade with the non-Chinese world. Tai Zong encouraged all knowledge from afar: Buddhist, Manichean, and Christian. In 635 he issued an edict allowing the propagation of Christianity, and he also gave room for monks to translate their texts on the grounds of the royal palace. A church was soon built in Xian, and monks were dispersed throughout the expanding empire. Both the pull factor of the emperor's thirst for knowledge and the push factor of the missionary zeal of Persian monks were involved in the rapid spread of Christianity along the Silk Road and throughout China.

Much has been made of the imprecise theology of earliest Chinese Christianity. These monks were east Syrian and thus Diophysite, and not orthodox by European standards. They did not translate the whole Bible; in fact we don't have even one complete book of the Bible translated into Chinese from this early period (in contrast to Syria, Armenia, the Roman Empire, and Georgia). Finally, this earliest Chinese Christianity has been criticized for building monasteries and not churches. And so, the reasoning goes, what spread in China in the early period was not a healthy form of Christianity.[10]

However, this earliest movement of Christianity in China is far more complex and rich than has often been appreciated. Monastic religion was very appropriate in Asia, especially China, and this may have been reason for the early acceptance rather than cause of Christianity's decline. Although we do not have record of books of the Bible being translated, it is clear that much was written about Jesus ("Jesus the Messiah Sutra," ca. 638), almost in the pattern of Buddhist Jataka stories (stories of the former lives of the Buddah). Most of the writings in Chinese were apologetic in nature. We continue to find more Christian sutras into the twenty-first century, indicating there was more of a Christian movement in Tang China than we had realized. One of the strongest criticisms of early Chinese Christianity—that it was a syncretism with Daoism or Buddhism—can be seen as positive trait. Rather than bringing Persian forms of Christianity, Chinese forms were developing from the very beginning.

As in all newly encountered cultures, it takes centuries for local theological lines to develop. In China, the church did not have the luxury of developing, for persecution began with the rise of Empress Wu Zetian (Wu Hao or Wu Zhou, 625–705) in the last decade of the seventh century. The empress selected another foreign religion, Buddhism, as the national faith for China, and thus persecution of Christians began in earnest in 691. Persecution lasted over two decades. Churches were then rebuilt, and there is evidence of much more translation, dialogue with other religions, and the spread of monasteries. Once again, peace did not last for the church. By the

---

[10]Dale T. Irvin and Scott W. Sunquist, *History of the World Christian Movement* (Maryknoll, NY: Orbis Books, 2001), 1:321-22.

middle of the ninth century, persecution returned, and this time it did not abate. The persecution was expressed, beginning in the 840s, as a nationalistic revival of Chinese religious belief against all followers of foreign religions: Manicheans, Christians, Zoroastrians, and then Buddhists. Although some small Christian communities survived, and some forms of royal Christianity developed among the Mongol tribes,[11] it is generally agreed that the extensive rejection of Christianity by Chinese rulers silenced Chinese Christianity. When envoys of Franciscans and Dominicans in the thirteenth and fourteenth centuries arrived in China, they confirmed this assumption.

In 1623, workers near present-day Xian unearthed a nine-foot stone monument—stele—with writing in both Chinese and Syriac describing the first arrival of Christian missionaries to China in 635. This came as news to Christians in the West, indicating the eradication of the first wave of Chinese Christianity and even the loss of the memory of this important chapter in Christian history. The monument, commonly called the Nestorian Monument, is a public, even political, statement that tells the story of the coming of the first missionary monks led by Alopen the Persian. Erected in 781, the monument tells the history of the coming of the first missionaries from the West, explains a little about the theology of this new religion, and then describes a history that shows the value of this "luminous religion" for the Chinese Empire. At points the statement is clearly orthodox Christian, at other points sounding strangely Chinese ("Twenty-seven sacred books [the number in the New Testament] have been left, which disseminate intelligence by unfolding the original transforming principles . . ."). Much ink has been spilt over the meaning and purpose of the stele. What it does indicate is that Christianity had a public standing at the end of the eighth century in China, and Christians saw it as important to make a public statement in the pattern of Chinese cultural norms. In the history of Asian Christianity it is one of the most important reminders of the constantly changing fortunes of Christianity in Asia: one moment publicly proclaimed by royalty, the next crushed by that same class.

---

[11]Moffett, *History of Christianity in Asia*, 1:422-70.

3

Ecumenism in Asia

Movements of Christian Unity

Introduction: Unity and Cooperation Before the Pacific War

The earliest movements of Christian unity in Asia were more of a pragmatic than a theological commitment. As early as 1810, English Baptist missionary to India William Carey had proposed a conference for Protestant mission cooperation in South Africa, but rather than a grand global meeting, national and regional missionary conferences were held in the second half of the nineteenth century. In China, for example, there were three major mission conferences that were all held in the very international city of Shanghai: 1877, 1890, and 1907. Almost all foreign missions were represented, and major issues of unity in translation, education, and other areas of missionary work were decided on at these meetings. These gatherings developed patterns of dividing up fields of service (or regions to "occupy") in a region or country to avoid duplication in some regions and missed opportunities in other areas. Called comity arrangements, this type of cooperation signaled a very early theological commitment to accept others' sacraments and orders of ministry long before such agreements were made by churches in the West. The Comity Agreement of 1901 for the Philippines was unique in that decisions were made before Protestant missionaries could officially enter the country. It was earlier cooperation between church and independent missions in other Asian countries that made such an agreement possible. Decisions were made in London, Berlin, or New York, but the cooperation and movements toward unity were expressed in local contexts in Asia.

In Japan the first major missionary conference (called the second) was held in Osaka in April 1883, uniting groups as different as Anglicans,

Friends, and Baptists in common study and cooperation. Later that same year a national Christian Conference was held by the Japanese churches, in which missionaries were observers. This conference, more revival than a working conference, ended with Joseph Hardy Neesima[1] preaching and a joint communion service with over three hundred participating. From this perspective we can say that indigenous leaders were often way ahead of the ecumenical curve in the nineteenth century. By the time of the famous 1907 Centenary Missionary Conference held in Shanghai, missionaries were identified by their place of service more than by their denomination. However, it was the national Christian councils that grew in importance in the early twentieth century as the missionary councils and conferences ever so slowly declined.

Another foundation for unity and cooperation in Asia was the work of the YMCA and the World Student Christian Federation (WSCF). These organizations for young people—mostly university students around the world—brought together leaders from many denominations to cooperate in reaching young people for Christ. After the 1910 World Missionary Conference, held in Edinburgh, Scotland, John R. Mott, representing the Continuation Committee, traveled to Asia. He began his travels in Ceylon and India, where he brought together local churches, student groups, and mission societies. His travels focused on bringing all Christians in each region together in unity for the church's missionary task. Evangelization was the main task. In all, Mott and his traveling team organized eighteen regional and three national conferences in Asia: Ceylon, India, Burma, Malaya, China, Korea, and Japan. In India Mott organized and led the India National Conference for Christians in mid-December of 1912, and then immediately afterward he led the All-India Student Conference at Serampore. Thus, the student work of unity was held in parallel with the development of national church councils. As a result, most of the early ecumenical leaders came out of the WSCF, where they had their first experiences of unity in mission, often in evangelizing future national leaders. In all of these countries in South and East Asia, Christian unity took a major leap forward with these regional meetings and the follow-up evangelistic rallies held by Mott and his associate Sherwood Eddy. Early Asian ecumenical leaders such

---

[1] Joseph Hardy Neesima is a very important figure in early Protestant Christianity in Japan.

as Bishop V. S. Azariah and Cheng Jingyi (Ching-yi) surfaced at these important gatherings held between October 1912 and May 1913.

At the same time Christian leaders were cooperating in the formation of Christian colleges and training schools for pastors and missionaries, and in some cases in indigenous missionary work. One of the earliest cooperative institutions for theological education in Asia was the United Theological College of South India and Ceylon. In this early prewar period of cooperation, a college for providing "sound theological education" was created by the good graces of the London Missionary Society, the Wesleyan Methodist Missionary Society, the United Free Church of Scotland, the Arcot Mission of the Reformed Church in America, the Trustees of the Jaffna College Funds, and the SPCK in Scotland, all of whom gave their support. Although most cooperative leadership work was pioneered by Western missionaries, in 1903 V. S. Azariah and others founded the Indian Missionary Society in Tirunelveli District of Tamilnadu. Very few indigenous works of cooperation were founded so early, but this became the model for later cooperation in Asian mission.

Ecumenical cooperation in Asia had many push-and-pull factors influencing the course of events. Among the forces working toward union were denominational and theological similarities, common ethnic identity, political pressure, and persecution. In Indonesia the earliest movements toward unity were ethnic: Chinese as outsiders cooperated and sought greater unity in their work and worship. In 1926 Chinese Christians formed the *Bond Kristen Tionghoa* (Chinese Christian association). In a similar way Tamil immigrants in Malaya and Singapore, and Chinese in Indochina, often worked together more closely with their own ethnic neighbors than with their denominations. As we will see, after the end of Western colonization in Asia the push factor of religious pressure and political isolation became more important.

Pacific War Period

There are two great paradoxes in ecumenism. First, when churches unite—whether churches that were formally one or that were never united before—the energy from the union quickly dissipates, and the united church is almost always smaller than the total of the two churches. In this regard it seems that union causes churches to decline. A second paradox is that union, a reconciling and peace-making process rooted in Christology, is often forced on people by governments or through war and violence. This was certainly the case during the Pacific War. The United Church of Christ in Japan (UCCJ) came about as a result of the imperialistic movement of the Japanese government.

In Japan church unity was a concern, with some limited success as early as mission cooperation in the 1870s, but little was accomplished until the 1930s. A national Federation of Churches had been formed in 1911, which later (1923) became the National Council. However, actual church union, in the end, was precipitated through a mixture of nationalism, imperial pressure, and theological commitment. In 1940 the *Nihon Kirisuto Kokai* (Church of Christ in Japan) came into existence, and the union was celebrated at the same time as the "legendary" founding of Japan twenty-six hundred years earlier. The previous year the imperial Japanese government passed the Religious Organizations Law, which necessitated the union of thirty-two churches that formed the NKK. Thus, unity was a mixture of submission to government pressure and theological conviction. After the Pacific War, with political pressure no longer a factor, some of the churches left the union, and newer churches were formed from the rapid rebuilding and remissionizing of Japan by Western churches and governments.

Japan's imperial expansion in East Asia forced the cooperation and at times unification of churches throughout the region. In Malaya Christian cooperation was moving toward the formation of a Federation of Christian Churches in Malaya, but it was not until after Japanese occupation that the federation actually came into existence with the consent of Lt. Ogawa, Japanese director of religion and education, himself a Christian. Organic union was not part of the development because of the emigrant nature of Christianity in Malaya (Christians were mostly Tamil-speaking Indians and Chinese of many dialects). In Indonesia, regional unions were almost wholly a result of Japanese initiative during Japanese occupation. The *Celebes Kiristokyodan Rengokai*, for example, was a forced union of Protestant churches in central and southern Sulawesi. Other unions that were forced created social service agencies or new church structures. Many did not continue after the war, since they represented Japanese imperialism more than Christian unity.

However, some of the forced unions and councils catalyzed further cooperation in education, especially in theological education, as well as promoting regional and national councils. The experience of imprisonment at Changi Prison in Singapore led the leaders of the Methodist, Anglican, and Presbyterians to found a union seminary upon release. Thus, in 1948 Trinity Theological College was founded: a three-in-one seminary. Union or united seminaries were also founded in China, Japan, Sri Lanka, India, and Indonesia. Such seminaries became important for the development of national conciliar cooperation and for ecumenical responses to government pressure and religious self-definition.

Decolonization and Ecumenism: 1944 to 1970

As colonial powers began to exit Asia, the transfer of church leadership followed a similar pattern to the transfer of political power. In some areas leadership of the churches was transferred before political power was handed over, but in most places church leadership continued in the hand of Europeans and North Americans well into the 1960s and 1970s. Ongoing concerns of global ecumenism, which were at their height from the late 1940s throughout the 1960s in the West, were very much alive in the leadership of the missionaries working in Asia. As a result a number of church unions and national and regional councils developed more rapidly than before or since.

One of the most hopeful signposts of ecumenical commitment was seen on September 27, 1947, when the newly formed Church of South India was finally officially celebrated at a worship service in St. George's Anglican Cathedral in Madras. This historic church union came in the wake of the national celebrations and religious violence related to the independence of India from Great Britain in August 1947. This celebration was the culmination of a long process that began in 1901 when two Scottish Presbyterian churches and an American Presbyterian church united and eventually formed (1904) the Presbyterian Church of India. After a series of other organic unions with congregational and other Reformed bodies, the Tranquebar Manifesto was signed in 1919, which expressed the larger ecumenical goal of uniting both episcopal and nonepiscopal churches. It was not until 1947 that such a union finally took place, but when it did it was an historic event. Former Presbyterian and Congregational churches accepted bishops (J. E. Lesslie Newbigin, the English Presbyterian, being one of the first CSI bishops), and Anglican churches soon began to recognize Presbyterian "priests."

The formation of the Church of North India was in some ways a delayed and anticlimactic ecumenical event. Negotiations began in 1929 and dragged on until 1970, when the union was finally celebrated at a worship service in Nagpur. Even in the last months there were negotiations to keep the Methodist Church of South Asia in the union, but they eventually withdrew from the agreement. Later, other communions joined both the CSI and the CNI, but there was never the push for organic union, in India or elsewhere in Asia, after this union. From the 1970s on conciliar and cooperative unity has overshadowed the concern for organic union.

In the Pacific Islands, 1961 was a significant date. In that year the important Malua conference (Western Samoa, today Samoa) was held, which helped to establish greater cooperation and unity among all Christians in the Pacific. Christianity in the Pacific had grown rapidly in the late nineteenth century, mostly by the initiative of Pacific Island evangelists and missionaries. Until the Pacific War most of the senior leadership was still in the hands of Westerners, but after the war this quickly changed. During the war many of the Western church leaders were evacuated, and some of them met in Australia and planned for both greater unity and local leadership for the postwar period. As a result, the important Malua meeting also established the Pacific Council of Churches, a council that today has both nine national church councils and twenty-eight national church bodies as members. In 1976 the Pacific Bishop's Conference of the Roman Catholic Church also joined the PCC, making one of the most active regional Christian bodies with Roman Catholic involvement. A saying developed among Pacific Island church leaders: "Denominations divide and culture unites." This has very much been the mindset of Christian leaders in cases where there might be four or five different churches on the same island. Pacific Theological College was founded in 1966 in the wake of the strong spirit of cooperation that developed after the 1961 Malua gathering. As noted above, cooperation in ministerial formation was at its height during this period.

Regional cooperation was also accelerated during the period of decolonialization and independence movements in Asia. The work of the International Missionary Council and then the formation of the World Council of Churches in 1948 gave some structure as well as experience for the formation of the East Asia Christian Conference at Prapat, on the island of Sumatra in Indonesia in 1957.

One of the greatest surprises in ecumenical cooperation came out of the aftermath of the Second Vatican Council (1962–1965) and the formation of national and regional gatherings of bishops. Although the Indonesian bishops' conference had been established in 1925, it was only after 1966 that its meetings began to bring together the Catholic Church as well as other Christians in united responses to pressing social issues such as abortion, seminary education, family life, *Pancasila* (the fivefold principles of Indonesian society), and even general elections in East Timor. The Federation of Asian Bishops Conferences came into existence as a result of the visit of Pope Paul VI to Manila in 1970. The gathering of bishops from many countries in Asia for this event revealed the common issues before the bishops of East Asia, and this culminated in forming a transnational body of Roman Catholic bishops from fourteen national bishops' conferences in Asia.

Unique in this period of independence and nationalism in Asia is the ecumenical experience of the People's Republic of China. Prior to the communist period in China (1949), church unity and cooperation was mostly directed by missionaries bringing their experiences from the Student Volunteer Movement and then the International Missionary Council. Suddenly, with the birth of the People's Republic, the missionary era ended, and Chinese Christian leaders came to the fore, even as Christian hospitals and schools were taken over by the state, and seminaries were combined and others closed. In this new context the government removed certain Christian leaders, appointed others, and launched the Three-Self Reform Movement. The First National Christian Conference was held in Beijing, and one of the most important results was the formation of the Three-Self Patriotic Movement (TSPM; 1954). All Christian churches were required to join this "ecumenical" church body, and those that refused were arrested. The number of churches and leaders dropped dramatically, and during the period of the Great Leap Forward the Church Union Movement was initiated, further reducing the number of churches and Christian leaders. In parallel with the changes in the government, theological education was also centralized (one seminary, Nanjing, remained), and church leaders at the highest level retained excessive control.

After the death of Chairman Mao ecumenical relations began to be restored, and slowly regional seminaries and churches began to reopen. Many people began to talk about a postdenominational era in China. With the founding of Amity Press for printing Bibles in China, global and national cooperation reached its height. Although the church was still "centralized" more than it was ecumenical in its expression, cooperation and unity were presented as a models for the rest of the world. However, by the mid-1980s it became clear that there were new challenges to Christian unity in China. Christians from East Asia as well as from the West began to flood into China, looking for ways to support the Chinese Christians. What became evident very soon was that the church had actually grown dramatically in the Mao period, even though the formation of the China Christian Council (CCC) in 1980 indicated that the Christian population was very small. Christian growth was stifled in the official TSPM churches, and so most of the new Christians had only local or regional awareness through networks that had developed. The great challenge of Christian unity today in China continues to be an issue of trust, going back to the period of growth of unregistered Christian groups. The TSPM and CCC function as national Christian bodies with good relations with the government and with overseas partners. However, a larger group of Christians has developed their own networks of relationships within China and with their own overseas partners.

End of the Twentieth Century Changing View of Unity

In the last decades of the twentieth century the vision of ecumenical unity in Asia changed dramatically. In general, the movement toward greater organic and conciliar unity evolved into a movement to cooperate in the social, cultural, and political spheres. Ecumenical organizations suffered support from their constituencies, and yet there was still vigorous support for ongoing and newly emerging social problems in Asia. Some of the issues that have brought Asian churches together, both Protestant and Roman Catholic, include the protection and care of migrant workers, human trafficking, environmental concerns, religious persecution, poverty alleviation, and response to natural disasters. Environmental concerns have been an increasingly important issue in church relations because much of the strip mining, deforestation, and air pollution is caused by companies run by Christian businesspersons, both Asians and Westerners. Similarly, many of the Filipina *amahs* and Sri Lankan, Bangladeshi, Filipino, or Indonesian construction workers are Christians themselves or are hired by Christians. Thus, these are issues that bring the ecumenical church together in solidarity. For example, the Christian Conference in Asia, the major ecumenical body uniting Protestants across Asia, has programs in the following areas:

1. ecumenical formation, gender justice, and youth formation
2. faith, mission, and unity
3. justice, international affairs, and development and services
4. HIV and AIDS concerns
5. emergency and solidarity fund

Even though the CCA does not have the broad support of Asian churches that would enhance its impact on Asian societies, this list is representative of many of the concerns that bring Christians together in Asia.

One of the main reasons for the weaker impact of ecumenical groups such as the CCA and even the WCC in Asia is that the classic ecumenical movement has been challenged by the increasing numbers of Western evangelical missions working in Asia with little or no background in ecumenical cooperation. Other forces, such as the growth of Asian missions, mostly from wealthier countries to poorer countries, began to increase the diversity of Christian communities in Asia starting in the 1980s. The newer concerns include finding ways for Singaporean, Malaysian, and Korean Methodists and Anglicans to cooperate in countries such as Vietnam, Laos, Cambodia, India, Indonesia, and Myanmar. Many of the earlier cooperative arrangements and unions began to pale in comparison to newer churches and institutions. New cooperative (not usually called ecumenical) structures developed that identified themselves as evangelical or Pentecostal. Their concerns in cooperation are more in the areas of evangelism and church growth and less in the social concerns listed above. The Asia Theological Association was formed in 1970 as an evangelical accrediting agency working in parallel with the ecumenical theological bodies such as the Synod of Serempore in India and the Association for Theological Education in Southeast Asia.

However, even though new realities of globalization seemed to work against historic ecumenical cooperation, other forces worked to bring Christians together. Both communism and threats of religious persecution have had the effect of uniting Christians in countries such as Malaysia, Indonesia,

Vietnam, and China. In Malaysia, the Christian Federation of Malaysia was formed in 1985 as a "super council" of Christian churches. The federation brings together Roman Catholic, evangelical, and ecumenical groups to provide a united Christian witness, especially in areas of Bible distribution (and translation) and religious restrictions (property disputes, etc.), as well as to respond to secular and political trends. Thus, the minority status of the larger Christian community in Malaysia has brought about a larger unity than has been possible through councils and unions.

There have been other newer and creative dimensions to Christian cooperation that were not evident earlier in the twentieth century. In the areas of music, art, liturgy, and literature there have been great ecumenical advances. The Asian Institute for Liturgy and Music in Manila has provided a place for the development of Asian Christian theology to be expressed in indigenous forms in a way that has brought about greater unity in worship. An Asian Christian hymnal was produced in 1990 ("The Sound of Bamboo"), bringing together Asian music from many regions and uniting Christians in worship through indigenous forms. Bible publishing has been another highlight of ecumenical cooperation and Christian unity. The large Amity presses in Nanjing, China, have not only been producing Bibles for all Christians in China, but they have also been printing Bibles for other countries in Asia. International cooperation in leadership development has been evident through the ongoing work of bodies such as the Association of Theological Education for Southeast Asia. Such cooperation has blurred the lines of theological divisions brought from Europe (often ethnic in origin) and helped to establish Asian Christian leaders who are free to respond to theological concerns that present themselves in various Asian contexts. In all of these areas we can say that the new contextualization of Christianity that is developing is a major theme for ecumenical life in Asia into the twenty-first century.

Ecumenical Hope and Hindrances for the Twenty-First Century

New forms of Asian Christianity that are now developing both unite and divide the church. Indigenous forms of expression must be in local languages, and these local languages unite "like" people, but they also separate outsiders. This is true of all movements of contextualization; they deepen the understanding of the faith for particular contexts, but at the same time specific contextual forms separate Christians from Christians. Other movements have worked against Christian unity in the early twenty-first century. Although Pentecostalism is not new to Asia, its rapid growth in recent decades has created a problem for Christian unity. Many of the Pentecostal churches do not have a history of ecumenical cooperation, and many of the new Asian leaders are developing relationships and alliances that are newer forms of cooperation. Thus, a form of unity is developing, but once again it is often running in parallel rather than running with existing ecumenical bodies. In addition to newer Pentecostal bodies, there are indigenous forms of Christianity developing in most every country. Many of these indigenous forms, like the early indigenous churches in China (e.g., Jesus Family, True Jesus Church), are formed in reaction to existing churches. Thus, they are born out of division and struggle with issues of unity. This trend throughout Asia is a challenge to cooperation in the future.

However, the great hope of the ecumenical movement for the future is not to be found in any particular ecumenical agency or organization. In Asia, Christians are a minority in every country except the Philippines, and as a minority among other religious majorities, certain social, political, and religious pressures will always exist, and these pressures act as a collective or uniting force for Christians. As Asians are involved in neighboring nations in mission, cooperation becomes necessary at times and is a natural outgrowth of common experiences and training, much like the earlier ecumenical leaders who worked in Asia. In China, as the one national and twenty-two regional seminaries grow and equip more and more leaders for churches, cooperation will continue to be enhanced. But this growth in unity continues to be challenged by other networks that provide parallel training for church leaders in unregistered churches. In local contexts unity is more of a reality than perceived from afar. Christians share the same Bible (for the most part) and worship in similar patterns, in the same language, and this all works toward greater unity, if not through official councils. Asia's ecumenical future will be found more in such basic concerns as sharing Scripture in local languages, and then in turning to care for the least and most oppressed in each context.

4

Evangelicalism in Asia

Protestantism in Asia began with the evangelical awakenings in Europe and North America, which means that the true roots of Asian Protestantism are found in evangelicalism. Protestant and Spiritual Christian families[1] existed from the second decade of the sixteenth century, but Protestant presence in Asia did not begin until the advent of German Pietism (beginning in the last decades of the seventeenth century) and the awakenings in North America and Britain in the early eighteenth century. Thus evangelical forms of Protestant Christian witness, whether through mainline churches or not, have been the dominant stream up to the present time. This is a great contrast with Protestant Christianity's beginnings in North America and the Caribbean, where Christendom Anglican, Lutheran, and Reformed churches generally came before the advent of evangelicalism. It would be accurate to say that evangelicalism is normative Protestant Christianity in Asia, both because of its genesis and because of its recent developments through indigenous movements.

In this chapter we will first look at early evangelical missionary movements in Asia, movements that began in the first decades of the eighteenth century in India and in the first decades of the nineteenth century in China. These early movements set patterns and established values that have continued to be characteristic of Asian evangelicalism. Then we will note the development of indigenous leadership and indigenous movements, discussing how evangelicalism, as a global movement, has had to be redefined in the light of evangelical movements in the non-Western world. The next sections will look at

---

[1] We use "Spiritual families" for those Christian communions that came out of the Reformation era and that rely on direct inspiration of the Holy Spirit as either the primary or the secondary source of authority. The other three Christian families would be Protestant, Roman Catholic, and Orthodox.

themes that have developed in and through evangelical Christianity in Asia: revivals and political resistance, Pentecostalism, the place of women, persecution and martyrdom, and interreligious relationships. In our final section we will look at what these characteristic developments of evangelicalism in Asia tell us about the possible future of this expression of Christianity for Asian cultures. As we will see, Christianity has developed more slowly in Asia than on any other continent, and yet its influence on governments, religions, and cultures has been historically significant.

Evangelical Beginnings in Asia

Although Protestant presence in Asia began with the British East India Company (founded in 1600), the Dutch United East India Company (1610), and with the Danish East India Company (1616), these early companies had little missionary interest. They were companies with business concerns. It is important to note that the door was open to Asia for Protestant missions in the first decades of the seventeenth century, but without the evangelical impulse there was no concerted Protestant missionary activity until a century later. The Dutch established their center in Batavia (Jakarta), East Indies; the British in India; and the Danish in a small strip of land on the southeast coast of India centered on the village of Tranquebar (a name meaning "song of the waves"). Since evangelical missions could not start on lands owned or controlled by Roman Catholic nations (Spain and Portugal), it was not until the twentieth century that evangelical missionaries began to work in places like Indochina and the Philippines. Other Asian countries resisted all foreign intervention until late in the colonial period: China was "forced open" during the "Opium Wars,"[2] Japan was confronted by Admiral Perry's steamships in Edo Bay (1853), and the first resident missionary did not arrive in Korea—the "Hermit Kingdom"—until 1884. Thus, evangelical Christianity came very late to many regions of Asia.

Evangelical missions in Asia mark their beginnings with the international and ecumenical initiative called the Danish-Halle mission to Tranquebar.[3]

---

[2] 1839–1842 and 1856–1860. For a brief overview see G. Thompson Brown, *Earthen Vessels and Transcendent Power, American Presbyterians in China, 1837–1952* (Maryknoll, NY: Orbis Books, 1997), 25-27.

[3] See Dennis Hudson, *Protestant Origins in India: Tamil Evangelical Christians, 1706–1835* (Grand Rapids: Eerdmans, 2000).

King Friedrich IV of Denmark controlled a small colony on the southeastern coast of India called Tranquebar. It was reported that Catholic kings were propagating the Roman Catholic faith on their colonial lands, and so, in consultation with his court preacher, the Pietist Franz Julius Lütkens (who in turn consulted with August Hermann Francke in Halle), King Friedrich became the first Protestant to send out missionaries in the same manner as the kings of Portugal and Spain. (This model, in imitation of Roman Catholic missionary cooperation of mission with kings, was short lived for Protestants.) The good court preacher Lütkens chose wisely. The first young evangelical missionaries were the German duo of twenty-four year-old Bartholomäus Ziegenbalg (1682–1719) and twenty-nine-year-old Heinrich Plütschau (1677–1752). On these young German shoulders were carried the first evangelical missions in Asia. Without any formal training in missions, these young men established trends and concerns that would mark most evangelical missions. They were the pioneers in Protestant missionary work in Asia.

Their evangelical anthropology taught them that all people were made in the image of God and therefore all Indians had some knowledge of God, even though that knowledge was imperfect and distorted. It was their responsibility to present the gospel to those in south India in a way they could understand most clearly. Thus, Ziegenbalg and Plütschau studied local languages (especially Tamil) and local religions. In Ziegenbalg's earliest letters he is involved in dialogue with his language teacher, who taught him much about local religious piety, including the four types of religious practices or approaches (disciplined behavior, liturgical ceremony, unified consciousness, and esoteric knowledge). One of the first and the most outstanding works that Ziegenbalg produced was titled *Genealogy of the Malabar Gods*. However, the Pietists in Germany were more concerned that their German missionary translate the German Bible for the Indians than that they receive the Indian gods in German. The volume was not published for over 150 years.

Other trends in evangelical missionary work that the early Germans established included Bible translation (1715 for the New Testament and 1727 for the whole Bible), schools for both boys and girls (focusing on literacy and basic biblical knowledge), establishing local churches, and training local leadership for the new churches. This early work, as we noted, was ecumenical and international. Through the "Halle Reports" sent out from Germany, Protestant leaders in England, Scotland, the Netherlands, and even North America were keeping up with this early Protestant work in Asia. Anglicans from the Society for the Promotion of Christian Knowledge (SPCK) donated a printing press that revolutionized literature production in India. The first ordained Protestant in India (1733) was a Velalan convert from Shaivism named Arumugam Pillai. Ziegenbalg gave him the name Aaron (which presumably made Ziegenbalg Moses). With a strong foundation built on translations and writings in Tamil, the Evangelical (Lutheran) Church that developed under the Danish-Halle missionaries sprang out of Tamil life and with Tamil sensitivities. In the nineteenth century the famous Tamil poet convert Vedanayakam Sastri produced a wealth of Tamil poetry and epic songs that expressed the gospel in ways friendly to the Tamil ear. Evangelicalism began to develop as a Tamil religion.

In this early period of Protestant missions in Asia it was the colonial powers that were the major hurdle in evangelical missionary work. Revivals had awakened Protestants from their missionary slumber, but the new resistance to mission was the very political powers of these same "revived" nations. Even the Danish authorities in Tranquebar made missionary work difficult for Lutheran missionaries. In Dutch lands, the Dutch United East India Company (VOC) made missionary work all but impossible in the East Indies. When the VOC went bankrupt in 1799, things began to change: it took the bankruptcy of a Dutch multinational corporation to make Dutch missions possible. In 1806 freedom of religion was proclaimed, and only from that point did evangelical missions (along with Catholic) begin to extend their work in the East Indies. Ceylon (Sri Lanka) followed a similar pattern, although freedom of religion came much later and after much more persecution of the Roman Catholics by the Dutch Reformed rulers.

Beginnings of English-Speaking Evangelicals

English-speaking evangelical presence began in Asia with the great pioneer missionary William Carey (1761–1834).[4] Carey, a self-taught and self-made man, was not only a pioneer Protestant missionary to Asia, but he was also one of the early advocates for the English-speaking Protestant world to begin

---

[4] There were a few evangelical chaplains, such as David Brown (1763–1812), who worked on British lands overseas, but their work, though well meaning, did not have a major impact. One of the most influential was Henry Martyn, whom we will briefly look at later.

to take initiative in missions. A strange hyper-Calvinism seemed to have hamstrung Protestant missions as a convenient excuse since the late Reformation period.[5] It is reported that Carey was told by a Baptist preacher as early as 1786, "Young man, sit down. . . . When God pleases to convert the heathen, he'll do it without consulting you or me." Carey was convinced from Scripture of the continuing relevance of the call to carry the gospel to all nations, and was convinced of the pressing need to go after reading some of the reports from the travels of Captain James Cook. Carey made a reasoned defense of the church's missionary responsibility in a small 1792 publication with a large title: *An Enquiry into the Obligation of Christians to Use Means for the Conversion of Heathens, in Which the Religious State of the Different Nations of the World, the Success of Former Undertakings, and the Practicability of Further Undertakings Are Considered.* The title said it all. Christians were responsible to actually do something ("use means") to bring about the conversion of the heathen. Carey used statistics to bolster his theological argument.

Carey and two close associates, schoolteacher Joshua Marshman (1768–1837) and printer and preacher William Ward (1769–1823), made up the famous Serampore Trio. Guided by their own missionary covenant, the three founded a college (1819), translated the Bible into numerous languages, began to develop horticulture as part of the missionary work, and took on social reform such as education for women and working to end the practice of sati (1829: burning of widows on the deceased husband's pyre), all while founding the Baptist Church in India. Four issues here are of special note. First, Carey believed missionary work, like all Christian work, should be self-supporting; thus he and others in the mission carried on work as teachers and printers. Second, Carey's top priority was planting churches of Indian converts, led by Indian preachers. Despite all of the education, horticulture, and translation work, the trio never wavered from this sense of purpose. Third, Carey's and Marshman's translation of the Bible was remarkably extensive, if not so remarkably accurate. They completed a remarkable six translations of the Bible and another twenty-three complete translations of the New Testament. Other languages had portions of the Bible translated. Carey had no university education, nor did he have mentors in the translation work to guide him. He learned as he went along,

---

[5]For a broader perspective on this see Dale T. Irvin and Scott W. Sunquist, *History of the World Christian Movement* (Maryknoll, NY: Orbis Books, forthcoming), vol. 3, chapter 25.

revising the important Bengali New Testament eight times. The Bible, rather than the foreign missionaries, would be the foundation for their churches.[6] Fourth, we should note the broad understanding of mission that these pioneers held and how similar their priorities were to the early German Pietists. Carey developed new plants in India, both for income and to help enhance the Indian diet, and he founded the Agri-Horticultural Society of India for ongoing research. Although the Serampore Trio believed that Hinduism was a false and "heathen" religion, they worked on a translation of the famous Hindu epic poem, the *Ramayana*, into English, and Ward wrote a book on the manners and customs of Hindus. The college provided a broad education and was called the "College for the Instruction of Asiatic, Christian and Other Youth in Eastern Literature and European Science."

A major theme in evangelical missions in Asia was Bible translation. From the time of Martin Luther, evangelical faith has been built on biblical knowledge available for all people. Luther's Bible was a central plank in his platform of reform. Evangelical missionaries stood firmly on this plank in their missionary work. The first goal for evangelical missionaries was not to plant a church or start a school, but to learn the local language and to translate the Bible. In fact, most of the early missionaries in Asia ended up being Bible translators, even if they did not leave for the mission fields with that goal in mind. An important product of Bible translation was the conversion of early local assistants. Bible translation brought the missionary and the missionized in close relationship. Most of these early translation assistants became the early converts, evangelists, and, at times, early Asian Christian writers. By 1900 the New Testament or the whole Bible had been translated into at least sixty-three languages of Asia.[7] This phenomenal translation project—a project almost solely of evangelical missionaries and Asian scholars—more than anything else marked evangelical Christianity in Asia. With ever increasing numbers, Asian Christians were hearing God's Word in their own language, carried by their own idioms, and they were thus able to pioneer Asian reflections on Christianity without Western dependency.

---

[6]Carey's translation work is all the more impressive when one notes that by 1920 the New Testament was completed in only nineteen Indian languages.

[7]Taken from "Bible Translation," in *A Dictionary of Asian Christianity*, ed. Scott W. Sunquist (Grand Rapids: Eerdmans, 2001), 81-88.

Beginnings in China, East Asia, and the Middle East

India, with its ecumenical and international beginnings of evangelicalism in Tranquebar, was only slowly followed by other evangelical missions working in China, Burma (Myanmar), Malaya, the East Indies, and the Middle East. China would quickly become the main preoccupation among European and North American evangelicals, and China's pioneer missionary hero was Robert Morrison (1782-1834) of the London Missionary Society. Prevented from traveling to China by the British East India Company, this pioneer Scotsman traveled to New York to get to China in 1807. Morrison's strength of character and evangelical convictions helped him to carve out the earliest evangelical mission in China, at a time when the penalty for advocating Christianity in China was death by strangulation.[8] Compromises had to be made to attain the goal of evangelizing the Chinese. Morrison's first years were spent in seclusion and disguise while studying Chinese with the help of Roman Catholic priests. Later he was able to stay in south China by taking up employment with the very company that blocked his entrance just two years earlier. Walking the very thin and dangerous line between obeying the law and obeying his Lord, Morrison, working in the employ of the East India Company, chose to devote his time to translation of the Bible, a less public and thus less dangerous ministry. By 1822 Morrison had translated a Chinese grammar (1815), the Bible (1819), and a Chinese-English dictionary (1822). Evangelical commitment to the Bible and to vernacular translation kept the conversion rate low (only ten converts in twenty-five years!), but Morrison and others were committed to building strong indigenous congregations, and this could only happen through Chinese Bible readers.

Public missionary work was, at this time, lethal in China. Morrison and later colleagues William Milne and Dr. Walter Henry Medhurst from the LMS made the difficult decision in 1815 to surround China with a "wall of light," by working with the Chinese diaspora (*Nanyang* Chinese). To this end, the LMS set up their base (the Ultra Ganges Mission) in Malacca (Melaka) on the west coast of Malaya, evangelizing and educating Chinese to go to China as missionaries. The strategy had little success until China

---

[8]See Samuel H. Moffett, *A History of Christianity in China* (Maryknoll, NY: Orbis Books, 2005), vol. 2, chapter 13, on early Protestant work in China.

was forced "open" at the end of Western guns during the "Opium Wars" (1839–1844; 1856–1860). Then missionaries began to flood into China. Many missionaries abandoned their work in the East Indies and Malaya to concentrate on the real goal: China. Under the first treaty (Treaty of Nanking, 1842), missionaries were restricted to five treaty ports: Guangzhou (Canton), Xiamen (Amoy), Fuzhou (Foochow), Ningbo (Ningpo), and Shanghai. But at the end of the second Opium War (1860), missionaries were allowed to reside inland. The great compromise, however, was that the same treaty that protected missionary presence also protected the trade in opium. Most evangelical missionaries spoke against the use of opium and the opium trade, but for the Chinese, Christian identity was foreign identity, and foreign identity included forcing opium on China.

One major transition in evangelical work during this period was developing modern medical missionary work as a viable way of opening a "mission field." It was said that Peter Parker (1804–1888) was the medical doctor who "opened China to the gospel at the point of a lancet." Parker pioneered missionary medical work as an ordained Presbyterian minister who also studied medicine. Parker quickly saw the great need for medical work in China, so he put out a call for more medical missionaries and, more importantly, he began to train Chinese in modern Western medicine. Parker's record mirrors many of the ambiguities of early evangelical missionary work in China. He was concerned to proclaim the evangelical message to Chinese, and yet he spent most of his time in medical, educational, and even political work. He established the first medical training center and undertook the first major surgery in China, he was the first ophthalmologist in China, and he established the first medical missionary society in China. However, because of his knowledge of Chinese and Chinese culture, he later was recruited and then enlisted as the US commissioner to China. In this capacity he acted more as an expansive Western imperialist, to the degree that he even supported Western military intervention to expand Western trading and residential rights in China. He helped to write, translate, and negotiate the Treaty of Tientsin in 1858, which opened up China to Western traders and missionaries. At times evangelical missions were caught in reprehensible methods while clinging to more admirable goals.

China became the greatest and most sought after of all mission fields after the 1850s. Two major developments occurred in evangelical work in China after the mid-century. First was the pioneering work of James Hudson Taylor (1832–1905). Taylor, son of a Methodist pastor, had a transforming spiritual experience when he was seventeen that propelled him toward missionary work in China. Although he started with the Chinese Evangelization Society (at the age of twenty-four), he left to begin his own work, which would be marked by pioneering work inland, trusting God through prayer for financial support ("faith missions"), and working as closely as possible in and with the local cultural contexts. His newly formed China Inland Mission (CIM) was undergirded by evangelical piety and strong evangelistic passion. The CIM promoted a type of piety and approach to mission that spread, in part, through Taylor's extensive travels and his prodigious recruiting. After the communist victory in China in 1948, CIM missionaries relocated to work among Chinese in East and Southeast Asia. Thus the faith mission and contextual approach of Taylor's CIM continues throughout East Asia under the new banner of the Overseas Missionary Fellowship, today dominated by Asian missionaries. Its penetrating influence occurred not only directly through its missionaries and Asian Christian leaders, but also through its model and example for other Protestants working in East Asia.

A second major issue that enhanced the development of evangelical Christianity in Asia came from John L. Nevius (1829–1893) of the American Presbyterian Mission. Nevius worked in Shandong Province in east China, where he noted that sending young converts off to Bible schools far away from their home villages weakened church leadership. Church leaders were detached from the very people they were to minister to. His ministry of church planting and leadership development led him to the conclusion that church leaders should be kept in their local contexts so that they grow as local witnesses. Each Christian should be a witness in his or her own community, with his or her own friends and family. Training leaders should be done on a short-term basis in a central location. These ideas were published in a series of articles in the *Chinese Recorder* in 1885. In 1890 Nevius spoke about his method to American missionaries working in Korea, whereupon Presbyterian missionary Horace Underwood described the basic lessons from Nevius in the following way: "Let each man 'abide in the calling wherein he was found'; teaching that each was to be an individual worker for Christ, and to live Christ in his own neighborhood, supporting himself by his trade."[9] Presbyterians in Korea followed this model closely, especially in the north, where the city of Pyeong Yang became known as the "Jerusalem of the East."

Connected with this idea of Christians remaining in their contexts to be a living and connected witness was the idea that local Christian converts then are fully accountable for their churches. Each church must be self-supporting, self-propagating, and self-governing from the beginning. This "three-self" principle had been discussed earlier by Rufus Anderson of the ABCFM, but in Nevius it is clearly connected to the idea of local leaders not being removed to a far-off seminary or university for training. When these ideas were applied, local Christian communities tended to be more evangelical: they were dependent from the beginning on their own study of the Bible, prayer, and evangelism. Evangelicalism is marked by biblicism, personal piety, activism, and conversionism, or taking the Great Commission as a primary task for the church. These ideas of Nevius may seem obvious to some, but even today it is difficult for a "missionary" to let go of a new Christian community, especially when that community is poor, persecuted, and very naive about the Christian faith. However, when the young church has this localized identity and independence from the start, it does not have to work at being contextualized or indigenized, for it never has the chance of developing as a "foreign religion." The local church also naturally expresses its biblical faith as local leaders apply Scriptures to local contexts. This was the experience throughout Asia as evangelical Christianity moved from shoreline ports and trading centers to highlands and outlying islands.

India and China were among the earliest and largest fields of evangelical missionary outreach, but evangelical theology is driven by the Great Commission, "Go therefore and make disciples of all nations" (Mt 28:19). "Nations" does not mean modern political nation-states, but every language or ethnic entity. Evangelical missions began work among the ethnic Burmese in British Burma in 1807, and by the 1820s they were working among the Karen, but not until 1899 was work initiated among the ethnic Chin. In Thailand, missionary work began among the ethnic Thai (1833) and later among the Thai-Lao and even among the Chinese. The same concern for

---

[9] Allen D. Clark, *A History of the Church in Korea* (Seoul: Christian Literature Society of Korea, 1971), 114-15.

indigenous churches speaking indigenous languages, led by indigenous leaders, drove evangelical missionaries to move farther and farther inland as they translated and established schools. The last South and East Asian countries to receive evangelical missionaries were Japan (1859), Korea (1884), the Philippines (1899), and Nepal (1952).

In west Asia evangelical Christianity met a very different context, but was guided by the same principles mentioned above. The earliest Protestants to reach out in regions of the Ottoman Empire were Congregationalists, Wesleyan Methodists, and Episcopalians. Episcopalians and Anglicans, though inspired by evangelical revivals in Europe and North America, struggled with what it meant to do mission among the Orthodox. High Church Anglicans resisted witness to Orthodox churches, even if these churches seemed listless to evangelicals. In true evangelical fashion, the main strategy for the early missionaries was to work with the Orthodox churches to try to bring about revival and missionary concern for Muslims through biblical literacy and preaching. Orthodoxy, in their reasoning, needed to become more evangelical to engage in witness.[10] The strategy had little success, but over the years many Orthodox churches received a new impetus for their ongoing witness.

Earliest evangelicalism in all of Asia carried with it the essential DNA we have seen that came from the Protestant movement in the sixteenth century and the evangelical revivals in the eighteenth century. In each place the translation of Scripture was a priority, and from this followed the need for schools to teach biblical literacy and basic theological concepts. Indigenous Christian leadership soon followed. One of the most dramatic results of this translation priority was the early contextualization of evangelical Christianity in Asia, and thus greater diversity rooted in evangelical piety and theology. We will see other fruits or results from these primary evangelical concerns in mission in the following sections.

Indigenous Movements and Indigenous Leaders

The Protestant principle of access to the Bible, along with the more specifically evangelical concern for conversion, combined early on to create indigenous leadership as well as indigenous movements in Asia. For example, one of the

---

[10]In a similar fashion, early Roman Catholic witness to Orthodox, Coptic, and Ethiopians sought to bring them under the authority of the pope, making the Orthodox more like them (Catholics).

first Burmese women to convert, Ma Min Lay, learned to read the Bible from Ann Judson and then turned around and started the first school in the country for women (1820). Thus, in the first generation indigenous leaders were beginning to assert themselves in imitation and extension of what they had experienced. This was not always the case among all Protestants. Some High Church Anglicans and other nonevangelical missionaries relied on a well-trained church hierarchy, and therefore indigenous leadership was longer in coming. However, evangelical piety and missiology resisted more extreme forms of colonial missionary domination, facilitating the spread of evangelical forms of Christianity in Asia. A few examples will help us to understand how Asian forms of evangelical Christianity became the main expression of Christian faith in most of Asia.

The first example comes from the very province in China, Shandong, where John L. Nevius was working. A residential seminary had been founded in the last decades of the nineteenth century in Shandong, but by the end of the second decade of the twentieth century much of the theological education reflected modern American trends, many of which had no place in China. This was a time of antiforeignism in China, and in that light a group of Chinese Christians took theological education in their own hands and established their own North China Theological Seminary (December 1919). The seminary was started in reaction to the Western university model of theological education that was developing in China. The Chinese were clear about what they wanted in theological education: more Bible, less criticism of the Bible, more spirituality, and they wanted the seminary under the control of the Chinese.[11] It was the strong indigenous identity of the Chinese church in this particular area that gave them the confidence to say no to more liberal education (explicitly rejecting Union Theological Seminary in New York) and to seek their own more evangelical teachers and teaching. The new seminary insisted that all teaching be in Chinese.

Many other independent Christian movements in China rejected the liberalizing and secularizing tendencies of Western missionaries that came about in the first decades of the twentieth century. Until the last decade of the nineteenth

---

[11] John J. Heeren, *On the Shantung Front: A History of the Shantung Mission of the Presbyterian Church in the USA, 1861–1940 in Its Historical, Political and Economic Setting* (New York: Board of Foreign Missions of the Presbyterian Church in the U.S.A., 1940), 116-18.

century, Western missions expressed a broadly evangelical approach and held onto evangelical goals. Churches developed evangelistic ministries in Asia in the pattern taught from the West. Western theological "modernism" was exported to Asia, creating a rift between indigenous Asian evangelical churches and some of the newer missionaries who no longer endorsed conversion and who emphasized modern Western educational theory and sociology over established evangelical patterns of preaching and care for the poor. Thus, Asian resistance to modern theological movements was the catalyst to Asian church independence, creativity, and indigenous movements.

These indigenous movements of Christian renewal were further promoted by revivals and mass movements in the early twentieth century, creating resistance to Western imperialism and ideologies. Nee To-sheng, known to the West as Watchman Nee, is another example of this resistance that helped to shape Chinese evangelicalism. Raised to respect the Confucian classics, Nee attended an Anglican high school, but it was the more revivalist approach of evangelical Methodism that touched his heart in 1920. He studied for a year at Dora Yu's Bible school in Shanghai. Yu has been considered one of the most important Chinese evangelists of the early twentieth century. She not only led Watchman Nee to faith, but she discipled him, giving him the spiritual nurture and confidence that was Chinese from first to last. Nee was then influenced by literature from the Keswick movement and from the Welsh Revival (1904–1905), as well as a broad range of Protestant evangelical literature from Martin Luther to George Müller to Jonathan Edwards and John Wesley, and D. L. Moody, Charles Finney, and Charles Spurgeon. His motto for his great evangelist ministry would be, "I want nothing for myself; I want everything for the Lord." Other Chinese evangelists, church planters, and missionaries followed in this same evangelical stream: deeply engaged in biblical texts, a passion for evangelism, and resistance to Western imperialism, denominations, and theology. Great Chinese Christian leaders such as John Sung (Song Shangjie) and Wang Mingdao come to mind. Their evangelical faith was expressed only in the Chinese language, and it was strong enough to endure great suffering. Resistance to the West was an essential ingredient in indigenous evangelical movements in all of Asia.

Another way this evangelical indigenization accelerated the growth of Christianity in Asia was through mass movements. Evangelical development in Asia was more democratic than either Roman Catholic or later mainline Protestant missions. For example, the work of many evangelical missions was more extensive—beyond major cities—reaching out into villages and therefore among the poor. In South Asia this outreach to Dalits and tribal groups at times turned into mass movements of conversion. Andrew Gordon, working in the Punjab, came to the conclusion that trying to reach Punjabis through modern education and science was effective only for a few of the high-caste Urdu speakers. Thus, Gordon reasoned that direct preaching in the local languages would bring about conversion, and then education would come later. Conversions did come, and then mass movements began when local evangelists were trained. Mass movements began among the Megs and Chuhras in the 1870s and 1880s. These south Indian Christian communities grew at times 100 percent or more a year, making it unlikely that they would reflect Western structures or theology.

Indigenous leadership also arose in resistance to Western ideas and Western control of churches. One important example from India—both because he reveals a pattern and because he became a pattern for others—is Sadhu Sundar Singh (1889–1929?). Raised by a devout Hindu mother and a Sikh father, Sundar Singh attended Christian schools but ridiculed Christians until in 1904 he had a vision of Jesus Christ, who asked him, "Why do you persecute me? See, I have died on the cross for you and for the whole world." Upon his conversion after this vision, Sundar Singh was persecuted by his own family, and so he escaped and became a wandering pilgrim, studying the Bible as his own sacred book. He attempted to fit the Western Christian norms by studying at St. John's Seminary in Lahore, but a residential seminary was too confining for him. Sundar Singh became an Indian holy man, called a Sadhu, wandering in bare feet through India and even into the mountains of Tibet as a witness to Jesus Christ. His rejection of Western theology for Indian spirituality was his strength and the secret to his very important and influential ministry. Other indigenous Asian evangelical leaders began to arise in the twentieth century, and in each case resistance to Western models, structures, and theology was a major push factor in their development.

When Asian Christian leaders rose to lead churches, they also developed their own institutions. We noted above the North China Seminary as an example of Asian initiative and resistance to the West. Educational institutions were one form of indigenous initiative, but there were others. In 1903, in response to the great transformation that the gospel had brought to his life, and coming out of a series of revivals in Tirunelveli, YMCA Indian Secretary V. S. Azariah gathered together eight Anglican clergy and twenty-two laymen in Tamil Nadu to form the Indian Missionary Society (IMS). Through the international associations available in his work with the YMCA, Azariah had a larger vision to bring the benefits of the gospel especially to the oppressed in India. Founded in 1903, the IMS was a completely indigenous movement. All of the missionaries were Indian, their mission field was India, and their support came from Indian Christians. Much of the support came from local sextons or church workers collecting handfuls of rice. Later, Azariah would become the first Indian Anglican bishop.

After Indian independence, another significant Indian missionary society was formed, the Friends Missionary Prayer Band (1959). This indigenous missionary society also reflects basic evangelical themes in Indian dress (or more accurately, it expresses Indian evangelicalism). It focuses on a fourfold objective:

1. proclaiming the gospel in the mother tongue of the people[12]

2. planting indigenous congregations among these peoples

3. producing local leaders

4. providing wholesome development

Indigenous leadership development within evangelicalism in Asia came much earlier than in Roman Catholic missions or in the nonevangelical Protestant missions. In Korea the first resident missionaries arrived in 1884, and by 1907 the first indigenous presbytery was established by the Presbyterian church, and the majority of the leaders were Korean. There was no looking back. The Korean church has always been very evangelical, with an emphasis on Bible knowledge and Christian witness, and its indigenous

---

[12]"Those Indians who can understand major languages such as Hindi or Telugu, no new translation of the Bible is needed. But tribal people who do not understand these languages should have the Bible in their own mother tongue because they can hear Jesus Christ and his apostles speak their language and better understand the content of the Bible. Full New Testament is already available in *Vasavi*, *Malto* and *Chodri*. The New Testament is being translated into *Varli*, *Pawri*, *Kurux*, *Hariyanvi*, and *Khandeshi*." Daniel Jeyaraj, "Christian Message in Life and Action: Two Case Studies from India," unpublished paper presented at Pittsburgh Theological Seminary, December 11, 2009.

leadership came very early. Evangelical leadership in Asia, like in the West, often received revivals as an expected outcome of faithful preaching.

Evangelical Revivals and Political Resistance

As we have noted above, one of the main catalysts for Protestant mission and for indigenization was the occurrence of revivals. Revivals reinforced the evangelical character of the Asian churches, strengthened indigenous cultural themes, and at the same time empowered Asians to lead. The empowerment directed by the Holy Spirit acted as a more direct route for Asian leaders to be discipled. There was no long-term training dominated by Western forms and structures. But revivals also have had a political characteristic to them, often fueled by oppression and therefore allowing Asian Christians to express themselves as a type of resistance to other authorities. One good example of this is the Korean Revival, beginning in 1907. This revival seems to have been directly related to other revivals, including the Welsh Revival (1904–1905), the revival in northeast India, the revival in the Mukti Mission in India, and the Shandong Revival.[13] All of these revivals had the effect of deepening the identity of Christian communities with the local contexts, strengthening the Christian communities, and empowering them for crosscultural witness. The Korean Revival, although similar to other revivals of the period, did have expressions that were unique to Korea. First, when the revival began missionaries were more observers than leaders. The revival began in Pyongyang and touched church leaders, women's groups, and even children in primary school. Second, the revival initiated Korean unity and cooperation for evangelistic outreach. By 1909 a bold Korean Christian initiative was announced called the Million Souls movement, to begin to pray and work for the conversion of one million Koreans. Third, Korean leaders who began to come forward were raised up by the rising tide of revival waters. Kil Sun Joo, the nearly blind preacher of the revival, became a nationally known evangelist and church planter. Kim Ik Du became a great evangelist with a gift of healing. He eventually died as a Christian martyr under the communists. Finally, the Korean Revival, coming

---

[13] For the relationship between the Korea and Shandong revivals, see Lian Xi, *Redeemed by Fire: The Rise of Popular Christianity in the Modern World* (New Haven, CT: Yale University Press, 2010), 87-88. J. Edwin Orr, Baptist historian of church revivals, identifies the period from 1900 to 1910 as a period of a global "Fifth General Awakening." See Orr's *Evangelical Awakenings in Eastern Asia* (Minneapolis: Bethany Fellowship, 1975).

at a time of increased oppression from the Japanese Empire, expressed identity with Jesus Christ as uniquely being Korean, standing against the foreign Japanese hegemony. Korean Christianity, from this revival, identified Korean Christians as real Koreans in opposition to foreign domination. Evangelical Christianity was being shaped by indigenous leaders who were responding to the social, religious, and political contexts that were their own.

Other revivals or periods of rapid growth were even more directly related to political events. Christianity in Singapore, especially after independence from Great Britain, has been strongly evangelical, whether as expressed in traditional Western denominations or through newer evangelical churches. When the Singapore government made the decision to redistribute the population of Singapore in order to ensure a mixing of races and religions, this had a positive, almost revivalistic, impact on Christianity. In the anxiety caused by the disruption to families, many people lost their religious moorings that were attached to a local temple or mosque. The "new towns" and housing estates grew rapidly in the 1970s, and this was a period of very rapid growth of Christianity—from about 6.5 percent in 1970 to about 13 percent in 2000.[14] Technically speaking, many would not call this a revival or awakening, but after 180 years of Christian witness, this sudden growth had many of the marks of a true revival. Similarly, social policies in neighboring Indonesia, this time to resist the communist insurgency threat, also helped to create the environment for very rapid church growth. In 1965 the Indonesian government faced a coup d'état. The response was to weed out the communists, who at the time were the largest political party in the country. Since communists were understood to be atheists, all Indonesians were required to identify their religion and carry with them religious identity cards. The five recognized religions in Indonesia were identified as Islam, Protestantism, Catholicism, Buddhism, and Hinduism. Those who had no religion before, or who had attended Christian schools, often chose Christianity. The result was a large influx of Christians into the churches, and where Christians were strongly supportive of conversion the preaching and teaching stimulated rapid growth. Evangelical presence in Indonesia grew

---

[14]According to *Operation World,* ed. Jason Mandryk (Milton Keynes, UK: Authentic Publications, 2010), evangelical Christianity in Singapore during these thirty years grew from 1.8 percent to 7.8 percent.

from 1.5 percent in the mid-1960s to over 5 percent by 2000.¹⁵ Political disruption, forced migration, and even communist threats (and communism itself) have tended to promote revival of evangelicalism in Asia.

Pentecostalism in Asian Evangelicalism

It is not historically accurate to divide Pentecostalism in Asia from evangelicalism, since historians are now clear about the origins and precursors of modern Pentecostalism. Asian Pentecostalism originated in Asia and was soon linked with similar movements from the West. Pentecostalism in Asia borrowed from Western movements and ideas, and it created its own unique forms, structures, and institutions. Soon it became a new stream of Asian evangelicalism.¹⁶ Since Pentecostal-like movements occurred in Asia as they did in the West in the late nineteenth century, it is not helpful to talk about borrowing or direct influence. It is more accurate to talk about the global cross-fertilization that occurred with the rise of Pentecostalism. For example, in both Asia and the West there was a very close relationship between the Holiness movements and Pentecostalism. In 1901 a Holiness movement began in Japan, initiated by one of the most famous Japanese evangelists, Nakada Juji, in partnership with Charles and Lettie Cowman¹⁷ and Ernest and Julie Kilbourn. This movement, emphasizing indigenous leadership training, self-support, the imminent return of Christ (premillennialism), and holiness as a second experience of the Holy Spirit,¹⁸ was both a precursor of Pentecostalism and an Asian-initiated missionary movement: the Oriental Missionary Society. Without tracing the lines of the various movements, some general themes can be lifted up for a better understanding of Asian Pentecostalism as an Asian evangelical movement.

First, evangelicalism in Asia in the nineteenth century often looked more like the book of Acts than like Calvin's *Institutes of the Christian Religion* or the Anglican Book of Common Prayer. What I mean by this is that European and North American evangelical missionaries encountered spirits and demons,

---

¹⁵Ibid.
¹⁶Michael Bergunder, in his important study of Pentecostalism in south India (*The South Indian Pentecostal Movement in the 20th Century* [Grand Rapids: Eerdmans, 2008]), discusses the historiography of Pentecostal origins in his introduction (pp. 1-19).
¹⁷Lettie Cowman was the author of the enduring devotional classic *Streams in the Desert* (1925).
¹⁸Or as a series of subsequent experiences.

dreams and visions, throughout Asia, even though most did not have a theology that included such occurrences. For some of these missionaries experiences of the Holy Spirit were part of their heritage, and the more direct spiritual encounters were simply a new dimension of the Spirit coming with power. John L. Nevius, the Princeton-educated missionary to Shandong province, China, heard and observed so much about the spirit world that he wrote a book called *Demon Possession and Allied Themes*. He was not at all a Pentecostal, but he dealt with Pentecostal themes, including healings, casting out demons, and other "supernatural" expressions of the Spirit of God. As with the development of Christianity in Africa, many Asian societies were culturally and spiritually closer to the world of the Bible than the Enlightenment world of the North Atlantic missionaries. Thus, the spiritual experiences during worship or prayer meetings of revivals often did not follow Western theology, but traversed spiritual terrain that was indigenous. When the Great Revival in Korea broke out, it was among Presbyterians and Methodists for the most part, but the experiences were nothing that Calvin or the Wesley would recognize. Missionaries describe it as being disorderly, filled with impassioned cries of repentance, and later marked by miraculous healings. Even though classic Pentecostalism (with attendant speaking in tongues) did not arrive in Korea until 1930, many of the connections with worldwide revival and Pentecostalism were already present. Asian cultures were ripe for Pentecostal Christianity even without Pentecostal leadership or theology.

A second characteristic we might call the Indian connection. Most of the features of classic Pentecostalism were first seen in India, beginning with an unlikely pioneer: Pandita Ramabai, a Brahmin widow, Christian convert, and founder of a home for orphan girls. Ramabai teamed with American Minnie Abrams beginning in 1897, and in 1905 a revival broke out among the Mukti Mission girls and spread throughout the Maharashtra state. Girls were overwhelmed by their sin and cried out to God for forgiveness, and there was weeping followed by great joy. Two manifestations of this revival—speaking in tongues and evangelistic outreach—were recorded by Minnie Abrams. Even though later Pandita Ramabai stepped back from the Pentecostal movement, this revival marks the birth of Pentecostalism in South Asia, and soon missionaries from the Azuza Street Revival in Los Angeles were working alongside Indians in Pentecostal missionary outreach. The

Indian connection is also important in the missionary outreach that began from Pentecostalism in India. Missionary outreach from India spread to Ceylon (Sri Lanka), as well as to Southeast and northeast Asia.

Indian Pentecostalism also is a catalyst to indigenization and ministry to the poor. Ramabai channeled the spiritual power and awakening of the revival at Mukti into famine relief efforts and other ministry to the poor. The Pentecostal experience, as an empowering event, enabled indigenous Christians to resist foreign leadership or domination. Having experienced the power and grace of God, they were free to engage in ministry without dependence on foreign missionaries. In this way Pentecostalism, spread by indigenous leaders (including many Bible women), advanced church independence and indigenization.

A third characteristic of Asian Pentecostalism is its immediate missionary outreach. In this regard, global Pentecostalism has a certain homogeneity; Pentecostalism everywhere breaks out of old patterns and focuses its energy on both personal transformation and missionary outreach. Empowerment is for mission. The origin of the modern missionary movement from China, "Back to Jerusalem," can be found in earlier revivals (Pentecostal, Holiness, and evangelical) in Shandong and other provinces in China.[19] It was revivals (both Charismatic and Pentecostal) in Korea, beginning in 1907, that have inspired Korean missions overseas, and other island revivals such as in Nias (1916–1922) and Timor (1965) led to island-wide missionary outreach. Pentecostalism in Asia continues to inspire and empower Asians for crosscultural outreach in Asia. Although Pentecostalism is not as dominant in Asia as in Africa or Latin America, it still has been a vital ingredient to Christian growth in Asia.

According to the Pew Forum on Religion and Public Life, Pentecostals in Asia went from 1 percent of the population of Asia in 1970 to over 4 percent in 2006. Four percent of four billion is 160 million, and that is a lot.[20] Pentecostalism is still a young movement in Asia, and it is still more movement than institution, which means that it is not as organized and unified as older movements are. In one state of India, Tamil Nadu, there are presently over

---

[19] Its earliest history is most likely found in a vision that came out of the early Jesus Family community in Shandong in the 1920s.

[20] Quoted in David H. Lumsdaine, ed., *Evangelical Christianity and Democracy in Asia* (Oxford: Oxford University Press, 2009), xi. See also "Overview: Pentecostalism in Asia," Pew Research Center, October 5, 2006, www.pewforum.org/2006/10/05/overview-pentecostalism-in-asia/.

thirty-three Pentecostal bodies, and twenty-seven of these are indigenous, or founded by local leaders. In many countries in Asia it is difficult to distinguish Pentecostal churches from non-Pentecostal by their worship, missionary work, or organization. Many churches in Asia have been influenced by the Pentecostal immediacy and intimacy of the Holy Spirit. Pentecostalism continues to grow, both as a distinct movement and as a spiritual dimension within Asian evangelicalism.

Women as Subjects in Asian Evangelicalism

Pentecostalism, as we have just seen, has been a movement for the empowerment for women in Asia. In fact, evangelical missions have done more for women's liberation and advancement than any other single force or cultural movement in Asia. Islamic regions in Asia provided no education for young girls or women, and in most Hindu regions women were also kept at home, living in *zenanas*, parts of houses in South Asia where women were to reside. In South Asia for over a millennium before the arrival of Protestant missionaries, there had been *devadasis*, or temple prostitutes, who were dedicated to a particular god in a local temple. These *devadasis* started out as young girls and were taught ritual Hindu dance as part of their role in the Hindu temple. In China, the feet of upper-class women were bound from a young age to keep them small ("little flowers") and beautiful, and to prevent the woman from traveling away from home. All of these structural elements in Asia—keeping women ignorant, isolated, temple prostitution, and foot binding—are evidence of how women were treated as inferior to men in most of Asia. Although evangelicals have not always treated women as equal, evangelical Christianity had always treated girls as equal to boys in basic knowledge of literacy and study of the Bible. For example, the first law regarding education in the Puritan Colony of Massachusetts required every town to have compulsory education for both boys (up to twenty-one) and for girls (up to eighteen). The law was called "the Old Deluder Satan Act," since the reason for education was to fight against Satan, who could less easily delude a person who could read the Bible (1647). Puritanism, from both England and New England, is one of the major tap roots of evangelicalism. Equal treatment of women began with literacy for girls, so they could read the Bible, and this evangelical conviction was carried to Asia.

The early exposure of evangelical Christianity in Asia was to married couples and families serving through their homes. The contrast with the earlier Roman Catholic priests, monks, and friars was immediately evident. By the middle of the nineteenth century, single women were serving in Asia, often, but not only, to reach women in the *zenanas*. However, other Christian women pioneers were "Bible women," traveling through villages distributing and teaching the Bible. Thus, for many Indians, Indonesians, Chinese, or Thai, their first exposure to Christian teaching was from Bible women. Asian women learned from what they saw and heard. They received a message that was every bit as important for them as it was for the men in the villages. Evangelical Christianity had a democratizing and a gender-equalizing effect. One of the examples we have already mentioned is Ma Min Lay, the early convert among the Burmese. Other Asian converts recognized the need for social reform, especially the treatment of women, which came from Christian teaching. The Hindu convert Krishnan Mohan Banerjea (1813–1885) wrote an influential essay in support of women's education, "Native Female Education" (1841). Such a conviction challenged Indian cultural norms for decades. "In those days of child marriage, female infanticide, the burning of widows, and, in the North, the Purdah system, there was little thought of the emancipation of women. . . . The idea was prevalent that education was not for respectable women. When, therefore, the Calcutta students, in 1831 debated the subject of female education they were handling a new and revolutionary idea."[21]

As in the early church, the gospel proclaimed to women meant liberation.[22] Women were often attracted to consider Christianity both because it was often proclaimed by women and because of its radically democratic approach to humanity. We have already mentioned one of the great examples of the changed status of women, Pandita Ramabai (1858–1922). Ramabai was raised by an enlightened Hindu father who taught her to read Vedic texts in Sanskrit. Married only briefly, when her husband died she traveled to England, where she became a Christian. With a new view of humanity, sin, salvation, and

---

[21] Cyril Bruce Firth, *An Introduction to Indian Church History* (Serampore: The Senate of Serampore College, 1968).
[22] See Rodney Stark, *The Rise of Christianity: A Sociologist Reconsiders History* (Princeton, NJ: Princeton University Press, 1996). See chapter 5: "The Role of Women in Christian Growth."

responsibility before God, she became a poet, writer, social reformer, and advocate for the most needy girls and women in India. In 1881, Ramabai founded the Arya Mahila Sabha, which was the first feminist organization in India. Her Mukti ("liberation") mission, rescuing widows and young brides, is still in existence today.

One of the signs of the impact of evangelical liberation for women (in addition to the end of sati, foot binding, and other traditional practices) is the strong leadership of women in churches in Asia today. China, a traditional Confucian society with two generations of communist rule, is one of the fastest-growing churches today, and much of its leadership is female. In fact, even where traditional patterns of gender roles continue in the church, women are educated and are actively involved as evangelists and missionaries. Asian societies have been transformed in large part by the pioneering work of Asian Christian women reached through evangelical witness.

Persecution, Martyrdom, and Political Influence

Persecution has been more a part of Christianity in Asia than in any other continent. From the Mediterranean to the Pacific, Christian communities have lived almost exclusively as minority communities among major religions (which are often supported by governments).[23] When Christian witness challenges long-held traditions, such as the role or place of women, tensions often escalate into violence. Conversion, one of the identifying characteristics of evangelicalism, becomes a flashpoint for tensions and subsequent persecution. These persecutions are sometimes popular and at other times political. Whether government sanctioned or not, we can identify four major types of persecution of evangelicals in Asia in the past three centuries. The first, as we have noted, was persecution, or at least resistance from colonial multinational companies and colonial governments. It may seem odd, but with the primary concern to make money and to control trade, Western leaders often resisted the work of missionaries, especially among Muslim communities. During the first half of the twentieth century it was not a European but an Asian colonial government that caused much persecution and suffering: Japan. Empires, whether

---

[23]The one exception is the Philippines. But even in this predominantly Christian country, persecution continues in the southern island of Mindanao, which is predominantly Muslim.

Western or Asian, have resisted evangelical witness, especially to the poor and uneducated.

The second type of persecution has come from the newly independent Asian governments whose independence was often an affirmation of their religious heritage. Nationalism and independence flourished with historic religious identity. Thus, Pakistan's Islamic identity and Burma's Buddhist identity challenged Christian freedom and especially evangelical witness. Decolonization of Asian nations (all Asian nations except Thailand, Bhutan, Afghanistan, and Saudi Arabia had been colonized) not only restricted international connections with indigenous Christian groups, but it also stoked the flames of religious revivals of national religions. Movements such as Hindutva in India promote Indianess as Hinduness and interpret Christian conversion as opposed to this Indian identity.

Third, Christian persecution has been greatest not from other religions but from newer secular ideologies. The rapid growth of communism in East Asia brought about the largest and most extensive persecution since the early persecutions in Persia. Christians were one of many groups that were persecuted under the Cultural Revolution in China (1966–1976), but in proportion to their numbers, their suffering was probably the greatest. With the rise of communism in Vietnam and the reunification of Vietnam, there was an exodus of many Christian leaders from that young Protestant church. Many other Vietnamese Christians were imprisoned, but as is often the case, the persecutions in these communist countries have, in due time, had the remarkable effect of increasing the rate of growth of Christianity.

Finally, modern persecution of evangelicals has been through both governments and popular uprisings. Anticonversion laws (often called "freedom of religion laws") have been proposed and passed in at least five states in India. The enforcement is uneven and imprecise, but the message is clear: we want to keep Hindus as Hindus as a matter of Indian identity. It is estimated that there were only seven hundred Christians in Cambodia and Laos after missionary work from 1923 to 1970. In 1965, Prince Sihanouk expelled all missionaries from Cambodia as CIA agents. When they returned in 1970 Christianity began to grow, but the rise of the Khmer Rouge in the mid-1970s meant the collapse of the church in Cambodia. This was a largely secular, communist vision of remaking all of society as an egalitarian, strict, and austere state. All religion was outlawed, and the Christian population quickly dropped from ten thousand to about four hundred.

Popular persecution is also common, and it is often encouraged by the state. One example is the Boxer Rebellion (1900) in China. "The Society of Righteous Harmony Fists," as the Boxers were known, was a nationalistic and religious uprising against both Western colonial powers and Christianity. The decline of the Qing Empire and the failure of the reform movement in the 1890s led Empress Qixi to encourage rebellion against foreign powers. The Boxers were willing and able to respond. Violence was greatest in certain regions of the East, but even Muslims from western China were encouraged to join the Boxers in their revolt against foreigners and foreign religion. More Chinese Christians were killed than missionaries, but the loss of mission property and lives led to an Eight Nation Alliance to put down the rebellions. The "Boxers" had many slogans, but one of the most popular expressed a primary concern of the movement: "Defend Chinese Religion and Get Rid of Foreign Religion."

Persecution of evangelicals continues to be a major theme in Asia, both because of their strong commitment to conversion and because of their emphasis on the Bible. Biblical preaching and small groups studying the Bible often lead evangelicals to patterns of ministry among the neediest, and this may lead to direct social engagement. This social engagement—on behalf of the poor, the oppressed, for women and children—does not always translate into political engagement, but at times it does. We seldom see public protest and other types of direct confrontation with governments in Asia (approaches that are more Western), but Christian resistance to injustices and oppressions is evident throughout Asia.

The twentieth century began a century of persecution of Christians in Asia with the Boxer Rebellion, and the persecution continues today. The communist advance in China, Vietnam, and Laos, along with the revived Muslim nations of Iran (Iranian Revolution of 1979), Afghanistan, Malaysia, and Pakistan, has increased the suffering of Christians in Asia. One of the main causes of suffering is the perception that there is a loss of social order or social harmony when many people convert to Christianity. Today mass movements (or even the perception of these) among Dalits in India continue to cause persecution. Christian converts are rewarded for conversion back to Hinduism (though many were never Hindus to begin with), and Christian leaders and buildings are often targeted when Christians do not convert. In east Malaysia, tribal people are "encouraged" to convert to Islam by being offered free (or reduced) tuition for education, access to the university, or new housing. Christians are excluded from basic social services in many countries of Asia as a form of passive persecution. In west Asia Islamic law may prescribe death to the person who leaves Islam, but this is seldom carried out. Thus, it is still true that in most countries of Asia, evangelical witness continues in creative and careful ways in the context of persecution.

But persecution is not the only political story of evangelicalism in Asia. One of the most observable byproducts of evangelicalism in Asia is the development of democratic movements. The assumption that evangelicalism is apolitical or "otherworldly" is inaccurate both historically and globally. Evangelicals (especially of the Pentecostal variety) tend to be activist in their piety—meeting to study the Bible, pray, and develop social networks—and in their social networks they begin to engage society. Informal associations of evangelicals are often the seedbed of democracy. Thus, with the spread of evangelicalism has come less hierarchical associations and greater participation in social collectives. This is an often overlooked but essential quality of evangelicalism: Christian communities, under the guidance of the Holy Spirit, congregate, debate, decide, act, and engage their world.

In addition, evangelicalism has had a more direct impact on politics in Asia through the participation of evangelicals in the democratic process where that is viable. More than any other continent, Asia has been dominated by non-Christian religious states that have often excluded and persecuted Christians. However, this is slowly changing. It has been noted

> that evangelicals participated in national and regional politics with important consequences for democracy and civil society in several parts of Asia, including the Philippines, Korea, Indonesia, and Northeast India. In the Philippines, Korea and Northeast India, evangelical politics has proven especially significant largely because evangelicals have been more numerous than in almost all other parts of Asia.[24]

---

[24]Timothy Samuel Shah, from the preface, in Lumsdaine, *Evangelical Christianity and Democracy in Asia*, xiii.

Christian participation in China today reveals another way evangelical life contributes to political engagement. Evangelical witness before the communist "liberation" laid a foundation for Christian life that included participation in the social witness in each local community. When persecution increased, especially under the Cultural Revolution (1966–1976), Christian communities organized locally and through networks. On one level, a very dangerous and fragile, but massive, democratic experiment was carried out. Christianity, in fact a very evangelical and vital form of Christianity, emerged in the 1980s in the form of regional and even national Christian societies. Today these vital communities have grown, for in all places it is necessary to have some relationship with governing authorities. Christians are negotiating their place in social and political matrix of modern China and in doing so are promoting public discussion and debate—the foundations of democracy. As evangelical Christianity grows and matures, its place in society will be a major theme, whether in persecution or in participation.

EVANGELICALS, ASIAN RELIGIONS, AND SUB-CHRISTIAN CULTS

Of all the continents, Asia is unique in Christian history because of its religious encounters. Only in Asia did Christianity encounter major multicultural and even continent-wide religions. In all other continents, most all of the religions that Christianity encountered were limited to a particular culture or ethnic group. Larger intercultural religions such as Buddhism, Islam, and Hinduism are more resistant to Christian witness, and so the interreligious encounter is longer and more complex. The earliest evangelical missionaries encountered these major faiths in India. Searching for ways to relate the gospel, they studied the texts and experimented with newer patterns of Christian witness. Adoniram Judson, pioneer missionary in Burma (Myanmar), studied the ancient Pali Buddhist texts and set up a *zayat* (rest house) alongside a road where he would sit and engage Buddhists in discussions about religion. His approach was positive, dialogical, and attentive. Not all evangelicals were so quick to listen, however. Especially later in the nineteenth century, at the height of colonialism in Asia, many missionaries became more critical and judgmental, especially of Hindu temples and their depiction of the Hindu gods.

By the twentieth century evangelicals were encountering many of the religious and cultural issues in their witness that the Roman Catholics had encountered centuries earlier. Asian religions were totalistic, directing every area of life and even death and beyond. How, for example, could a Chinese young man become a Christian and abandon his responsibility to carry on sacrifices for the ancestors? How could a good Hindu girl become a Christian and refuse to participate with family worship at a local temple? Could a Muslim girl profess faith in Christ and still live with her family? Would they accept her, and if so, how must she dress? It was such webs of cultural meaning that hampered evangelical witness, especially among the Buddhists, Hindus, Sikhs, and Muslims in Asia. Where there were conversions, they were predominantly among mountain people, or tribals in the highlands of Thailand, Myanmar, and Vietnam, or among Dalits, who were excluded even from Hindu temples.

Even while evangelical witness developed new forms for witness—distributing Christian tracts, YMCA/YWCA, Sunday Schools, and so on—Buddhists and Hindus began to respond. The response was both rejection and imitation of evangelical missions. Hinduism was transformed by its encounter with evangelical missions. "Hinduism [began] to be defined in western fashion as a religion, but the various responses to Christianity and western education show that Indians were appropriating Christian teaching on their own terms."[25] Hindu social reform movements began with India's encounter with missionaries. But also, many Hindus began to study the life of Jesus, and they found him very attractive. Ram Mohan Roy (1772–1833) argued for monotheism behind the many gods and avatars of Hinduism and, like Mahatma Gandhi many years later, he studied and followed many of the ethical precepts of Jesus. By the end of the nineteenth century Buddhism was responding to Christian missions by starting a Young Men's Buddhist Association (1899) and Buddhist Sunday school classes for both boys and girls.

As Asians appropriated some of the teachings and structures of evangelical witness, evangelicals searched for contextually appropriate ways to relate in Asian religious cultures. In India, a Christian ashram movement began in the late nineteenth century: a Hindu religious model of retreat and

---

[25]Irvin and Sunquist, *History of the World Christian Movement*, vol. 3, from chapter 5.

religious reflection, but now focused on the teachings of Jesus. One of the pioneers in this type of Indian Christian witness was the Methodist missionary E. Stanley Jones (1884–1973). Whereas much evangelical witness began with teachings, Jones would often start with listening to the spiritual experience of the Hindu or Buddhist, and then encourage the Christian to explain their experience of God through Jesus Christ.[26] His "round table" discussions attracted many religious leaders in a nonthreatening environment and provided an environment where more people heard the Christian witness. In Korea, it was a Korean convert who adapted an indigenous Korean religious practice of going to a mountain temple and praying to the spirits before daybreak and used it for Christian worship. As part of the 1907 Great Korean Revival, Reverend Kil Sun Ju initiated daybreak prayer meetings, which continue to be a mark of Korean Christianity today.

Asian evangelicals continue to struggle with witness to the great blocks of religious adherents in Asia. Secularization has had both a negative and positive impact on Christian witness in this continent of "world religions." In Singapore, the Christian population is about 15 percent, the same percentage as there are of "free thinkers" (no religion). In China, a half-century of secular communism has left many people questioning life without religion. In both of these countries Christianity is growing. However, in Japan, Thailand, and Taiwan, where secularization is also having a great impact, Christianity is not growing rapidly. While evangelical Christianity is growing in most countries of Asia, there is also a revival of certain forms of Buddhism, and there are vigorous new movements within Islam.

Not all encounters with religions in Asia have been as neat as a meeting of Christian with Hindu or Buddhist. Evangelicalism, with its more diffuse authority structure and greater propensity to contextualize, has unwittingly spawned many sub-Christian cults. The mixing of essential elements from religions we call syncretism, and many newer religions in Asia (or in the West, but that come from Asia) have mixed religious elements. In Asia, it also must be recognized that evangelical witness has at times led to the formation of sub-Christian—usually chiliastic—sects. In each case a charismatic leader has risen to give a definitive interpretation of Scripture and

---

[26]E. Stanley Jones, *Christ at the Round Table* (New York: Abingdon, 1928).

of the times. The most obvious example is the Unification Church of Moon Sun Myung.[27] At the age of fifteen, Moon, while praying at daybreak, had a vision of Jesus, who spoke to him and asked him to complete the work of Jesus in bringing unity and peace to the church in the world. Raised a Presbyterian, Moon began his own church in North Korea and eventually moved his ministry to South Korea (after the war) and then to the United States. Although evangelicals are marked by a devotion to Scripture, Moon soon developed a new scripture for his followers called the Book of Divine Principles. We are not interested here in the myriad of unusual teachings, ministries, and businesses of the Unification Church, but we do want to note that Moon himself, like many other indigenous leaders of the colonial era, came out of the very evangelical Presbyterian Church of North Korea, but he then recentered his church on his own teachings and personal kingdom.

An earlier and far more lethal sect that came out of evangelical missions was the *Taiping Tianguo* (Heavenly kingdom of eternal peace and prosperity) of Hong Xiuquan (1814–1864). Hong, after failing his civil service exams many times, turned to Chinese Christian literature produced by one of the first Protestant Chinese evangelists, Lian Fa (Leong Kung Fa). After reading Lian's "Good Words for Exhorting the Age" and portions of the Bible, he had a series of visions and he began to construct his own religion. "He believed he had received a divine mandate to lead the people."[28] From the Bible he picked up the need to destroy idols and to be fully devoted to God. From Chinese culture he retained morning prayers, burning paper containing confessed sins, lunar New Year celebrations, and other practices. Most significantly, Hung elevated himself to the status of brother of Jesus who was called to clean China of demons. More Old Testament law than New Testament grace, Hung spread his teachings through an earthly kingdom, and soon his army numbered in the hundreds of thousands. By the time Hong's kingdom was crushed, the Taiping Rebellion had lasted fifteen years and had resulted in the death of about seventy million people.[29] Having spent some time

---

[27] The full name of the church is the Holy Spirit Association for the Unification of World Christianity.
[28] Patricia Siew and China Group, "Hong Xiuquan," in Sunquist, *Dictionary of Asian Christianity*, 349.
[29] For a full discussion of the theology, the rebellion, and statistics, see Jonathan Spence, *God's Chinese Son: The Taiping Heavenly Kingdom of Hong Xiuquan* (New York: W. W. Norton, 1996).

studying the Bible with a Baptist missionary and being devoted to the Bible, Hong had many evangelical advantages. However, missionaries would not baptize him because his motives were unclear. It was immediately after he turned his back on evangelical teaching that he began to shape his own earthly kingdom using Christian resources.

Examples of eccentric cults spinning off evangelical structures can be found in most Asian countries. Two other quick examples will help to illustrate the trends. Indian Pentecostalism, we noted, is easily traced back to the earliest years of the twentieth century, but indigenous Pentecostal evangelists came much later. One of the earliest and most controversial was Paulasser Lawrie (aka Shree Lahari Krishna; 1921–1989). Lawrie came from an Anglican and Salvation Army background in both south India and Ceylon; however, until later in life he endeavored to remain a Church of South India communicant while preaching Pentecostal sermons and while being engaged in a ministry of healing. Lawrie's ministry developed, he traveled and gathered a US following, and eventually he claimed that he was Jesus Christ. Strongly eschatological in the mid-1970s, Lawrie eventually said that he himself would fulfill other religions as well. By the time he finished his ministry, he was revealing other formerly hidden (gnostic) teachings. He claimed to be an avatar who would return again after his own death.

Another chiliastic or millenarian group is the *Dongfang Shandian* (Eastern lightning sect) of eastern China. This sect is also an eccentric Christian group that only began about 1989. According to their teachings, the Messiah has returned as a Chinese woman to release people from evil. They also have an additional sacred book called *Lightning from the Orient*. The Chinese government considers this fairly large group an illegal cult because of its strong millennial hopes and longings. What do these and many other sub-Christian sects tell us about evangelicalism in Asia? We must be careful not to make quick conclusions, assuming that the causes are all found in the genetic makeup of evangelicalism, because Roman Catholicism in Vietnam and the Philippines and throughout Latin America has also engendered numerous syncretistic movements. And yet the combination of democratizing social movements (and the free-market structures), the priority to contextualize (or translate) the message, and interaction with many Asian religions continues to produce new religious movements in Asia.

Evangelical Future

It has been said that Asia is the one continent where Christianity has failed to win allegiance of great populations or groupings of people. On one level this is true. In countries such as Japan, Taiwan, and even the subcontinent of India, Sri Lanka, Pakistan, and Bangladesh, the Christian population remains under 5 percent. In western Asia the Christian population remains even smaller, Christianity never having recovered from the Arab Muslim invasions of the seventh and eighth centuries. The two countries that stand out, neither of them have a large evangelical population, are located at the far eastern and far western ends of Asia: Lebanon (over 70 percent Christian in 1900 and about 40 percent Christian today) and the Philippines (over 92 percent Christian). It is true, evangelical Christianity has not broken through the large bloc of Muslim communities that spread across western and southern Asia, and it has barely started to reach the largely Buddhist and Hindu regions. The exceptions to this generalization are that Christianity has spread rapidly among Koreans, Chinese, and southeastern Buddhist regions where communist rule (or the communist threat) has caused a great disruption in societies. Thus, in China, Vietnam, Cambodia, Malaysia, Singapore, and Indonesia, the Chinese diaspora in East Asia are coming to faith, and this is happening mostly through Asian evangelical outreach.

Although statistics don't tell us everything, they do tell us something. In 1900 the Protestant population in Asia was mostly all evangelical, but it was less than 1 percent of the population of the continent. Roman Catholics were also about 1 percent of the Asian population. In 2005 about 3 percent of Asians were Roman Catholic, and 6 percent were Protestant. In countries such as Nepal, Vietnam, and Korea, where there were very few Christians at all, there are now vibrant evangelizing communities. The growth is uneven, but the witness to unreached areas is overwhelmingly Asian and evangelical (including Pentecostal) today.

"Evangelical" looks and sounds very different in Asia than in North America or Europe. In countries such as Vietnam or Malaysia, or China, or Singapore or Korea, where most of the Christians are recent converts, the evangelical aroma is very strong. There is great zeal for evangelism and discipleship of young converts, and there is an activism that most Western Christians find more in their history than in their churches today. Conversion is a central element in defining evangelicals, and since the overall growth of Christianity in Asia has been from conversion in the past two generations, most Christians talk about conversion as part of the normal Christian life. In countries such as China, Vietnam, Cambodia, Nepal, Malaysia, Indonesia, Singapore, and Korea, where Christianity has experienced its greatest growth ever since the 1960s, most of the Protestants would be described by outsiders as evangelical, even if it is not their own self-designation. What Western Christians would call "mainline" churches (Methodist, Presbyterian, Lutheran, and Anglican) are growing, confident, and very evangelical in Asia. Thus, identifying evangelicals in Asia is more than counting self-identified evangelicals in evangelical churches. Still, the Asia Evangelical Alliance claims that nearly one half of the three hundred million Christians in Asia (140 million) are evangelical.[30] The number is probably much higher.

Many of the themes we have looked at above will continue to be key themes for evangelicals in Asia. Their encounter with major religions will be an issue, as will their concern for the poor, women's issues, and translation of texts and worship patterns. However, some more recent issues are becoming more important. In East Asia there is a growing minority of very wealthy Christians who are using their financial resources for evangelistic outreach. The great disparity of rich and poor in Asia creates a context similar to that of evangelical missions in the late nineteenth and early twentieth century. Rich Taiwanese or Chinese engaged in mission to Vietnam or Indonesia or Nepal may have trouble adapting to the different economic standards. Some groups of well-connected Asians raise money from rich Asians and from rich Westerners to support Asian pastors and missionaries. Money issues are beginning to be a problem again, but now from newer money sources. The rise of militant and violent Islam is not a new issue for Christians in Asia (it dates back thirteen hundred years); however, the new dispersed and popular forms of violence creates a new missional context that is less clearly defined.

Another ongoing issue that is at the heart of modern evangelicalism is the issue of unity. Evangelicalism in the modern world has promoted more new churches and has been less of an agent for renewal in existing churches. For example, Pentecostals in India have a difficult time working together, and then

---

[30]David Barrett's *World Christian Encyclopedia* (Oxford: Oxford University Press, 2001) estimates 312,849,430 Christians in mid-2000, and of these about 166 million are evangelical or Pentecostal.

other evangelicals may or may not work with all Pentecostals. Even though restrictions and persecution in countries such as Vietnam, Laos, Malaysia, China, and Myanmar force Christians to work together, Christian unity continues to be a major problem among evangelicals. Evangelicals from outside these countries often promote their own kingdoms at the expense of the unified body of Christ. In China, where sporadic, localized persecutions continue, Christians often resist cooperating in areas such as pastoral formation, worship, and mission. Evangelical divisions, however, are often linked to economics. Will there be missionary fidelity in unity when many countries are becoming wealthy? We might also ask, will evangelicalism continue to care for the poor and the outcast as evangelicals become wealthier in East Asia?

It may be that the unity and wealth issues are even more closely related. As the church in Asia holds together, the witness of the poor Dalit Christians in India and outcast Christians in Pakistan and Bangladesh will help to recenter the wealthier Asian Christians back at the foot of the cross. Evangelical witness will continue to thrive as the suffering servant makes his home in the suffering church of Asia.

PART II

History

5

Missio Dei

Christian History Envisioned
as Cruciform Apostolicity

INTRODUCTION: HISTORY IS TELLING A STORY

In the popular tale of an Indian boy and a tiger, *The Life of Pi*,[1] the narrator whets the appetite of the reader in the first page by saying that the following tale will make you believe in God. That is a pretty tall order for the telling of a tale, but what Yann Martel has in mind is that in this tale you will see evidences of God's presence in what you are about to read. By the end of the novel, French investigators are interviewing young Pi, and they find his story a little too fantastic: a tale about a hyena, rat, zebra, and tiger on a small lifeboat on the open seas. So, he invents a tale that is more gruesome, but it does not include a fantastic story about animals. After hearing such an awful human tale of murder and cannibalism on a lifeboat, the investigators decide to reluctantly accept the fantastic story of a tiger and a small boy together surviving on that same lifeboat across the Pacific Ocean for 227 days. It is enough to make you believe in God, or to recommend a Pulitzer or Booker Award.[2]

Martel's novel is a masterpiece of choosing and telling. In his story he cannot tell everything about young Piscine Molitar Patel (aka Pi), but he tells what the reader needs to know to understand the reality of God in the intersection of the mundane and the miraculous. All history, like all storytelling, involves choosing what to ignore, what elements to tell, and how to weave the elements in such a way to tell a meaningful story, a story that tells what it promises to tell. When facts and inferences are poorly chosen, with no

---

[1] Written by Yann Martel (New York: Alfred A. Knopf, 2001).
[2] In fact it did win the Man Booker Prize in 2002.

understanding of the story they tell, we are either misled or bored to tears as we read a history that is just fact upon fact, event upon event, date upon date. History must be told with "historical flow not just assemblages of events."[3]

Many students are anesthetized by teachers who have taught "assemblages of events" and called it history. *Columbus got royal support. Columbus sailed to Hispaniola, thinking he was in Japan. Columbus sailed home, leaving some of his less-than-exemplary sailors on the island. All the sailors were killed by the time Columbus returned.* And so we build one fact on another and we call this history. Most students of history find this pretty boring because there is no real story. And as we all know, we are created in and for story; we understand reality as story. The mechanistic type of history that has evolved from our appropriation of modernity[4] also has no real way of evaluating the past and no way of understanding or interpreting God as the subject of history. Until recently much of our history was taught this way, under the guise of science and objectivity, but that is not our main problem with the writing and teaching of Christian history today. We have moved beyond thinking we can really be objective ("Just the facts, ma'am") in history, and like a mad pendulum, we have swung wildly in the opposite direction, so most of our church history today wallows in its own personal (or community) perspective. Before we go further, let me outline the issue with more precision.

There is no commonly accepted way of telling the history of Christianity today. The academy is dominated by various ideological trajectories, and most of our Christian historians learn how to read, write, and teach Christian history in these environments. Thus, we have a great variety of historical approaches to Christian history that find their unity more in sociology of religion (or even economics) than in the theological realm. Because of the variety of ideologies, church historians have to give lengthy prolegomena before they begin telling their story. However, such ideologies, as helpful as they may be in some respects, carry with them much unwanted baggage. Marxist or feminist or postcolonial critique is just that, a critique. Some of

---

[3] Andrew Walls, "Eusebius Tries Again: The Task of Reconceiving and Re-visioning the Study of Christian History," in *Enlarging the Story: Perspectives on Writing World Christian History*, ed. Wilbert Shenk (Maryknoll, NY: Orbis Books, 2002), 1-21.

[4] The Enlightenment produced dichotomies between fact and faith or science and belief. See one of the best discussions of this issue for the *missio Dei* in Lesslie Newbigin's "Can the West Be Converted?," *Princeton Seminary Bulletin* 6, no. 1 (1985): 25-37.

these same ideologies are buoyed on the assumption that mission history is the history of oppression and the imposition of unwanted beliefs and powers forced on the marginalized. Such assumptions put Christian historical writing on the defense before the first word is penned. It is my thesis that the history of Christianity must be studied and taught differently than in the past; it must be taught as a centered-set religion with the perception of the two eyes of the cruciform and apostolic church. This is what the Christian story is about, and this reveals the essential unity of ecclesiology and missiology. Good Christian history must be grounded in good theology.

The two reasons that we have discovered (or rediscovered) these lenses for the writing of Christian history are the recent great changes that have taken place in Christianity (globally considered) and the developments in ecclesiology and missiology. Both the recent history and the recent theology are expressions of the two major movements of trinitarian reflection on God and the incarnational nature of Christianity. They are not only closely related; they find their common taproot in the simple truth that God revealed in Jesus Christ is love. This should become clearer as we look at exactly what we mean by *cruciform* and *apostolic*. First, by way of introduction to our topic, I offer two stories. Following these stories, I will outline some of the main features of historical research and writing in the recent past before explaining the meaning of telling the story of Christianity with the two eyes of apostolicity and cruciformity. I conclude with a few examples of how such a perspective will look when writing Christian history. What might the future of Christian historical writing look like with this bipolar emphasis?

Two Stories: Shanghai and Princeton

In 2007, I was doing a lecture for master's-level history students at one of the large secular (Marxist in ideology) universities in Shanghai. The professors (seven out of ten) were mostly interested in studying the history of Christianity. Post-Maoist China has opened up to what many communists had considered the Pandora's box of Christian studies. Like children in a candy shop, they are zealous to turn over every item and taste to see what is there. The faculty members were studying late Roman Empire Christianity ("because China is just like the declining Roman Empire," I was told), missionary history in the nineteenth century ("Did you know almost all of our scientific terms were coined by missionaries?" "Did you know all of our earliest universities were started by Christians?"), and indigenous Christian movements that began in the 1920s ("This was a truly Chinese form of Christianity that rejected Western imperialism"). My lecture was on how to study Christianity as a historical movement. I relied on Latourette, Walls, and our own work coming out of the *History of the World Christian Movement* project. My main point was that Christianity must be studied on its own terms. If one is studying the history of American musicals, the subject matter will guide the research and writing. If one is studying the history of a banking enterprise, one will ask questions of fiscal policy, board members, guidelines for loans, and other financial questions. My main point in this regard was that Christianity must be understood more as a centered-set movement than as a bounded-set institution. The great diversity of Christianity through history is held together by its center and only secondarily by its boundaries. Boundaries are important, but they develop out of the various historical movements pulling away from the center: movements that become eccentric or are labeled heretical.[5]

Only one of the twenty-five students and faculty was Christian. They had little understanding of Christianity, but they had much interest in its cultural impact. To illustrate my point about centered-set faith, I then asked the class, what is the symbol that you will see on all churches that will identify them as churches? Only two students knew the answer: a crucifix (or cross). I asked what that symbolized, and no one knew. After explaining the centrality of Jesus Christ, his passion and glory, the professor jumped up and gave a five-minute impassioned speech in Chinese, leaving me very anxious and with no interpreter. He apologized for interrupting me and then said, "That is wonderful. That is what I have been trying to get them to understand, that they have to understand more about Jesus if they are going to understand the historical movements of Christianity. Christianity is about Jesus, and all of

---

[5]There is no space to develop this point here, but the contrast with Islam should be self-evident. Buddhism, I think it can be argued, is closer to Christianity in that not laws, but the Buddha and what he represents as one who lived the middle path and one who was enlightened, is what holds the various schools of Buddhism together. For another way of talking about Christianity as being centered set and at times as bounded set, see Paul G. Hiebert, *Anthropological Reflections on Missiological Issues* (Grand Rapids: Baker Books, 1994), chapter 6, "The Category *Christian* in the Mission Task." He adds the concept of fuzzy sets to the discussion, which is particularly helpful for his purpose of discussing missions and church planting. For a study of how to write Christian history, the two categories of centered and bounded set provide enough definition for our subject.

his followers are trying to imitate him." The professor then turned to me and with knitted brow inquired, "How can they learn more about Jesus?"

My second story is about an experience in Princeton, in the United States, with mostly European and American scholars. All were Christians. I was presenting a paper on how to do Christian history in the twenty-first century when a South African ethicist caught me off-guard and asked the global question, "Scott, you have been studying the history of Christianity in the whole world for years. Writing these two volumes, what have you learned about Christianity? In other words, you are in a unique situation to talk about what Christianity is like, not just as a Western religion, but what its nature really is globally considered over twenty centuries. What have you learned?" Without a pause I quickly said, "I have learned just how fragile Christianity is and yet how it has been central to the transformation of so many cultures. In other words, I have learned the paradox that Christianity is just a thin red thread running through history, and yet it is a major actor on the stage of world history."

What I meant by this is that Christianity at times has been spread at the end of the sword, but for the most part, Christianity is spread as a simple message, just words spoken into the air or recorded with a few strokes of the pen: "Jesus died to bear your sins and guilt, and he liberates you to participate in God's redemption of his creation." It is a simple message that illiterate Punjabis can comprehend, and yet the greatest minds of the world have spent their lives trying to explain its implications and explanations. This simple little message of death and life, of God's relationship with humanity, is so fragile, so easy to pervert or misuse, and yet all the diverse Christian movements are held together in this simple kerygma. Cultures and nations are transformed and threatened by these simple words.

The cross and kerygma might be shorthand for these two little stories. What they illustrated for me is that those in China who are just beginning to learn about Christianity in history, and those in the West who are watching Christianity decline all around them, recognize these themes of cruciformity and apostolicity. Christianity is a story centered on humiliation and suffering. Christianity is a story of followers moving out with a message. However, this has not been the focus of our teaching of Christian history in the past, and to that we now turn.

Overview of Recent Christian Historiography

Modern historical writing about Christianity, until recently, was dominated by confessional and geographic factors. In fact, in most seminaries today there is still a sense that teaching church history is in part an apologetic for the Lutheran or Reformed or Roman Catholic Church (vis-a-vis other churches). If the history is not written to defend a particular confession outright, the overwhelming content of the volume (or the course) will pertain to one's own confessional tradition. Most seminaries want a church historian who majors in the confessional history of the seminary (when appropriate), to prepare young priests or pastors to defend their tradition. This is understandable. The second and closely related theme has been geographical. Most church history volumes have been written by Europeans or North Americans, and the overwhelming amount of the volumes cover Europe (mostly Western) and North America (mostly the United States). Christianity is assumed to be a Western religion. This tradition has been carried over even into much of the teaching of church history in the non-Western world today, where confessional histories and local histories are both taught. A seminary might teach church history (meaning Western and denominational history) and then Indian or east African church history, as if the two were not connected (except by Western missionaries). Andrew Walls notes that church history in Scotland used to involve three years of study: early church (first year), Reformation church (second year), and Scottish church (third year).[6] This type of vision of Christianity, seen through these lenses of church history, reinforces the perception that Christianity divides people (Reformed, Thomist, Orthodox, Lutheran) and Christianity is a tribal religion (the Scots, the Irish, the Tamils, the Vietnamese).

One of the most used and translated church history volumes, first published in 1918 and then revised and updated for decades, was Williston Walker's *A History of the Christian Church*.[7] To illustrate our point about

---

[6]Shenk, *Enlarging the Story*, 6.
[7]Williston Walker, *A History of the Christian Church* (New York: C. Scribner's Sons, 1918). A standard German introduction to the history of Christianity is even more confessional and geographic-centric: Kurt Aland's 1980 German edition *Geschichte der Christenheit*, band 2, *Von der Reformation bis in die Gegenwrart* (Gütersloh, West Germany: Gütersloher Verlagshaus Gerd Mohn, 1980), has 221 pages on the Reformation (to 1648) and less than ten pages on non-Western Christianity (including about three pages of statistics for the twentieth century). The volume is 479 pages of text.

geographical and confessional perspectives, we can look at this popular volume. Walker (updated by Norris, Lotz, and Handy) spends 28 percent of the volume on the Reformation period (mid-fifteenth through late seventeenth centuries). This is very important for a Protestant historian, because this period gives clear identity to particular confessional identities. Non-Western Christianity is covered as mission history, but Ignatius of Loyola is not even mentioned in the glossary. There is only one paragraph on the Jesuits in Latin America and Asia from the sixteenth through the eighteenth centuries. The final chapter, "Church in the World," focuses on the Western ecumenical movement and does not include Africa, Asia, and Latin America (where most Christians live today). Many other history volumes show the same predisposition to geographical and confessional foci.

With the rise of postmodern, postcolonial ethnic studies, and at the same time the rise and maturing of the non-Western churches, this all changed. Cultural and non-Western church histories began to appear in the 1970s, and today historical studies are a rich kaleidoscope patterned by ethnic and postcolonial perspectives. The centuries-long Western captivity of church history is over. However, not everyone has been informed of this. A new center, focus, or uniting narrative has not yet been developed, but it must be done soon. Christianity, after all, is a faith that has a unity based in a common genetic makeup, and that is the point of this chapter. The fragmentation of Christian history telling can be illustrated by a new series of Christian history called *A People's History of Christianity*.[8] The volumes tell about a period of history (mostly all Western) from the perspective of different communities: Johannine community, the poor, slaves, women, "Matthew's people," and so on. Themes of empire and power dominate, but the concern is not to find a cohesive narrative, or lens, except possibly the theme of diverse peoples who were engaged (or oppressed) by religion and empire. All of this history, along with the historical writing coming out of EATWOT,[9] has begun to describe areas, concerns, and perspectives that have long been neglected. It is very important to understand why Muslims from Nigeria become Christian and to ask how they understand what their conversion means. It is also very important to ask how

---

[8] Richard A. Horsley, ed., *A People's History of Christianity*, vol. 1, *Christian Origins* (Minneapolis: Fortress, 2005).
[9] Ecumenical Association of Third World Theologians.

women in China (or colonial Brazil for that matter) came to hold together Christian communities from their homes. Our concern is the next step of telling a meaningful single story, and that brings us to our present topic.

Cruciform: The Ongoing Story of the Body of Christ

The Christian story begins with Jesus, looks back to the history of Israel, and moves forward as the ongoing story of the body of Christ. As the Chinese professor (and Communist Party member at that) recognized, this Christian history is a lot easier to understand if we know about the life and teachings of Jesus Christ. Central to the meaning of the Jesus event is his humiliation and passion, focused on the cross. The Gospel narratives all build up to the passion, and the Epistles describe the continuity of Jesus' sufferings with those of the church:

> By making peace through the blood of his cross . . . he has now reconciled [you] in his fleshly body through death. . . . [This is] the gospel that you heard. . . . I am now rejoicing in my sufferings for your sake, and in my flesh I am completing what is lacking in Christ's afflictions for the sake of his body, that is, the church. (Col 1:20-24; cf. 2 Cor 4:5-18; 5:1-15)[10]

Andrew Walls discusses the serial nature of Christian expansion, noting that Christianity generally withers from its "heartland." I would modify that and say it withers where it has worldly strength and power, and then it develops on the margins and from areas of poverty and weakness. Walls goes on to say about Christianity, "It has vulnerability, a certain fragility, at its heart—the vulnerability perhaps of the Cross, and the fragility of the earthen vessel."[11] If this is true, if Christianity is built around this cruciform meaning and message, then how should that shape our writing of Christian history? I offer three issues that come from the cruciform nature of Christianity.

The most obvious implication when cruciformity is emphasized is that we ask more questions about the marginalized and powerless in our research and then in our telling of the story. Cruciformity begins with Philippians 2 and the kenotic identity of Jesus Christ. "Have the same mindset," the Christians are commanded (Phil 2:5 NIV), and so history is filled with this theme

---

[10]See also Michael Gorman's *Cruciformity: Paul's Spiritual Narrative of the Cross* (Grand Rapids: Eerdmans, 2001), especially chapter 4, "The Triune God of Cruciform Love."
[11]Walls, "Eusebius Tries Again," 19.

either expressed or resisted. Much of our history in the past has focused on the powerful and self-fulfilled rather than the self-emptied. There are obvious reasons for this, including the abundance of physical evidence provided by the wealthy and powerful. In a context where many or most Christians are illiterate, there will be little in the way of physical evidence to tell the story of the marginalized. Still, the questions about the poor and oppressed need to be asked, and what stories are available need to be preserved and woven into the Christian story with clear intentionality, not as sidebars to the major theological debates, but as the heartbeat of the central story.

Second, the cruciform life's origin in the incarnation will become more important in Christian historical writing. This theme has become more important in postmodern approaches to Christian history, looking at particular ethnic or national communities and their appropriation of Christian teachings. As Latourette noted in his 1940 volume *The Unquenchable Light* (William Belden Noble Lectures), Christianity, more so than any other religion, takes on the local culture, adapts to its environment, if you will. The words *contextualization, incarnational, translation,* and *adaptation* are all common Christian parlance.[12] Christianity, as it crosses cultural barriers or begins to expand in regions beyond the direct influence of more powerful churches, develops local customs, ideas, and practices that make Christian sense *in situ*. At times outsiders talk about many different Christianities, not realizing that the center still holds even though many of the practices are in conflict with one another. Insiders will talk about such diversity as one of theology or of ideas. But the correct category is the incarnational nature of Christianity, stemming from its cruciform nature. After recognizing that diversity of expressions does not necessarily mean a difference in essence, we then must also recognize that at other times diversity, understood as

---

[12]As a Presbyterian, I feel compelled to note John Calvin's wonderful expression for this incarnational work of Jesus Christ (taken from his *Institutes of the Christian Religion*, ed. Ford Lewis Battles, trans. John T. McNeill [Philadelphia: Westminster, 1960], 2.12.2) for our salvation: "Relying on this earnest, we trust that we are the sons of God, because the natural Son of God assumed to himself a body of our body, flesh of our flesh, bones of our bones, that he might be one with us; he declined not to take what was peculiar to us, that he might in turn extend to us what was peculiarly his own, and thus might be in common with us both Son of God and Son of man." In other places Calvin often talks about God's "adaptation to our weaknesses." Darrell Guder mentions that the gospel must be retranslated for each culture and for each new generation (see *The Continuing Conversion of the Church* [Grand Rapids: Eerdmans, 2000], 91-92).

incarnational, may indeed be a matter of difference of essence. There may be a new center if the local context becomes the dominant partner. Is Joseph Smith a prophet of contextual American Christianity, or is he a prophet of a new isotope? The language of incarnation and contextualization, with Jesus Christ as the center, helps us to talk about Christianity as it develops in a place over time and as it develops across cultural barriers.

A third, but not final, implication of cruciformity in Christian historical studies is transformation. The whole purpose, or even the meaning of self-emptying and dying to self for the Christian, is to bring about transformation of the self (repentance) and then transformation of other individuals and societies: laying down your life for your friends. The cruciform life is not an end in itself; if it were, then Christianity would be a religious form of masochism. Love is the motive, kenosis is the means, and transformation is the goal. Chinese communist historians have seen the goal (or the results) in the form of medical clinics, schools, feeding programs, and orphanages. They also see the means, as they have remarked how "interesting" it is that so many people left their homes and family to risk their lives in small villages in China, helping local people with schools or clinics. So much of Christian history in the past has focused on institutional history, and yet this institutional history is replete with institutions set up for transforming lives and societies; they incarnate the Christian concerns for holiness, justice, and mercy. It is in the Sermon on the Mount where we see the life of self-denial leading to transformation of others. Even Mahatma Gandhi recognized how important these teachings were; his followers were often motivated by Gandhi's teachings on the Sermon on the Mount to protest the oppressive rule of Great Britain. Cruciformity brings a transformation of holiness to the individual, but of justice and mercy in society. In sum, cruciformity in historical writing will raise questions of the marginalized, issues of contextualization, and transformation. The root of these three, however, is in the first of the two poles of our bipolar approach, the cruciform life.

Apostolicity: Overflowing Love of the Triune God

The second pole of Christian history is that of apostolicity, which finds its origin in the very nature of the triune God. God is love. His triune community expresses love to overflowing. It is the communal nature of God and

Missio Dei

the ongoing, unlimited love, or the superfluity of that love,[13] that moves out to his creation in incarnation and reveals him in the resurrection and ascension. Therefore in God's own self-revelation is reconciliation. There is no revelation from God that does not bring reconciliation. Thus, the Christian community, as a called-out community, is also called to the world, to represent the very reconciling and, we might add, self-emptying love of God.[14] There is no way to talk about the church or any local community of the church without recognizing its formation as being an apostolic formation. Barth goes as far as to say that

> the community which has not existed in the interim period as a *missionary* community as such, whose witness has not been *invitational* and *persuasive* according to the measure of her power, with the return and final revelation of her Lord will be banished into the darkness, where there can only be wailing and gnashing of teeth instead of the promised banquet.[15]

Here we see the strong word of affirmation—even a threat if there is denial—that the church exists in mission, and this mission is more than passive presence. In its welcoming and persuading, it is continuing the active presence of God to and for the world. The church is always confessing and missionary, or always declaring the glory of God (a phrase that captures the confessional and missionary aspects of its identity).

What this means for Christian history is that the temptation to research and write a history that ignores basic questions of Christian existence as missionary existence will be truncated at best and misleading at worst. In any area of being or in any area of obedience the church has never fully lived up to its identity, and yet that does not excuse us from asking the right questions in studying its history. As we noted in the previous section, we must ask questions of the marginalized, and we must ask how the church exists in self-emptying reality. Here we must ask a different set of questions:

---

[13]See John G. Flett, "God Is a Missionary God: Missio Dei, Karl Barth and the Doctrine of the Trinity" (PhD diss., Princeton Theological Seminary, 2007), 390-92, for a discussion of the superfluity of the resurrection. Here we add that the same is true in trinitarian discussions of God's love in the triune community (Barth, *Church Dogmatics*, trans. Geoffrey W. Bromiley and T. F. Torrance [Edinburgh: T&T Clark, 1962], IV/3.1, p. 79).

[14]Flett, "God Is a Missionary God," 455-56.

[15]Quoted from Flett's translation, ibid., 457 (citing Barth, *Church Dogmatics*, trans. Geoffrey W. Bromiley and T. F. Torrance [Edinburgh: T&T Clark, 1962], III/2, p. 610). Please note that this is from his doctrine of creation.

questions about how the church exists as apostolic community, confessing, inviting, persuading, and reconciling even as it bears the death of Jesus to the world (2 Cor 4:10). There are three themes that we should look for in Christian history that come out of the apostolicity of Christianity.

First, we will see and look for crosscultural interactions. The historian of Christianity will look for places where Christian communities cross cultural barriers or encounter new cultures. This naturally follows from the cruciform love mentioned above, but here, more specifically it follows from the movement out from self and local community. As the church expresses its missionary nature it will encounter the other—people and communities that are new or different. Moving out is both spatial (geographic) and cultural (ethnic). The church's apostolic nature may mean tracing the movement of Fijian missionaries paddling to neighboring islands and then all the way north to the Sandwich Islands, and it will also mean watching the North Carolinians find ways to serve and confess their faith to Vietnamese refugees and Mexican farm workers. Historically, these cultural meetings (whether they be clashes or serendipitous associations) express both the apostolic essence of the church described and the eschatological community prescribed (Rev 7). On the negative side, when we ask these questions about crosscultural interactions and we come up empty, that also tells us something about the story in a particular context.

Second, and coming out of this first theme, is the responsibility of the historian to describe apostolic activity, with all of the movement and diversity that it will experience, as a single essence: the church, the body of Christ. What we are saying here is that the historian must resist the contemporary, and temporary, temptation to see the various Christian movements and incarnational realities as different religions. We must not talk about different Christianities, even if we have a difficult time seeing all the various forms and divisions as actually being of the same body. At times we might ask, "Does the center hold?" Especially we ask this when we see the divisions becoming so great, and even so violent, that it may be tempting to study and receive the divisions as if they are only that: divisions and therefore new faiths. And yet, and now we speak of the *Christian historian* specifically, the theology must guide the historiography. And then more generally speaking for the *historian of Christianity*, the understanding of

Christianity as a centered-set faith must guide the historical work. Most of the divisions and diversity will involve issues of apostolicity and contextualization. Some of the most fertile historical soil, and some of the most enlivening theological debate, will relate to these two issues working together. What is appropriate in terms of being an apostolic community in a Muslim context? What is appropriate contextualization in the midst of an increasingly materialistic (or hedonistic) culture? Is baptism necessary if baptism will cut off apostolic witness in important areas of culture, government, or the larger society? "What language can I borrow?"[16] to express the message in rap, Latino, or reggae culture? It is of great importance to resist past historical approaches that gave priority or favor to particular confessions or contextualizations, because to do so cut out major segments of the church and painfully denuded the full story of Christianity.

A third apostolic theme of Christian history is derived from the simple commission given in the Gospel of John: "As the Father has sent me, so I send you" (Jn 20:21). Apostolicity must be understood in concert with the foundational commission of the church. This means that Jesus' sentness in some sense is our sentness. Jesus was sent as the Word of God, communicating on the most intimate level of humanity (human speech); so is the church's sentness. The apostolic message is a specific message with content (the Word) and power (the Spirit). Jesus also touched the lame, healed the blind, spoke to power, and depended on the life of others for his own life. So should we expect to see this or look for this in our study of the history of Christianity. In the terms of modernity and its propensity to dichotomize, the apostolic life of the church is expressed in both the verbal and social witness. It is best to avoid that dichotomy and say that Christian history will show the fullness of the marks of all of Jesus' life in its institutions, movements, and confessions. When we do not see those expressions of apostolic life in the pattern of Jesus Christ—one might think of the Protestant side of the Reformation—then we will raise questions and look for issues that prevented such Christian development.[17] Eventually, Christian life through time self-corrects. The lopsided and

---

[16]From "O Sacred Head Once Wounded," attributed to Bernard of Clairvaux.
[17]Although much has been written on the mission theology of a few of the Reformers, such as John Calvin, in fact, there was little to no apostolic trajectory to the Protestant Reformation.

truncated forms dissipate in light of ecumenical relations and biblical literacy, even though the dissipation of such truncated forms may be much too slow for us. In summary, the apostolic nature of Christianity in history will be revealed in these three ways: (1) crosscultural interactions, (2) unity in Christ with great diversity in cultures, and (3) in the holistic, apostolic pattern of the life of Jesus Christ.

Summary and Examples

This bipolar or two-eyed perspective of writing and telling Christian history is true to the essence of Christian teaching and theology, but it also has a practical theological function. With these dual poles guiding the process, it becomes possible to critique Christian communities or movements at a particular time and place as being more or less true to these guiding principles. At various times and in various places the cruciform nature of the church is all but obscured by economic, imperial, or ideological concerns. At times the persecution and violence is not received by the church (the cruciform identity), but is delivered by the church against outsiders (an oppressive identity). It is important to recognize these times and then draw attention to these as departures from Christianity as found in the very nature of God and as revealed in the primal Christian story, the crucifixion.

One of the losses in writing Christian history with this pattern might be the grand tradition of telling doctrinal history, or the history of Christianity as the story of competing theological claims. Is this, which has been our dominant story of the past, completely lost? I don't think so, although it may not be a bad thing. What happens is that the story of doctrinal development and conflict is seen in its proper perspective, described and viewed as it is part of the ongoing story of the life of Christ, as we have mentioned. Eucharistic controversies may be more or less significant, or even more or less "Christian," if we can say so, as they reflect on the humiliation and suffering of Christ and at the same time have an apostolic trajectory. After all, the Eucharist is a celebration and remembrance of Christ given for the nations. The same elevation of themes during historical developments in history would be possible for christological controversies, trinitarian controversies, and others. In a sense, this is a recovery of what we would like to see as essential elements of the Christian life and practice.

Historical writing and research that will include the theological diversity in the context of cruciform and apostolic understandings of Christianity are more than a single historian can muster. It should be obvious by now that the emphasis on diversity of cultures and contextual practices with the attendant variety of languages will necessitate that Christian historical writing be a community endeavor. We accept the postmodern critique that communities of interpretation require multiple readings and interpretations of texts, but we do not leave it there. Such a critique brings us only half the way home. With this perspective on telling the Christian story, we can in fact communicate between communities, and the church is in fact able to see itself as bigger than any local assemblage. Therefore local stories, local incarnations of these apostolic communities, will need to be told and interpreted so that the whole and broader story can be woven together as a single story. When we hear others tell their stories, we begin to see and hear others identify their own self-emptying on behalf of the world. We begin to understand how we are part of the same apostolic community of God. Even when we disagree with their theology or their cultural practices, we begin to see something of the truth we also seek to reveal. As historian Richard Lovelace would say at the beginning of his church history classes, "The problem with studying church history carefully is that you often find that God blesses people who you know have bad theology." When we do Christian history in community we are forced to hear and honor Christ as more fully the sacrifice for the world.

A few examples from Christian history will help show how this bipolar perspective helps to shape the story of Christianity according to its own nature. Jesuit missions in China beginning in the last years of the sixteenth century are well-known by Christian historians for their imperial or top-down approach to reaching the Chinese. Most of the studies of the Jesuit mission focus on the great missionary scholars, such as Matteo Ricci, Johann Adam Schall, and Ferdinand Verbiest. These scholars represent the cruciform ministry under the particular concerns for translation or incarnation of the message to the local culture. However, one of the key elements that we mentioned, reaching the marginalized and outcast, is not evident in these Jesuit scholars. A second concern that is related to contextualization and the translatability of the message is the reverse impact of translation. As Christianity was being adapted to the Chinese, the Chinese expression of Christianity was changing the way Europeans thought about Christianity. A recent volume has corrected these omissions. Liam Matthew Brockey's *Journey to the East: The Jesuit Mission to China, 1579–1724* explains and verifies that most of the Jesuit missionaries were actually working in smaller villages, not in Beijing, and their converts were fairly ignorant farmers and village dwellers. He notes that the Jesuits were "motivated by a firm conviction that the Christian language had an elasticity that permitted it to conform to the contours of even the most widely disparate cultures."[18] In their adaptation, however, the Christianity they presented often was so Confucianist in its ethics and Buddhist in its use of images that something of the cruciform nature of the faith was lost. In fact, "the Jesuits did not employ depictions of the crucifixion when explaining Christian teachings to new audiences."[19] This was a temporary measure, for they later talked about and had pictures of the crucifixion, but just noting this fact reveals a great deal about European understanding of how the apostolic and cruciform nature of the faith is to be expressed.

Another, more positive example of the bipolar nature of Christianity comes from the nineteenth century in the Punjab, on the border between present-day Pakistan and India. A mass movement to Christianity began among the Chuhras about 1873, when a "dark little man, lame of one leg, quiet and modest in his manner" heard the Christian message, found out that Jesus accepted outcasts, was baptized, and returned thirty miles to his Hindu village.[20] He was an impoverished outcast who only had one name: Ditt. He was severely ostracized for his conversion, but he remained faithful and in about three months' time brought his whole family to be baptized by the missionaries. To this day the largest number of Christians has come from the lower castes and from the Dalits. Ditt and the thousands of Dalits who followed in his wake were welcomed by the bipolar nature of Christianity, and they developed an Indian Christianity that both has been welcoming of the marginal and outcast, and has sent missionaries across the subcontinent.

If we had space, it would be helpful to look at examples from Africa, central Asia, the Americas, and the Pacific. However, we just don't hear much

---

[18]Liam Matthew Brockey, *Journey to the East: The Jesuit Mission to China, 1579–1724* (Cambridge, MA: Harvard University Press, 2007), 6.
[19]Ibid., 307.
[20]Scott W. Sunquist, *A Dictionary of Asian Christianity* (Grand Rapids: Eerdmans, 2001), 245.

about New Zealand, land of the Kiwi, Maori, and the best rugby team in the world, the All Blacks. When the earliest Protestant missionaries came to New Zealand they encountered both the new language of the Maori and the new commercialism of the British: rifles. The missionaries responded to both by translating the New Testament and the Book of Common Prayer into Maori (1837). What happened?

> In the past, the local chief was the law for the people. With the advent of writing and published sacred scripture, even chiefs stood under the new law. The written word had a power of its own for the Maori like few other places and times. Along with translation and literacy came the need for schools. If Maori learned to read, they could read the Bible, and then knowledge of the Bible would be the basis of a new Christian Maori civilization. This in fact happened, although not always as the missionaries had envisioned. When frustrated missionaries sought the help of the British military to put down local violence in the 1840s, Chief Rawiri Kingi,
>
> "... ran forward with his New Testament in his hand and exclaimed, 'See! See! This is my weapon; the white man's book. You sent us this book and it tells us not to fight: you have got other weapons—weapons of blood: use them not; fight not; or my heathen relations will fight too. Remember your book! Remember your book!'" (Lineham 1996: 21)
>
> The Bible gave the Maori a new sense of authority, even over the missionaries. Literacy spread like wildfire, some of the early Roman Catholics noting that Maori who had never seen Europeans had learned to read and had portions of scripture for themselves. For many Maori, the Bible was a person's greatest possession.[21]

Finally, this bipolar concept helps to explain the decline of Christianity in the West. Christianity, as we noted earlier, seems to lose its center when that center has taken on the world's power and authority, even in the name of Christ. Christian preoccupation with power and property was the story of much of modern European history. We can see renewals of the two poles coming most often from the edges (monks and friars) and seldom from the center (papacy). The Reformation, viewed this way, is both a Christian tragedy (as militant forms of Christianity took up the sword against one

---

[21]Taken from Dale T. Irvin and Scott W. Sunquist, *History of the World Christian Movement* (Maryknoll, NY: Orbis Books, forthcoming), vol. 3, chapter 25.

another) and a Christian revitalization (as we tell the story of efforts to return to a cruciform ecclesial existence). When any Christian community becomes preoccupied with self-existence (rather than missional existence) and with power (rather than self-emptying), the Christian identity is waning. Christian history, like the history of Israel, is both the tale of God's cruciform and apostolic life and the story of human hubris and self-arrogation.

Such an approach to the telling of Christian history as I have described should be faithful to the church as it was first formed, and to a theology that is in harmony with a vigorous trinitarian theology. The first will reveal the continuity from Jesus, to the apostles, through the apostolic age, to the present. The second will ensure that the story comes from, or reflects the nature of, the God of history, the God whose humanity is present in community with the Father and the Spirit. In this way our history will tell the story that is specifically Christian, even as it uses the various tools and approaches of the academy. Since God remains active in reconciling the world to himself, we do see glimpses, shadows of the triune God in the suffering and apostolic servant in history. This is the church. In fact, it may be that such a story, filled with marvelous tales of sufferings, martyrdoms, reconciliation, and transformation, will lead a person to believe in God. Well, stories can have such power.

6

The Century That Changed the Religious Map

1910–2010

> *Our Western civilization, borne upon the wings of modern science, has shattered the ancient ways of life, breaking up tribes, extinguishing the old customs and religions, the old beliefs and the old moralities.*
>
> JAMES BRYCE

Six months before moderating the World Missionary Conference at Edinburgh, John R. Mott chaired another missionary meeting on the other side of the Atlantic. The Sixth International Convention of the Student Volunteer Movement, held in Rochester, New York, dealt with many of the same missionary issues. For Mott and others, it was like a trial run before the more important Edinburgh meeting. The SVM Convention was held from December 29th, 1909, to January 2, 1910, and it focused on issues of special concern to students (preparing for missionary work, money, qualifications, etc.) as well as on issues central to the Edinburgh Conference (regional studies, the present world situation, the promising time for missions, etc.). Mott presided over this SVM Convention, which had many of the same great minds who would soon be on the other side of the Atlantic talking about how to complete the task of world evangelization. The theology, historical awareness, and understanding were all of the same fabric, and so we can look at both together to fill out our understanding of the time and thinking about mission.

It was a time of great optimism, in spite of the recent uprisings against foreigners ("primary hairy men") and Christians ("secondary hairy men") in China, and the uprisings against the Armenians in the Ottoman Empire.¹ Speeches at Rochester and at Edinburgh were filled with confidence, the confidence of a businessman with a near monopoly on a particular commodity (religion) more than the confidence of the gospel of hope. Just six days after the end of the Edinburgh Conference, John R. Mott, who had chaired the important conference, wrote in the preface of a volume soon to be published (*The Decisive Hour of Christian Missions*), "In the history of Christianity there has never been such a remarkable conjunction of opportunities and crises on all of the principle mission fields and of favorable circumstances and possibilities on the home field."² As Brian Stanley has noted, the adjective *great* was used to describe the opportunity for global evangelization at the conference itself, but the memory of the conference has been more about the foundations for ecumenical cooperation and unity.³ The conference is significant today both for its missional zeal and its ecumenical pioneering, but on both accounts it saw the future only in a mirror darkly. In fact, the conference can be seen as an example of how difficult it is for the greatest church minds both to perceive the future and to distance themselves from contemporary movements. In this brief essay we will look at the historic understanding of Christianity and Christian mission that permeated Western church leaders in 1910. Next we will look at seven developments that reconfigured Christianity in the twentieth century—some were predicted, but most were not—and then we will conclude with how Christianity must now be understood, and how Christian history must be researched and written for the twenty-first century in light of the past one hundred years.⁴

Christian History and Christian Mission Identity: 1910

In 1910 Christianity was like a roller coaster at the top of a great incline: filled with great hope, but on the cusp of a wild ride. The twentieth century was

---

¹The worst uprisings against the Armenians would come later, but in 1909 angry Turks killed close to twenty-five thousand Armenians in Adana.
²John R. Mott, *The Decisive Hour for Christian Missions* (New York: Student Volunteer Movement for Foreign Missions, 1910), v.
³Brian Stanley, *The World Missionary Conference, Edinburgh 1910* (Grand Rapids: Eerdmans, 2009); see chapter 1.
⁴For a more detailed look at the twentieth century and the misplaced hopes of Western Christians, see Scott W. Sunquist, *The Unexpected Christian Century* (Grand Rapids: Baker Academic, 2015).

that wild ride. Western Christians confidently rode Western civilization as their vehicle in confident "expansion" of the faith to the far corners of the world. James Bryce expressed the mindset of the time in words only a little stronger than most when he said at the sixth SVM Convention,

> This is a critical moment in world history, and it is also an auspicious moment. ... Never since the discovery of this continent, now more than 4 centuries ago, has there been any time of such change, or such advance in the exploration and development of every part of the earth's surface as we see now in our own time.... Nine tenths of the habitable globe are under the control of civilized powers.... There is scarcely a spot in which the influence of the white races is not felt, and in which the backward and uncivilized races are not being penetrated by the ideas and habits of those more advanced nations. The old religions are being shaken.[5]

Technology was seen as a special gift of God for the Western "civilized races" to help bring about the evangelization of the world. In fact the great advances in the natural or hard sciences, as well as the newer "soft" or social sciences, were God-given gifts. Supported by Western science, the delegates also shared a common Christian conscience. As one writer said of the Edinburgh Missionary Conference, "The missionary conscience is assumed here. The church's duty is taken for granted. Every delegate is already an ardent missionary believer."[6] This missionary obligation was shared across theological and denominational lines, and Western Christians believed modern science was a gift of God to help complete the task. This consensus in both Christian duty and an understanding of civilization's gifts would never be as strong as it was in 1910. Civilization, however, was identified with a "race." This was one of the unfortunate themes that Christians did not critique from the larger discourse of Western secular scholars.

In terms of historical awareness, we also have to add that the "obligation" at its best was expressed as Christian duty that had not been carried out as Jesus commanded. At its worst, the obligation took on nationalistic, imperial, and

---

[5]James Bryce speaking at the Rochester Student Volunteer Movement Quadrennial meeting, 1910; see "Responsibilities of Christian Nations Toward the Backward Races," in *Students and the Present Missionary Crisis* (New York: Student Volunteer Movement for Foreign Missions, 1910), 112. "This continent" is North America. Bryce was the British ambassador to the United States!

[6]Charles Clayton Morrison, "The World Missionary Conference, 1910," *Christian Century*, July 7, 1910.

racist tones. Many of the speakers at both conventions used language like that of Julius Richter, pastor, missiologist, and future professor in Berlin: "The evangelization of primitive races, all those dark, dull peoples, low in civilization, even lower in religious and moral standards . . . what a disadvantage it is for modern missions that their spheres of work among the primitive races are so widely scattered and diversified."[7] Richter would be one of the key continental delegates at Edinburgh. His language of primitive races and of low and high civilization expressed the evolutionary assumptions that most all scholars had at the time. Missionary history or Christian advancement was understood almost in Hegelian terms, but certainly as superior (Christian) civilizations or races helping other inferior people to move out of darkness. Richter was a German, and he was playing with the same ideas, in a Christian and missionary form, that would lead to the racist policies of the Third Reich. In a volume he published just two years before Edinburgh 1910, Richter describes how, in order to better understand different cultures, "there are two sciences which have largely contributed to clear up the question of the origin and mutual relationship of the people of India," philology and more recently, anthropology.

> The last named, claims to have found a sure test of the relationship of the various races in the comparative measuring of those parts of the body which largely remain unchanged (anthropometry). In this science three proportions are largely called in question—the proportion borne by the length of the head to its breadth, the proportion borne by the length of the nose to its breadth, and the angle formed by the line by two corresponding points on the upper eyelids and the root of the nose.

An appendix is added to the book to elaborate on this introduction. The author describes four basic races in India, which are identified by language, but more "solidly" by "nasal index" and "skull index" sizes.[8]

Progress, evolution, and *science* were the key words behind the SVM and later Edinburgh Conference leaders. These were all understood to be in service to the Edinburgh watchword: "the evangelization of the world in this generation." Before condemning this whole missionary approach, and the "scientific racism" of Richter, we must remember two facts. First, this was the view of the world

---

[7]Julius Richter, "The Decisive Hour in the History of Protestant Missions," in *Students and the Present Missionary Crisis*, 119.
[8]Julius Richter, *A History of Missions in India* (New York: Fleming H. Revell, 1908), 437-38.

and of Western civilization that was shared by most of the greatest and most liberal minds of the time. Missionaries, as part of this civilization, understood the world this way; however, for the most part they were less racist than the highly educated scholars such as Richter. Second, in missionary thinking and in motivational speeches at missionary gatherings, such racist and paternalistic language tended to take a back seat to the language of *Christianization, evangelism,* and, at times, *repentance and humility* before the task. Thus, the racist and imperial language was less pronounced among missionaries than among the general scholarly communities. James Bryce reminded the young people that mission would help to revive the languishing faith of Western Christians. "This movement of yours seems to me a movement so wholesome and so noble not only because it has great promise for the outer world which you are seeking to evangelize; but also because it stimulates that renewal of Christian life which is so needful in order that the Kingdom of Heaven be made more of a reality in our own lands."[9] Thus, missionary rhetoric was more aware of the need for humility in the face of global concerns, and even the need for greater conversion of the West.

In 1910 there was a broad but very fragile consensus in the Christendom West. At the most basic level it was a consensus that cooperation was needed to "complete" the task. We can complete the task of evangelizing the other "races," so it was reasoned, because of the great advances we have in science and technology: these were very pragmatic (mostly) Anglophile assumptions about mission. An orthodox Protestant foundation supported this consensus, and so Baptists, Anglicans, Presbyterians, and even Hudson Taylor's China Inland Mission could all come on board. At times it seems like their trust was put in human science or human inventiveness to complete this task, but eventually all speakers would acknowledge that mission is a work of God.[10]

---

[9]Bryce, "Responsibilities of Christian Nations," 116.
[10]John R. Mott's widely read book coming out of Edinburgh, *The Decisive Hour for Christian Missions* (London: Young People's Missionary Movement, 1910), has eight chapters, beginning with "The Non-Christian Nations, Plastic and Changing." It was only three years earlier that a process for economically manufacturing "plastic" was invented, so this modern term was put in the service of the church. It is only the seventh chapter that really talks about theology, and the rest of the book reads like a business manual on how to corner the religious global market. Chapter 7 is titled "The Requirements of the Present Situation: The Superhuman Factor." The superhuman factor is the Spirit of God.

The consensus, however, would quickly break down both theologically and in terms of science and evolutionary optimism. World War I, the collapse of the Christian nation of Russia to atheistic communism, the decline of "Christian" empires, the rise of Nazism in Germany, the violence of Turks against Christian Armenians, and the rise of communism in China all came about within twenty-five years of the conference. The evolution of Western civilization could no longer be assumed. Ironically, it was the best of modern Western science that helped to bring about all of these disasters that hamstrung the Western missionary movement. The theological consensus also quickly broke down at the end of the conference. In America a theological battle was being waged at the time of the conference, by many of the same men who attended the conference. From 1910 to 1915 a series of edited volumes was distributed to every English-speaking missionary, pastor, and education worker: *The Fundamentals: A Testimony to the Truth*. Thus, a controversy surfaced that would prevent ecumenical unity and would highlight divisions that would soon take place across the global church.[11] Edinburgh was a time of hopefulness, confidence, and consensus that was more emblematic of an age than prophetic of the church in the future age. Like a reverse image of the collapse of the Berlin Wall, no one was prepared to see how Christianity would develop after 1910. It is to that development that we now turn.

Christian Movements in the Twentieth Century: Six Themes

As we mentioned earlier, Christianity in 1910 was at the top of a roller coaster on the cusp of a wild ride. The wild ride of the twentieth century was a ride that was out of the hands, and beyond the vision, of Western Christendom. Christianity's vitality and strength suddenly moved from the West to "the rest" and from the centers of power to the margins. It was assumed in all the talks given at Edinburgh that the evangelization of Africa and Asia would occur under the leadership and wisdom of Western missions, but this was not the case. For example, in 1910 Latin America was left off the agenda, and yet Christian development in Latin America has been a major twentieth-century Christian theme. There was little protest that Latin America was not

---

[11]For example, there were articles written in *The Fundamentals* by Robert E. Speer and Charles Eerdman, both Presbyterians who attended Edinburgh 1910.

represented at all in 1910. Few people even noticed that there was only one African representative and eighteen representatives from Asia. In the early twentieth century, these "marginal" and often liminal areas of Christianity became the new center of Christianity. In this section we would like to look at the transformation that actually did occur in the twentieth century in terms of six major shifts or themes.

First, at Edinburgh Christendom seemed to be coming together to accomplish something great for God, but in fact Christendom was on the verge of completing its 250-year-long collapse. As a result of two European wars and what J. H. Oldham would call "a new Paganism in Christendom,"[12] Western Christendom collapsed in the twentieth century. It was not just the European wars that killed Christendom (Europeans had fought in earlier centuries and come out very religious), but it was two vicious wars along with the victory of Enlightenment (secular) ideas that killed the centuries-long Christian-cultural matrix. Christianity, after the Second World War, was no longer the soul of Europe, nor of Europeans. A hundred years after the 1910 Conference, Europe has gone from 95 percent to 77 percent Christian. According to Gallup, only 20 percent of western Europeans and 14 percent of eastern Europeans attend worship services in a given week.[13] In some countries, fewer than 4 percent now attend church in Europe on any given Sunday. Christianity no longer has a holding power on Europeans. The story of the decline of Western Christendom has been told many times,[14] but the fact is that any way one measures it, Christianity has become a small annex to the cultural palace of Europe, whereas it was the ancient foundation of its morals, ethics, and even its politics a century ago.

Second, the mission fields that the Edinburgh Conference most neglected ended up being the most responsive to Western missionary work. The hope, organization, manpower, and money that were poured into East and South Asian work ended up being the least responsive mission fields. Protestant Christianity did not develop in these favorite mission fields among "higher

---

[12]J. H. Oldham, "The International Review of Missions After 25 Years," *International Review of Missions* 24, no. 95 (July 1935): 300-301.
[13]Robert Manchin, "Religion in Europe: Trust Not Filling the Pews," Gallup poll, September 21, 2004, www.gallup.com/poll/13117/religion-europe-trust-filling-pews.aspx.
[14]See, for example, Noel Davies and Martin Conway, *World Christianity in the 20th Century* (London: SCM Press, 2008), chapter 12, "Europe."

races." Instead it was the neglected continents of Africa (only one guest at Edinburgh) and Latin America (not officially discussed at all at Edinburgh) where the great twentieth-century miracle of Christian development occurred. Protestant Christianity grew from 1.4 percent to over 9 percent in Latin America in the twentieth century, and Pentecostals and Charismatics grew from about zero to over 25 percent of the Christian population. This could not have been predicted in 1910, since the Pentecostal movement was barely out of the starting blocks at that time. Latin America, in fact, is now sending missionaries throughout Latin America as well as to Europe, Asia, North Africa, and North America. About five thousand missionaries are overseas today from Brazil alone.[15] By comparison, in 1920 the number of Western missionaries in China peaked at about seven thousand. Latin Americans have taken the seeds of Protestant Christianity and brought new life, whereas a century ago they were intentionally ignored by the Edinburgh Conference.

Africa is the second major story that Edinburgh could not see. In 1910 at the SVM Conference in Rochester, Reverend Thomas Moody clearly identified the situation of Africa at that time in his address, titled "The Urgency of the Situation in Africa": "Three great religions are now in conflict to win Africa—Paganism, Mohammedanism and Christianity. Paganism is passing away, but the great conflict is with Islam with its 58 million followers, against which we have two million Christians; and the question today is, which will win Africa?"[16] In fact, Africa's growing and most organized religion in 1910 was Islam, and most of the non-Muslims were not Christians, but they were people who continued in traditional patterns of worship. John R. Mott himself, optimist that he was, fully expected Islam to take over Africa.[17] In 1900 there were only 8.7 million Christians (9 percent of Africa's population) after nearly nineteen centuries of Christian witness. There were 34.5 million Muslims, which amounted to 32 percent of Africa's population. Christian witness in 1900 didn't seem to match the advance of Islam in Africa. However,

---

[15]For a discussion of the developments of Latin American missions, see Todd Hartch, *The Rebirth of Latin American Christianity* (Oxford: Oxford University Press, 2014), chapter 10, "Universal Christianity: From Latin America to the Ends of the Earth," 184-206.

[16]Thomas Moody, "The Urgency of the Situation in Africa," in *Students and the Present Missionary Crisis*, ed. Robert J. Cole (New York: Student Volunteer Movement for Foreign Missions, 1910), 211. The two million figure may be speaking only of Protestants.

[17]See Lamin Sanneh, *Whose Religion Is Christianity? The Gospel Beyond the West* (Grand Rapids: Eerdmans, 2003), 14-15.

the great reversal that we are describing in these first two points became most pronounced in Africa. By the year 2000 there were 360 million Christians in Africa (46 percent of the population) and 317 million Muslims (40.5 percent). As Lamin Sanneh and others have pointed out, the greatest growth occurred after the collapse of the colonial empires.[18] No one in Edinburgh could see this coming, for their priorities and hope were placed in East Asia and South Asia. It seems that their evolutionary view of cultures (Confucianism was more advanced than African tribal faiths) blinded missionary scholars from seeing that civilization is in the eye of the beholder. Within a few years the most "civilized nations" of Western Europe would be slaughtering each other with the greatest and most civilized minds and their scientific advances. Africa and Latin America, the neglected and "less civilized" continents, were the places of greatest Christian growth and vitality.

Third, the Western intellectual assumptions about evolution, social evolution, and race were quickly put to rest with the rise of National Socialism in Germany and their racist critiques of non-Aryans. The language all seems so strange to us today, and yet the greatest minds of the time shared some of the basic assumptions of race that supported colonial empires overseas and the Third Reich in Europe. In fact these were global assumptions among intellectuals, which explains the similarity of the treatment of Chinese and Koreans by the Japanese and the treatment of Jews by the German Aryans and black Africans by the Afrikaners. What made the more civilized Victorian version of race turn demonic was the "scientific" support of the theory, as we saw expressed by Bryce and Richter above. No longer was racial superiority an assumption, but now it could be proven scientifically.

A fourth major shift that occurred in the twentieth century was the shift from centered, rational, and hierarchical Christianity to Pentecostal, Charismatic, and indigenous forms of spiritual Christianity. Global Christianity after the Edinburgh Missionary Conference was moving toward greater organization and global order. The International Missionary Council and the future World Council of Churches represent this global ordered and centered (Geneva and New York) church. Ordered and centered Protestantism became fragmented by many of the spiritual

---

[18] This is part of the total argument in *Whose Religion Is Christianity?*

movements of the twentieth century: Pentecostalism, Charismatic movements, and both African and Chinese independency.

Pentecostalism was not even a factor in 1910, even though Pentecostal missionaries had already spread to fifty countries by the time of the Edinburgh conference. Early Pentecostals were not a "civil" lot when compared to the highly organized business, scholastic, and academic meetings held at New College, Edinburgh. A quick look at the classic photo of the gathering[19] shows a very different Christian culture from that of the Azusa Street Revival. The beginnings of Pentecostalism are varied and global, but the early adherents were described in the *Los Angeles Times* in the following way: "Devotees of the weird doctrine practice the most fanatical rites, preach the wildest theories, and work themselves into a state of mad excitement." This form of Christianity, with all of its "mad excitement," was to become one of the major stories in the twentieth century. It is difficult to overestimate the impact that indigenous and Pentecostal forms of Christianity have had in the twentieth century.

In Africa, for example, resistance to European colonialism and missionary domination of church life seemed to fuel indigenous church movements. These indigenous movements were not dependent on Western Pentecostalism but shared many of the characteristics. These churches, often led by local prophets (male and female), were beyond the control and even the understanding of most Western mission agencies.

> Revivals from the Protestant churches (such as the mostly Anglican East Africa Revival) produced or stimulated other indigenous movements. In the 1930s the East Africa Revival was the catalyst to the indigenous *Balokole* ("saved ones") movement in Uganda and the surrounding countries. In the 20th century these AICs grew from about 40,000 converts to an estimated 54 million at the beginning of the 21st century.[20]

This global "spiritual" movement of Christianity has been a major theme of the twentieth century, not only in Africa. David Barrett estimated that there were over 525 million Pentecostals and Charismatics in the world in 2000. This is a group that was not even counted or discussed in 1910, but today is a major factor in global evangelization.

---

[19]Found, for example on the cover of Stanley's volume, *The World Missionary Conference.*
[20]From Sunquist, *Unexpected Christian Century*, 159.

Fifth, in 1910 no one saw that atheistic communism was on the rise and would have such a major global impact on politics and religion. Communism's impact was not anticipated at all. The 1905 revolution in Russia was much more important than any of the Western missionary personnel could have guessed. However, by the time of the founding of the International Missionary Council in 1921, the largest Christian nation in the world, Russia, had become the largest secular (or atheistic) nation in the world. In the 1920s the same ideas were spreading in China, and by the end of the Second World War atheistic communism was closing churches, mosques, temples, and shrines from Germany to the Pacific Ocean. Reading over the records of mission societies in the late 1940s, I don't believe there was ever a missionary disappointment like that of the "closing" of China. Western missionary work in China had become a huge Christian empire of schools, universities, hospitals, YMCAs, YWCAs, and, of course, churches. The Japanese invasions were a terrible setback, but the communist victory was devastating. Western missions hoped to rebuild their hospitals and schools, but slowly they realized that the new communist leaders would not allow this. The "three-self" approach discussed by missionaries and mission theorists in the mid-nineteenth century was now being forced on the church in China by communist leaders and accepted by some Christian leaders.[21]

When communist Russia expanded its empire to become the Union of Soviet Socialist Republics (USSR), churches throughout eastern Europe were closed and, depending on the local communist leadership, persecution was more or less extensive. Many of these countries (Latvia, Lithuania, Estonia, Germany, Poland, etc.) had very strong Christian communities that were now languishing. Upon the collapse of the Iron Curtain in 1989, churches did not quickly recover. In fact generations of communist rule had a devastating impact on Christianity in eastern Europe. Secularization and materialism advanced with little sign of abatement under communist rule.

The impact of communism in the pre-Christian countries of China and eastern Asia (Vietnam, Cambodia, Laos) was very different, and this is our sixth theme of the century. Those sitting at New College in Edinburgh in 1910 not only could not envision the communist empire of eastern Asia, but they

---

[21]The July 1950 "Christian Manifesto" written by Christian leader Y. T. Yu prepared the way for the end of the missionary era and the beginning of the Three-Self Patriotic Movement (1951).

certainly could not have predicted that such an atheistic "empire" could have a *positive* influence on the development of Christianity in East Asia. But that is indeed what happened. When the Protestant missionary force slipped away from China to relocate in Taiwan, Malaysia, Thailand, and other regions, it was assumed that the less than one million Protestants in China would now be greatly reduced. It was a time of missionary mourning.

In the early years of Mao's rule in China some Western mission executives wanted to believe the best concerning Christian life under the communists. The move to self-support was seen as a good for Chinese Christians, even if Western mission agencies did not believe the church could survive without them. As late as the 1960s and early 1970s there were some ecumenical writers who believed that the Mao could be seen as a type of Moses, leading his people to freedom and preparing the way for the Messiah.[22] The 1972/1973 World Mission Conference of the WCC, held in Bangkok, had as its theme "Salvation Today," and therefore emphasized the horizontal dimension of salvation as seen in societies and cultures. Raymond Whitehead of the United Church of Christ (USA) wrote an article for the *International Review of Mission* built around this theme titled "Salvation in the Chinese Revolution."[23] In this article, and in the minds of many other ecumenists, there was a tendency to look over the tragedy of the Great Leap Forward and to overlook the great suppression of the Cultural Revolution to hear about the social salvation that was brought on by Chairman Mao. "Salvation terminology is used extensively by followers of Chairman Mao. Mao Tse Tung is referred to as '*da-jiou-xing*' or saving star. . . . In stories it is not uncommon to find the words 'Chairman Mao saved me,' a phrase that is verbally parallel to the Christian declaration, 'Jesus saved me.'"[24] However, the salvation that would come to China would be classic Christian salvation through Jesus Christ, and Mao was instrumental not directly, but indirectly. Zhao Fusan of the Chinese Academy of Social Sciences, director of the Institute for the Study of World

---

[22]A 1951 *Time* article described how the "Vatican's semiofficial newspaper, L'Osservatore Romano, published a new Decalogue, said to be the first step in a new 'Chinese' theology developed for Chinese Roman Catholics by the brain trust of Communist Leader Mao Tse-tung." "Mao as Moses," *Time*, April 23, 1951, http://content.time.com/time/magazine/article/0,9171,821566,00.html.

[23]Raymond Whitehead, "Salvation in the Chinese Revoluion," *International Review of Missions* 61, no. 244 (1972): 327-41.

[24]Ibid., 327.

Religions of the Academy, commented in 1985, "Suffering was the experience of the decade of the cultural revolution. . . . The cultural revolution helped one to really understand what the Christian faith means in its challenge to one's life."[25] He then went on to comment that the suffering of the church helped the church to draw closer to Chinese culture, and this both deepened the church and gave courage and focus in Christian witness.

The suffering of the church in China and Vietnam had the effect that Zhao described above. Christianity grew when most assumed it would struggle to even survive. From less than a million Christians in 1948, it was commonly assumed to be at least five times that by the end of the 1970s, and today is estimated to be over 50 million (including Roman Catholics).[26] In Vietnamese Christianity, both Roman Catholicism and Protestantism are growing in most regions of the country. In both China and Vietnam, the growth is much more rapid than before the collapse of Western colonialism and than before the rise (and now the diluting) of communism. Edinburgh predicted that great civilizations of Asia would be evangelized by the Western missionaries. Western missionaries laid a foundation, but the evangelization of East Asia has been completely an Asian affair, through suffering rather than through Western civilization.

The final theme of the twentieth century we would like to look at is less scientific and historically verifiable than the other six; in fact, it is a theological statement that the twentieth century has brought back to our consciousness. Christian missions is a work that all of the church is invited into, but in fact it is God's work. The development of global Christianity is a work of God that generally takes place through suffering and marginalized human agency. Our power and technology has little to say about the kingdom of God, the mustard seed that Jesus spoke of. Mott knew this about Christianity, but his excitement about modern communications, colonial Christendom empires, and modern science drowned out the fact that mission is really God's work, not ours. It was

---

[25]From an interview by Jean Stromberg, "'We Live as We Are Led by Christ,' Interview with Zhao Fusan," *International Review of Mission*, April 1985, 179.

[26]This number is an average from the more extreme estimates of 100 million to the more conservative numbers of about 35 million. We assume that the publication and distribution of over 100 million Chinese Bibles in China gives some indication of the number of people reading the Bible. In most areas the Bible is now available, but there are still Christian communities in rural areas without Bibles.

almost an afterthought rather than a foundational statement in his 1910 volume *The Decisive Hour for Christian Missions* when Mott said,

> No lesson of missionary experience has been more fully impressively and convincingly taught than that apart from the divine working all is inadequate. The hope and guarantee of carrying the Gospel to all the non-Christian world do not rest principally on external favoring advantages which Christianity may possess in certain fields nor upon the character and progress of the civilization of Christian countries nor upon the number strength experience and administrative ability of the missionary societies nor upon the variety and adaptability of missionary methods and the efficiency of missionary machinery nor upon an army of missionary evangelists preachers teachers doctors and translators much as these are needed nor upon the relation of the money power to the plans of the Kingdom nor upon aggressive and ably led forward missionary movements either in the home Churches or on the foreign field but upon the living God dominating possessing and using all these factors and influences.[27]

In fact this was only partially correct. Christian statesmen of the period (for they were mostly men) could only see God using "external favoring advantages which Christianity may possess." They could not imagine that the power of the gospel to transform peoples would be found in weakness and suffering. It was from the margins and from the weak that Christianity transformed itself and transformed the world. Africa is and was the poorest continent, and Chinese peasants were the least powerful in East Asia. Dalits or those outside the scheduled castes have been the greatest force in the evangelization of India, not the Brahmins or Kshatriyas. The greatest power in the evangelization of Latin America, Africa, and Asia in the past century has been dedicated and consecrated indigenous evangelists, not well-educated scholars either from Asia or from the West. But, if we have been paying attention to the history of Christianity, then we will not be surprised, because this has always been the case from the days of Stephen the martyr and Paul the prisoner for the gospel.

Christian Identity and Historical Understanding Today

It is important not to stop here but to take time to evaluate what has happened in the past century in, through, and in spite of the greatest Christian minds of

---

[27]Mott, *Decisive Hour for Christian Missions*, 194.

the period. The voices at Edinburgh were more the voices of church executives, bishops, and moderators than the voices of missionaries and indigenous church leaders. This may help to explain the misperceptions of the evangelization task and its future. Edinburgh's discourse reflected European Christendom's understanding of the church, mission, and culture. More voices from the margins—Africans, Latin Americans, missionaries, and women—may have corrected that perception some. For example, the earlier SVM meeting in Rochester and the 1900 Ecumenical Missionary Conference held in New York had more women than Edinburgh 1910.[28] Edinburgh was dominated by male church and mission executives who were enmeshed in the Western academic and organizational models for understanding the church in mission. It is very hard to hear the countercultural message of Scripture when the cultural expressions are so dominant, appealing, and vocal.

We, like the participants in 1910, live in a culture that has a mental environment, or a mental world, of assumptions, values, and views of reality.

> Our mental environment is the surrounding climate of ideas by which we make sense of the world. It includes our moral environment since our ideas about how to live are a prime way we make sense of the world. But our mental environment is broader still. It includes our ideas about what exists, what can be known, and what counts as evidence for our beliefs. It assigns value to our life and work. Above all, it determines our plausibility structures—what we find reasonable or unreasonable, credible or incredible, thinkable or unthinkable.[29]

In 1910 the best and the brightest shared the basic plausibility structures that led them to great optimism: *God will do the work of evangelizing the world, through our "civilized" culture*. It was hard to think any other way. And so the deeper truths of salvation through suffering and the meek inheriting the earth were drowned out by the larger mental environment. Even the devout and devoted leader John R. Mott was sure that it was God's mission, but he could only see God working through human excellence and strength, not through human failure and weakness. We might surmise that a missiology of suffering would have been considered heretical at the time.

---

[28]See Timothy Yates, *Christian Mission in the Twentieth Century* (Cambridge: Cambridge University Press, 1994), 20.
[29]William A. Dembski, *The End of Christianity, Finding a Good God in an Evil World* (Nashville: B & H, 2009), 1.

Christianity in the twentieth century has been a clear demonstration that the gospel message for the nations is carried in clay jars, not in ocean liners or trans-Atlantic jets. The twentieth century has also shown that God's order is not always our design.[30] In 1910 it seemed like Western executives could design the evangelization of the world, but the great irony is that God's disorder came in the person of the Holy Spirit and did a much greater work of evangelization than "man's design." Gospel imperatives will be carried out, but not as we might expect—not according to careful plans and strategies. The evangelization of the world in this generation did not occur, but the cry did focus on the will of God, if not the means for effecting that will. Still the watchword is much closer to being fulfilled in 2010 than in 1910, but not in a way that anyone could have predicted. History teaches us, above all, that we are so limited, forgetful, and self-oriented. If we look carefully, if we read with one eye to God's suffering and the other eye to God's glory, we can also see the power of the gospel to save, through death: "always carrying in the body the death of Jesus, so that the life of Jesus may also be made visible in our bodies. For while we live, we are always being given up to death for Jesus' sake" (2 Cor 4:10-11). We are not that different from the delegates who met in 1910 at New College, Edinburgh. It is equally difficult for us to die to those parts of our cherished mental environment that give us meaning and hope. If, however, we learn anything from what has happened in the past one hundred years, it should be that it is only through great humility that we can see clearer into God's future. That may be enough.

A Hesitant Postscript: Lausanne 2010 in Cape Town

There were four major conferences held in 2010 to celebrate or at least to commemorate and remember Edinburgh 1910. Christians around the world recognized some significance of that conference held a century ago, even though there is little consensus as to what that significance is for the twenty-first century. I did not attend all four conferences, but I did attend one (Cape Town), and some ruminations in light of my reflections on 1910 will reveal a few other issues. I will make a few observations about what it seems to indicate about global Christianity in the past century. All of these comments must be

---

[30]The title of the first General Assembly of the World Council of Churches in Amsterdam was "Man's Disorder, God's Design."

understood with some understanding of the Lausanne movement, a movement that finds its heritage in Billy Graham's 1966 Berlin Congress on Evangelism and the follow-up 1974 Congress held in Lausanne. Lausanne produced a "covenant" that is still very interesting reading today. In short, the Congress—as well as the next-generation Lausanne leaders—promoted a recovery of the priority of evangelism in mission, a focus on finishing the task of reaching every "unreached people group," and in this task a focus on demonstrating as well as proclaiming the liberation that is offered in Jesus Christ. This is the nature of the movement.[31]

First, the Cape Town Congress demonstrated with gusto that Christianity has been recentered in Africa, Latin America, and certain regions of Asia. The delegates came from more nations than there are in the United Nations, and they included thirty from Nepal and fifty-five from Ethiopia. This would have been absolutely unthinkable one hundred years ago. I don't believe there were even thirty believers in all of Nepal at that time. Africa was represented in artwork, music, preaching, teaching, and developing ongoing and new partnerships for mission. Over two hundred delegates were expected from China, but only three or four made it out of the country. However, they paid their own way. This in itself is remarkable.

Second, the Congress reminded us of the divisions of global Christianity that were coming to the surface in 1910. At that time there was the Anglican problem (they would not talk about mission to Latin America). At this conference there was confusion over the relationship that evangelicals might have with the Orthodox and Roman Catholic churches. *Evangelical* was never clearly defined, but everyone seemed to know what it meant. At one point, according to Fr. Ioan Saucca, an observer from the WCC noted (with a twinkle in his eye) that he was apparently an "unreached people group," but then later in the conference Egyptian or Coptic Orthodox were described as brothers and sisters in mission. Surprisingly, large icons were displayed in times of worship on the huge illuminated screen. This looked very unevangelical and I am sure was not part of the worship one hundred years ago in Scotland. It did mark a broadening of evangelicalism and a development in global church leadership.

---

[31]The leaders at the Cape Town meeting repeatedly noted that Lausanne was not an institution, but a movement dedicated to stimulating new ideas and partnerships.

Third, the conference relied on massive amounts of finely tuned technology, even using online chats and discussions beforehand, but the messages that were given indicated that Christian witness is not a matter of money or technology, but of suffering and humility. Like a century earlier, the best in human technology or human science was brought to bear on missionary work. The question to be asked is whether this technology is seen as the promise of mission as science and innovations were in 1910. We hope not.

Fourth, Edinburgh 1910 was a male movement, but at Cape Town, from one of the more conservative elements of global Christianity, close to one-third of the official delegates were women, including a liturgist, preacher, and a number of teachers. Women were full participants at all levels. Still there were side debates about how women in leadership are to be seen. This shows that much of the movement is still too much in the pockets of Western leaders (and probably money), for outside the West these arguments about women in leadership are very different. In places of suffering and rapid growth there is not time (and no real reason) to argue about a woman complementing a man's leadership or being able to lead in her own right.

A fifth observation from this important conference was that the Anglican presence was very large from the Middle East, Asia, and Africa. For an evangelical conference the presence of a liturgical church—the church of the Middle Way—was a signpost. This seems to indicate that the leadership of global churches like the Anglican Communion are not in Western hands. The conference was influenced by the Anglican and therefore more traditional liturgy. Many of the attendees were from Bible churches, independent and indigenous churches, and from Baptist churches. Liturgical worship, even singing the creed, was certainly a new experience for many delegates. The overall sense of worship with this strong Anglican presence was more like charismatic, African Anglicanism.

Many other observations may be made, but one stood out, and that is that Arabic was one of the official languages that lectures were translated into. The engagement of Christianity in the Islamic world was also indicated by the large numbers of delegates who attended very sensitive (no pictures, no recordings) break-out sessions on Christian witness to Muslims. The sessions were at times very heated, and both the complexity of the issues and the large and diverse group of observers pointed to a major theme in Christian witness for the future.

Do any of these indicate the future of Christianity and Christian missions for the future? We should be careful. We missed it by a long shot a century ago. We should do better now, but we will only do so by embracing, I believe, a missiology of suffering and of humility. This should be the task of the global church in the coming decades.

7

Time, Lectures, and Redemption

The Princeton Student
Mission Lectures

This chapter seeks to understand better this compound question: "What is Christianity as a historical movement, and how can we best understand and explain Christianity as God's redemptive work in history?" I want to be clear from the start that this compound question—focusing on a historical movement, linked to the faith commitment that in Christianity we see something of God's redemptive work—is being asked on the other side of modernity. We now publicly admit that scholarly neutrality is a myth. I have commitments and assumptions that I believe are more liberating than binding, more general than specific, and less Presbyterian than Christian. I know and you know that history and context influence perception. Our question has two lines of vision, and how we answer this compound question will have both a pedagogical line of development and a practical line. It will influence how we teach and how we live. How we understand Christianity as a movement in history will determine how we teach about Christianity, how we prepare pastors, and how we equip people for Christian mission. What do we focus on, and what do we leave out? What are we looking for in our research? Any historian will tell you that the art of the historian is mostly a matter of deciding what to leave out, so how we answer this question will help us in the art of historical excising.

Thus, our question has an ethical dimension. Having majored in education decades ago, I am still aware of the truth that education is not a neutral science. Jesus talks about the misuse of pedagogy resulting in having a millstone strung around your neck and being thrown in a lake. Teaching is less a matter of throwing facts out into the air and more a matter of shaping, directing, and guiding. Jesus realized that education is a moral undertaking, as did Karl Marx, in fact. Politicians running for office also realize this. Minds can be corrupted or corrected; lives can be saved or starved by teachers and scholars. In universities and seminaries we are often so far removed from the "end product" (e.g., the pastor applying the Word to an individual's or family's life) that we seldom recognize our responsibility and accountability, but I believe that how we answer the above questions about teaching focus and research has moral and ethical implications. It would be much safer if our historical and theological scholarship could be as "neutral" as the description of a slug or as boring as watching grass grow. However, when we teach Christian history, especially in a seminary, we are directing minds and affections; we are building an image of "church." In all honesty, at times we may just be putting people to sleep. This also has moral implications.

This may seem like an odd topic for a students' mission lecture, so let me explain. I have been involved in two major history projects, both collaborative with a global community of Christian scholars.[1] While deeply involved in researching and writing about the eighteenth and nineteenth centuries in Africa, Latin America, and South Asia, I presented a paper at the Center for Theological Inquiry in Princeton on historiography. There were only about fifteen scholars at this evening presentation, all scholars in residence and a few local faculty. The paper I presented was to be an introduction or epilogue (I am often nor sure whether I am coming or going) for volume two of *History of the World Christian Movement*. It was a well-researched paper tracing historiography in the past two centuries that timidly and hesitantly worked toward the conclusion that all of the nineteenth- and twentieth-century historiography was leading to our book. The paper was both premature and self-serving. It fell flat, and everyone, including the presenter, was uncomfortable at the conclusion of the paper, looking down at their feet and adjusting napkins and picking at crumbs on the tables. The paper deserved to be ignored. However, my bad paper and everyone else's evening was redeemed by an insightful question from a South African ethicist: "Scott, you have been reading about

---

[1] Dale T. Irvin and Scott W. Sunquist, *History of the World Christian Movement*, 3 vols. (Maryknoll, NY: Orbis Books, 2001–); Scott W. Sunquist, ed., *A Dictionary of Asian Christianity* (Grand Rapids: Eerdmans, 2001).

church history globally for the past eight years or so. Few people are forced to read so widely about Christian history: the Pacific and the Potomac, the Balkans and Batakland, and of course Pretoria and Princeton. You have had to tell all of this as a single story, to make some sense of various movements as all part of the fabric of Christianity. Tell us, what have you learned?"

Thin Red Thread

It was not the question I was expecting. With this question he graciously swept my paper from our gaze and put on the table something much more solid, precious, and important: the question of meaning, if not purpose. On one hand I was in shock and wanted to crawl under the table. All of these great scholars from around the world, and I am supposed to answer the global question about the meaning of Christian history? On the other hand, it was a very simple question to answer.

"What I have learned is that Christianity is so fragile, and yet it is powerful enough to change the world." That is it.

As I explained this, scenarios from across the centuries and across the seas came to my mind. The scenes all revealed something of the missional meaning of Christianity. Christianity—even under terrible conditions and for sloppy reasons, or with uneducated leaders—is constantly moving out. But as it moves out it transforms cultures. As I was concluding my brief exposition an image came to mind that I will stick with and that I now want to stick on you.

Christianity is a thin red thread woven into history, a thin red thread that has changed the world.

The thin (and fragile) red thread is the message of Christianity. It is fairly simple. It does not have to be written; in fact, it is usually spoken. It is something like this:

> God created all things, and in Jesus Christ he came to forgive sin and to show us how to live. His message was rejected. He was killed on the cross and was buried, rose from the dead, and now, through his Holy Spirit, he continues his work of liberation and redemption of all things through Jesus Christ.

We may quibble with some of the words here, but this is the basic message. It has been translated, spoken, acted out, sung, and preached, and people and their cultures have been transformed. During the past few years I have expanded that simple image into three concepts of time, cross, and glory.

In exegeting this answer about the meaning of the Christian movement, I will first set the context. I will use the history of the Princeton Student Mission Lectures as my canvas, and the early speakers, especially James Dennis, for my paint. After looking at how Christianity was understood in his historical and cultural context of the early twentieth century, we will turn to look at history itself, or more exactly the concept of time. At a future time the whole concept of time, cross, and glory will be expanded, but for this chapter we will only look at the meaning of time for Christian faith and history.[2]

HISTORY OF THE LECTURES AND HISTORY ITSELF

I have long used James Dennis's three-volume *Christian Missions and Social Progress: A Sociological Study of Christian Missions* as a case study in the problems of contextualization and historical understanding.[3] In preparing this lecture I found out that Dennis, a Presbyterian missionary to Syria and a historian of mission, gave the first Students Mission Lectures at Princeton.[4] These were later published as *Foreign Missions After a Century*. Later Dennis (a favorite of Princeton, apparently) gave the fourth lectures, which were later expanded into the massive three-volume work *Christian Mission and Social Progress*. Dennis was a guiding light for mission scholars and one of the leaders of Presbyterian mission over a century ago. Thus, we can use his understanding of mission and the Christian movement as a starting point. His views seem so strange and optimistic to us today, so imperialistic and even arrogant, and yet his idea of progress was as natural and common in his time as our commonly held ideas that technology holds the answers for the future. Dennis was a progressive—a nineteenth-century progressive

---

[2]I am developing this further in a forthcoming book titled *Time, Cross, and Glory: How to Read Christian History* (Downers Grove, IL: InterVarsity Press, forthcoming). The other two concepts further expand on the core meaning of Christian history and the necessity of keeping them in view in both research and in reflection on Christian history. Christianity is cruciform in its essence, pointing toward a future of glory. All this is found in the life of God.

[3]James Dennis, *Christian Mission and Social Progress: A Sociological Study of Christian Missions*, 3 vols. (New York: Fleming H. Revell, 1897–1906).

[4]An early form of this chapter was delivered as the first of three of the Princeton Student Mission Lectures at Princeton Theological Seminary.

evangelical rooted in the American Protestant tradition, the confidence of this Student Volunteer Movement, and the sense of duty that was at times expressed as the "white man's burden."

In the introduction to his first volume of *Social Progress* Dennis notes the following:

> That there is a striking apologetic import to the aspect of missions herein presented is evident. It is not merely a vindication of the social value of mission work, but it becomes, in proportion to the reality and significance of the facts put in evidence, a present-day supplement to the cumulative argument of history in defense of Christianity as a supreme force in the social regeneration and elevation of the human race.[5]

His view was illustrated in the wealth of facts, stories, and pictures that fill the volume.

Figure 1. In these and other pictures in *Christian Mission and Social Progress*, Dennis shows that the need for mission is in part to bring about social progress such as ending slavery.

---

[5]Dennis, *Christian Mission and Social Progress*, 1:ix.

For Dennis the missionary message is for "worldwide reformation . . . or . . . regeneration." Listen to his evaluation of history and reform:

> We have had local reformations in religious history; we had them in Hebrew history, before the coming of Christ. The result of early Christian labors was the conversion of the Roman Empire, and in the sixteenth century came the great historic Reformation of Europe. Now, for the first time in the history of our earth, this great movement in the direction of regeneration or reformation is beginning to shape itself into a *world-wide enterprise*.[6]

Figure 2. Social progress in these pictures shows Christianization as almost identical with Westernization.

The sixteenth-century Reformation was only in Europe; thus, he says, "may we not expect that a reformation so extended as that contemplated in modern missions will produce world-wide fruit, especially since it has all the advantages afforded by modern inventions, and facilities and methods of communication and international relations and the almost magical expedients for disseminating knowledge?"[7] He and his age had great trust in technology and human inventions. This is what gave him confidence in Christianity. I do not

---

[6] James Dennis, *Foreign Missions After a Century* (New York: Fleming H. Revell, 1893), 18-19 (emphasis is mine).
[7] Ibid., 18.

believe we are that different today, although we express it differently.[8] His views, however, were not as chastened by the world wars and genocidal obsessions of the twentieth century. In the preface to volume three, he notes, referring to his previous lectures, "It has been asserted, for example, that missions are a forceful dynamic power in social progress, a molding influence on national life, and a factor of importance in commercial expansion, as well as a stimulus to the religious reformation not only of individual lives, but of society as a whole, through many and various channels of influence."[9]

What may cause us to pause is his seemingly imperialistic view of Christianity ("national life, commercial expansion"), which sounds like a domination of the world by Christian cultures and nations. And yet the evangelization of cultures or penetration of Christian values of justice and peace is something we should affirm. Jesus' life and death was not just a private and privileged act for our own therapy. It was identification with the lost, lonely, and oppressed in order to usher in new relationships, life, and a new society called a kingdom. The problem with Dennis from our perspective is not how expansive his vision of mission was, but how it was woven with national aspirations (a particular society) and reliance on human efforts. Here we see some pictures that help us see through Dennis's eyes how he understood the progress that Christian missions promised. The global situation outside Christendom was marked by slavery and by extreme religious practices that kept people poor and ignorant (the Hindu holy men whose life prevents social progress, such as can happen with boys' training schools). The contrast is dramatic and clear in his three volumes. I cannot emphasize enough that this was the common understanding of Western nations and Western theologians, even (or especially) the more progressive and better educated of the time.

The phrase *Western nations* includes France. In 1899, as the Ottoman Empire was collapsing, France, England, and Russia were moving into the Middle Eastern neighborhood. The opportunity arose for the Benedictines to rebuild a Crusader church in Palestine. In a September 11, 1899, letter from D. Drouhin, OAB (Ordem dos Advogados do Brasil) to French Consul Ernest Auzépy we read the following: "In this surprising concourse of circumstances,

---

[8]We can end global warming, the energy crisis, human trafficking, cancer, etc.
[9]Dennis, *Christian Mission and Social Progress*, 3:vii.

there is for us, Mr Consul, a very precious encouragement: we will gladly say, with our generous crusaders of the eleventh and twelfth century, 'God wants it. God wants it! Especially as our consciences and our hearts give their testimony that, like them, we are *looking for the greatness of our dear France and the extension of God's reign*, which for individuals and for peoples is the real, the unique source of civilization and happiness.'"[10] Our Presbyterian James Dennis is much less imperialistic than the good French Benedictine brother, but that should give Presbyterians little solace.

Dennis and Grouhin and, for that matter, other great Christian leaders of the early twentieth century—people such as John R. Mott, Robert E. Speer, Bishop William Oldham, and Samuel Zwemer—viewed Christianity through their cultural lenses, and when they looked they saw progress—social progress, in fact. Christianity was advancing and bringing with it a better life for all, a life for the West African or Chinese that would be like the best of Western civilization (including the clothes). This basic view was an academic view—the view of the academy—but it was also the fundamentalist and the Pentecostal view of Christianity. The great historian Kenneth Scott Latourette reflects a similar view, although he was more chastened by the long historical record he traced. Still, he saw each advance of Christianity as progressing a little further and each recession as receding a little less. Optimism, progressivism, and human ability were themes in the historical writing of Christianity. It was easy for them to see the kingdom of God revealed in modern technology, better health, and the missionary movement.

We now live in a new century, and I would like to propose that we need to recenter or re-view Christianity today. In light of the presence of Christianity today as mostly non-Western, and in light of the errors of the past in equating human technology and empire with Christian mission, meaning must now come out of the biblical story, the experience of the global church, and it must be in continuity with its founder. Neither Wesley's quadrilateral[11] nor the Reformation cry of *sola Scriptura* is adequate for the twenty-first century. Again, these convictions come out of studying the Christian movement

---

[10]Dominique Trimbur, "Between Eastern and Western Christendom: The Benedictines, France and the Syrian Catholic Church in Jerusalem," in *Christianity in the Middle East: Studies in Modern History, Theology and Politics*, ed. Anthony O'Mahony (London: Melisende, 2008), 379.

[11]Scripture, tradition, experience, and reason.

through the ages and throughout the world: the biblical story, global Christian experience, and faith as defined by its founder. These are our sources.

TIME AND REDEMPTION: HISTORY

It should have been clear in looking at the pictures from Dennis's book, and in hearing his attitude of progress for all nations, that the Christian idea of hope was driving his theology and understanding of history. In fact, for all of our criticisms of nineteenth-century progressivism, social gospel optimism, or Student Volunteer triumphalism, we can see that the hope of the gospel is expressed in all of these.[12] In Jesus Christ, hope is offered. It is described as forgiveness, liberation, and redemption, and it comes in many forms. However, in Jesus Christ we believe there is a future, which includes a purpose and a goal. History as an ongoing and purposeful story is important.

One of the great tragedies of the modern and now postmodern era is the disdain we have developed for history. In a sense we have ourselves to blame for this, since the antihistorical bias that developed in the Enlightenment was very much a result of the betrayal of religion by Western societies. Religion—which is supposed to give solace and comfort, meaning and understanding—had become the crusader against the East and the inquisitor in the West. As Descartes looked over the seventeenth-century battlefields, where Christians were killing other Christians over political power and interpretations of the Eucharist, he believed that all knowledge was misleading. And here was the rub: what we have known through history and tradition has misled us, and so we need to start afresh. What we have been told from history cannot be trusted, so (he reasoned) I have to begin with myself. I can trust myself, reasoned Descartes. Actually, two revolutions occurred at the same time, and we still live with these today.

The first revolution was a turn away from history and a turn toward the future. This meant a turn away from Christian tradition or the past as being a source of truth.[13] Truth was to be found now in what was modern and what

---

[12]"The evangelization of the world in this generation" became the watchword or mission cry of the SVM and of the 1910 Edinburgh Missionary Conference, indicating that it was a mainstream, mainline understanding of mission.

[13]Christian tradition is the dynamic life of the gospel, rooted in Jesus Christ and participating (with faithful continuity) in history. The tradition at times becomes captive to cultural expressions, and when this happens it becomes necessary that it be freed through rediscovery and recommitment to its life-giving Spirit. See John McGuckin, *The Orthodox Church: An Introduction to Its History, Doctrine and Spiritual Culture* (London: Wiley-Blackwell, 2008).

was to come, for the past had betrayed humanity. The second turn was a turn away from God and God's church to the "self" as the measure of truth. Thus, the scientific method developed, even among well-meaning Christians, at a time when history was on the decline. The Reformation cry of *"Ad fontes!"* (to the source) turned into the Enlightenment cry of Kant, *"Sapere aude!"* (dare to know). And knowing involved daring to discover and think something new. In fact, one of the proofs of truth in the modern era is simply that it is new. And so we live with this modern epistemological heresy, where history does not contain knowledge. This makes it difficult to entice young people to study the past while they are texting to their friends back home: "History is so boring." "Kill history before it kills me."

History, or more exactly, the Christian view of history, is the exact opposite. With the coming of Christ as the Sent One of God came a new view of reality, one that confronted the cyclical views of reality that were common in the Roman Empire as well as among many of the religions of the world at that time. We might say that for the earliest Christians, there was a great interest in the discovery that history was God's idea.[14] The cycle of birth, growth, decay, death, and rebirth was broken when God came to usher in a new kingdom on earth that pointed to a fulfillment of time in the future. The earliest Christians rightly found the origin of salvation in creation, and so creation became a central, or at least foundational, salvific event. Athanasius begins his discussion of the incarnation (*De Incarnatione Verbi Dei*) by talking about creation: the one who created humanity is the only one to redeem humanity. This helps to explain why there are so many patristic commentaries and homilies on Genesis and more specifically on the *Hexameron*[15] (Ephrem, John Chrysostom, Diodore of Tarsus, Basil, Narsai, Origin, Ambrose, Augustine, Cyril of Alexandria).[16] The early defenders of the faith would agree with Martin Luther: *Nihil pulchrius Genesi, nihil utilus*. Nothing more beautiful than Genesis, nothing more useful.[17] The creation of time—

---

[14]See Andrew Louth, who has a section on Maximus's cosmology in his book *Maximus the Confessor* (New York: Routledge, 1996), 61-76.

[15]The six days of creation.

[16]See Fr. Seraphim Rose, *Genesis, Creation and Early Man*, rev. ed. (Alaska: St. Herman the Brotherhood, 2011), for other commentaries.

[17]Assuming James Strahan's attribution is correct: *Hebrew Ideals: A Study of Genesis 11–50*, 4th ed. (Edinburgh: T&T Clark, 1922), 5. Stanley L. Jaki says the saying is from a nineteenth-century French exegete (see "Genesis 1: A Cosmogenesis," *Homiletic and Pastoral Review*, August 1, 1993,

expressed as a movement from chaos to order through fall and redemption and then to the new creation—continues to be important today for those whose lives are still cyclical.

This new understanding of reality, where God created all things (including time), was a radical break from the common understanding of the ancient world, as we see in the patristic commentaries. This view of time, purpose, and a goal of time continues to be a key issue in Christian witness to Hindus, Buddhists, and those who worship according to the cycles of nature. Missionaries teaching people who view time as nonlinear always turn to a single God as Creator of all things. Creation becomes the main, or at least the foundational, doctrine to be discussed. For example, the much-persecuted, exiled, and imprisoned Jesuit Alexandre de Rhodes, who worked in both Annam and Cochin China, began his "Eight Day Catechism" with a long discussion of creation, explaining each day of creation. Then he talked about the "three religions" of Vietnam and how they were false, and then he got around to talking about Jesus.[18] Lesslie Newbigin remarks in his book *Gospel in a Pluralist Society* that the Tamil language, dominated by Hinduism, has no word for hope. Creation, time, and fulfillment of time carries with it hope.[19] Newbigin then comments that this is one of the main marks of a Christian community: it has a future hope. In a number of ethnic groups, such as the Karen (in Myanmar), there are myths or national stories about a Creator God who is far away. Embedded in their cyclical lives, measured each year by the seasons, is a timeless hope of redemption. For the Karen, it is a lost book; for some West African groups there is a Creator God, but he has been forgotten or has moved far away, usually because humans have offended him. This is not an empirical study, but it has been my experience that when Buddhists become Christians, they are particularly interested in the stories of creation. Creation *ex nihilo* was understood to mean time (*kronos*), which meant the possibility of development, change, progression, and fulfillment. Jesus' coming marks time and marks humanity. Therefore, the key to time and, by extension, the key to humanity is found in Jesus Christ.

---

www.hprweb.com/1993/08/genesis-1-a-cosmogenesis/).
[18]See Peter Phan's *Mission and Catechesis: Alexandre de Rhodes and Inculturation in Seventeenth Century Vietnam* (Maryknoll, NY: Orbis Books, 2006).
[19]Lesslie Newbigin, *The Gospel in a Pluralist Society* (Grand Rapids: Eerdmans, 1989), 101.

Closely connected to the creation of time was the new concept mentioned above of *creatio ex nihilo*. Ancient Christian writers wrote about creation to show that God's redemption is in fact a creation and creative work that God alone has done. We can see how important it was to understand God's absolute creation out of nothing when we look at the response of patristic authors to Origen. Origen's theology of creation was seen as semi-Platonic, and so his views were criticized and his works on creation were not included in the *Philokalia*.[20] Creation out of nothing was a radical departure from the Greek view of the world, a world where intermediaries moved between the divine and physical plane. The implications of this radical claim have been spelled out by Andrew Louth. He notes that

> both Athanasius and Arius have a very clearly defined doctrine of *creatio ex nihilo*. This may seem very surprising until it is realized that the doctrine was unknown to pagan philosophy and only emerged slowly and uncertainly in early Christian theology. . . . With Athanasius and Arius, there is no doubt, for they enumerate the alternatives and reject them (see *De Inc*.2 and Arius's Letter to Eusebius of Nicomedia.)[21]

What this means, says Louth, is that there is a complete contrast between God and his creation or between the divine (uncreated) and that "which is created out of nothing but the will of God." Therefore, there is no intermediate zone; there are no aeons or emanations. It was this intermediate world (posited by Middle Platonism, e.g., Philo) that contained the idea of *Logos*, but because the Christian view of creation had no middle zone, the *Logos* had to be identified fully with God (Athanasius and the Orthodox) or with the world (Arius).

The soul, it was soon understood—in contradistinction to Origen—also was created *ex nihilo*. Thus, Christian mystical theology does not see the soul as part of God. For Athanasius the soul is a mirror of God. Louth comments,

---

[20] Origen's view of creation and time has recently been reevaluated by Panagiotes Tzamalikos (*Origen: Cosmology and Ontology of Time*, Supplements to Vigiliae Christianae [Leiden: Brill, 2006]), but the historic fact is that Origen's interpretation of the Bible was appreciated by Orthodoxy and is included in the *Philokalia*, except for his writings about creation. The Cappadocian Basil of Caesarea explicitly rejected his interpretation of Genesis as being too Platonic. Origen's disembodied eschatology or idealism does not provide adequate basis for social activity on behalf of justice, nor does it promote the cultural mandate, which has been a central pillar of Christian history.

[21] Andrew Louth, *The Origins of the Christian Mystical Tradition, from Plato to Denys*, 2nd ed. (Oxford: Oxford University Press, 2007), 74.

Time, Lectures, and Redemption 139

"There is no ontological continuity between the image of the mirror and of that which it is the image; so, in the case of the soul reflecting the image of God, this similarity discloses a much deeper dissimilarity at the level of substance."[22] For Athanasius the soul is created—it is not part of God. It is something new and different but reflecting something much greater: the image of God. What does this have to do with us?

I believe that as Christians, we may be helped to regain for a moment the wonder of creation and time. Stop arguing about what cannot be known (the how) and affirm afresh the wonder of creation itself (the what) and of the Creator (the who): "I believe in God, the Creator of the Universe and of all things visible and invisible . . ." Western societies readily accept the concept of time and hope of a better future. Can we also see in a James Dennis, or in the 1910 Edinburgh Conference, the long influence of time, of hope of a creation absolutely dependent on God the Creator? And yet we also see in the first Students Lectures on Mission misplaced hope. But I believe there is more.

What does this view of time and creation have to do with mission? Everything. We have already seen how the teaching of creation was seen as foundational for teaching about redemption. The message that the church bears to the world is a message of hope, and this hope begins with the knowledge that God, the Creator of all, has entered into God's creation to restore the image, redeem God's people, and bring forth a new creation. The gospel message is a message of hope that is being fulfilled in linear time. Time began, and time will end. And the end of time means judgment, promise, and glory. We have a sure hope that there will be a time when nations will no longer make or teach war, when God will cover his own with his tent, when his glory will be revealed to the nations, when they will thirst no more, and when God will wipe away every tear from their eyes (Rev 7). Creation, time, redemption, and glory are of a fabric, and they are the fabric that has become our mission, the mission of God. It is important to remember God's work in the past and to fully enter—to participate in Christ—in God's future, leading to a sure hope.

Before concluding, we must be honest and note that *time* and *hope* can be misused. Thus, it is important for us to be clear about Christianity and time

---

[22]Ibid., 77-78.

as we look at disparate movements that claim the title *Christian*. There is a view of time that believes that the future hope can be realized in our very missionary work today. This is the voice of James Dennis and many of our church leaders in the progressive era. There are others who see the future hope of the gospel, but they do so without embracing its humility and patience. During the period of sixteenth-century reforms, they were known as revolutionary radicals. In China in the nineteenth century, they were known as the Heavenly Kingdom of Great Peace, or the Taiping (1850–1864). The Taiping was a separatist kingdom that tried take over Qing China, but ended up in a long-fought civil war. The Taiping Rebellion (as it is called) was a revolt against the oppressive rule of the Qing, and it was inspired by the apocalyptic Christian-influenced teachings of Hong Xiuquan (1814–1864). As with most religious renewals, there was a concern for justice. However, this "renewal" movement can and must be judged for its misunderstanding of the message, the Messiah, and meaning of hope.

Hong was a Hakka Chinese ("guest people") from near Canton who read Chinese-produced materials about Jesus Christ: *Good Word for Exhorting the Age*, written by London Missionary Society missionary William Milne's assistant translator and convert, Liang Afa.[23] Hong was influenced by these writings, by visions, his readings of Confucian texts, selective reading of the recently translated Bible, and of course the social oppression and poverty of late Qing China. Hong's Heavenly Kingdom of Great Peace became a unique Chinese religion based on a realized eschatology: the kingdom of heaven was here, and Hong, who was elevated to the place of Heavenly King (*Tian Wang*), was the younger brother of Jesus. The Heavenly Kingdom developed a massive army of soldiers who memorized the Ten Commandments and who were copying Bibles by the thousands. The Kingdom was first centered in a strong Hakka region (Guangxi province, where Karl Gützlaff's Chinese missionaries had made many converts in the early part of the nineteenth century), but then they captured Nanjing with over 750,000 soldiers. For a decade the Kingdom attempted to conquer all of China from this base: the southern Chinese capital. The movement was strongly biblicist—opposed to idolatry, foot binding, and corruption—and very communal (sharing

---

[23]See Samuel A. Moffett's *A History of Christianity in Asia*, vol. 2 (San Francisco: HarperSanFrancisco, 1995) for a full discussion of the historic context of this movement.

goods). The Kingdom collapsed as much by internal disorder and murder as by Qing government pressure. It is estimated that between 20 and 30 million people died in this massive civil war, making it one of the most destructive wars in history. It was clear that many of the elements of Christianity found a home in the Chinese heart, but at the core of this movement was the hope that both Qing and warlord corruption and violence could be ended and a Kingdom of Heavenly Peace could become a reality.

Nearly thirty million deaths. The United States Civil War, which occurred at about the same time, resulted in about two-thirds of one million dead. Unless we have clarity about Christian history, we will have a hard time giving a clear critique of Hong's Heavenly Kingdom or Dennis's earthly kingdom. We can describe these events, but future generations need for us to give moral and ethical guidance. What went wrong? On what basis can I judge his zeal for righteousness and justice? These are the questions that the historian must answer, but the answers must be guided by a clear understanding of Christianity's core identity, an identity rooted in time, the central historic event of the cross, and the hope of future glory.

8

World Christianity

Transforming Church History and Theology

World Christianity—its recent surprising developments and global connections—has transformed the study of church history. No one predicted it, and most historians have yet to embrace the new reality. For centuries it has been common to see church history as the history of the Western church (mostly Roman Catholic and Protestant) with some discussion of Orthodoxy and missionary work to the non-Western world. However, when Christianity outside the West is discussed, the assumption is that eventually Western forms and ideas will develop in every village and among every language. Church unity has been understood as all churches, in each context, becoming Western and thinking Western, theologically speaking. Most people would not express it this way today, but old habits die hard, and the habit of rooting normative Christianity in Western theological statements, Western liturgies, and Western creeds still dominates the church ecumenical.

The Christianity of today, as Dale Irvin explains in the first chapter of *World Christianity: Perspectives and Insights*, is not what we thought it was.[1] What we are talking about is not just the writing of church history, but the very understanding of Christianity. The great theological debates and ecumenical traditions of most of the twentieth century had no language or concepts for what world Christianity was becoming in Africa, China, or Brazil. The basic debates regarding Christology, the Eucharist, church unity, ethics, and ecclesiology were all using the discourse and assumptions of the

---

[1] Jonathan Y. Tan and Anh Q. Tran, SJ, eds., *World Christianity: Perspectives and Insights* (Maryknoll, NY: Orbis Books, 2016).

Western church. The framework of these discussions assumed the history of the Western church as normative. But the big surprise is that Christianity could develop, almost bubble up or emerge, from non-Western cultures, with no Western initiative. Many of these indigenous expressions have come to challenge our basic assumptions of what Christianity really is. Christian life in community is not as rational or scholastic as we thought.

My argument in the following pages is twofold. First, I would like to argue that the newer writing of church history as world Christianity is foundational for the task of doing theology today. Thus, we must understand the history of Christianity in Ethiopia and China on their own terms if we are going to be involved in honest ecumenical or ethical discussions. The nature and meaning of the church (ecclesiology) is not just a Western discourse, but it requires some knowledge of the understanding of the church traditionally held by Coptic and Persian as well as French and Caribbean Christians. All of these discussions must be historically grounded in a more globally inclusive, less Western-dominated, Christian story. Even our reading and study of the Bible requires a more inclusive historical awareness of the history of interpretation. History is important.

My second argument relates to diversity and unity. I posit that the newer study of church history as world Christianity requires newer questions to be asked (mostly related to local cultures), yet this preoccupation with diversity does not mitigate the early church assumption that Christianity is one ("one, holy, catholic, and apostolic"). Let me explain.

It is common today to emphasize that the great diversity of Christian expressions in the twenty-first century—a diversity that we are far more aware of than ever before—points to essential differences. To express it with a biological analogy, it is like these different Christianities have different DNA strands and are therefore genetically or essentially different. I think it is more accurate to describe the great diversity (as with plants) as an expression of the same genotype but expressed in a variety of phenotypes. In other words, we are talking about the same plant, but the different expressions of that plant (here, the diversity of Christianity) are determined also by environmental and epigenetic factors. Plants with the exact same genetic structure may look and behave differently depending on the environment and which genetic codes are turned on or off (epigenetic factors). So Christianity, as it may be expressed in different contexts with a variety of languages and cultures, is still Christianity. This argument does not take away from the obvious truth that there are expressions of the Christian tradition that are not truly Christian, but that debate and the various ways we identify what is Christian do not take away from the fact that we can study Christianity as *a particular belief-life system*. Still, we know that biologists often have to retract decisions about plant families and species; historians are no different.

Church History as the Study of World Christianity Will Transform Theological Disciplines

When teaching pastors and missionaries from ten countries who were working in seven different countries in Southeast Asia, I was amazed to discover the variety of ways these men and women were involved in outreach and ministry. One of the pastors, who was also a professor, told me he was working on a book on systematic theology from the Thai perspective. This would be one of the first theology books written in Thai. Still thinking about our discussions in class, I asked, "How are you going to handle ancestors and spirits? Do you have a separate chapter on spirits?" His response showed me how much the dominant Western story (history) has shaped local theologies. "I haven't thought about the spirits. But I guess you are right, I need to talk about a theology of 'spirits' since that is so much a part of Thai culture."

What good is a systematic theology if it does not answer questions presented by a local culture, and how could a Thai Christian think of writing a theology that does not mention what every Thai sees every day: spirit houses? The answer is both simple and troubling. Most theology that has been written, even by Asians, assumes a Western historical tradition and thus deals with themes related to Greek philosophy and the Western church tradition. I have found that when Asian Christians study church history as a worldwide Christian movement, they are more able to engage their local culture in thinking about the nature of the church, liturgy, and biblical interpretations. Church history as the history of the world Christian movement enables theological studies for each context.

What follows are themes in the newer study of church history and a brief presentation of how these themes will redirect the theological enterprise. My point is that each of these important themes of world Christianity must now guide historical Christian studies. The inclusion of these themes will change the way we do theological studies.

End of Christendom. Christianity flourished in the West in the context of governments and empires that worked with or in some way supported Christian teachings and practices. Much has been written on the mixed history of Christendom, but more important than studying this mixed history is recognizing what it means that Christendom is now gone. For the first time since the fourth century, Christianity is now flourishing in places where governments and local authorities only tolerate, restrict, or persecute the church. In Africa and Asia, where Christianity seems most vital (numerical growth, new institutions, etc.), Christians live under rulers and constitutions that at best tolerate and at worst persecute Christians. In most places there are restrictions on Christian life and practices. Western Christians are just beginning to experience what has been the normal Christian life in Asia as Western governments drop Christian identity from their historic memories.[2] Historians were lulled into the assumption that Christianity works toward Christendom with all of its shared power and shared ideals. We had forgotten that from the beginning Christianity grew and flourished under great opposition, as a minority faith resisting majority narratives of life.

This new understanding will determine how we teach ethics. Under Christendom, the church saw it as the responsibility of Christians to speak prophetic words to power, to participate in the marketplace of ideas in bringing about more just societies. The approach of previous generations, such as the invitation for theologians to speak on important public and political issues, will no longer be possible. I first learned the difference between Christendom and what we see now in the marginalization of Christianity in non-Christian societies while living in the Republic of Singapore. Issues of justice came before me when I heard about the treatment of foreign workers, especially of female *amahs* from the Philippines. Roman Catholic priests spoke up about this and provided free legal counsel for foreign workers who had been mistreated. These priests were exiled from the country. Soon the Protestant ecumenical body, the Christian Conference of Asia (CCA), was also sent out of

---

[2]See Michael O'Neill, *The Struggle for the European Constitution: A Past and Future History* (New York: Routledge, 2009), 244-46.

the country on twenty-four hours' notice. Is it not possible to engage in public debate and service, I thought?

Christian ethics in a Buddhist or Muslim country will look very different from ethics in a Christendom context. Teaching and writing about ethical concerns will be more of an interreligious task as well as a missional task. The contexts will determine the issues and the expression. Christians in Kenya, both Kikuyu as well as missionaries, have had to deal with the issue of female circumcision, a cultural trait of the Kikuyu. Contexts shape theological and ethical discourse.[3] Writing about ethics and the Christian life in northern Nigeria, where children are kidnapped and churches burned, will be very different. But it will not only be very different for those living in Nigeria, but it should be different for all Christian communities. The global context should inform parochial parish thought and life, and these local discussions should in turn reshape global theological awareness.

Culture and theology. The writing of Christian history must now pay more attention to the cultural contexts of Christian life. This has always been true, but only now do we see how important this is to explain the diverse expressions of Christianity. What this means is that when writing about the early church we must continue to pay attention to Roman values, deities, and philosophies, but we also need to pay attention to astrology and Zoroastrian dualism of the Persian Empire, and Buddhism, Taoism, and Confucianism in the Chinese realm. In the past it was the more exotic regions that drew the attention of mission historians (ancestor worship and foot binding in China or Indian practices of settee and child brides in India). But it is more than the exotic that requires our attention. We must understand basic myths, cultural values, and cultural histories in which Christianity develops.

Following the indigenizing or incarnational principle described by Andrew Walls, historians must make sense of local incarnations of Christianity by giving greater attention to indigenous customs, beliefs, and practices. In writing about Christianity in West Africa, the Christian historian must first explain basic beliefs that are held in common from various ethnic groups. There are some common beliefs regarding a Creator God, ancestors, the spirit

---

[3]Kevin Ward, "African Identities in the Historic 'Mainline Churches': A Case Study of the Negotiation of Local and Global Within African Anglicanism," in *African Identities and World Christianity in the Twentieth Century*, ed. Klaus Koschorke (Wiesbaden: Harrassowitz Verlag, 2005), 54-55.

realm, and the use of charms or fetishes. All of these local customs and beliefs are part of the context that will help to explain the growth and conflicts that occur in Christian development. Language and translation is one of the most important cultural issues. Christianity in East Asia develops very differently than in West Africa because of the deeply ingrained Confucian values of most East Asian people. Christianity in India develops differently than in Indonesia because of local *adat* or customs, as well as the dominant overlay of Islamic culture in Indonesia. Thus, theological development, interpretation of Scriptures, and ethical concerns will all be shaped by local cultural contexts. Both macro cultural themes (such as views of ancestors, or Islamic heritage) and micro (local) cultural themes are important in explaining historical developments and practices.

The local contexts of Christian development include social and political realities as well. Church histories of the past were generally alert to social and political movements, but today the movements are not just local rulers and governments; global movements also shape the church. Christian history writing must be alert to issues of international trade, human trafficking, and migration, all which connect church developments in distant regions. The growing economy of China, which is related to trade sanctions and permissions, has created a whole class of global Chinese. Many of these Chinese are Christian, or they become Christian when they are involved in education or trade in the West or in Africa or South Asia. African and Asian migration to the United States today is related to the 1965 Immigration and Nationality Act, which removed the preference for European immigrants and opened the door to Asians and Africans for the first time since 1921. As a result, Christianity has become more global in the United States than ever before. Globalization is a dimension of cultural awareness that is required in church history writing today.

Indigenous movements. Another major theme of world Christianity and therefore of historical writing is the remarkable number of indigenous movements that were nurtured under colonialism and its aftermath. Most of the earliest movements were in Africa, beginning in the late nineteenth century. By the early twentieth century, the new phenomenon was occurring throughout Africa, Asia, and in some regions of Latin America. Some of these movements were closely related to the rise of Pentecostalism, but most were catalyzed as a resistance to colonialism. In China indigenous movements such as the Jesus Family, Jesus Church, or Christian Tabernacle were started by Chinese leaders who were often overlooked or undervalued by missionaries and their missions. Indigenous leadership began to bubble up apart from the Western-dominated mission structures. In Korea the rapid indigenization was related to Japanese imperialism, and in Africa it was related to British, French, and Belgic imperialism. Prophets such as William Wade Harris proclaimed a Christian faith that resisted American domination of Liberia, and Simon Kimbangu, son of a traditional healer, proclaimed a faith of conversion and healing that resisted the Catholic Church and the Belgic authorities. The Kimbanguist Church was seen as a nationalist movement. Many indigenous movements of recent history are closely related to independence movements: independence from missionary control and independence from colonial powers.

Other indigenous movements have challenged Western and traditional understandings of the church (ecclesiology). China has witnessed a movement of "culture Christians": believers who meet in homes for Bible study, fellowship, and prayer, but who do not share in the sacraments and do not "join" a church. Political and social considerations are reshaping Christian identity. In India there are movements of "unbaptized believers": believers who follow Jesus and read the Bible, but do not get baptized because of the social or religious stigma in a conservative Hindu or Muslim community.

Indigenous movements in Islamic contexts are more complex. Only in the past four decades have we now seen movements of people who follow Jesus, but who do not drop the name *Muslim* from their identity. These movements of Muslim followers of Jesus have been a challenge for Western theologians as they try to make sense of a church where members attend the mosque rather than church and do not get baptized (or only do so secretly at night). Some of these Muslim believers' groups eventually become a church, but others never will. They are emerging as embedded followers of Jesus in Muslim villages and neighborhoods.

The variety of indigenous movements that have sprung up in the past century is not like anything witnessed before. In the past millennium, indigenous movements have come from Christians who sensed that they were to reform the church. Lutheran and Reformed movements were "indigenous" and often nationalistic, but they were not like the indigenous movements of today that spring up out of non-Christian cultures. Recent indigenous movements have come about within other religions (or ideologies, as in China) or as resistance to the Western church. It will be necessary to include these movements, describing both what they oppose and how they express themselves as Christian. Again, this will have a great impact on theological study today since it comes as new evidence regarding ecclesiology, missiology, and pneumatology.

Can historians and theologians be friends? This means that the teaching and writing of theology, ethics, ecumenics, and other theological disciplines is going to have to change. We are not talking about replacing systematic theology with contextual theology. All theology must be more explicit in its cultural engagement and still be systematic in its presentation. The change is much more profound and simple. Theological discourse built around the Western frameworks of the past, answering questions of the past, will not do for the future. Theological discourse must ask the questions and describe the situation of all of Christian history, but particularly the recent history. Again, what happened in the twentieth century was never predicted because our theological language and our theological frameworks were inadequate. Historians must help theologians write with this newer understanding or mindset, and theologians must remind historians that ideas about God need to develop in ways that are still fully trinitarian and connected with the Great Tradition. We cannot afford to jettison the tradition that we are part of, but we must see it as a developing (not static) tradition involving the worldwide church.

One simple example may help: pneumatology. How do we write about the Holy Spirit in writing Christian history, and how do we write about the Holy Spirit when writing theology? Earliest Christian histories were quick to see God at work through the Holy Spirit in every miraculous or seemingly miraculous event. It is a little uncomfortable for us today when we see some of these histories and how they give credit to God's Holy Spirit for battles won and natural disasters coming on God's enemies. After the Enlightenment, historical writing was much more scientific, and mention of the Holy Spirit for most historians today (Christian or not) has been eschewed. We ignore the Holy Spirit except when describing how a church or leaders explain what has happened in history. We do not claim that the Holy Spirit did anything specific but merely report what people say when they make spiritual claims.

Theologians, until very recently, spoke little about the Holy Spirit. The Spirit was the small, shy person in the Trinity. This is changing today as Spiritual forms of Christianity grow and develop throughout the world. Amos Yong[4] and Veli-Matti Kärkkäinen[5] are two Pentecostal theologians who are developing theologies that are centered on the Holy Spirit (Yong) or are infused with the Holy Spirit and global concerns (Kärkkäinen). These and, I would argue, all theology today must take into account indigenous movements that have no other explanation for their genesis and continued existence except for a dream or series of dreams. Some indigenous movements are rooted in a vision, a voice, or a dream that points to Jesus and the concern for a more rigorous and dedicated life in a particular context. Can such visions and words that have changed whole communities become the "stuff" of theological reflection—the "facts" that will begin to reshape our Reformed and Anabaptist and Thomist theologies? I hope so. If our systems do not explain such Christian existence, they are too small.

CHRISTIANITY AS ONE: CHRISTIANITY AS DIVERSE

As a reminder, my second thesis relates to the unity and diversity of Christianity: I posit that the newer study of church history as world Christianity requires newer questions to be asked (mostly related to local cultures), yet this preoccupation with diversity does not mitigate the early church assumption that Christianity is one ("one, holy, catholic, and apostolic"). We are concerned with the greater diversity that comes about when we look at all the new questions and all the areas of the world, but looking for what holds it together: unity and diversity.

History reveals that Christians have a hard time staying united. It is easier to call our neighbor a heretic (or so it seems) than to try to understand differences and learn to love. Religious wars in the Christian past are not all that different from religious wars of the Muslim present. We can learn from

---

[4] Among the many books and articles Yong has written regarding a systematic theology centered on the Holy Spirit are the following: *The Spirit Poured Out upon All Flesh: Pentecostalism and the Possibility of Global Theology* (Grand Rapids: Baker Academic, 2005) and *The Spirit of Creation: Modern Science and Divine Action in the Pentecostal-Charismatic Imagination* (Grand Rapids: Eerdmans, 2011).

[5] Kärkkäinen's works include *Pneumatology: The Holy Spirit in Ecumenical, International and Contextual Perspective* (Grand Rapids: Baker Academic, 2002) and, edited with Jürgen Moltmann, *The Spirit in the World: Emerging Pentecostal Theologies in Global Context* (Grand Rapids: Eerdmans, 2009).

both about how to write history. Often these wars are about power, control, and ethnic identity, all masked as religious conflict. Still, differences persist within Christianity, and these differences, whether they create conflict or not, are of many origins. Some differences express the rich variety of languages and cultures. Other differences reflect a decentering of Christian teaching and practice by secular rulers or even by Christian leaders. In this section I would like to suggest how we can understand Christian unity and diversity through the newer study of church history. Our overriding concern is to tell a more accurate and complete Christian story, a story that includes what is necessary and releases what is extraneous. This has always been the challenge of historical writing, but the process has changed. That is what the section seeks to explain.

Writing history is a matter of what to throw out. In our work on writing *History of the World Christian Movement*,[6] we had to decide what to include as "Christian" and therefore what to "throw out." This becomes more of a problem when we are trying to write a thicker description of history than when a more exclusively Western history is written. Do we include movements that claim to be Christian and yet are not included in any Christian list of major churches? Is it enough to say you are Christian to actually be a Christian? Of course the dominant American splinter groups come up in all of these discussions: Jehovah's Witnesses, Mormons, various Adventist groups, and Christian Science. But what about other African Initiated religions, and what about the apocalyptic "Christian" movements such as the Taiping Heavenly Kingdom in nineteenth-century China? Christians may not want to claim all of these splinter groups (and many others that are considered more orthodox), but on what basis can (or should) we include or not include? Everyone is not in the same story, even though our stories are not absolutely exclusive.

I believe there are two ways we have sorted this out in the past. One way is to establish our own orthodox filter that filters out all groups that do not fit our standard of what it means to be Christian. Groups that have done this in the past have ended up with a very small fellowship of other Christians. This tendency we might call the *minimalist* approach. Lutherans,

---

[6]Dale T. Irvin and Scott W. Sunquist, *History of the World Christian Movement*, 3 vols. (Maryknoll, NY: Orbis Books, 2001–).

Reformed theologians, Brethren, Catholics, Methodists—we have all been guilty of a minimalist approach to Christian unity, and all of these approaches are based on an inadequate history that is dishonest with the facts. One of the most helpful pieces of advice I received in how to study church history was given to me by Richard Lovelace in the first church history class I took. I must admit my Reformed heritage was severely bruised by this reminder: "One of the most difficult lessons we will learn in the study of church history is that God often blesses the people who have bad theology." What he meant here is that the minimalist approach to church history, built around our particular theology, is inadequate to explain the facts. What Lovelace calls bad theology is often the theology that we and our tradition have resisted or have rejected. Catholics find that Lutherans and their missionary work are often blessed (or so it seems). Reformed Christians find that Arminians and Catholics are blessed. If we have a minimalist approach to what must be included in the Christian story we end up with a small church and a small God.

The second tendency is the *uncritical* approach to historical Christian studies. This approach uncritically wants to include all who claim to be Christian. However, we find that even though this sounds reasonable, inclusive, and open, it is in fact an impossible position to hold. The Taiping Rebellion (causing over 20 million deaths) and the Unification Church have a different center and a different goal (eschatology) from most Christian traditions and yet have claimed to be part of the larger Christian story. Although greatly influenced by Christian teaching and even the reading of the Bible,[7] groups such as Jim Jones's People's Temple were centered on something very different and had a very different understanding of purpose and "end." We know this intuitively, but how can we write about it historically?

It is neither accurate nor possible to include every group that has been influenced by Christian teaching. On the other hand, it is both helpful and necessary to be honest about our study and writing of Christian history in order to ask critical questions before we end up including wolves in sheep's clothing. Some religious groups have certain elements of the discourse and resources of Christians, but that does not make them a Christian group.

---

[7] See especially Jonathan Spence, *God's Chinese Son: The Taiping Heavenly Kingdom of Hong Xiuquan* (New York: W. W. Norton, 1996).

Church histories have always had to make decisions about who is in and who is out of the Christian family, and many times we have had to repent of bad decisions. The newer openness of the Vatican to the Protestant Church, beginning with Pope John Paul II on the anniversary of the birth of Martin Luther, is an indication that our judgments can change. The Roman Catholic Church declared Lutheran and the earlier Waldensian movements as heretical, outside the Christian story. In the past Protestants included Waldensians as Protestant forerunners, but until recently these same Protestants have had great difficulty including the Roman Catholic Church. But today many evangelical Protestants claim Pope Francis as their pope! Judgments change, but on what basis do we change our judgments?

Looked at from another angle, most Christians have consistently seen the Unification Church as outside the Christian family. This judgment has changed very little. In contrast, some groups start as Christian-influenced groups, outside the Christian family, but then they later recenter and become part of the Christian family.[8]

Historians can and should provide guidance for the church in these questions. Historical writing is not a neutral science. What we include, what we exclude, how we describe, and how we decry are important decisions that cannot be avoided. These decisions are part of creating the discourse for all other theological discussions. Below we will look at four major themes that help us understand the nature of Christian diversity in historical writing. This section concludes with a brief discussion of where we find the unity in Christianity as we write about it as a diverse, worldwide movement.

Migration: Forcing the issues. As a number of authors have shown us in recent years, migration is a major issue in understanding the development of Christianity.[9] Although migration has always been important in Christian history, it has taken on new meaning today with the massive numbers of people moving and the large distances they travel. We now find that in major

---

[8] I am thinking here of the Worldwide Church of God (Herbert W. Armstrong), later to become Grace Communion International. Upon the founder's death, theological statements were rewritten, and under the new theology and openness to other Christian organizations what was a marginal group has become part of the worldwide Christian story.

[9] See Jehu Hanciles, *Beyond Christendom: Globalization, African Migration and Transformation of the West* (Maryknoll, NY: Orbis Books, 2009), and Mark Gornik, *Word Made Global: Stories of African Christianity in New York City* (Grand Rapids: Eerdmans, 2011).

cities of the West it is common to find Asian, African, and Latin American churches. Cities such as New York, Toronto, London, Munich, and Los Angeles have growing West African as well as Korean and Chinese churches. These churches fit into the local Christian climate only uncomfortably. They bring with them different ways of worshiping, different questions and answers, and they often worship and teach in different languages. They quickly change their patterns as the second and third generations express different cultural forms of Christianity.

One way of looking at this is that migration brings together the ecumenical church in local proximity like never before. Rather than ecumenical discussions being held only among an elite group of Christian leaders in a special space, migration forces ecumenical discussions at a local and common practice level. We observe each other, pray together, sometimes we worship together, and this forces us to rethink commonly accepted Christian norms. We absolutely must adjust our understanding of what it means to be Christian in light of our new locally present global Christian life. One example will help us see how this will affect our understanding of what unites the Christian global community.

My wife and I attended a multicultural church in the east end of Pittsburgh for about eight years. During our time there, our church leadership was approached by Christian leaders who migrated from Francophone Africa. Their numbers were growing, and they were looking for a local church where they could meet for worship, education, and prayer. Most of these leaders were Presbyterian or at least had some type of Reformed background, so they came to our Presbyterian church. We had some wonderful meetings learning to listen to each other. They were surprised at how short our worship service was, and we were surprised about their all-night prayer meetings ("fire night"). The real conflict that we all remember was about the possibility of combining our youth fellowship groups. It seemed to be obvious that since all our children, African and African American, spoke English, they could combine forces: a wonderful place to ground our Christian unity.

However, no sooner was it suggested by our pastor that we could combine youth groups than all three African leaders said, "No. That will never work." Their point was clear. The African American youth did not want to gather only for Bible study and prayer meetings like the African youth. The cultures, values, and understanding of the Christian life were too different for them to work together. Hopefully this situation will change in a generation, but it may not. Migration brings up new themes for the church to study and new challenges and opportunities for Christian unity.

Some migrant communities are large enough that they can plant their own "Presbyterian Church of East Africa" in Philadelphia or London. Other groups worship with people of their own language, even if they have to compromise some on the worship liturgy, music, and even sacraments. I recently ran into a group of Malabar Christians from Austin, Texas, who worship together as Roman Catholics, Eastern Catholics, St. Thomas Christians, Mar Thoma, and Orthodox Syrian. They do not all worship together each week, but they come together quite often for worship and meals and celebrations, mostly for the sake of the children. Migration creates new theological issues and new issues and opportunities for church unity.[10]

Power and the poor. Most of the Christians in the world are not *for* the poor; they *are* poor. Christian growth has been greater among the outcasts and the powerless than among the powerful and influential. It has always been the case, but the past centuries of colonial and Christendom Christianity have clouded our memory. Before the middle of the twentieth century, we thought of Christians as Western people living in modern and fairly wealthy cultures. The great shock in nineteenth- and twentieth-century missions was when missionaries discovered the great poverty and disease of many tropical and subtropical peoples. Thus, missionary work during this period was framed as a theology of progress and advancement, even civilization. Becoming Christian required social progress.

The focus on the poor came from two directions: from Latin America and from Africa. In Latin America, the church leadership was very much a Christendom leadership working closely with powerful and wealthy rulers. Many of these rulers were corrupt, and many of the church leaders were complicit in their support of an unjust social and political structure. Theologies of liberation developed as expressions of the gospel with and from the poor and oppressed. A model of theological reflection also developed

---

[10]Space does not allow here for a full discussion of Korean churches and Chinese churches in the West. Issues of unity, division, different generations (first versus 1.5 and 2.0), language, and their Confucian heritage are very complex.

that required theological reflection to be rooted in identity with the poor and in praxis. Theology is not theology unless it is lived theology, and it is not lived unless it is lived with and for the poor.

In Africa, the rapid Christianization that took place in the last half of the twentieth century was not dependent on missionaries, colonial empires, or large institutions. A church developed rapidly among the poor, both through missionary churches and the newly instituted churches.[11] These churches were indebted to, but not dependent on, mission schools and mission hospitals. Many of the converts were very poor subsistence farmers whose literacy was very low. However, churches grew, and forms of Christian ritual and life began to develop through, rather than opposed to, local customs and beliefs.

The rapid growth of the church of the poor has created other challenges for Christian unity. Theologies of liberation often develop out of opposition to the traditional church. Theologies of liberation are also very costly, as they develop a discourse that exposes false beliefs and oppressive structures of a military elite. The church of the poor is the majority church. How can this church express unity both in local contexts and with the churches in the West who often represent what is resisted by the poor? Can a liberationist church from Latin America be in fellowship with a church rooted in Western capitalism in the West?

Spiritual Christianity. Not even recognized or known in 1900, barely recognized by historians in mid-century, the Spiritual family of Christians is now a dominant form of worldwide Christianity.[12] At this time we do not need to go over the statistics or the many streams of Spiritual Christianity that have developed in the past century.[13] Suffice it to say that this is one of

---

[11] There is much writing on the various movements of spiritual renewal, Ethiopianism, and independency in Africa. One of the more insightful is Ogbu Kalu's "Ethiopianism in African Christianity: Power and Contested Identities—'Princes Shall Come Out of Egypt; Ethiopia Shall Soon Stretch Out Her Hands unto God,'" in *African Identities and World Christianity in the Twentieth Century*, ed. Klaus Koschorke (Wiesbaden: Harrassowitz Verlag, 2005), 19-48.

[12] We use the phrase "Spiritual Christianity" here, as we use it in *History of the World Christian Movement*, to mean one of the four major families of Christianity: Roman Catholic, Orthodox, Protestant, and Spiritual. We include those churches who primarily find authority and guidance in the Holy Spirit (Pentecostal, AICs, many indigenous churches in the non-Western world, as well as Charismatic churches).

[13] See Sunquist, *The Unexpected Christian Century: The Reversal and Transformation of Global Christianity, 1900-2000* (Grand Rapids: Baker Academic, 2015), 124-33.

the three most important transformations of Christianity that took place in the twentieth century.[14] Spiritual Christianity has a power and influence that has brought about changes in individuals and societies. Some of this power, however, brings about divisions, as many loyal Pentecostals or Charismatics have left their traditional churches. For example, many of the Spiritual Christians in the West were raised Anglicans, Presbyterians, or Lutherans. Many from the Church of South India have become Pentecostal, and we could go on and on.

There are at present a variety of approaches to writing about the Spiritual family of Christians, but there is no one agreed method or style. In some ways it was easier when we had a limited number of mainline and traditional churches with only a few "splinter groups." The fragmentation that has occurred in institutional Christianity makes it difficult to tell about Christian history as a story. We can no longer tell the story of the newer Spiritual family as a side story, or as an annex of the church universal, for in many regions these churches and movements are now the main story of Christianity. Some of these churches start out as Christian movements, but then they move away from the main story—they focus on themes or practices that oppose commonly accepted Christian teaching. How do we talk about these movements when they move away from continuity with the Christian story?

Women. A final important theme that must be explicitly included, but that seems to invite further division, is the role and place of women in the church. Three major historical themes have made the place of women central to our history today. First was the modern missionary movement, which was often (after the middle of the nineteenth century) dominated by women. In unprecedented numbers women, many very well educated, were sent out by mission societies to work with their husbands as equal partners planting churches or running schools. Later, single women were sent out to work with women who could not be reached through traditional methods. Often called *zenana* missions, they were devoted to reaching Hindu and Muslim women who were isolated to the *zenana* region of the house.[15] Thus, the overwhelming majority of Protestant missionaries sent out before World War II were women, maybe as many as two-thirds.

---

[14]The rise of non-Western Christianity and the ecumenical movement would be the two others.
[15]The region of the house reserved for women only.

Second, as the concern for reaching women increased, a whole movement of women's mission ("women's work for women") developed, and these new institutions were led mostly by women. Thus, women were running missionary institutions and establishing schools, hospitals, and churches. Missionary gatherings included women leaders who often spoke on an equal level with the male missionary leaders.

Third, the recent growth of Christianity in the non-Western world is at the heart a women's movement, according to Dana Robert.[16] Many Christians in Africa or Asia know this through their daily experience. The Chinese church, the fastest-growing church in the world for decades, is dominated by women in leadership. Even with the resistance of women in leadership that is often part of Confucian societies, women are leaders in large numbers of churches throughout East Asia. In Africa, many of the African Initiated Churches have been started by women who had dreams or visions that they identify as their call to evangelism or to lead churches.

Of course, such a strong movement of women in church leadership puts pressure on churches that have traditionally not supported women in the highest levels of leadership (not only Roman Catholic and Orthodox). What does church unity mean when women are leading church movements in some cultures and countries, but in other church traditions women are not to teach, pastor, or lead men in any area of the church? Again, where do we find unity, and how do we write about such movement in our newer historiography?

Unity: What holds Christianity together? What the above discussion should make clear is that as these newer issues in the worldwide Christian movement become larger in our Christian discourse, we will be forced again and again to ask, "Where is our unity?" Can we write about "Christianity" as a story? The answers of the twentieth-century ecumenical movement, of the nineteenth-century Roman Curia, or of the Orthodox Church are not sufficient. These issues today, studied through our newer historical awareness, force the church to find unity in ideas, practices, and traditions that empower the Jesus story to continue to make its historical impact in a unified witness (Jn 17).

Many approaches to church unity have filled library shelves in the past century or so. Ecumenical discussions (the reversal of the Reformation)

---

[16]Dana L. Robert, "World Christianity as a Women's Movement," *International Bulletin of Missionary Research* 30, no. 4 (2006): 180-88.

have been a major theme of twentieth-century Christianity. Unity has been sought after in missionary work (the foundation of modern ecumenism[17]), in common witness and service in society, in common confession, and in shared liturgy and sacraments. All of these are difficult and have particular histories of successes and failures. Our approach here is not to bring about some type of corporate unity, either theoretical or organic. Instead I would like to offer a simple explanation for what holds Christianity together. For even if we talk about "Christianities," we can and must still talk about Christianity.

Another way of framing our concern here is to answer the questions, "What is the absolute core of Christianity without which we would not have Christianity? What is essential in the Christian faith and tradition?" These questions have been answered by using confessions, but all confessions are ad hoc, written to and in a particular context. Other answers have started with particular doctrines that have come out of particular cultural contexts: belief in God as triune, or Jesus as fully human and fully divine, or belief in the inerrancy or infallibility of the Bible (or of the pope!). We may believe one or most of these, but this does not answer our question. Our question must be asked of the whole church, this church that we see now is both incarnational and pilgrim.[18] What is it that holds together Christianity in all of its diverse expressions throughout time and throughout the world? Looked at from another angle, we might ask, "What is it that is only true of Christianity, but not of other beliefs or other communities?"

The World Council of Churches has an answer to this, as do most church traditions.[19] What is helpful about the WCC "basis" is that it is not limited to beliefs (a weakness of most of the Western Christian tradition), but it points toward participation or embodiment of those beliefs. Andrew Walls gives a suggestive description of what gives coherence, connection, or continuity to Christianity. In an oft-quoted paragraph, he says,

---

[17] Willem A. Saayman, *Unity and Mission* (Pretoria: University of South Africa, 1984).

[18] It is really not possible to discuss this issue without reference to Walls's famous essay, "The Gospel as Prisoner and Liberator of Culture," in his *The Missionary Movement in Christian History: Studies in the Transmission of Faith* (Maryknoll, NY: Orbis Books 1996), 3-15.

[19] The Basis of the World Council of Churches is expressed in the following manner: "The World Council of Churches a fellowship of churches which confess the Lord Jesus Christ as God and Saviour according to the scriptures, and therefore seek to fulfill together their common calling to the glory of the one God, Father, Son and Holy Spirit."

> Our observer is therefore led to recognize an essential continuity in Christianity: continuity of thought about the *final significance of Jesus,* continuity of a certain *consciousness about history,* continuity in *the use of the Scriptures,* of *bread and wine,* of *water.* But he recognizes that these continuities are cloaked with such heavy veils belonging to their environment that Christians of different times and places must often be unrecognizable to others, or indeed even to themselves, as manifestations of a single phenomenon.[20]

We might summarize this as man, story, book, bread, and water. Again, this is very suggestive and minimalist, but it comes from a historian who has held together the church, in all of its diversity, in his historical writing over the past four decades. We should take this very seriously, knowing that each of these words requires expansion. Walls has done us a great service in opening up an awareness of Christian coherence that is not found in Western theology or Western Christian practices.

After working for the past decades on writing Asian Christian history and the history of the worldwide Christian movement, I would like to suggest a framework for understanding the essential elements of Christian continuity. There are elements in Walls's "essential continuity" that I believe are missing. Two of the most important that I believe give clearer coherence are the *Holy Spirit* and the *mission of God.* Throughout history, as Christian presence develops in each place and language and culture, the missionary nature of the story and awareness of God's active presence through the Holy Spirit provide coherence and continuity. Therefore I would like to suggest the following five elements as giving the church in each context a common story and a common family identity.

> Christian coherence is found in that Christians, in all their diverse beliefs and practices, find *their identity in Jesus Christ, they look to the Scriptures* to explain who he is and who they are to be, as *they gather to remember, honor, and spread the teachings and practices* that Jesus commends, and they are aware that *God is somehow active through his Spirit* in what they do and say.

To expand this a little, continuity according to this coherence model would mean that the local Christian community would see itself as part of the tradition that points back to the life of Jesus of Nazareth. It would not see itself

---

[20]Walls, "Gospel as Prisoner," 7. The italics are mine.

as absolutely unique, but as part of a larger story. It is hard to find a community in the history of Christianity that does not find its primary identity in and through Jesus Christ, or that does not see that in light of Jesus' life: it as a local community is part of the continuing life of Jesus in its context. Mission, social witness, evangelism, and public theology are all indications of this life in Jesus. Any of these tones may become weak and hardly audible, but they are still present if a community is a Christian community.

In addition, the phrase "remember, honor, and spread" expresses the integral relationship of worship (remember and honor) and mission (spread). Christians gather to do both, and we see it throughout history and throughout the world. Historical Christian writing, I believe, recognizes the great diversities of Christianities, but at the same time remembers the coherence that holds them together.

Finally, I believe Christians in all places and time recognize the ongoing work of God through his Holy Spirit. This is a major theme in Orthodox liturgy, and indigenous churches in Africa, Asia, and Latin America, and it is inescapable in Roman Catholic and Protestant teachings and practices. Can we really call a community "Christian" if the community sees that all that it does and says is purely this-worldly, "secular"? Certainly the emergence of the Holy Spirit in the twentieth and twenty-first centuries should remind us that Christian coherence is in some way or in some dimension a Spirit and spiritual matter.

Reconception, re-vision, and retradition.[21] What was beginning to be recognized by Henry P. Van Dusen[22] in 1945 and by Walbert Bühlmann[23] in

---

[21]These three concepts come from Andrew Walls's essay "Eusebius Tries Again: The Task of Reconceiving and Re-visioning the Study of Christian History," found in *Enlarging the Story: Perspectives on Writing World Christian History*, ed. Wilbert Shenk (Maryknoll, NY: Orbis Books, 2002), 1-21, and Dale T. Irvin, *Christian Histories, Christian Traditioning: Rendering Accounts* (Maryknoll, NY: Orbis Books, 1998).

[22]Van Dusen wrote about world Christianity and endowed two chairs at Union Theological Seminary in the areas of ecumenics and world Christianity. But his understanding of what was happening was very limited. Van Dusen still saw this "world Christianity" as somehow Western Christianity now finding greater unity as led by the West. Thus, most of his volume *World Christianity: Yesterday, Today, Tomorrow* (New York: Abingdon-Cokesbury, 1947) focuses on the (now waning) ecumenical movement. His vision of world Christianity was a Western vision empowered by Western institutions and thinking. He could never have guessed, writing during World War II, what would happen in the shadow of global imperialisms. The above book was first delivered as lectures in 1945 at Emory University.

[23]Walbert Bühlmann, *Es Kommt die dritte Kirche: Eine Analyse der kirchlichen Gegenwart und Zukunft*, original German edition of 1974, published in English as *The Coming of the Third Church* (Maryknoll, NY: Orbis Books, 1976).

1974 has become much clearer with the reflections of writers such as Andrew Walls, Dale Irvin, and Peter Phan.[24] What they call for, and what historians are now engaged in, is reconceiving, re-visioning, and retraditioninig the past with an understanding that the Western Christian tradition is not the only norm. The challenge is to embrace the full diversity of Christian life and belief, the many cultural expressions of followers of Jesus, and to tell a story that is still a single story. Like the migrant family from Ireland who, a few generations after migrating to North America, finds that it has Italian, Swedish, Hispanic, and Afro-Caribbean relatives, Christianity is no longer Western. Actually it never was.

The retraditioning that is needed involves recovering the many lost themes mentioned above, but it also involves recovering the topographic diversity that has been part of the original DNA of the followers of Jesus. Christianity was born at the intersection of three continents and on the border of two empires.[25] From the beginning, followers of Jesus spoke different languages (see Acts 2), ate different foods, and lived under different rulers and governments. Theology developed as it always does, answering questions posed by local cultures, in and through a community seeking to be faithful to Jesus and all his teachings. Worship patterns and patterns of living also were Christian responses to local cultural customs and assumptions. In the Greek-speaking world of the eastern Mediterranean, it was important to make sense of creation and the cosmos in light of Christian teaching. Thus, statements like the Nicene Creed and theologies like those of the Cappadocians made perfect sense. However, these were not the questions or concerns of Persian Christians, nor of Ethiopians, nor even of Latin-speaking Christians of Italy or England. Earliest Chinese theological developments, dating back to the seventh century, were responding to another set of issues. They did not develop a "Nicene Creed," but they responded to Buddhism and Daoism in their earliest writings.

Writing Christian history today involves "norming" the story as a global story, both recovering the variety of traditions of the distant past and reciting

---

[24] Among others, Peter C. Phan, *Vietnamese-American Catholics* (Mawhah, NJ: Paulist, 2005), and Peter C. Phan, edited with Elain Padilla, *Theology of Migration in the Abrahamic Religions* (New York: Palgrave-Macmillan, 2014).
[25] See Scott W. Sunquist, *The Unexpected Christian Century: The Reversal and Transformation of Christianity, 1900–2000* (Grand Rapids: Baker Academic, 2015), 1.

the diverse stories of the recent past. It is neither helpful nor accurate to follow the Western theological tradition alone. From the start, and throughout the narrative, Christian diversity and lines of unity must both be carefully traced by the historian. In the end we find that the fabric of the Christian church is more of a paisley or plaid than it is a solid color. Still, it is a single fabric.

PART III

Missiology

9

Underwood, Moffett, and Korean Liberation

Making Sense of Early Korean Protestantism

KOREA 1880-1900

"The 19th century was not a good one for Korea."[1] So begins Martha Huntley's *History of the Protestant Mission in Korea*. Well, yes and no to Ms. Huntley. It was a terrible century in terms of disease, famine, persecution, and foreign and domestic oppression, but it was a great century regarding Protestant Christian missions. After shutting out the world for centuries, the Hermit Kingdom finally, slowly, and begrudgingly opened itself up to modern medical practices, the development of a Korean *koine* literature, orphanage work, and education. This smaller and often mistreated younger sibling of China had been a very advanced East Asian culture. Moveable type in Korea dates back to 1232, and a Korean (Hangul) script was developed for the masses by good King Sejong (Seijong) in 1450. However, after the Japanese invasion of Korea by Hideyoshi in 1592, Korea turned inward, resisting all social intercourse, and as a result it slowly but steadily declined. Nations thrive with international relations and atrophy with isolation. During the very time that the northern Atlantic nations were reaching out in political, economic, and religious expansion, Korea was trying to limit Chinese influence, discourage Buddhist practice, and once again fend off Japanese penetration. In the midst of these protectionist battles, the royal family and provincial rulers oppressed the peasants as much as human endurance

---

[1] Martha Huntley, *Caring, Growing, Changing: A History of the Protestant Mission in Korea* (New York: Friendship, 1984), 1.

would allow. No, all things considered the nineteenth century was not really a good century for Koreans.

And yet, there were intellectual and social movements that were active below the normal historical radar for centuries before the first Protestants ever arrived. Although most contact with the outside world was discouraged, Confucianism, especially a very conservative Neo-Confucianist school from China, was encouraged. Many Confucian priests made pilgrimages to China, even to the capital in Peking, to bring back manuscripts and new ideas. Some of these new ideas were not from the Neo-Confucianist tradition, but from the *Sohak* or Western Learning tradition. On some of those trips (beginning in 1777[2]), Korean Confucian priests, hungry for new ideas, returned with more than they sought or than they thought: among their exotic Chinese *Sohak* manuscripts were Chinese Jesuit manuscripts. These were some of the Chinese writings of Italian Jesuit Matteo Ricci (d. 1610). Copies of these strange new "Confucian" texts were made in Korea and can be found today in at Chol Du San Martyr's Shrine along the banks of the Han River. Two of Ricci's manuscripts, *The Truth About God* and *A Symposium of Ten Famous Scholars*, were widely read, translated, and distributed. Korean Confucianists almost inadvertently became Korean Catholics and spread the teachings of Jesus of Nazareth in Chinese-dominated Seoul. Thus, the first known movement of Christianity in Korea was started by Koreans bringing in the Chinese Christian writings of an Italian Jesuit Confucianst. The movement was severely persecuted for over a century, reaching a climax with the March 10, 1866, edict to kill all Christians. Within a few years an estimated ten thousand Christians were killed (mostly beheaded) both for accepting a foreign religion and for the greater crime of supporting a foreign country: France. Contemporary writers talk about the Han River turning red from the blood of the martyrs.

The French connection, which seemed to have offered the most hope for the Catholics of Korea, very quickly became the most oppressive and costly relationship. Korean Catholics, who had been introduced to Christian faith

---

[2] Actually the trips were ongoing, as Confucian ideas and texts were constantly passed between Korea and China. The Christian Neo-Confucian texts were returning with Korean priests as quickly as they were being written in Beijing. See Cornelius Osgood, *The Koreans and Their Culture* (New York: Ronald, 1951), 250.

from China, sought Catholic priests to baptize and teach the faithful. In the early Roman Catholic years, all of the help came from Chinese priests. Father James Chu of Peking came to help the Koreans in 1801, but he was quickly executed, and his arrival precipitated a massacre of about three hundred Korean Christians. Catholic Christians were persona non grata in Korea, in large part because of the antifilial piety stance of the young Christian converts. Under Clement XI, ancestral worship was banned for all Catholics. The Korean Catholics were remarkably zealous in their application of this papal proscription, burning ancestral tablets and refusing to conform to any Confucian ceremonies.[3] Thus, in the first introduction of Christianity in Korea the religion came as a new Chinese belief (as had Buddhism and Confucianism centuries earlier), but its particular breed was both anti-Korean and anti-Confucian. Chinese Roman Catholicism in Korea on one level came as a reformist, unpatriotic challenge to conservative Neo-Confucianists. The French connection made matters even worse. In December of 1835, Korean Catholics surreptitiously brought in Father Pierre Maubant to Korea across the frozen Yala River. Two other priests came within the next two years, but persecution soon followed.[4] The great affront to Korean sensibilities was the denigration of the family. Roman Catholicism was considered the religion of "No-father and No-king." Any foreign ideas that encouraged celibacy and discouraged honoring ancestors could not be tolerated in Korea. Nonetheless, French priests continued to enter Korea, often in the guise of Koreans in mourning, which in turn increased the French interest in Korea.[5] By the time of the Civil War in America, there were about 23,000 Korean Catholics served by two foreign bishops and ten priests. Foreign residence in Korea was still unlawful in the "Hermit Kingdom," but the Catholic influence on upper sections of society—both Confucian elite and the royal family—gave some protection to the priests. That protection, however, was not sufficient. In 1866 the largest massacre of Christians took place. The flames of anti-Christian

---

[3]See In Soo Kim, *Protestants and the Formation of Modern Korean Nationalism, 1885–1920* (New York: Peter Lang, 1996), 14-15; and Charles Dallet, *The History of the Catholic Church in Korea* (New Haven, CT: Human Relations Area Files, 1952), 1:3.
[4]Father Jaques Chastan (January 1836) and Bishop Laurent Marie-Joseph Imbert (January 1, 1838).
[5]To "save face" when in mourning, Koreans would often hide their faces with cloth on long bamboo sticks and refuse to talk. This was a convenient disguise for foreigners. See Huntley, *Caring, Growing, Changing*, 6.

passion were stoked by the appearance of a Russian war vessel near Wonsan harbor, followed by the United States ship *General Sherman*; both ships were seeking trade with this shy nation. The Koreans understood that these ships were proof of the Christian attempts to overthrow the government. After all, Roman Catholics were "antiking." Politics, trade, and religion all worked against the spread of the Roman Catholic faith at this time.

Tonghak Interlude

The religious and political landscape of the late nineteenth century in Korea was quite complex and unusual. Although Korea was still a Hermit Kingdom, fighting off foreign intrusions, it had also existed religiously and politically for centuries as it looked geographically: as an appendage to northeast China. Korea had followed the Chinese in their social order and education (Confucianism) and in accepting and adapting the foreign religion from the West: Buddhism.[6] And yet, Korean shamanism, the oldest and most Korean form of life, existed and permeated both the Chinese (Confucian) social order and the Indian religion (Buddhism). The Chinese never dominated Korea politically as the Japanese Empire soon would, but their cultural presence was felt by all. The main language used in both religion and politics was Chinese. This excluded the masses or *minjung* from the decisions of both religion and politics. The cultural isolation of the rulers from the masses created a strange paradox: most of the *minjung* were supportive of the royal family, but they were at odds with all of the rest of the court and the officials. The corruption of the government, with ever-increasing taxes, raised the ire of the masses. The *minjung* were reaching the limits of their toleration.

In the last decades of the nineteenth century the frustration of the people bubbled over into a revolt that, had it not been for the ever-feared foreign intervention, would have created a new antiforeign Korean government. Foreign intervention did take place (Japanese), and, ironically, this helped

---

[6]Buddhism had reached its zenith of influence in Korea during the Mongol period in China and began a long and slow decline with the advent of the Yi Dynasty in Korea (1392). Buddhist monks were turned back to the world, women were told to marry, and Buddhist prayers were removed from funerals. By the eighteenth and nineteenth centuries, Buddhists were considered a corrupting influence on society. See Osgood, *Koreans and Their Culture*, 245-51; William Ellion Griffis, *Corea: The Hermit Nation* (New York: Scribner's Sons, 1894), chapter 37, "Religion"; and Erik Zürcher, *Buddhism: Its Origin and Spread in Words, Maps and Pictures* (New York: St. Martin's, 1962), 62-64.

to facilitate the rapid Protestant Christian growth. The popular revolt was rooted in a new indigenous religion: the religion of a Korean scholar and patriot, Choe Chei Woo (Ch'oe Cheu). Choe's Tonghak (or Donghak) or Eastern Learning was a syncretistic religion that combined elements from Neo-Confucianism, Taoism, Buddhism, shamanism, and Christianity to create a uniquely Korean form of political and religious ideology.[7] This was a religion that affirmed Asian values, opposed political oppression, and accepted (or adapted) some Christian teachings as Korean. Central to his teaching as recorded in the Tonghak Bible ("The Great Canon of the East": Tong Kyong Dae Chun) is the belief that heaven and humanity are one. This is a direct affront to Chinese religiosity, where heaven is far above all earthly existence. But if heaven and humanity are one, then there is a basis for a radically democratic, even communalistic orientation to politics.[8] By 1894 the Tonghaks had developed a strong network of support throughout the country, and the revolt took hold and spread. When the revolt bore down on the capital in Seoul, King Kojong and Queen Min requested more troops from China to help defend the nation. This marked the beginning of the Sino-Japanese War. Chinese were sought to protect the corrupt Korean government, but the Japanese came in as "liberators." As fate would have it, the foreign liberators proved to be far worse oppressors than the domestic ones. Protestants, who had been at work in Korea now for ten years, were caught in the middle of the bloody conflict. Their letters reflect the terrible slaughter of the Chinese, the stench of human flesh and the spread of disease. At first there was an appreciation of the new Japanese presence, and even after the social upheavals of 1919 there still were a few missionaries who supported the constructive work of the Japanese on behalf of the Koreans. After the terribly oppressive and corrupt rule of the Chinese in Korea almost anything

---

[7] Tonghak theology borrows the following from the various religions: Confucianism, the importance of upholding the five relationships; Buddhism, the "heart cleansing" or removal of desire; Taoism, the law of cleansing the body of moral and natural filth; shamanism, the use of charms and magic to control the evil spirits; and Christianity, the belief in one God. The Tonghaks also borrowed the idea of burning candles from the Roman Catholics!

[8] Clearly, the parallels, if not direct influence, with the Taiping movement in China are self-evident. Both were radically democratic movements in the midst of government corruption and the oppression of the masses. Both also benefited from the areas of Christian teaching that value the individual over the state. In China it was the Protestant teaching from Chinese Christian tracts (Liang A-Fa), and in Korea it was from the Roman Catholic teachings that emphasized monotheism: the Lord of Heaven can be known.

new looked good. Protestants quickly learned, though, that their enemy's enemy was not necessarily their friend.[9]

UNDERWOOD, MOFFETT, AND THE PRESBYTERIANS

Enter the Protestant missionaries. Both Presbyterians and Methodists first came to live in Korea in 1884, at a very critical time in the history of the nation. These pioneers were dedicated men and women who came to learn the language and culture of Korea, and to help mostly in the areas of education, literacy, medicine, and in religious training. Inspired by the revivalism of Moody[10] and the later Student Volunteer Movement, these missionaries were conservative both religiously and socially. Their text was the Bible,[11] and their goal was to see Korea reformed through becoming a Christian nation. We should not be surprised by the language of one of the earliest missionaries, Miss Lillian Horton, who was the first woman medical doctor in Korea.[12] Her first letter of April 1, 1888, summarizes very succinctly about her new home, "This is par excellence, a heathen land." The heathendom, poverty, and oppression were all related in the minds of the missionaries. The seldom-articulated assumption was that only clear Bible teaching and the spread of Christianity would remove the scourge of the nation.

We may be able to understand the conservative theology of these early missionaries, but what may be somewhat surprising is their equally strong penchant for the poor and the oppressed; their understanding of missionary work was more integral or holistic than we often give them credit for. There is no question about this strong commitment, for it was argued in the missionary correspondence with poor Mr. Ellingwood back in New York. Ellingwood, the general secretary for the (Northern) Presbyterian Board of Foreign Missions, had the difficult task of trying to sort out why the small

---

[9]This phrase is from Samuel H. Moffett's lectures describing the Persian Christians' response in welcoming Arab invaders as friends against the oppressive Sasanian rulers.

[10]The 1920 curriculum of Moffett's Presbyterian Theological Seminary of Chosen includes *Moody's Sermons* (senior year) and Torry's *How to Lead Men to Christ*. Both were translated into Korean. From the February 2, 1920, Board Report of the Seminary, found in Princeton Theological Seminary library archives.

[11]Moffett was pleased in the 1920 Board Report "that not counting a Personal Evangelism course which will be largely bible, or the Theology courses, there is over 34% of straight bible teaching in the [curriculum]."

[12]Miss Horton arrived in March of 1888.

missionary community, starting with Dr. Allen and Rev. Underwood, was so quickly at each other's throats. After the arrival of the intermediary and medical doctor Heron (who "called Allen '*an ass*' on one occasion and on another shook his fist in his face and acted in a violent manner generally"[13]), all three tried to resign. It took two years to straighten out the problems, but the root of the problem was summarized very well by a government teacher (and another Presbyterian), Rev. George W. Gilmore. Gilmore takes Allen's side: "The Koreans must be converted from the *Head* downwards. . . . They [Underwood and Heron] do not appreciate the fact that they are tolerated here largely because Dr. Allen has prestige at the palace and among the nobility."[14] Another government teacher, George C. Foulk, confirmed this evaluation. He summarized that Dr. Allen's approach was to reach the rulers and the leaders, paving the way with good relations with royalty. Underwood, on the other hand, worked to reach "the common folk." This is quite accurate. Underwood is constantly writing about his "school" and orphanage for young boys. It must be free so that it does not become an elitist school. There must be an orphanage and school started for girls also. We need women teachers.

It is only a little bit simplistic to see Dr. Allen and his friend Gilmore as bright scholars who assessed East Asia, specifically Confucianist societies, in a similar way to how the Jesuits had centuries before. "From the head downwards" is a nice, neat expression. Underwood, and just a few years later Moffett, would tolerate only a part of this. They did want good relations with the king, but they could not stand to hobnob with the more elitist dignitaries of the foreign community in Seoul. Moffett was always on the road, going out to the villages, always pushing for permission to take up residence in that den of thieves, Pyeng Yang. Many letters are filled with petitions for more evangelists to move into new areas, more teachers to equip village Christians, and "one medical doctor" for Pyeng Yang. Underwood is constantly defending his school, working with boys on the streets to bring the good news of Christ and of education. It is no accident that these two pioneers were also the best Korean language students. They lived closer to the

---

[13] Emphasis is in the original letter, dated January 29, 1887. From the Presbyterian Mission archives on microfiche at Pittsburgh Theological Seminary.
[14] December, 24, 1886, letter from Gilmore to Ellingwood in New York. Clearly the problem had become so great that nonmissionaries felt compelled to enter the fray to help solve the problem.

common people. Moffett remarked in a letter of 1893, just three years after his arrival, that with Underwood gone, he was now the best person at spoken Korean.[15] In part this must have happened because Moffett refused to ride in a "sedan chair" or even a bicycle. He spent most of his time on the road walking with the people and talking about Korean life.

In the end, Allen took the government job representing the US government to Korea, a position that was of great value to missionaries, and thus the Underwood and Moffett approach became the accepted pattern. Presbyterian work became centered in the north, far away from the international community, and it was widespread among the common folk: the *minjung* in the villages. Foreign Protestant missionaries were known, even by the local shamanists, as being friends of the poor. During the Sino-Japanese conflict Moffett returned to Pyeng Yang and noted, "However, we ran across one old man who was so delighted to see a foreigner who he knew to be in sympathy with Koreans that he gladly hunted up some rice for us, and food for our horses and gave us a room to sleep in."[16] With all of the foreigners (now Japanese) flooding the land, the tall American Presbyterian was known to "be in sympathy with Koreans." Moffett's identity with the oppressed Koreans is even better illustrated in his own reflection on the Tonghak, the very movement that precipitated the Sino-Japanese conflict. He recorded in the widely read periodical of the time *The Missionary Review of the World* (1894) that he entered a village in his travels in the north where the Tonghak were agitating for support for their rebellion. Moffett engaged the leader in conversation about his complaints, analysis, and goals. After the conversation, where the leader negotiated to use a Christian building for a rally, Moffett commented, "I realized that we were very much in sympathy with the Tong Haks. I told him so and only encouraged him not to use means of violence. I then realized that these Koreans are more sinned against than sinners." This language clearly identifies the missionary sympathies that help to explain the events of 1919.

It is a great irony that this "grassroots" missionary approach was systematized by, among others, Presbyterian John L. Nevius of Chefoo, China. It is not our place here to discuss where Underwood, Moffett, and others

---

[15]Underwood and his wife were on medical leave.
[16]Letter from Samuel A. Moffett (Pyeng Yang) to Ellingwood (New York), November 1, 1894. From the Presbyterian Mission archives on microfiche at Pittsburgh Theological Seminary.

developed their ideas, but in the summer of 1890 Nevius spoke for two weeks to the missionary community at a special annual missionary conference in Seoul. This certainly strengthened the resolve of the bottom-siders over the top-siders. The idea of inviting Nevius to speak, however, was not Underwood's, but it was that of the respected Dr. Allen. Nevius had a great influence on the missionaries as a community, but, oddly enough, Moffett makes no mention of him in his extant correspondence.

March 1, 1919: Korean Christians as Theologically Conservative and Socially Liberal

We now jump ahead to the events of 1919. A steady course of conservative Bible teaching and preaching had continued with a focus on the poor, oppressed, women, and children. Correspondence reveals these priorities, along with the Nevius language of "self-support," "native evangelists" (self-propagation), and "native preachers and elders" (self-governance). The nature of this subversive teaching was not made clearly known until 1919.[17] Japanese control of the peninsula had continued to increase over the decades, and Koreans, who had been dominated by a corrupt Chinese-Korean rule, now found themselves under a more direct but equally oppressive Japanese rule. Among the most patriotic and nationalistic were the Christians. This meant that they were also among the most independent and liberationist minded. Anticipated by Moffett's earlier appreciation of the Tonghaks, an interesting bond developed between this group and the Christian (mostly Presbyterian) leaders. Choi's group was now called the Chongdokyo (Religion of the heavenly way), and they, with Christian leaders, drafted a Korean Declaration of Independence.[18] This declaration was signed by thirty-three: fifteen Chongdokyo, fifteen Christians, and three Buddhists. Copies were made on every available mimeograph machine. Even Moffett's secretary and cook were involved in making and distributing copies. In Pyeng Yang a peaceful rally was held. Actually an independence worship service would be a better title for the event. The

---

[17]The subversion in part had to do with language. Moffett and Underwood honored the Korean language and spoke it with all the Korean. The Japanese insisted that the Koreans learn Japanese.
[18]It is worth noting that this declaration was inspired by Wilson's 14 Points after World War I. Wilson's fifth point was the self-determination of smaller nations must be respected. Koreans understood what this meant.

service was held at the Presbyterian Boys' School and was led by many of the leaders of the Presbyterian Church (including moderator Rev. Kim Sun-du). Pastors spoke in honor of the late emperor, they sang the doxology, a benediction was given, and Scriptures were read (Rom 9:3; 1 Pet 3:13-17). Next, the Declaration was read, and instructions were given as to how they were to carry flags, shout *mansei*, and not resist arrest.[19] Moffett attended as an observer and was seated at the side. He was not informed about the details of the meeting but attended out of curiosity. These leaders were, after all, his students. They honored him as their teacher, but on this day they were teaching their teacher what they understood of Christian leadership in Korea.

Moffett refused to become involved politically, both out of personal necessity and theological conviction. And yet, his leadership of Koreans made it clear to the Japanese that he was the instigator of this whole affair. A Japanese newspaper, the *Osaka Asahi*, wrote in a March 17 editorial that the center of the independence movement was really in Pyeng Yang and the Presbyterian missionaries. "They pretend to be here for preaching, but they are secretly stirring up political disturbances, and foolishly keep passing on the vain talk of the Koreans, and thereby help to foster trouble. These are really the homes of devils. The head of the crowd is Moffett. . . . This is the centre of the present uprising. It is not in Seoul but in Pyeng Yang."[20] Missionaries were called in before the Japanese judge Watanabe and Mr. Katayama to explain what they had done to start this movement. Moffett's defense was carefully crafted:

> I have come to find that they [Koreans] place a higher value on spiritual and moral things than on material. My teaching has been to elevate the spiritual and have been greatly satisfied with the results. One must recognize the worth of the Koreans along this line. The thing which appeals to the Korean is justice and justice has a greater appeal to him than anything of material nature. Impress him with the fact that justice is rendered him and he will value and receive it gratefully.[21]

---

[19] *Mansei* is the Korean shout of cheer.
[20] "Editorial: The Evil Village Outside the West Gate," *Osaka Asahi*, found in records transcribed from Samuel A. Moffett files and letter by Eileen Moffett (author's copy).
[21] From Samuel Hugh Moffett collection of the Samuel Austin Moffett papers.

After the investigation, the Japanese were sure that the connection was direct. Christian missionaries and their teaching had brought on this movement. In a sense they were right. Churches were closed (not temples), and seminary students, even before they entered the classroom, were arrested and beaten. Church leaders were called in, detained, some arrested, and large numbers were tortured. Political nationalism, in the form of an independence movement, worked in tandem with Christian teaching to produce a nonviolent protest like that of Martin Luther King Jr. Only this nonviolent protest was in 1919, and it was in Asia. It was built on very conservative protofundamentalism, but it was expressed as liberation theology.

10

The Importance of Shandong

A Missiological Evaluation of *Place*

> *The Master said, "The study of strange doctrines is injurious indeed!"*
>
> CONFUCIUS, *ANALECTS*

INTRODUCTION

Robert Morrison never stepped a foot in Shandong, but I would argue he should have. Robert Morrison tilled the soil of Chinese culture to plant the seed of Protestant, Bible-centered Christianity, and in later generations, the seed Morrison planted developed. The development of Christianity has been quite diverse in China, but of special significance are a few locations: Shanghai, Nanjing, Hong Kong, Beijing, and, I would argue, the province of Shandong. Most are major cities, Shandong a more rural province.

Missionary intercourse with local cultures is part of the story of local societies and cultures. Perspective is everything. If we were looking at the missionary endeavors in China from Europe or North America, we would see interactions, glories, or tragedies as expressions or extensions of Western culture. Even if we have great empathy for the Chinese, we would still be expressing Western interpretations of the Chinese context and the Chinese psyche. In this essay, we shift the historical perspective, not from Western missionaries to that of the Chinese, but from that of institutions to that of a province. What can we learn about cultural interactions and Christian missionary expression by focusing on a diachronic study of a

---

This chapter was first delivered as a lecture in Hong Kong at the bicentennial of the arrival of Robert Morrison to begin Protestant missionary work in China. It was later published in *Ching Feng*, n.s., 8 (2007): 131-52.

province? Although we could choose any province or even a number of major cities for our study, I have chosen a province that has been remarkable in the history of China and in the history of Christianity. Whether we are studying climate, geography, cultural history, colonial history, indigenous church development, or Christian missionary activity, Shandong stands out as an interesting case study.

Our approach may seem a little unusual, but I would like to suggest that such a pattern may bear fruit in other areas of mission history as well as other studies of indigenous Christian development. First, we will take a brief look at the historical geography of the region. Climate and topography, as we will see, have had a decisive influence on the history of Shandong. Second, we will look briefly at some of the cultural history of the province. Its proximity to the northern capital, Beijing, and its geography have had an influence on this cultural history, but as we will see, there are other reasons that the province has had such a rich history. Third, we will look at some of the historical Western figures who have worked in Shandong, trying to answer some questions about how their Christian endeavors were channeled by their relationships with the environment and history of the region. Fourth, we will look at a few indigenous Christian movements that developed in Shandong from 1900 to 1938, and even before. Again, we will ask some questions about the relationship of the history (cultural, geographical, political, and religious) to the development of these indigenous churches. Finally, we will draw some tentative conclusions about what we have learned by taking this angle or perspective to study Christian history.

Historical Geography of Shandong

Geography does not completely determine history, but it is one of the major factors. In the case of Shandong, geography and climate together are major factors in the history of religion there. Shandong's geography has a few unusual features that have led to some extreme natural occurrences. We will look at its coastline, the Yellow River, and its location. From these three we will see that important events follow such as the building of the Grand Canal, the flooding disasters, and great droughts and famines. More than any other province, geography has both blessed and cursed Shandong. The mighty Yellow River, for example, is called both "China's Pride" and "China's Sorrow."

Shandong is a peninsula situated between the northern capital, Bei-Jing, and the old southern capital, Nan-Jing. It contains uplands in the central west and ever-so-slightly raised plains, and then most of the province is a massive peninsular floodplain. The coastline is the second longest in China and contains many natural harbors (but also many dangerous reefs). Being situated between the two ancient capitals, Shandong is a crossroads for traveling both north and south and east and west.[1] The Grand Canal, a project mostly done at the end of the Sui and the beginning of the Tang dynasties,[2] is the longest and most important canal in the world, traveling through western Shandong. The Yellow River is the second-longest river in China and is considered the cradle of Chinese civilization.[3] This mighty river descends much too slowly through Shandong, and it carries too much of the loess soil from Shanxi, and so it is constantly shifting direction as it annually carries over one billion tons of soil to and through Shandong; it is truly a yellow-looking river. Because of this "crossroads" location, and due to particular climatic conditions, this province has been unusually enriched, but more often in the past two centuries unusually impoverished. Because southern China is the more productive region for wheat and rice, it became necessary to transport those grains more easily to the north, and so the Grand Canal was built.

The Grand Canal was a huge and lengthy human undertaking, but there is a second massive human undertaking in Shandong, and that has been the thousand-year attempt called "Controlling the Dragon."[4] Annual summer rains along with thawing snows in the mountains cause periodic flooding. What makes it much worse for this lazy river is the constantly rising riverbed, causing the river to "seek lower ground" and causing engineers to build containing dikes and levees. At great cost of both human labor and money, Confucian engineers worked for centuries to minimize flooding and control the mighty dragon. In spite of the grand bureaucracy of Qing China working to control the river, in the years following 1853 the mighty river finally turned

---

[1] Even today, Shandong has the densest highway network, again explained by its location.
[2] As early as the fifth century BCE the canal was started to bring grains north. The canal was not completed until the Yuan Dynasty (1279–1368).
[3] Other river basins that have been "cradles of civilization" are the Indus, Nile, and twin rivers of the Tigris and Euphrates.
[4] Randall A. Dodgen, *Controlling the Dragon: Confucian Engineers and the Yellow River in Late Imperial China* (Honolulu: University of Hawai'i Press, 2001).

north, to an earlier emptying place, into the Bohai Sea. For a brief period of seven hundred years the Yellow River had passed Shandong and emptied farther south into the Yellow Sea.[5]

In the century between the First Opium War (1842) and the Japanese War of Aggression, there were four major tragedies related to the Yellow River. The first was the major course change that took place from 1853 to 1855. During this time millions of people were displaced. The second major disaster has been considered the worst natural disaster up to its time: the 1887 Yellow River Flood. Estimates of the number of people killed (mostly in Shandong) go from eight hundred thousand to 2.5 million. Again, millions were dislocated and lost their homes. The third major disaster was even greater, and that was the 1931 flood, whereby between nine hundred thousand and four million people were killed.[6] This was the worst natural disaster of the twentieth century. The fourth disaster of the Yellow River was not a natural disaster. With the Japanese advancing by sea and then through Shandong in 1938, the Guomindong decided to secretly slow down or prevent their advance by destroying the major dikes and levees of the Yellow River and flooding major portions of Shandong. Citizens were not notified, so they slept quietly in their homes as the waters rushed through their villages. An estimated nine hundred thousand people died.[7] In each and every one of these disasters, massive movements of people were necessary. Death, migration, homelessness, and despair reigned far too much in this one province from 1842 to 1942.

As significant as the floods have been for Shandong and the surrounding regions, droughts have been just as disastrous in Shandong, as well as elsewhere in China.[8] Shandong has not been the only province hit by some of these droughts and famines, but because of the impact on the Grand Canal and the river basin, the droughts have had wider repercussions than the loss

---

[5] It is estimated that the Yellow River has breached levees over fifteen hundred times and had major course changes eighteen times.

[6] Death estimates are very difficult to quantify because many people will die within the following six months to a year from cholera and typhoid outbreaks.

[7] Estimates range from 500,000 (from more recent research) to 12 million (when the Guomindong blamed the flooding on Japanese bombing). Actual deaths were very likely under 1 million.

[8] Estimating deaths from drought is a risky business, but globally most people would agree that four of the worst six droughts and accompanying famines in the world occurred in China (the 1900 famine in India and 1930-1931 famine in Russia would be the other major ones, each with over a million deaths).

of grain. We could speak of other famines in the past century or two, but the Great Famine of 1876–1879, both because of its time (rise of Protestant missionaries) and its impact (some regions saw a reduction in 90 percent of the population) will be used as an illustration. The droughts in Shandong and nearby provinces generally occur when the monsoon rains in the south do not move. These clockwise spinning winds will pump water into southern China for months, bringing long-term dry winds from the west (Gobi Desert) into northern China. When this happens, the ground gets parched like a rock, and, if it occurs for a few years in a row, as it did beginning in 1875, the reserve grains are quickly consumed. Eastern Shandong had also had dry years for two years preceding, so the famine hit them hardest and earliest. The results were devastating, and the letters and articles written by missionaries are, to this day, among the most heartrending you will ever read. They talk about people dismantling their homes to sell wood for fuel. Parents would sell their children into servitude or sell their daughters into prostitution. There were stories of people becoming cannibalistic, sometimes not waiting for babies or starving adults to die before they began preparations. Bark was stripped off trees for food, and many, in complete despair, used their last strength to leap off of a building to their death. Suicide was common. Cholera and typhoid exploited the weakened condition of people in a five-province area of Shandong, Hebei, Henan, Shanxi, and Shaanxi. The British legation estimated seven million died in the first winter of the Great Famine: 1876–1877. Estimates from the China Relief Fund, an international fund set up by missionaries, estimated 9.5–13 million died in the three-year famine.[9] Those who could fled to the cities of the south where there was still food. Farms and homes were abandoned in an effort to stay alive. The migrations became a new problem for the already overtaxed government. A trade imbalance, due to the enforced trade in opium, the economic drain of a thirteen-year civil war (Taiping Rebellion, 1851–1864), and now famine and uncontrolled migration just about brought the dynasty to ruin. Over 70 percent of China's budget was being spent on military, to keep down rebellions, triad gangs, and now to control masses of migrants. The government had neither the will nor the foresight to keep the water system (dikes, levees, and canals) in good

---

[9]At the same time, a similar though slightly less tragic famine was occurring in India. See David Arnold, *Famine: Social Crisis and Historical Change* (London: Wiley, 1988).

working order, nor to keep large granary inventories. The climate made things terrible for China, but political decisions and British imperialism made this apocalyptic. It was into this situation that the first generation of Protestant missionaries flooded into China after the Second Opium War.

Cultural History of Shandong

Chinese culture developed in the Yellow River basin, in part centered in Shandong. The earliest dynasties were all centered in the Yellow River basins moving out to the north and south from the river. In these earlier dynasties the Yellow River emptied to the north, and so it traveled through much of what is presently Shandong.[10] It is here, then, in present-day Shandong, Henan, and Shanxi that Chinese civilization and culture first formed. In fact, the Chinese culture that Western missionaries from the seventh century on would encounter was the culture being formed for a millennium or more in the Yellow River region.

This is not the time or place for a detailed discussion on Confucianism, but a few comments should be made, if for no other reason than to acknowledge some historic irony. Confucius (Kongzi, 551–479 BCE) was born during the later Spring and Autumn Period (approximately 770–476 BCE), in the city of Qufu, which was in the fragile state or dukedom of Lu. For our interest, it is important to know that Confucius never claimed to be teaching anything new, only to remind people of truths they already knew, and to remind them that lessons of *li*, or what is righteous, are found in our past. In this sense, he was an archtraditionalist who, according to tradition, spent three years mourning his mother's death and who taught that honoring your father is to imitate him when he dies. The afterlife is of no consequence; doing what is right in this life, and learning how from the wisdom of the past, is what is important. Two generations later, his greatest follower, Mencius or Mengzi (372–289), was born just thirty miles south of Qufu in the impressive capital city of the Qi Kingdom, Linzi. This was not a state but a kingdom, and Mencius carried on the teachings of what some have called early Neo-Confucianism. His teachings were long monologues and dialogues, whereas Confucius would give aphorisms and proverbs. There are

---

[10]The twelfth century was the first time that the silt built up so much that the river flowed to the south, emptying in the Yellow Sea.

differences in their teachings, but what is remarkable for twenty-first-century ears, whether Eastern or Western, is the constant concern to learn from the past, preserve the past, and show reverence and honor to family (especially parents) and rulers. Children also are to be trained properly, raised not near a graveyard, nor near a market, but near a school.[11] One element that is new in Mencius is his teaching about the "enemy" of the old, established traditions. Mencius, unlike Confucius, makes room for revolutionary behavior against a ruler who has "lost the mandate of heaven." When violence and corruption persist, or when famine and floods abound, it is clear that the ruler has lost the mandate from heaven. In times of national disaster, kings and other rulers must make proper sacrifices to retain the mandate for their rule. In Confucianism, both women and children are to be cared for. This is acting justly or in harmony, according to *li*.

There are many other cultural and historic events and people associated with Shandong, but I would like to mention just two more. Buddhism also is important to Shandong. In 412, the Chinese Buddhist monk Faxian (Fa-Hien according to James Legge) returned from a twenty-year trip to the West, traveling to India and Sri Lanka, and bringing with him Buddhist scriptures and circulating his famous *A Record of Buddhistic Kingdoms*.[12] When he returned, he first landed in Shandong, where he began his translating of one of the lives of the Buddha from Sanskrit into Chinese.[13] Thus, he is one of the greatest historical figures in the translation of south Asian Buddhism to Chinese Buddhism.

One final historical note is worth mentioning, and this is an occurrence during our time period: the Boxer Rebellion.[14] The "Fists of Righteous Harmony" were aroused first in Shandong with the post–Sino-Japanese War settlements

---

[11] Taken from one of the most quoted phrases of Mencius: *mou bo san sen*; literal translation: "Mencius's mother, three moves." These are the three moves she made, ending up near a school.
[12] The full title is *A Record of Buddhist Kingdoms: Being an Account of the Chinese Monk, Faxian, of His Travels in India and Ceylon*, trans. James Legge (Oxford: Clarendon, 1886).
[13] It appears from his biography that he later did most of his translation in Nanjing, being prevented from returning to his home in Xian, to the west.
[14] An interesting study related to Chinese rebellions would be to compare and look for some direct relationships between the White Lotus rebellions at the end of the eighteenth century, and the Nien Rebellion (1851–1868) and the Boxer Rebellion. All have strong religious components (Pure Land Buddhism and some Daoism), along with various concerns for national identity (opposing the Manchus, British, Germans, etc.). The Nien Rebellion, however, was clearly catalyzed into semiorganized "bands" by two major floods of the Yellow River, in 1851 and 1855.

whereby Germany gained control over the important port of Qingdao. German Catholic missionaries were very strong in this region already, and Society of the Divine Word (SVD) brothers were working throughout Shandong. Although antiforeignism was mounting throughout the country at the time, Shandong seemed to be the flashpoint. The SVD missionary John Baptist Anzer (1851–1903) was more confrontational than most of his missionary brothers, trekking to the home of Confucius in Qufu and stating his purpose: "My one aim, and the end of all my struggles and tribulations, was to lift high the standard of Christ in Qufu, Confucius' birthplace."[15] Anzer's imperialistic approach had sudden and dramatic repercussions: on November 3 of 1897, two SVD missionaries were killed in Shandong. At the time, Anzer was back in Berlin, possibly conferring with the kaiser about extending German influence in China. This was the final impetus to the regional and then empire-wide movement against both foreigners (both businesspeople and Christians) and against Chinese who became Christian. The initial slogan was "Overthrow the Qing; destroy the foreigner," but later it was a call to resist "primary, secondary, and tertiary hairy men" (foreign traders, Christians, and Chinese Christians). Nationalism, Buddhism, and indignation combined to create a national explosion against foreign communities. Most of those who were killed, however, were Chinese Roman Catholics.[16] The Boxer uprising began in Shandong.

Missionary Christian History

Roman Catholics up to 1800. Christian history in Shandong goes back to the early Jesuits, who mostly passed through Shandong, going from port cities in the south to the imperial center of the Middle Kingdom, Beijing. In the early 1600s some Jesuits did toil away for twelve years, but with no response, they left.[17] Shandong was not the type of place for Jesuits who were committed to

---

[15] See Gianni Criveller, PIME, trans. Betty Ann Maheu, "Freinademetz and Anzer: Two Missionaries, Two Styles," from the web site of the Holy Spirit Study Center, Hong Kong: www.hsstudyc.org.hk/en/tripod_en/en_tripod_131_02.html.

[16] Samuel H. Moffett, *A History of Christianity in China* (Maryknoll, NY: Orbis Books, 2005), 2:486, gives statistics from K. S. Latourette of 1,912 Protestant Chinese killed, but thirty thousand or more Roman Catholic Chinese. This fits well with the thesis that Anzer and others had provoked the Boxers, since there were far more Protestant missionaries working in China at the time. The Protestant community was a little more than one-third of the Roman Catholic Chinese community in 1897.

[17] For a summary of the early Roman Catholic work, see Nicholas Standaert, *Handbook of Christianity in China*, vol. 1, *635–1800* (Leiden: Brill, 2000).

reaching the rulers so that the masses would follow. It was no longer the center of Chinese civilization, as it was in the Spring and Autumn Period and in the Period of Warring States. Shandong was poorer, with no major cities like Beijing, Nanjing, or Wuhan. Next, in the early decades of the eighteenth century, the Franciscans came, and these friars, more suited to work among the poor and on the underside, had amazing ministry results.

> The friars indeed sometimes took on work in a particularly tough territory, sometimes even in places that the Jesuits had given up as hopeless. The latter, after twelve years' fruitless work in Shandong, abandoned the area, and the friars remained alone there in the 1650s. They worked for fifteen years almost in despair, then suddenly the tide turned and by 1670 they had 4,000 converts. Within a few more years they reported that for Christian fervor it was the best province in all China.[18]

For less than ten years, Dominicans labored in Shandong as well as in Shanxi. Then, after a period of absence, the Franciscans returned and labored under very difficult conditions, including the general exile of all missionaries from China (1665–1671). Antonio de Santa Maria Caballero (1602–1669) is one of the more interesting of the friars of this period, and he gives us a window into the approach that was required at the time. He describes the difficulty relating to any of the literati, and then he talks about the overwhelming majority of the people in Shandong:

> The second are the country people. . . . From these our Christians are drawn. They appreciate the things of this world well enough and that which concerns life here on earth; but to comprehend the way of eternal life these people are so ignorant, awkward and dull that it requires the above-mentioned exertions to prepare them for holy baptism and even greater ones to maintain them in the truth.[19]

Most of the Christians are "awkward," "ignorant," "country people." Roman Catholic work at this period was little concerned with training Chinese priests. Their concern was to baptize, catechize, and order Christian communities that would be under Spanish or French or Portuguese priests.

---

[18] J. S. Cummins, *A Question of Rites* (Aldershot, UK: Scholar Press, 1993), 110.
[19] From R. Gary Tiedemann, "Christianity and Chinese 'Heterodox Sects': Mass Conversion and Syncretism in Shandong Province in the Early 18th Century," *Monumenta Serica* 44, no. 9 (1996): 340.

Until Spanish funding could no longer provide support, the Franciscans continued their ministry in China, up to the first years of the nineteenth century, about the time of the arrival of Robert Morrison.

Protestant missionaries in Shandong. Shandong was only entered by Protestants after the Second Opium War, when foreigners were "officially" permitted to reside beyond the approved treaty ports.[20] These early missionaries were little different from missionaries from the same societies already working in South Asia and Africa. They were motivated by a desire to see Chinese come to faith in Christ, for churches of Chinese to be worshiping the triune God, and for Chinese to eventually evangelize their own country. They believed in the importance of learning local languages and dialects and in translating the Bible into those local languages. The Bible was the primary source and subject. Supporting this work of conversion and church development were the twin tools of education and medical care. But medical care was more than just an evangelistic tool; it was also a very personal concern. In 1861, within just a few months of each other, the Southern Baptists Reverend and Mrs. J. B. Hartwell, Presbyterians Reverend and Mrs. Samuel Gayley, Reverend and Mrs. J. A. Danforth, and Reverend and Mrs. John L. Nevius arrived in the port city of Dengzhou (Tengchow). G. Thompson Brown puts things in perspective: "In the mid-nineteenth century it [Shandong] was desperately poor, and far removed from the Western commercial penetration. Both the Gayley and Danforth families had suffered from the heat and humidity in Shanghai and it was thought the five-hundred mile move north would be good for them."[21] Helen Nevius also became very sick on the ship, and the south China weather was very hard on her, so the Neviuses almost moved permanently to Japan, but John Nevius's clear sense of call brought them back to China. However, they returned to the north, where the climate might be more favorable for his wife. John Nevius himself never had health problems, something his wife attributed to

---

[20] Although the "peace treaty" opening the ports to foreign residence was signed in 1858 (Treaty of Tianjin), China refused to allow foreign embassies in Beijing, and so fighting continued up to the capture, looting, and destruction of the emperor's "Summer Palace." Thus, 1860 or 1861 was the very earliest Protestant missionaries could "legally" reside in China outside the treaty ports.

[21] G. Thompson Brown, *Earthen Vessels and Transcendent Power: American Presbyterians in China, 1837–1952* (Maryknoll, NY: Orbis Books, 1997), 54.

his exercise and "Sabbath keeping."[22] I believe his imported fruit trees and seeds may also have helped.[23] A cholera outbreak greeted the earliest missionaries, and this dominated their first few years of letter writing, that is, along with language learning. Nevius, driven by health issues to Shandong, developed an approach to missionary work that, though not completely novel, is world famous. His "Three-Self Principles," as they are commonly known, are really about the deprofessionalization of the ministry.[24] In his famous article, published in 1886 in the *Chinese Recorder*, "Methods of Missionary Work," Nevius focuses on the problems with the "old way" of doing missionary work and contrasts this with the "new methods." The old way involved paying Christian agents and thus taking converts out of their environment and out of their place of greatest effectiveness. Nevius contrasts this with the need to leave people in the occupation and location where they were first found and then to provide training in each local context. This also meant that the missionary work would not be as dependent on foreign capital (paying Chinese to do the ministry), nor on foreign leadership. Nevius lived this idea of entrusting the ministry to local people. He and his wife had a nice mission house that was both a launching pad for his two- to three-month trips and a type of school for young girls. He traveled constantly around central and western Shandong from the home base (first in Tungchow [Dengzhou] and later in Cheefoo [Yantai]). His approach was not the basic approach used in China by the larger denominational churches, but it was the pattern of the Shandong missionaries: Hunter Corbett, Calvin Mateer, and others.

Supporting this approach was the establishment of schools for both boys and girls. Julia Mateer imitated Helen Nevius by starting her own school, as weak as she was. Both Julia and Calvin had run their own schools in the

---

[22]Helen S. Coan Nevius, *The Life of John Livingston Nevius: For Forty Years a Missionary in China* (New York: Fleming H. Revell, 1895). Helen Nevius remarked on the move north, "It required but a few months to prove the comparative salubriousness of the climate" (213).

[23]Part of Nevius's response to the Great Famine was to bring in a variety of fruit trees from the United States. It worked in providing an important source of nutrition. Even today, the Shandong government website acknowledges the importance of fruit in Shandong: "The apples produced in Yantai, pears from Laiyang, peaches of Feicheng, and Leling's golden-threaded jujubes are all famous specialties." "Shandong Natural Resources," www.china.org.cn/china/shandong/2010-03/12/content_19595872.htm.

[24]See the next chapter in this volume.

States before leaving for Asia. They were energized by thinking of how to better communicate, educate, and transform young lives. Julia could not have children, so her educational ministry, a ministry that did in fact transform hundreds of young, poor Chinese boys into Christian men, was her life. The Mateers, but mostly Julia, set the pattern for the famous network of Shandong schools: these schools were basic schools of literacy, Christian knowledge, and modern sciences, where all the teaching was done in Chinese.[25] This meant that the first standard books on geography, Western science, and mathematics were the translations and writings of the Mateers. The goal for the first two decades was not to train scholars but to train well-informed Christian young men. Parents would sign their children up for a nine-year basic education that included the best of the West and of China.

Calvin Wilson Mateer and Julia had arrived in 1863, just two years after the first Protestants in Shandong, and while Julia stayed at "home" in the Kwan Yin Temple, Calvin tried the Nevius approach of vast itineration for nine and a half years (until 1873). The childless Julia, who was still a gifted mother and educator, quietly established a school in her home for orphaned and poorer boys. Eventually, Reverend Mateer gave up on exercising a gift he did not have, and he soon followed his wife and became a leader in education. However, their educational model supported the Nevius method of providing basic education for boys and girls, as opposed to training an elite class of Westernized Christians. Mateer had traveled an estimated fifteen thousand miles by foot and donkey before he settled down to educational work. When he did settle down, he and Julia wrote what became a standard book for learning Chinese, *Mandarin Lessons*, an indication of their commitment to doing all work in Chinese and in making sure that all missionaries knew Chinese well.[26] The little school that Julia founded and ran became the Tengchow College and later the Christian University of Shandong. Mateer's Christian college trained all students to be

---

[25]"Mr. and Mrs Mateer included in their curriculum of studies the Chinese trimetrical classics (which were explained as soon as committed), geography, mental and written arithmetic, natural philosophy, 'Peep of Day,' *Pilgrim's Progress*, *Evidences of Christianity*, and the 'Church Catechism'; later were added algebra, geometry, astronomy, chemistry, etc. They early began, also, giving their students practice in writing compositions, a new feature of school life to them. As early as the summer of 1867, drill in debate was established as one of the regular features of the school." From the aptly titled biography of Julia written by her brother-in-law, Robert McCheyne Mateer, *Character-Building in China: The Life Story of Julia Brown Mateer* (New York: Fleming H. Revell), 50.

[26]Julia refused to take any credit. From *Character-Building*, 38-39.

Christians in word and in deed, and they would also be thoroughly Chinese, doing all of their studies in the Chinese language. A Baptist friend once observed after hearing formal addresses delivered at graduation from students at the Mateer school (1876), "These accomplished and earnest young men have learned no English and have not been lifted above their natural position or in any way denationalized."[27] This was in concert with the Nevius plan, but it was also clearly swimming against the missionary tide, for educators working in China felt that modern science had to be taught with Western languages; the Asian languages were not suited for these new ideas.[28] Over half of the graduates became teachers themselves, making possible a self-propagating educational system, if not a self-propagating church.[29]

Time does not allow for a full discussion of three other important missionaries who worked in Shandong—Charlotte (Lottie) Moon,[30] Gilbert Reid, and Timothy Richard—but to illustrate our thesis, we must briefly look at the third of these three. Timothy Richard (1845–1919) was a Baptist Welshman whose Christianity was flavored by Welsh revivalism.[31] Although he later became a missionary to many provinces of China, his early and formative years were spent in Shandong, working alongside men such as Nevius and Mateer. In fact, Mateer's educational leadership, doing some of the early chemistry and physics experiments in classes, was a model for what Richard would later advocate for all of China.[32] Richard began his work as an evangelist distributing Scripture in far-off villages in 1870, but within his first six years he had two major transformative experiences. He began to talk to people of different religious loyalties (Daoist, Buddhist, Confucianists, and Muslims), and he encountered the Great Famine. This first turned him

---

[27] Mateer, *Character-Building*, 50.
[28] When Henry Winters Luce became principal of the school, he moved it to Jinan and introduced English-language education. Luce later moved to Beijing and became vice president of Yenching.
[29] Irwin T. Hyatt Jr., *Our Ordered Lives Confess: Three Nineteenth Century American Missionaries in East Shantung* (Cambridge, MA: Harvard University Press, 1976), 140.
[30] Lottie Moon, because of the annual "Lottie Moon Mission Offering," is the best known of all Southern Baptist missionaries. She is also well known because of her effective long-term work in Shandong; this work is not without its problems, but it was strong and persistent.
[31] It is of interest that Richard, who developed a highly social and political theology, died the year after Washington Gladden and Walter Rauschenbusch.
[32] From the less-than-objective work by William E. Soothill, *Timothy Richard of China: Seer, Statesman, Missionary and the Most Disinterested Adviser the Chinese Ever Had* (London: Seeley, Service, 1924), and Hyatt, *Our Ordered Lives Confess*, 193 and 217.

toward the study of religion and what we might call early interreligious dialogue. The famine caused Richard to quickly make the assessment that the problems in China were so great they demanded a good understanding of the politics and religions of the country. Changes that Christians wanted to see in individual lives would not take place unless the larger societal problems were confronted. Chinese would not understand the message unless it was shown to them, not just told to them. Richard began to make contacts with local officials to get food to the poorer regions. Then he began to organize relief efforts, channeling money from Europe and Shanghai to Shandong and Shanxi provinces. His work with Chinese officials convinced him that the role of the missionary was to open doors of understanding among the elite leaders of China. The traveling evangelistic work must be done by the Chinese. In this regard he strongly supported the Shandong-Nevius method. However, educational work for Richard and others like him (W. A. P. Martin and Young John Allen) must reach the scholars and literati class. Richard was a modern Protestant Matteo Ricci in his approach. "Inquire for the most worthy. There was to be no stealthy progress by keeping in the shade, but open dealing with the most open-hearted and even-minded of the people."[33] Richard was redirected by his ten years in Shandong, and he became a global advocate for educational and relief reform for China.

Indigenous Christian Movements in Shandong

A common theme of Christianity in the twentieth century is the development of indigenous Christian movements. In Africa and Asia these indigenous movements developed in response to or opposition to oppressive Western dominance of Christianity; in this case, in response to foreign domination of the church in China. Such was the case in many other areas of the world. Slaves in the Americas developed their own churches in opposition to white churches and as a matter of Christian self-definition. In Africa, African Initiated (Indigenous) Churches began developing in the late nineteenth century, and these churches, using African languages and religious rituals, resisted foreign domination and even foreign culture. In China this also happened,

---

[33]From Soothill, quoting from Richard's handwritten note on a published sermon of Edward Irving, where Irving argues for missionary work in the pattern of Jesus, "seeking the most worthy." *Timothy Richard of China*, 77.

but I think it is of note that many of these movements were initiated by or developed in Shandong. The great Chinese evangelist John Sung (Song Shangjie) is an example of an indigenous leader rising up and throwing off the blanket of Western Christianity, but he did not start a church: he was a prophetic figure. Andrew Ji and the others in the Bethel Evangelistic Band did evangelistic work, but they did not repudiate the Western church and Western institutions. Thus, the number of truly indigenous movements that became institutionalized before the Japanese War of Aggression is relatively small. We will briefly mention four churches, one revival, and one modern development rooted in Shandong origins.

The Jesus Family was founded by a former Taoist and Confucianist, Jing Dianying, at Mahzhuang, Shandong, in 1927. Although he attended a Methodist middle school in Tai An, Jing was not converted until eight years later, in 1920, when he was struggling with a failed marriage. He then formed what he called the Saints Cooperative Society (Shengtu She) to call together other Christians to live a more Christian life in contrast to the corrupt lives around them. His second conversion, we might call it, came from a Pentecostal revival that occurred in 1925 in Tai An, and he now began praying for a full manifestation of the Holy Spirit and repented of sending off his wife by arranged marriage. Jing, now reconciled to his wife, focused on developing a Christian community that would manifest the leadership of the Holy Spirit. There were many influences on Jing to bring him to this point. First, he was greatly influenced by the Methodist missionary Nora Dillenbeck, who taught at the Methodist girls' school in Tai An beginning in 1913.[34] Second, we read of the influence of Hudson Taylor and the China Inland Mission on his thinking. Third, the newly formed Assemblies of God Church in town was the conduit for the Pentecostal revival that seemed to be the catalyst to a much broader Shandong Revival in the 1930s. Finally, Jing received support from Presbyterian medical missionary Dr. Thornton Stearns, who worked out of Jinan. Stearns provided needed financial support for a year or so after the Pentecostal experience.[35] However, the shape of the Cooperative Society

---

[34]Her photo album is now available online: http://hahn.zenfolio.com/dillenbeck.

[35]Stearns, it is interesting to know, presented a paper at the China Medical Missionary Association meeting in Shanghai in 1923 on the treatment of tuberculosis of the knee joint in China. He was chief surgeon in the Chinese Christian University Hospital: founded by Mateer, moved by Luce.

and later the Jesus Family was very much a product of Jing and his own background and Pentecostal experience with God. The Jesus family had four important aspects in the practice of the Christian faith: (1) break from your family (or leave) to join the Family; (2) a change of life since Jesus is Lord of the family; (3) do away with life essentials to actualize true life essentials; and (4) resolve to live and die for the Lord with all your heart.

Individuals came to the community handing over all of their worldly possessions, and they accepted the completely communal, even millenarian life. All of life was religious life, from morning, through the day, and even through the night. Much time was spent in prayers (out loud and often in tongues), interpreting dreams each morning, studying Scripture, and even in ecstatic worship. This movement was so independent that upon liberation in China under the communists, the Jesus Family was respected as a communal, anti-imperial existence. Later it was denounced by people from within. However, for our study, it is of note that this movement came from rural communities in Shandong and expressed much of the Confucian understanding of "family relationships" (now redefined, of course) and much of the ecstatic religious experience of Taoist Chinese worship, and it was all in Chinese. Jing never adopted an English name.

Other, less visible independent churches were founded in Shandong, such as the Gospel of Grace Church (founded by Sheng Mo-Du in 1881) and the China Christian Church,[36] founded by Zou Liyou, who was a Presbyterian and graduate of Mateer's school in Tengchow (Deng Zhou). Zou formed his own independent evangelistic organization, which eventually became an independent church, possibly encouraged by the 1911 revolution. The first land for his first church in Jinan was donated by the mayor, and soon other churches were starting throughout Shandong. Many independent churches were starting during this period in China, generally with friendly relations with the Western church families from which they were spawned, and so the Chinese Independent Church Federation was formed in Shanghai, with an initial membership of over one hundred churches. The Shandong churches of Zou, however, were earlier and unrelated to the Shanghai federation.

---

[36]Not to be confused with the China Christian Independent Church, founded about the same time in Shanghai.

One gets the feeling that with some careful research, many other indigenous independent movements would be discovered. Many of these movements seem to have been driven by a desire to separate from the West; others were influenced (possibly) by a Taoist background and a Pentecostal foreground, but some are less easily explained. The Christian Village of Nanbeiling, near to Qingdao, is one of those indigenous movements in Shandong that is hard to explain by resorting to secular "outside" influences. Recorded by Dong Ting Liang in the 1996 China Christian Council periodical, *Tian Feng*, this is one of the earliest movements, and it is, once again, tied to the earliest Presbyterian missionaries, in this case Hunter Corbett. The villagers used to follow the Daoist form of folk religion known as Jin Dan and were eager to seek after what was true. In 1873, about one hundred of the villagers signed a petition inviting Hunter Corbett to come and teach them the Bible. Corbett, naturally, took this as an important invitation. He went and did as he was requested, and soon thereafter there were three hundred baptisms, more than the previous thirteen years. This began a movement, and through the years many of the surrounding villages were evangelized by the Christians from Nanbeiling. Little has been written about this; in fact it is important to note that neither the Presbyterian Church's 1913 *Record of American Presbyterian Mission Work in Shantung Province, China* (edited by Hunter Corbett!) nor the 1940 history (*On the Shantung Front*) mention these villages. Both volumes write about, or are organized around, institutions and missionaries, and so many of these indigenous movement are not on their historical horizon. More on this later.

Although little is written about Nanbeiling, much has been written about the Great Shandong Revival. In fact this revival, in part promoted by Pentecostals, had an impact on the Southern Baptists, Norwegian Lutherans, Presbyterians, Methodists, and the Assemblies of God.[37] Although people

---

[37] Mary Crawford of the Southern Baptists collected many of the stories in her volume *The Shantung Revival* (Shanghai: The China Baptist Publication Society, 1933); Norwegian Lutheran promoter of revival Marie Monsen wrote *The Awakening: Revival in China, a Work of the Holy Spirit*, trans. Joy Guiness (London: China Inland Mission, 1959), a book published and promoted by the China Inland Mission in 1959; Foursquare Gospel missionary Paul Stephen Dykstra wrote his book on the experiences, *Triumphs of His Grace in Shantung China* (Los Angeles: Angelus Temple, 1936), in 1936, and even the Presbyterians acknowledged the revival, although with some concerns in their reports and finally in their history, John J. Heeren, *On the Shantung Front: A History of the Shantung Mission of the Presbyterian Church in the USA, 1861–1940 in Its Historical, Political and Economic Setting* (New York: Board of Foreign Missions of the Presbyterian Church in the U.S.A., 1940), 198-200.

had come to promote revival decades earlier, it was only in the 1930s that a general revival broke out that the missionaries finally recognized and wrote home about. All sources find the earliest expressions in 1928, and all sources have some common identifying characteristics. Suddenly, many people were interested in hearing the gospel preached. Numbers in attendance grew dramatically, almost overnight, and the number of conversions and baptisms grew tenfold and at times one hundredfold. Public confession of sin became a new common part of worship, and new commitments in giving money, volunteering to preach, and entering full-time ministry all became more common. Some of the groups had more visions, exercised gifts of tongues, healings, and visions, but all prayed much longer (sometimes all night) and out loud. The Presbyterians were rather concerned for the "extreme" group known as the "Spiritual Grace Society" (Ling'enhui) because this was newly organized Pentecostalism. The Presbyterian history devotes a full third of its report on the revival to the excesses of the Ling'enhui: "shaking dancing, jumping, loud wailing and rolling on the ground."[38] These excesses are avoided "where the foreign missionaries and the well trained native ministers kept in sympathetic touch with the revival," we are informed. And yet, even the cautious and well-educated Presbyterians are "touched." Later in the report we read, "The revival ... has been the harbinger of many blessings, the renewal for religious vitality, the bringing of hundreds into the fold, and above all has made the Chinese feel that this revival is an indigenous Christian movement." Even with this paternalistic rendering, we can see that this was something that was indigenous and that came from the Chinese Christians and those becoming Christians. Remarkable prison work began, mission societies were founded, "tithing" societies started, and even a "children's church," run wholly by children, was started. The movement spilled to other areas and was not unrelated to the work of the CIM, Jonathan Goforth, John Sung, Wang Mingdao, and others. Yet, the main flowering took place in Shandong.

Finally, as a way of looking forward from this period prior to the Japanese occupation, it is interesting to look at the present "Back to Jerusalem Movement." Jing and the early leadership of the Jesus Family had more than a vision for

---

[38] *On the Shantung Front*, 198-99.

revival; Jing had a missionary vision as part of his overall understanding of faithfulness to Jesus. As with other revivals and awakenings, the Jesus Family sent out others to start Christian communities and to spread around what they had found. In the 1930s there was either a split in the Jesus Family or a group was sent out called the "Northwest Spiritual Movement" that became an early missionary endeavor of the Jesus Family. I don't believe the language of "Back to Jerusalem" was used at the time of the founding of the Jesus Family, but there is a consistent thread of history from the Jesus Family of Jing to the missiology of the Back to Jerusalem movement of today. All these and more were movements that came out of the important province of Shandong.

Preliminary Conclusions

In our study we have seen that a number of contextual forces were at work that shaped the particular forms of Christian development that took place in China, radiating out from Shandong. I will comment on six conclusions from our study, none of which are exclusively true of Shandong, but all are very easily illustrated from the unique Shandong experience. First, one of the key elements in Christian development was geography and climate. The Great Famine of 1876–1879 was critical to missionary formation, and the earliest transformation of Christian missionary thought was in Shandong. In a fascinating 1975 essay titled "British Protestant Christian Evangelists and the 1898 Reform Movement in China," Leslie R. Marchant makes the following observation:

> The heaven sent sign British evangelists took to mark the end of the old regime and the awakening of the need to reform was the great famine of 1877. This event was too momentous for them to treat lightly or ignore.... It provided them with opportunities to point out to the Chinese why their Empire was in a depressed state economically, and to show that they, the evangelists, could provide the necessary enlightenment needed to better conditions.[39]

From that point on, Richard, along with other British and American evangelicals, turned to a different approach. They "presented themselves to the Chinese as men of science and men of reason as well as men of God who brought to China not only the words of Christ but also the benefits of the

---

[39]Leslie R. Marchant, *British Protestant Christian Evangelists and the 1898 Reform Movement in China* (Singapore: University of Western Australia, Center for East Asian Studies, 1975), 4-5.

Enlightenment."⁴⁰ Not only did the concern of many of these people change, but their approach also changed. They became concerned to reach people of education and people with authority who could effect provincial and national changes. I believe further study will show that the expanding fissure between evangelical and progressive approaches to Christian mission in China (illustrated by the Mateer and Luce differences) is found in the enormous natural disasters of the period primarily, and then later from Western (imported) theological formulations. But on a more positive note, some of the greatest missionary work done "for the nation of China" came from this early Shandong experience.

A second conclusion that we can make without much thought is built on the first. These disasters of epic proportions, being among the greatest in human history, caused great movements of people, both the poor, diseased, and dying, but also the missionaries. While Chinese were moving out of Shandong, or being relocated in Shandong, the missionaries were moving into Shandong. It might be hard to quantify, but we have found that movements of people, forced more often than by choice, are a catalyst for Christian growth and development. Whether it be the Irish Potato Famine (1845–1849), which brought many Christians to North America, or economic migration of Central Americans to North America, or the forced migration of Koreans from the north to the south (1950–1953), in all cases Christianity develops as a result. The point is historically Christianity benefits from forced migration, and it has since the earliest persecutions under the Roman Empire, as well as under the Persian Empire. But not only the forced migration of the poor caused by floods and famines but also the forced migration of the missionaries shaped Christianity in the modern period. It is interesting how many missionaries ended up on Shandong because of the tropical diseases in south China. It is easy to see why so many missionaries worked in the major cities of the east—Shanghai, Beijing, Nanjing, Wuhan, Guangdong, and Hong Kong—but why the concentration of some groups such as the Baptists, Methodists, Presbyterians, and later Pentecostals in Shandong? The major port city of Qingdao was German territory, so the missionaries we have looked at did not even center

---

⁴⁰See Timothy Richard, "China's Appalling Need for Reform," in *The China Mission Handbook* (Shanghai, 1893).

their work there. Instead, the most important cities for Christian work were not major cities but towns and small cities, some not even of provincial importance. Shandong illustrates the truth that Christianity is in two ways a "movement": it derives some of its health from the movements of people, and it resists "thick" rationalizations or institutionalization that restrain its need to be expressed as a movement.

A third conclusion, not directly related to geography and climate but something that came as a surprise in my research, was the importance of relationships between missionaries of theological and ecclesial diversity. Of course disease and tragedies helped to bring these people together, but even without such external pressures, missionary and national church relationships were very important. Lottie Moon was a fairly strong bourgeois southerner from the States, yet she worked with Presbyterians from the North soon after the Civil War. In her correspondence with the Southern Baptist Mission Board, she requested that they send an official thank-you note to Calvin Mateer for preaching in her Baptist churches.[41] She was not always happy with this, and she even had a competitive streak in her ("The odds of heathenism and pedobaptism, make it hard for Baptists everywhere"[42]), and yet communication and support between Baptists (both British and American), China Inland Missionaries, Presbyterians, Lutherans, Congregationalists, and others is important. In general there is nothing unique about this cooperation, but in Shandong it is clear that the great human tragedies augmented such interdenominational fellowship.

A fourth issue that is important in Shandong is the use of language. I look at this a few ways. First, the language acquisition of the missionaries themselves is worth noting. Second, the use of language in Christian development is consistently Chinese until the first decades of the twentieth century. We have seen that a few of our missionaries were excellent with languages, especially Chinese. Calvin and Julia Mateer wrote books on learning Chinese, and Moon was multilingual before going to China. In addition, unlike the education programs that were starting in the international big cities, all of the early education in Shandong was in Chinese. I believe this had a great

---

[41]Keith Harper, ed., *Send the Light: Lottie Moon's Letters and Other Writings* (Macon, GA: Mercer University Press, 2002), 36, 46, 70, 73, 76, 78, 335, 337, 375, 389.
[42]Letter from Lottie Moon to Dr. Tupper, October 5, 1888, in Harper, *Send the Light*.

impact on the type of Christianity that developed, and it both reflected and promoted the rural and more *koine* (common) form of Chinese Christianity. Shandong Christianity was village and rural Christianity. Again, this was true in many other regions of China, but in Shandong there was purposeful and intentional resistance to teaching English.

Fifth, and this is much more universal than the others, is the role of women. One of the most influential revivalist preachers of the early 1930s was the Norwegian Marie Monsen. The work of the Presbyterian women in founding schools (Helen Nevius and Julia Mateer) and pioneering in education, and of course the itinerant missionary work of Lottie Moon, among others, should be mentioned. Further study might want to ask whether single women and wives in tropical climates accomplished as much or stand out as much. Many of these early missionaries in Shandong kept their same wives for decades, whereas in the tropics many of the missionaries lost one, two, or three wives due to tropical diseases. A missionary has to live a long time in a single place to have much of an impact. Did women just survive longer in more temperate climates like Shandong?

Finally, I think the experience of indigenous Christian movements in Shandong is unique. There were many indigenous Christian movements in China beginning in the twenties and thirties, but in Shandong, there were even nineteenth-century movements. In addition, there were a number of movements that were completely independent of foreign aid or promotion, and yet they ended up having a national impact. Most of the missionaries who worked in China followed the Ricci method of reaching the best and brightest, realizing that China's Confucian sense of social order meant that influence would always be from the top down. The Shandong missionaries, at least those working with the Presbyterian and Baptist churches, did not seek to reach the scholars and then show them the better (Western) way to live. Instead, their approach was quite intentionally to travel widely, entrust early, and gather only briefly. What this means is that they gathered their pastors and evangelists for annual or semiannual training sessions in Chefoo (Yantai), rather than sending them away to a seminary to make them theologically proficient. It may have meant that many of them did not make good Presbyterians; in fact, many Presbyterians and Baptists and Methodists did go off and create their own church movements.

All of this happened in Shandong, the land of great disasters, home of the mighty Yellow River, and of course the home of Confucius, who warned that "the study of strange doctrines is injurious indeed."

11

Four Theorists, Three Selfs, Two Countries, One Goal

Missionary Practice in
China and Korea

It is impossible to talk about Korean history without talking about China, but it is less necessary to talk about Korea when writing Chinese history. This is the reality of being a small country, even a hermit nation like Korea. The Christian development of the two nations, however, is more closely related than the general political history. One of the major themes of this shared history is the missionary concept that is still remembered by the name of the Chinese church: the Three Self-Patriotic Movement of Protestant Churches in China. The concept of developing a self-supporting, self-governing, and self-propagating church was promoted by an American missionary working in China who developed the concept more fully for Korea.

That is the short story. The actual story of the development of the concept and the impact it had on Christian development in the two countries is much more complex and much more interesting. In the following pages, I help to tell that story and draw some conclusions from the divergent histories.

Introduction to the Chinese Church Situation Today

The Chinese church today, possibly more than any other church in the world, is in a postdenominational stage. The church unions that formally began in China with discussions among church leaders, both Western and Chinese, in the first years of the twentieth century and then again in the 1920s were accelerated under the Japanese occupation in the late 1930s. These church union discussions were accelerated not only in China, but also in Malaysia, Indonesia, Singapore, and of course in Japan. Japanese oppression accelerated the movement for Christian unity. The unions that were prior to those later mandated by the Japanese—the Church of Christ in Japan, the Church of Christ in Thailand, the United Church of Christ in the Philippines, among others—continued after the Pacific War as new forms of church order in an age of decolonialization.

However, at the beginning of the New China in 1949, Christianity was still a very fragmented community of approximately one million Chinese Christians, or 0.5 percent of the population. Twenty-three major denominational groups existed, all but a few coming from foreign origins. Of greater interest for us today was that there were about ten thousand Chinese Christian workers and four thousand foreign missionaries in 1949. The Protestant churches in China were running 322 Christian hospitals, more than 240 schools, thirteen Christian colleges, and 210 seminaries and Bible colleges.[1] Christianity in China was still very rural (between two-thirds and three-fourths rural), quite diverse, but as these statistics above indicate, the church was also saddled with large, and very costly, institutions. The new situation whereby the Chinese church became independent from all foreign influence demanded a change in Christian structures as well as in Christian theology.

In 1949, 1,527 Christian leaders signed the Christian Manifesto marking the beginning of a new era for Christian participation in Chinese society. Among the signers was the late Han Wenzao (1923–2006). To quote from the recent obituary of Reverend Han,

> After the foundation of the People's Republic of China, Christian churches in China adapted to the new situation and, under the guidance and leadership of Mr. Wu Yaozong and others, they launched the "Three-Self" campaign aimed at cutting the ties between Chinese churches and imperialism, and also at leading churches in China on the road of patriotism and faithfulness. Dr. Han was devoted to the "Three-Self" patriotic campaign, and was among the first group of 1,527 who signed the Christian Manifesto; he was also one of the 25 committee members of the Chinese Christian Churches' "Three-Self Oppose America and Support Korea Preparation Committee" which was formed in

---

[1] From Kenneth Grubb, ed., *World Christian Handbook* (London: World Dominion, 1949), 247-49.

1951. In August 1951, he was elected Secretary-General of the Nanjing Christian Churches Three-Self and Reform Promotion Commission, which was the first city-level Three-Self organization in China. Through his efforts, the church in Nanjing did well in the Three-Self patriotic campaign, and was noted as a progressive work unit.

The idea of three-self was promoted in light of the necessity for the Chinese church to stand on its own, as its own, and with its own people. The term *three-self* was used to emphasize two concerns, independence from Western imperialism and support for the new China. A third concern would also become clear in those early years; this concern was expressed in the December 1949 "Message from the Chinese Christians to the Mission Boards Abroad." Love Country—Love Church. Chinese Three-Self Christianity would not be built on American church-state separation, but on an ongoing dialogue regarding the role of the church to be a partner in building up the country.

In this chapter I would like to look briefly at the antecedents to the TSPM, since the concept of three-self is much older than the liberation of China. The concept goes back to nineteenth-century mission theorists, both administrators living in the West and missionaries developing their goals and strategies, *in medias res*. In the past forty years historiography has gone through three developments, and these shifts in historiography are critical to our assessment of Chinese and Korean Christian history. Before the Pacific War (WWII), Western history scholars gave very positive evaluations of Western missionaries: these were basically hagiographical and inspirational. The second stage, during the 1950s through the 1980s, was the age of revisionist historians, both from Asia and in the West, who were critical of the cultural insensitivity, unhealthy motives, and "imperialism mediated through religious rather than political channels."[2] In recent years—say the past two decades—there have been more nuanced critical studies done of missionary work and motive. One of the biggest shifts has been that now studies have been done both by Asians (Church History Association of India, Chinese University of Hong

---

[2]John Halsey Wood Jr., "John Livingston Nevius and the New Missions History," *Journal of Presbyterian History* 83 (Spring/Summer 2005): 24. Wood provides an excellent overview of the historiographic trends in mission history during the twentieth century.

Kong, Hong Kong Baptist University, Chinese Academy of Social Sciences, Centre for the Study of Christianity in Asia in Singapore, etc.)[3] and by Westerners.[4] Present scholarship is involved in a crosscultural discourse reading the contexts and the actors, both Asian and Western, to come to a clearer understanding of the mission process and Christian development. This study is part of this new, we might say, third wave of mission historiography. More broadly speaking, this is the shift from mission history to history of the world Christian movement.

In looking at the foundation and practice of the three-self principles, I will first look briefly at the four major theorists who have been given credit for developing three-self principles. Second, I will look at similar concerns expressed also in Korea, and then I will ask the question, "To what degree did the missionaries fail at this goal in China?" I will look at one very important letter from a veteran Presbyterian missionary working in Korea, as a single window into the three-self practice of the churches in China. Finally, I will conclude with some avenues for further research and make a few slightly provocative conclusions.

The Theories of Three-Self in the Nineteenth Century

There are four mission theorists—two administrators, one missionary, and one missionary and pastor theorist—who are generally given credit for developing the concept of three-self: Henry Venn of the Church Missionary Society in Britain; Rufus Anderson of the American Board of Commissioners for Foreign Mission; Roland Allen, who was an Anglo-Catholic with Pentecostal sensitivities; and John L. Nevius, missionary to Shandong from the American Presbyterian Church. We will look briefly at each and then note how these ideas were applied in Korea and how they looked in China to one person in 1926. First we will look at the American Congregationalist, Rufus Anderson.

---

[3]See, for example, Lian Xi's *The Conversion of the Missionaries: Liberalism in American Protestant Mission in China, 1907–1932* (State College: The Pennsylvania State University Press, 1997).
[4]Dana Robert of Boston University, William McLoughlin of Brown University, and William Hutchinson of Harvard University. Hutchinson puts the missionaries in their own contexts: "If deficient from a modern point of view in sensitivity to foreign cultures, the [missionaries] were measurably superior in that regard to most contemporaries at home or abroad." From Hutchinson's *Errand to the World: American Protestant Thought and Foreign Mission* (Chicago: University of Chicago Press, 1987).

Rufus Anderson (1796–1880) was a Congregationalist from Maine, son of the manse, who from the age of sixteen wanted to serve as a missionary.[5] He never did so. Instead he ended up serving for forty-four years as a mission administrator and became one of the best-known mission strategists in the world. Church leaders recognized that he would make a greater contribution to the newly started ABCFM,[6] and so he became the "tyrant who ruled the American Board, the Prudential Committee, and the missionaries with an iron hand." We gain some insight into his influence (which I do not think was that of a tyrant) as well as his theology of mission in his famous 1854–1855 deputation trip to visit mission stations (as they were called) in Syria, India, and Constantinople. In this trip he convinced the missionaries of the logic of his "recommendations to break up the large stations, found village churches, ordain native pastors for them, and give up English language secondary schools in favor of vernacular-language schools."[7] We can see reflected here the clear focus of the missionary task for Anderson, later expressed as the mission's policy: "Missions are instituted for the spread of a scriptural, self-propagating Christianity. This is their only aim."

When Anderson says "scriptural Christianity," he is using St. Paul as the paradigm for what is scriptural about Christianity, and more specifically Christian mission. Paul's method was to evangelize, gather together converts, and turn them over to "native" leadership. Anderson is very clear that the missionary goal, according to Paul, was not social transformation nor to promote civilization. This may be the fruit of local and indigenous church development, but it was not the goal for the missionary. All other institutional work—Bible translation, schools, clinics, orphanages—were to promote the single goal of evangelizing and gathering into churches under native leadership. By 1869 he was very clear about this process:

---

[5] Upon retirement, Anderson wrote some important books on the history of various board missions (two volumes on the Far East, one each on Hawaii and India) and about his mission history and theory: *Memorial Volume of the First Fifty Years of the American Board of Commissioners* (Boston: American Board of Commissioners for Foreign Missions, 1861) and *Foreign Missions, Their Relations and Claims* (New York: Charles Scribner, 1869). Most of his writing during his working life was published in the Board's Annual Report and in *Missionary Herald* and *The Tracts of the American Board*. Many of his writings were collected in a volume by R. Pierce Beaver, *To Advance the Gospel: Selections from the Writings of Rufus Anderson* (Grand Rapids: Eerdmans, 1967).

[6] American Board of Commissioners for Foreign Missions (ecumenical, but mostly Congregational).

[7] R. Pierce Beaver, "The Legacy of Rufus Anderson," in *Occasional Bulletin of Missionary Research* 3 (July 1979): 94.

The means employed were spiritual; namely the gospel for Christ. The power relied upon for giving efficacy to these means was divine; namely the promised aid of the Holy Spirit. The main success was among the members of the middle and lower classes of society; and the responsibilities for self-government, self-support, and self-propagation were thrown at once upon the several churches.[8]

Two items are of particular interest for us in this quotation. First, Anderson observed that the early New Testament churches were not elitist or upper class. The gospel was attractive to the poor, and the early churches were mostly made up of the poor.[9] This did not dissuade Paul from turning the churches over to local leadership. This also explains the recommendation he made after his missionary tour to cease with elitist English-speaking schools and teach only in the vernacular. Second, the three-self terms are used exactly as they would be used in 1949 and 1950—eighty years later—by Wu Yaozong, Han Wenzao, and others. We must remember, however, that this terminology was a product of proper missionary practice that would focus on minimal (foreign) missionary activity (preaching and training local pastors) and immediate devolution of missionary presence.

Henry Venn (1796–1873), born the same year as Rufus Anderson, was an Anglican from the other side of the Atlantic who independently developed very similar views to Anderson. Venn served for thirty-one years as the general secretary of the Church Missionary Society in London (1841–1872). Venn came to nearly identical conclusions to Anderson, but he did this by asking a different question. Venn was driven by one question: "What gives a church integrity?" What Venn meant by this was similar to what Anderson meant by looking to the New Testament example to see what Paul's churches looked like and why they developed as they did. Both were concerned with missional work that led to local churches and local church life that had its own spiritual and social integrity. Venn was convinced that local church integrity was dependent on local church self-worth. This self-worth, he later concluded, required simply that the church must be self-supporting, self-propagating, and self-governing. Of greatest importance, or at least what received the greatest emphasis for Venn, was

---

[8] Anderson, *Foreign Missions*, 61.
[9] We should note that there was no middle class in first-century Palestine, so it would be more accurate to identify the Pauline churches as mostly poor with some elites.

the first: self-support. A church that could not support itself lacked self-worth and integrity.

From the start, Venn told missionaries, they must see themselves as working themselves out of a job. His term for this was "the euthanasia of mission." There are many similarities between Venn and Anderson—in fact the similarities are quite remarkable—but most important is the shared assumption that missionary practice must have the vision of three-self from the start. Different national church leaders, missionaries, and executives emphasized different missional elements, but all three "selfs" were seen as critical for both of these early theorists.

John L. Nevius (1829–1893) was an American Presbyterian missionary who worked in Shandong Province. Nevius, educated at Princeton Theological Seminary, was a prolific writer about Chinese culture,[10] mission strategy, and theory. Arriving in China in 1854, he can be considered one of the second-generation theorists of three-self principles. From the very beginning of his missionary work in Ningpo (Ningbo) in Chekiang (Zhejiang) province, Nevius was committed to a "three-self" type of approach. First, he traveled widely to make contact with many villages. Second, he established a "station" at San-poh using no outside support, such as payment to Chinese for work. This out-station was established in 1857, and by 1861 Lu Sing-sang was ordained as the first ruling elder. A few years later two other elders (Zia Ying-tong and Tsiang Nying-kwe) were ordained as pastors. By 1859, though, Nevius had already moved. Thus the station was already fully self-governing, self-propagating, and self-supporting after only two and a half years.

Next, in 1861 Nevius and his wife, Helen, moved to Shandong, and within months he had written a letter to the New York offices explaining his strategy of immediately forming a synod for China and establishing a theological school for training pastors. The local synod was needed to oversee the school, and the school was needed to train "native pastors." Thus, from the beginning of his ministry Nevius was clear about his method—what he would later call the "new system"—and yet in the early

---

[10]It is telling that his first work written both for better understanding on the part of Americans and (we might guess) for his own understanding of his context was *China and the Chinese: A General Description of the Country and Its Inhabitants; Its Civilization and Form of Government; Its Religion and Social Institutions; Its Intercourse with Other Nations; and Its Present Conditions and Prospects* (New York: Harper and Brothers, 1869).

years he tried to introduce the Presbyterian form of government and worship as the only viable forms for all Christians. He later moved away from this ecclesial rigidity.

In 1886[11] he wrote a series of articles in the *Chinese Recorder* that were later (1895) reprinted as a book titled *Methods of Mission Work*. The articles, written for missionaries working in China, are very carefully nuanced in their understanding of work and relationships. It is in this interesting work that Nevius makes a direct attack on the old way: paying foreign agents, paying for buildings, relying on foreign missionaries to do most of the evangelism, and building large institutions.

Actually, Nevius notes that the whole "new system" stabs a dagger at the heart of the "paid native agency." He bases his arguments, in part, on the observations of Dr. Kellogg, formerly of the Theological Seminary at Allegheny, Pennsylvania (now Pittsburgh Theological Seminary), who was then working in India. Kellogg defends the "ancient and apostolic practice of ordering elders in each church." Thus, he reasons that too often missionaries have been quick to "hire" a lone pastor when the pattern of unpaid but ordained elders would be better and more consistent with Presbyterianism. This is a description of mission to the villages and less to the major cities. This is church development founded on lay leadership, not on paid clergy or missionaries. This is (again) identification in language and life with the common folk rather than the elite. After all, Nevius's first book was on Chinese culture and religions. Although it has seldom been noted, we might stand back from a distance and note both the great similarities with the old Jesuit approach, as well as some great contrasts. Nevius's approach was not elitist but *koine*. Both the Jesuits and those following the "new method" wanted to develop churches that were indigenous: a Chinese Christianity. Nevius, however started with peasants:

> [A paid agent] is placed in a position unfavorable to the development of a strong, healthy, Christian character. Some of these men, originally farmers, shop keepers, peddlers, or laborers in the fields, find themselves advanced to

---

[11] This was the year of the founding of the Student Volunteer Movement in America—which would send thousands of well-educated missionaries to China in the next decades—and just two years after Horace Allen left Shanghai to become the first medical missionary, and first Presbyterian, to work in Korea.

a position for which they are by previous habits and training unsuited. The long gown and the affected scholarly air are not becoming to them, and they naturally lose the respect of their neighbors and their influence over them.[12]

Nevius's articles were captivating and very popular, even though he was mostly telling what they had done in Shandong. The ideas were immediately picked up by the pioneer Presbyterians working in Korea, and so, in 1890, Horace Underwood of the American Presbyterian mission in Seoul invited Nevius to give an orientation to the Korea missionaries who had just begun their work six years earlier (1884). This 1890 summer conference, more than any other single conference, set the future for Christianity in Korea. As Underwood later remembered, the main points of the conference were the following:

> First, to let each man "Abide in the calling wherein he was found," teaching that each was to be an individual worker for Christ, and to live Christ in his own neighborhood, supporting himself by his trade. Secondly, to develop Church methods and machinery only so far as the native Church was able to take care of and manage the same. Third, as far as the Church itself was able to provide the mend and the means, to set aside those who seemed the better qualified, to do evangelistic work among their neighbors. Fourth, to let the natives provide their own church building, which were to be native in architecture, and of such style as the local church could afford to put up.[13]

Roland Allen (1868–1947) is remembered as a prophetic mission strategist, biblical radical, pre-Pentecostal Anglican (SPG),[14] and a difficult colleague. This is quite a reputation. Allen first went as a missionary to China in 1895, serving in Beijing, preparing young men for the ordained ministry. He quickly grasped the complex nature of preparing Chinese for an "Anglican" ministry, and then he was forced to think more deeply about foreign intrusion during the Boxer Uprising in 1900. He later reflected on the role of the missionary and the nature of the church:

> The continued presence of a foreigner seems to me to produce an evil effect. The native genius is cramped by his presence and cannot work with him. The Christians tend to sit still and let him do everything for them, denying all

---

[12]John L. Nevius, *Methods of Mission Work* (New York: Foreign Missions Library, 1895), 11.
[13]Horace G. Underwood, *The Call of Korea: Political, Social, Religious* (New York: Fleming H. Revell, 1908), 110.
[14]Society for the Propagation of the Gospel in Foreign Parts (Anglican, High Church mission).

responsibility.... I should feel disposed to group all foreigners together in one place to avoid having them reside in more places than can be helped. A visit of two or three months stirs up the Church. Long continued residence stifles it.[15]

This became an ongoing point of reflection for Allen. He spent the rest of his life working and writing to see church ministry brought more into the New Testament pattern, which for him meant greater freedom for the local Christians to develop and control their own church at the earliest stage possible. Another theme, for a later paper, was his emphasis on the work of and dependence on the Holy Spirit in mission and ministry, but it should be mentioned since the global church is becoming more and aware of the importance of the Pentecostal movement.[16]

For our purposes it is important to understand how thorough, radical, and threatening Allen's ideas were. His later working out of his missionary principles was written in his book *The Spontaneous Expansion of the Church* (1927). In this volume Allen argues that real orthodoxy—the development of real Christianity in a "mission field"—is not something that is enforced by rules or foreign powers. Real orthodoxy is chosen in freedom under the power of the Holy Spirit. Thus, his pnematology was the foundation for his missiology. His understanding of the Holy Spirit led him to the conclusion that the first work of the missionary should be to train his converts in real independence. In order to fulfill this responsibility, he put forward three key principles. First, "native converts" must be taught to recognize their responsibility as members of the church. The missionary must never do for the "natives" anything that they could do for themselves. Second, missionaries must avoid the introduction of any foreign element unless it is absolutely essential. When foreign elements are introduced (books, vestments, ornaments, building designs), then the church becomes the foreigners' church. Third, the missionaries must always be retiring from the people; they must work so as to be dispensable. If they become indispensable to the people, then they have failed. The missionary should patiently watch while the Holy

---

[15]USPG, *Africa and Asia*, vol. 2, 1902. Quoted from Raymond Eveleigh, "Roland Allen: Prophet of Non-stipendiary Ministry" (master's thesis, University of Hull, 1995), 23-24, www.revray.co.uk/ministry/nsm.html.

[16]See, for example, "Spiritual Churches: Independents and Pentecostals," in Scott W. Sunquist, *The Unexpected Christian Century: The Reversal and Transformation of Global Christianity, 1900–2000* (Grand Rapids: Baker Academic, 2015), 124-33.

Spirit transforms the young, local believers into a new form of Christian life that is different from that of the missionary.

Long before his ideas were fully developed, in 1903, Allen went back to China for nine months and, with his bishop's approval, began to put some of his ideas into effect. At the time he was basing his instincts on the work of John L. Nevius as it was applied in Korea. Although medical difficulties necessitated his returning to England, he had enough time to confirm his theories. Roland Allen came to the conclusion that missionaries in China should stay in one place no longer than one year—like St. Paul. Any longer and the people become dependent on them, and local Christians never rise to take leadership of the local churches. Allen followed Nevius also in his articles, where he tells stories of how he practiced what he was teaching. At one time he was asked to start a school, but he refused, saying that any school that is started must be their own, with their own teachers. As a mission secretary Allen had the advantage of traveling to diverse "mission fields" to test these ideas in different cultural contexts. In 1912, after reflecting on the work of missionaries in India and having met the (future) Bishop Samuel Azariah of Dornakal, he wrote his famous book, *Missionary Methods: St. Paul's or Ours* (1912). In this book he strings together his radical approach to missionary work; this is the approach that lost him his job in China and then caused him to step down from his vicariate in England. His thesis is based on the assumption that the Holy Spirit can direct the church in each particular context with a minimal of missionary work, a minimum of foreign support, a minimum of foreign theology, and a maximum of teaching in the Bible. In the following passage, he describes the typical missionary situation that needs correction through his carefully nuanced version of three-self principles.

> [The missionary] is assisted by a number of native clergy, catechists and teachers whose work it is his duty to *superintend*. These again will look to him for guidance and encouragement, and probably for definite and particular orders in every conceivable circumstance that may arise, even if they do not depend upon his initiative and inspiration to save them from stagnation. In the central station he will almost certainly find a considerable organization and elaborate establishment which the native Christian community has not created and cannot at present *support* without financial aid

from abroad. He will find that they have been more or less crammed with a complete system of theological and ecclesiastical doctrines which they have not been able to digest. He will find an elaborate system of finance which makes him in the last resort responsible for the raising and administration of all funds in his district. He will find that as regards *baptism*, the recommendation of candidates for office in the church, and the exercise of discipline, the whole burden of responsibility is laid upon his shoulders alone. He will find in a word that he is expected to act as an almost uncontrolled autocrat subject only to the admonitions of his bishop or the directions of a committee of white men.[17]

I have highlighted three words that show Allen's diagnosis of the problem is centered on authority (self-governance), money (self-support), and baptism (self-propagation, which was almost completely missing). Allen's concern for what he calls the independence or liberty of the "native" Christians was rejected by the Anglican Church in China, and his high standards for the Christian life later led him to the conclusion that he should step down from his vicariate. And so he did. This great theorist of missionary principles spent most of his days outside the very church and mission that he so loved and for whom he was speaking.

Three-Self Understandings in Korea

As we mentioned above, it was in 1890, just six years after the first resident missionaries arrived in Korea, that the young band of Presbyterians[18] decided to invite one of the most well-known Presbyterian missionaries in China, John L. Nevius, to speak to all of their missionaries at their annual retreat. Two of the great pioneers in Korea attended that "conference," Samuel A. Moffett[19] and Horace Underwood. It was a rare opportunity for a newly "opened" country to have all of the missionaries in a single retreat, so that they could benefit from a seasoned missionary who had worked in the "neighborhood." In this case, the neighboring country, China, was, at

---

[17]Roland Allen, *Missionary Methods: St. Paul's or Ours; A Study in Four Provinces* (London: Robert Scott, 1912), 152.
[18]Horace Underwood, first ordained Presbyterian missionary to Korea, invited Nevius.
[19]Moffett's body was returned to be buried in Korea (May 2006), showing the respect that the Presbyterian Church in China has for this pioneer and advocate of three-self principles.

that time, an unfriendly colonial regional presence.[20] It was an auspicious moment for Korea and for ecumenical Christianity.

What do we know about how Nevius was heard and understood by these Presbyterian missionaries? First, it is very clear that the Presbyterians working in Korea took the teachings about education—basic Bible training for pastors and evangelists—very seriously. Correspondence with the mission office in New York is filled with debate and final resolution that a university education is not the priority for Presbyterian mission. Basic training in Bible and preaching is what missionaries were to provide, and then they were to "get out of the way." In northern Korea, where Christianity was strongest before the Korean War, Moffett had semiannual Bible training or leadership training classes. These were held after the fall harvest for three weeks and then before the spring planting (again for three weeks). When the lay leaders returned, they spent the next five months teaching everything they learned, and then they would return for more. In addition, Moffett would travel around making pastoral visits (like a good "bishop") and reach out to new areas to invite others for the lay training. The founding of the Presbyterian Seminary in Pyeong Yang in 1901 was an extension of these Bible classes.

Second, we have evidence that the "self-support" principle was applied almost legalistically. For example, when Moffett was ready for the Koreans to build the first church in Pyeong Yang in 1895, the mission board wanted to send (or assumed that they had to send) money to build it. Moffett fired back a letter that said (in my paraphrase), "Absolutely not! If the Koreans want a church building, they will make the sacrifice and pay for it themselves. They will build a building which they can afford, they can keep up and that is theirs. If we want to encourage them by giving the last 10 percent, we can do that, but it must be their building." This was the principle applied in most all of the Presbyterian work. In that same year, he wrote an article for the *Missionary Review of the World*, "The Work of the Spirit in North Korea": "We heard their [Korean Christians'] plans for building churches, for which they had already begun the collection of money; and we rejoiced that the work was being undertaken on the basis of self-support.... Brother

---

[20]Korea had been a protectorate of China, sending embassies to pay homage for centuries. At this time China was decreasing and Japan was increasing its influence in Korea.

McKenzie wrote us, 'We are waiting for the snow to clear to begin building *the church, the first Korean church with Korean money alone.'"*[21]

Third, the Presbyterians formed a presbytery in 1907, less than twenty years after the first resident missionary arrived. Not only was an indigenous church structure established in less than twenty years, but the majority of the presbytery members were Korean. Thus, from the very first meeting, the Koreans had the majority vote in governing their own church.

It must be added that the Japanese helped in the development of "three-self" Christianity in Korea. The missionaries arrived just years before the Chinese were routed by the Japanese for control of the peninsula. This was the Japanese nation's second try to control the Hermit Kingdom, and this time they succeeded, for about fifty years. Thus, the Koreans went from Chinese oppression to Japanese oppression. In the transition, it was the missionaries who brought a message of liberation and self-worth through the gospel of Jesus Christ. Jesus, a poor and oppressed "peasant," or *minjung*, was one of them. The message was not lost on the people. It was the Christians, both Korean and American, who cared for the diseased (in the typhoid epidemic), visited the poor, educated the powerless, and preached peace in the midst of turmoil. Proof of this identification of Jesus Christ with the suffering of the Koreans is that the 1919 independence movement was led almost exclusively by Christians and former Tonghak liberationists. The Tonghak movement had been put down, but the same spirit of advocacy against oppression was shared into the twentieth century by Tonghaks and Presbyterian ministers and elders.

Was the Three-Self Idea a Failure in China?

It takes very little imagination to see that the three-self ideal as envisioned by the four mission theorists above and as practiced in Korea was far different from the experience in China. In China, church leaders met with Minister Chou En Lai in 1950 to discuss the ongoing imperialistic elements that were woven into the very fabric of the Chinese church. Christianity in China was

---

[21]Samuel A. Moffett, "The Work of the Spirit in North Korea," *Missionary Review of the World*, November 1895, 833, 836. Italics are in the original, indicating how significant this was for the Presbyterian missionaries in Korea. It is interesting that Roland Allen, writing twenty years later, will also discuss self-support in terms of pneumatology, the work of the Holy Spirit.

still a foreign religion with foreign control and foreign governance of large and numerous institutions. Many of the concerns of Roland Allen continued to plague the Chinese church. The reaction of Christian leaders after the liberation of China was to lead the church to liberation as expressed in three-self principles. Why was this necessary, since two of the four great three-self theorists had worked in China? Was the Chinese church similar to the missionary churches in Korea, or was the Chinese church in some ways unique? I believe the historical evidence is clear that the Chinese church was unique—at least it was unique in how strong the foreign control was after 150 years of missionary work. A complete reappraisal would require looking into Christian movements of resistance against missionary domination[22] as well as comparing missionary budgets, institutional development (especially the number of schools, colleges, and hospitals), and mission stations in China with other mission fields. I will make a humble start on such a study by looking at a single letter from a Presbyterian missionary working in Korea.

Robert E. Speer, the general secretary of the Board of Foreign Missions Presbyterian Church in the United States and one of the great promoters of Rufus Anderson's principles in mission, had great concern about the direction of the China mission. His concern was that Rufus Anderson's three-self principles that he had studied and promoted were not practiced in the China mission. To investigate the situation, he sent an outsider from a neighboring country, one firmly committed to three-self principles, to visit and make a report.

Samuel Austin Moffett visited China in 1926 on behalf of the board in New York, attending conferences and interviewing missionaries and Chinese church leaders (mostly pastors). Upon completion of his official visit, he wrote a nine-page letter to Speer that, I believe, is a rare window into comparative Christian contextualization and indigenization. Although Protestant missionary work had been going on in China for nearly 120 years earlier (1807), and work in Korea began seventy-seven years later (1884), the grasp and implementation of three-self principles were quite different. Moffett makes eight observations: the first and third of the observations are

---

[22]Antiforeignism produced more than revolutionary Boxers; it also produced antiforeign churches (the Little Flock of Xiaoqun, the Jesus Family, etc.) and antiforeign individuals such as evangelist John Sung Shang Chieh.

positive, and the other six are hard hitting and critical. All this came from a very positive, upbeat pioneer missionary to Korea.[23] First we will look at the positive observations and then the problems.

Moffett, coming from the small, relatively homogenous, peninsular nation of Korea, was overwhelmed by the size of the "work" in China. He is overwhelmed by the "vastness of the task" and calls for more, not less, work "(if properly used)." This little proviso is very telling and points to later, very deep, criticisms. Second, Moffett says he probably should have mentioned first his appreciation of the great work that had already been accomplished. He lists the great work done by both missionaries and Chinese leaders, mentioning many by name. It is interesting that he mentions five Chinese leaders by name and only two missionaries.

Then, the other seven and a half pages focus on criticisms of the missionary strategies in China. First, he says there is a loss of a positive message concerning the power and triumph of God in human lives. The missionaries have compromised and preach "the fruits of Christianity rather than Christianity itself." Here he is talking about the mission of civilization and social uplift that was very much a part of missionary theory in the early part of the twentieth century.

His second criticism is that the church in China is "lamentably dependent upon subsidies and has been greatly injured thereby." "Self supporting churches are pitiably few, and even many of those reported self-supporting are not really independent of foreign aid. . . . In private conversation almost all frankly admit failure along this line and acknowledge and regret the mistaken policy." With a mind for exactitude, he gives statistics: "After fifty years of work in Nanking they have but two self-supporting churches, only sixteen groups with 2,000 communicants one of these 'self-supporting churches' has fallen back on the mission for $150 a year for repairs." "Shantung," where Nevius had pioneered, "with 20,000 Christians reports but eight self-supporting churches, not all

---

[23] A copy of this letter is in the author's possession and is from the Samuel A. Moffett archives. Moffett's letters have been compiled by his daughter-in-law, Eileen Moffett, wife of Samuel Hugh Moffett. They are at present on electronic file, but if printed come to over one thousand pages of text. The letters reveal a positive, forward-looking family man who is unflappable in the midst of many petty concerns.

of these being really self-supporting."[24] "In Ningpo, of 20 pastors, two are receiving Chinese support and even this support comes largely from non-residents." In case the reader is not sure how Moffett is evaluating the China work, he makes it explicit in the next sentence. "I wish the missionaries could be induced to read sympathetically Nevius' 'Methods of Mission Work' . . . and Roland Allen's 'St. Paul's Methods and Ours.'" Then he comes up with a key sentence that links his whole theory and much of the three-self genetic double helix, the two foundational principles of independent churches and lay Bible training: "If short term classes and Bible Institutes could be provided so that earnest Christians (however few in number at first) could be encouraged to study with a view to personal voluntary work, I believe they would do more for the growth of the Church and for progress in self-support than the long term schools . . . where the prospect of employment is in the minds of all."

Third, Moffett focuses on something he is very upset about and that he sees as the enemy of real church independence. "I hardly know how to express in moderate terms my impression of the undue development of the educational institutions on a scale out of all proportion to the Church and in water-tight compartments almost wholly unrelated to the Church or the evangelistic work." Such large institutions cannot be self-supporting: "I more firmly than ever believe that the development of institutional work should be secondary to the development of the Church and should be made for the sake of contributing to the up-building of the Church." He then goes on to talk about the overdevelopment of universities and the loss of interest and "lack of sympathy for the development of the Church." To drive home his point, he lists a host of problems related to the educational work of the church and then lists many quotations from local church leaders and missionaries that prove his point. This is his largest criticism, and it takes up three pages of his nine-page letter.

Related to the previous two concerns, Moffett observes a lack of instruction in the Bible. He understands that a strong foundation for social

---

[24] This is a little off our topic at hand, but the Southern Baptists recognized early on that the Presbyterians in Shandong were very wealthy and had "imposing male and female schools, their host of native assistants and hospitals with other pecuniary attractions." These, they say, "have quite overshadowed our simple evangelistic labors." Nevius's influence in his home province seems to have been quite limited. From "Proceedings of the Southern Baptist Convention, 33rd Session, 43rd Year" (Atlanta, 1888), 40.

welfare must come from good grounding in Scripture. Without this, he says, "I do not see how a strong, self-sacrificing Church can be built up except as it is instructed in the Scriptures." He later remarks, "The foundations for this must first be laid in the possession of a Christianity which is to be applied to life and unless greater emphasis is laid on instruction in the Scriptures with faith in the power of great supernatural truths to transform life, I see little hope for a strong Church in China or anywhere. I was told repeatedly that the YMCA has largely given up its Bible classes."

Fifth, Moffett remarks on the need for a few outstanding pastors as leaders of the church: Chinese leaders who can build "up a Chinese Church as a self-reliant, self-supporting Church with enthusiasm for aggressive evangelism" (or self-propagation). He then at the close of the letter makes it very personal and specific: "I wish that such men as Lee Sung Lin, Chang Fang, and James Yih could be induced to set themselves to the task of establishing local churches which will definitely aim to become self-supporting, independent churches, unwilling to be dependent long upon foreign salaries." It appears that the more imperialistic model of mission and ecclesiology had clouded the minds of Chinese leaders from seeking the very goals that would make for—and later made for—healthy Chinese churches.

Finally, on a more structural level, there was still a question of the relationship of mission to church, something that should have been resolved years before. In Korea, for example, the local Korean presbytery was established under Korean control after only twenty years. Moffett's concern is that the demands for autonomy and control of foreign funds were being made with a concern for money, and not with the larger view of a Chinese church independent in all areas. The call for independence was too late, and it was coming from the wrong people.

An Observation, an Evaluation, and a Caution

Judged by the statistics given in our opening paragraphs, we would have to make the observation that "three-self" was not a reality—not even a distant dream—at the time of liberation in China. The church was dependent on foreign leadership, even after 150 years of Protestant missionary work, and the church was burdened with large institutions that required foreign leadership and funding. Although there was very important work that had been accomplished in the areas of scholarship, translation, famine relief, and other areas, the church itself was still mission dependent. Even though some of the most clearly articulated three-self theory came from Nevius and Allen, both people who worked in China, these principles were quickly sidelined by the newer possibility thinking of Western academics, businesspeople, and mission leaders. Clear evidence that the three-self ideal had failed comes from the comments of Minister Zhou En Lai in his meetings with the Christian leaders, May 17–19, 1950. To paraphrase, he said that the church must develop into a self-governing, self-propagating, and self-supporting organization; it must train its own leaders, develop its own methods of self-support, and learn to do without foreign money. Thus a sudden transformation of Chinese Christianity was required by the government because the early and deliberate transfer never took place.[25] Further evidence, of course, can be seen in the very candid and lucid letter sent by Moffett after he traveled around China, attended conferences, and interviewed both missionaries and local Christian leaders. What does this mean for our understanding of Christian development and missionary outreach, and for how we can best research these two issues?

First, we have seen that moving our vision from studying only one local context to studying the movements of people and their crosscultural relationships gives us new insights. In this instance it involves very little movement: Nevius to Korea and Moffett to China. As a result of these movements, Korean Christianity is transformed, and Christianity in China is given a new perspective. If we simply had information about Christianity from Chinese Christians, or just from missionaries in China, we would have had a very limited understanding. However, when we add the multiple crosscultural perspectives of an American who had lived most of thirty-six years in Korea who takes time to observe in China, new vistas of historical awareness open up. In our study of Christianity we must always look for these multiple cultural windows and look for the movements of people to better understand Christianity as a movement.

---

[25] Further evidence of the failure of Christianity to identify itself as Chinese (a central concern of three-self theorists) is the fact of the Boxer identification of foreign Christians as the primary hairy people to be opposed, and the antiforeign campaigns of the 1920s that were directed very much against the church.

Second, I believe we see here how China was always a special case for Western missionaries. Even though more liberal or progressive missional theory was available and practiced in other regions, China continued to attract the best, the brightest, and the wealthiest. It was so difficult for the missionaries and their agencies to resist the possibility to set up another university, to build bigger and more elaborate churches, and to hire more church workers. China was always the supreme mission field—the jewel in the mission crown—and I believe that being such a special case worked against commonly accepted three-self principles.

This bring us to an important evaluation of mission historians. To wit: "What is conservative and what is liberal regarding Christian and missional practice?" Missionaries working in Korea, according to most Korean historians, were conservative in their theology, often reacting against modernism and higher-critical biblical interpretation. And yet, these "conservative" missionaries were very liberal in their approach to local cultures and in working almost in a liberationist fashion with the poor in the villages. For example, in that same article written by Samuel Austin Moffett in the *Missionary Review of the World* (the article that identifies his commitment to early self-support), he also sounds like a modern liberation or *minjung* theologian. In writing about his encounters with the liberationist Tonghaks, Moffett finds that they have many of the same concerns as the missionaries for Korea. "They recognized the fact that Christians are the true friends of the oppressed Korea." The Tonghaks offered their large assembly building for Moffett's Christian meetings, and he even calls the Tonghaks "so called rebels." Like the missionaries, these "so called rebels" are opposed to the "unjust, wholly unprincipled and cruel officials." Moffett concludes this section of his letter saying, "Our hearts go out in sympathy toward the poor, misguided Tong Haks, who are more sinned against than sinning."[26] This came from a conservative, some might incorrectly say today, "fundamentalist" missionary who quickly turned over control of churches to poor farmers. We may have to reevaluate what we mean by conservative missionaries.

China, on the other hand, had many more progressive missionaries, people like Presbyterian missionary Pearl S. Buck and her husband, who

---

[26]Moffett, "Work of the Spirit in North Korea," 834.

taught agricultural science. By all measures they were progressive, downplaying the differences between religions and focusing on social progress (through education) rather than conversion, biblical knowledge, and church planting. Yet, many of these more progressive Christians were from elite academies in the United States, and they carried a fairly elitist, progressive approach. Their goal could more accurately be described as that of civilizing the Chinese and Chinese culture. Regarding culture and social transformation, this was very conservative and, at the same time, very elitist. As Dana Robert, missiologist from Boston University, has commented,

> Theological conservatism and cultural conservatism do not necessarily go together. He [Mark Banker] assumes that cultural flexibility and theological liberalism somehow accompany each other. . . . But as anyone who knows missionaries can attest, they seem out of step with the mainstreams of both left and right because they often combine evangelical convictions with cultural flexibility.[27]

Finally, a caution must be given as we conclude our study. Although we have been somewhat critical of the strategy of the missionaries in China, we must remember this important truth: Christianity did develop and even grew in China. Even under severe persecution and the closing of churches, schools, and clinics, Christianity became three-self under Mao's rule. So maybe we should end with Moffett's positive assertions regarding the church in China: "Let us be grateful for such men as Ding Lee Mei, Lee Sung Lin, Chang Fang, Kwang Lan Chun and doubtless many others—men of strong character, zeal and consecration, and for such a school for Bible instruction as that for women in Nanking, and such a school as the True Light Middle School in Canton." Sometimes the gospel takes root in the hearts of believers in spite of missionary efforts as much as because of missionary efforts.

---

[27]"Changing Perceptions of Missionaries and Cultures," *Journal of Presbyterian History* 81 (2003): 368. Mark Banker was a historian of Presbyterian mission work in the Americas, mostly among the Cherokees.

12

Mission and Migration

An Introductory Theology

A Migration Story

In 1979 my wife and I had a newborn baby, and we were involved in a small group Bible study with other young couples, all in their twenties. One evening after our study, we were sitting in the living room talking about the Bible study, and the conversation turned to our need to practice what we were studying and believed. We all felt guilty. We were "study" Christians, not really "engaged" Christians. Then one of our group members noticed on the coffee table a Christian magazine with the following advertisement on its cover: "Needed: Sponsors for Vietnamese Refugees." We were intrigued. We looked further. "Twenty-four-hour hotline to volunteer to sponsor refugee families." Still young, we did not think twice about impulsively calling the number. That one call started it all.

Less than two months later I was driving to the airport with a Vietnamese engineering student from the local university to pick up our family of five: a widow and four children. They were thin, scared, and silent. I was scared. What were we thinking? A widow and four children under the age of twelve were coming to live with me and my wife and our six-month-old baby. We had no idea what we were doing. However, in the next year we all learned a lot about war, violence, loss, hope, determination, and the importance of family connections. First it was one widow and her four children, and then another widow (a sister-in-law) and her two children lived with us. After one year they all boarded a bus and went across the country to live with two nephews on the West Coast. We showed them the *Jesus Film* in Chinese and Vietnamese, we gave them Bibles, and said goodbye.

Multiply this scene by tens of millions and you get a picture of the movements of people—mostly because of war and poverty—all around the world each year. This picture is not typical, however. Most migrants do not have small group Bible studies with plenty of resources from a local church to help them get established. Today all of the six children and the two former widows own their own homes in California. It is an atypical "success" story. Most migrants grovel in urban slums or live a scared existence in crowded, temporary shelters. Most migrants will not be introduced to Jesus; they exist on our margins as unwanted invaders. This is the reason for a new area of mission studies focused on migration, or what is often called "diaspora mission."[1] One of the purposes of this chapter is to help the church reverse the global trend of merely tolerating our new guests and to move toward relationship and engagement. It is imperative that we see immigrants and migrants as opportunities both for us to ministry to them and to receive ministry from them. Migrants are not just a burden; they are also gifted.

Some Initial Considerations

First, migration is as old as Adam and Eve being cast out of the garden, but only recently has migration been linked to mission. The two are strange partners. Migration is people or a people group moving out. Mission involves particular Christians going out to the nations. In one case we are in control, choosing to go, after sufficient preparation, to another's culture. In the other case, we are sitting still, and people come in our neighborhood . . . uninvited. We are usually unprepared. In either case, there is movement, dislocation, the need for translation and contextualization. But whereas we have a whole theology and tradition of sending missionaries, we have very little in the way of understanding how to prepare for mission as migration. This chapter is a humble attempt to fill some of this gap. We will look at the larger context of migration both biblically and historically, and then we will establish some theological guidelines for a theology of migration and mission. In conclusion we look a few stories and then we consider some more practical issues.

Second, from the very beginning, Christianity had been expressed in translation and border crossing. I believe this is not accidental, but integral

---

[1] The University of London established one of the first centers in migration and diaspora studies in 2003 (MA degree, and then the center in 2007) in its School of Oriental and African Studies.

to Christianity. In other words, Christianity is a faith that does not stay still. The *normal* Christian existence is one of movement to spread the glory of God over all the nations and in all the earth. In the garden of Eden God condescends to come into his creation and to speak in and to his creation; then he sends Adam and Eve out—they are migrants from the garden. As we will see, the normal historical trajectory of Christianity has translation and border crossing as a major subtheme.

Third, we need to consider the concept of borderlands. Borderlands are places where people and cultures collide. Borderlands are places where we negotiate identity (Do you have a passport? Do you have a visa? Do you have Malaysian Ringgit?). Borderlands are train stations, airports, and wet markets. Borderlands are refugee camps, squatter camps, and urban centers. Some areas of the world, because of location or natural resources, are always borderlands. The Old Silk Road (now becoming a superhighway) is a borderland. Singapore is a borderland. The meaning of the word *Ukraine* is "borderland." Borderlands are creative places, but they can also be hotly contested lands with much violence. Borderlands are historically significant places, and now we see they are missiologically significant places. It may be a little provocative to say this, but borderlands are really Christian homelands.

Wherever a variety of people come up against one another and need to communicate with one another, we have entered a borderland. In the past, mission stations were manufactured borderlands where European or North Americans lived in the midst of a Tamil Hindu or a Thai Buddhist culture. Today borderlands are growing faster than we can trace in the urban centers of Asia, as well as Africa and Latin America. Borderlands are growing, becoming more complex, and becoming more important if we are to reach unreached people today. This development in human existence is a hopeful sign for Christianity.

Fourth, borderlands, as I will soon explain, is a central concept to the vitality and the spread of Christianity. In places and times where Christianity embraced or entered borderlands it thrived. Where it resisted the diversity of borderlands and the richness of necessary translation, Christianity tended to turn in on itself. Where do we see resistance to borderlands (and border crossing) in Christian history? Whenever there is a strong dominant culture or where there is an empire—imposing the religious/cultural will on others. Medieval Europe, after the migration of Asian tribes into Europe, resisted borderlands. Christendom is a form of resistance to borderlands. Foreign elements were not engaged or received, nor their languages and cultures translated. Instead, medieval European culture resisted other cultures, and we see this through the imposition of the Latin language and the long history of the Crusades. In this historical period in Europe and western Asia, the church engaged in attempted political and cultural conquest rather than cultural engagement and translation.

Being critical of this history does not mean that we now see the many other options that Christians had. There just weren't many other options at the time of the expanding Islamic caliphate. It is not that Christians simply chose the most violent and un-Christian of the options out of many other choices. We must remember that the violence against Christians on pilgrimage left few options for European Christians. One of the only other options was also not a healthy Christian response, and that was to "stay home," isolated from the world. My point is not to condemn Europeans for the Crusades (necessarily),[2] but to point out that the power and cultural dominance of Western Christendom in the form of the Holy Roman Empire *prevented borderlands encounters*. There are many other times when Christianity did not spread or when it became less vital because of empire, but that is not the main point of this essay.[3] As we all know, we can live in a borderland situation and refuse to accept it. Many of the migrant communities from southern and eastern Europe who came to North America resisted accepting their borderlands status in eastern cities. We often resist the deep borderland encounters that allow the gospel of Jesus Christ to be liberated among the nations.

Let's start then with this simple affirmation:

Christianity is nurtured and grows on borderlands because of the necessity of **retranslating the message with each encounter**. *In these borderland encounters the Gospel is* **re-expressed and recentered even as it reaches more cultures**.

---

[2]Compare Desmond Seward's *The Monks of War* (New York: Penguin Books, 1972) with Rodney Stark's *God's Battalions, The Case for the Crusades* (New York: HarperOne, 2009).

[3]Or I can mention the British and German and French empires in Africa. Mission work was limited in its results because of the dominant European culture imposed on African societies. And yet, the translation work that was done alone made up for all the other problems. Because the message was translated into local languages, genuine encounters occurred, and Christianity began to thrive after the empires drew back. See Sunquist, *The Unexpected Christian Century* (Grand Rapids: Baker, 2015), 90-93, for a discussion on decolonization.

There are three concepts here that are important. First, retranslation of the gospel message and life must take place. When people move into the neighborhood who speak a different language and live a different culture, we are given the opportunity to rethink the meaning of our message and our community, *for* the foreigner in our land. Borderlands require constant translating. Second, and closely related, borderlands require reexpressing the message of Jesus. This reexpression may involve different media, methods, or manners. Again, as with translation, we have to rethink the meaning of what has been entrusted to the Christian and help to make sense of it for others. Finally, in the processes of retranslating and reexpressing will come a recentering of the gospel. We find that we, as a local church as well as individuals, need to return to the core of our life and message, which is Jesus Christ. We cannot afford to become too eccentric with our message. The core meaning of the gospel, centered on the cross, comes to the fore in our borderlands experiences. Borderlands need to be considered a gift to the church, if we will only embrace these three healthy processes that are required of us.

Let me summarize these four introductory points:

1. Migration is as old as Genesis 3, but has only recently been linked to mission.
2. From the beginning of the Christian faith, it has been rooted in translation and border crossing.
3. We need to carefully consider the concept of borderlands for mission today.
4. Borderlands is central to the vitality and spread of Christianity, as seen in the need to retranslate, reexpress, and recenter the message.

A concrete example may help. In 1987 I began my teaching at Trinity Theological College in Singapore. We had students from many countries in the English-speaking section. Chinese-speaking students were mostly from three or four countries. English-speaking students could be from Thailand, Malaysia, Pakistan, India, Indonesia, Sri Lanka, Myanmar, and later from Vietnam, Cambodia, and Nepal. Students from Indonesia came from many ethnic groups. In my first years we had a number of Karo-Bataks. The Bataks were sending their better students to study in Singapore to raise their standards of theological education. I quickly learned that, for historical, cultural, and geographic reasons, the Batak church was isolated and almost completely from a German Lutheran heritage. Many customs had developed within the church that looked more like native Batak practices than like Christian practices. The one practice that I remember well was the practice of "moving of the bones of the ancestors." It was a very important ancient ceremony that involved digging up the bones of an ancestor and placing the bones with the other ancestors in a family grave site. There were ancient purposes for such a practice, and if the practices were not carried out according to custom, the community could suffer, or the noncompliant person(s) could be isolated or expelled. There was nothing Christian about it—in fact, it pointed to a belief in the power of ancestors over our lives.

It was the borderlands experience of a number of Batak students studying with students from all over Asia in Singapore that began theological reflection on cultural practices. Batak Christian practices were brought more in line with the global and orthodox practices of the church. Some Bataks began discussions with Chinese about finding ways of baptizing some of the Batak practices. A second factor helped to recenter Batak Christianity, and that was the migration of Bataks to Java (especially to the larger cities) for education and work. In this intercultural (but not international) migration, Bataks became more missionary in their outlook, reaching out to Javanese and other Muslim majority and Chinese minority groups in Java. I am sure we could quickly collect many similar experiences where a place of borderlands became an opportunity for rethinking or for presenting the gospel. Sabah,[4] for centuries, has been a borderland. It was the province of pirates and traders, and it was the hope for migrants from the Philippines and China. We want to keep that in the back of our minds as we work to develop a theology of migration and mission.

In the following sections we will look at migration biblically and historically, and then begin to think about how our theology of the church and of God's mission need to change for the church to receive the gift of migration for today.

Migration in the Bible

We start with the simple observation that the record of God's mission and God's people in the Bible is one of the sending and moving of God so that

---

[4] This lecture was first delivered at Sabah Theological Seminary in Kota Kinabalu.

all of the nations and all of creation receive the glory of God. We read again and again in the Psalms about God's glory being revealed among the nations and in all the earth.

> All the nations you have made shall come
>   and bow down before you, O Lord,
>   and shall glorify your name. (Ps 86:9)
>
> May God be gracious to us and bless us
>   and make his face to shine upon us,
> that your way may be known upon earth,
>   your saving power among all nations.
> Let the peoples praise you, O God;
>   let all the peoples praise you.
> Let the nations be glad and sing for joy,
>   for our judge the peoples with equity
>   and guide the nations upon earth. (Ps 67:1-4)

We see in the history books and in the prophetic literature of the Bible that God's people *move*, *are moved*, or even are *removed*. We would like to look in this section about the movement of God's people in the Old Testament, and then in the next section we will look at the movement of people in the New Testament and the earliest church.

MIGRATION IN THE OLD TESTAMENT

The garden of Eden is where we start because it indicates for us that displacement is rooted in the human condition, and it is also rooted in human sin and redemption. This is not to say that all migration is a matter of sin or injustice, but if we look at economic disparity and war as the two main causes of migration, then we would have to say, yes, human sin is at the root of migration. What keeps us from staying home—or being able to stay at home—is often sin. And yet, the message of the Bible is not that forced or necessary migration is evil, or the less good, but that it can be redeemed for God's good purposes. Exile from the garden was a type of salvation; sin would not be eternal, and redemption might be possible (Gen 3:22-24). Abraham's migration from Ur of the Chaldees was called for by God, and the result was that a new people were formed who would reflect God's glory to the nations. The lineage of a migrant ancestor is a common theme in history, and it is at the very genesis of our faith: Father Abraham is the ancestor of our faith. Salvation history begins with a migrant patriarch: "A wandering Aramean was my ancestor" (Deut 26:5).

Another early forced migration was blessed or redeemed by God. This second major place of migration begins with slavery and family betrayal. Joseph was sold by his brothers into slavery. Again, the evil was redeemed by God, and it ended up being a blessing both for the receptor country (Egypt and especially for Pharaoh) and for those whose migration was forced by hunger. God worked through individuals to bring about redemption by means of migration.

We don't have time to look in depth at the other major migrations in the Old Testament, but let me just mention some of them here to underscore my point.

1. Moses led the Israelites on a migration out of oppression and slavery to a Promised Land. That migration, like the migration of Abraham, helped to shape the community of Israel and prepare them to be "wed" to their God. It is pictured as a long time of betrothal or a honeymoon where God fully gave himself to his bride, Israel. Israel wandered among the nations, as a glory presence, a sign, and a warning to the nations.[5] The pillar of smoke by day and the pillar of fire revealed part of God's glory for the nations. God's tabernacled presence with Israel and among the nations is a type or a symbol of Jesus walking among the nations, and the church now dwelling among the nations (Jn 1:14).

2. The second major migration is the division of Israel (divided monarchy) and the slow depopulation of God's people in the Promised Land. We should remember that Israel as a united monarchy, as the whole people of God, only existed in their homeland for about ninety years (1020–930). Most of Israel's history is of civil war, division, and either partial or nearly complete exile. The divisions of a country, or redrawing the national property lines (Pakistan and India, Nigeria and Biafra, Mexico and Texas, modern Israel and Palestine), always involve refugees and migration.

---

[5]The narrative of King Balak, son of Zippor, and Balaam, son of Beor, is a good example of Israel of YHWH being a light and warning to the nations.

3. The exile of course was a forced migration. It was a typical way that conquering empires exercised control over those they conquered. The conquering army would dilute the conquered nation by removing large sections of the population, including many of the religious and political leaders. They also did the reverse: they moved many from the conquering nation (Babylon) into the conquered nation (Israel). Thus, Samaria was a very mixed-race region in the time of Jesus. The Babylonians did this, the Romans did this, the Sasanians (Persians) did this, Britain did this, and of course Soviet Russia did this. When conquest moves out in one direction, migration moves in two directions.

4. Finally, we see the return of Israel to their land, to rebuild the temple and the wall of Jerusalem, in Ezra and Nehemiah. Some Israelites moved back. Going back "home" was not easy. We read in both Ezra and Nehemiah how the local people tried to get the Jews kicked out of their land (again) and sought imperial proscriptions against their wall-building program. When this did not work, they taunted the Jews and tried to discourage them from recovering their cultural identity: a city, a wall, and a temple. Their cry in the midst of local oppression is memorable: "'Let us start building!' So they committed themselves to the common good" (Neh 2:18).

Thus, some struggled to re-create their cultural lives in this new pluralistic setting, but others stayed behind in Babylon (later the Parthian Empire of Persia). The ones who stayed behind, by the way, produced the more exacting and comprehensive of the exilic Jewish literature: the Babylonian Talmud. It is written "with an accent" because their Aramaic took on a local flavor. The psalmist in exile, longing for home, wrote one of the most memorable songs of prayer:

> By the rivers of Babylon—
>   there we sat down and there we wept
>   when we remembered Zion.
> On the willows there
>   we hung up our harps.
> For there our captors
>   asked us for songs,
> and our tormentors asked for mirth, saying,

> "Sing us one of the songs of Zion!"
> How could we sing the LORD's song
>   in a foreign land?
> If I forget you, O Jerusalem,
>   let my right hand wither!
> Let my tongue cling to the roof of my mouth,
>   if I do not remember you,
> if I do not set Jerusalem
>   above my highest joy. (Ps 137:1-6)

Then in a fit of anger the psalmist prays one of the most frightening imprecatory prayers:

> Happy shall they be who take your little ones,
>   and dash them against the rock! (Ps 137:9)

Exile, forced exile, produced some of the great pathos of Jewish literature, and at the same time it helped to produce some of the clearest teaching about God for all of the world to read.

As a footnote, this very strong exiled Jewish community became the foundation for early Christian evangelism in Persia in the first four centuries of the Christian era. The city of Nisibis was one of the most important cities with a Jewish community in the third to fifth centuries BCE. It was from Nisibis that the exiled Jews produced the Babylonian Talmud (*Talmud Bavli*). Nisibis was also the site, in the fifth to seventh centuries CE, of the great Christian "School of Nisibis" or School of the Persians. It was a seminary of about one thousand students. Graduates from Nisibis ended up traveling to China in the seventh century. Great literature about Yahweh was produced by exiled Jews. Later great Christian literature about Jesus was produced by local Persian Christians, some of whom learned Chinese and wrote about Jesus in Xian. There is much more to be said about migration and exile in the Old Testament, but now we turn to see the continuity that there is in this concept as expressed in the New Testament.

MIGRATION IN THE NEW TESTAMENT

Many of the early Alexandrian church fathers noted something central that we often forget: Jesus was a migrant. As a child, because of political violence against the Jews, he lived for a period of time as an exile in Egypt. If you go to Cairo or Alexandria, local Christians or Muslims will show you maps of the Holy Family's migration through Egypt during their time of exile. I have seen them, and I have heard their detailed explanations. For many Christians this exilic period of Jesus is very important. Jesus, before he was old enough to read, was in exile with his family, in a foreign land, fleeing terrorism—mass murder and genocide. The Savior of the world begins life in a stable in Bethlehem (he wasn't even born in his hometown) and then flees across deserts to a foreign empire. This should tell us a great deal about God's identity with the migrant.

Jesus, the Missionary of God, did not stay still. Many of his followers wished he had, but he had a mission to do that necessitated his movement, along with a small group of his followers. They were more like pilgrims than migrants in the ministry that Jesus chose; but they were more like migrants than missionaries when compared to the apostle Paul. A missionary relocates to a place. A migrant or pilgrim often wanders. Jesus and the Twelve (and the women) were wandering. Jesus was a migrant teacher. He had no school building, but he borrowed local places where he could gather together people to teach them about the kingdom of heaven. They gathered on hillsides, on seashores, in homes, by trees, in the synagogue, and even along streets and in boats.

Jesus, as a wandering teacher was, alert to the diversity of nations and cultures, even as he focused his ministry on the Jews. The Nazareth manifesto (Lk 4:16-30) of Luke makes it clear that Jesus' work among the Jews (he was doing this teaching in a synagogue) had the nations in view. He ended his little teaching by talking about God blessing a Sidonian woman and a Syrian general (Na'aman) when many of the Jews were being oppressed. Jesus even wandered into non-Jewish territory as a sign of the future of his kingdom (Mt 8:28-34). Casting demons into pigs was a doubly unclean thing to do. Movement, fulfillment, nations, redemption, and prophecy can be described as his life of ministry.

The Epistles describe the continuing ministry of the Spirit of Christ through various apostles. The apostolic literature reflects the missionary encounters of those whom Jesus sent. Thus, they reflect the missionary, or apostolic, nature of the early church. And yet, in the pages of Acts and the

Epistles we also see the theme of borderland, migration, and exile. In other words, it was not only missionary activity that spread the teachings of Jesus. Thus, the Acts of the Apostles begins with a sermon given to a pluralistic religious gathering in Jerusalem. These were Jews who had gathered from three continents, representing the world and its movements of people. In this second "table of nations" in the Bible,[6] we can see the pattern of where Christianity would soon spread: from Afghanistan to Persia and from North Africa and Arabia to Europe. The church is, symbolically and actually, birthed amid the nations *among people who are on the move.*

Furthermore, when Peter writes his letters he does not write to a specific group of exiles or refugees; he writes to exiles in general: "Peter, an apostle of Jesus Christ, To the exiles of the Dispersion in Pontus, Galatia, Cappadocia, Asia, and Bithynia, who have been chosen and destined by God" (1 Pet 1:1-2). The *church was a community of exiles,* and *the church spread through such exiles.* Here we see expressed the mission of God, not by professional missionaries, but through ordinary people scattered because of persecution. In other cases in the New Testament, during times of drought, people are scattered because of famine. My point is a simple one: the earliest Christians were traders, migrants, exiles, and the persecuted homeless. Homes were the gathering points and the brief stops along the way. Bishops were traveling, trying to provide some encouragement and teaching, as if doing missional ministry. Movement, more than stasis, marked the community of early Jesus followers.[7]

Migration in the History of the Church

Here is a provocative statement that I think it is pretty accurate: *Christianity has been spread more by exile, migration, and political rulers than by missionaries—and yet missionaries are necessary for the spread of the kingdom.* What I am saying is that it would be a mistake to understate the importance of the modern missionary movement or the monastic missionary movement, but it would also be a mistake to miss the fact that most of the extension of the kingdom of God is about migration and exile. In the following brief

---

[6]The first being the sons of Noah in Gen 10.
[7]As seen in the Acts of the Apostles, the earliest disciples encounter borderlands (Philip the Ethiopian eunuch, Peter and Cornelius, etc.).

paragraphs I would like to show how this is true, beginning with the earliest church up to the present. This is just a small window into a huge topic.[8]

Migration in earliest Christianity. Birthed in a violent empire at odds with its mother (Judaism), Christianity's birthmarks were two: *persecution and migration*. We saw a similar theme with the birth of Jesus. Now we see it with the birth of the church, which is the body of Christ. We must remember, however, that this is true for Christianity only in the Roman Empire. In the first generation, Christianity, born at the conjuncture of three continents, had a different fate in Asia (the Persian Empire) and in Africa (the edge of the Roman Empire). Persecution lasted for over two centuries (intermittent, but real nonetheless) in the Roman Empire, and still the followers of Jesus grew. The faith was passed along trade routes, among the wealthy, but mostly among farmers, traders, slaves, and women. It was less than a noble start. With very few if any full-time missionaries, the teachings of Jesus spread more by storytelling and gossip than apostolic activity. Neighbor told neighbor, and traders and migrants carried in their bodies the death of Jesus so that the life of Jesus would be made visible in their bodies (2 Cor 4:10). Some of the persecuted, especially after the destruction of the temple in 70 CE, fled to the much safer region of Persia: the Parthian Empire.

In Persia there was a genuine peace built on tolerance of beliefs with a Zoroastrian undergirding. Christianity grew rapidly as earlier migrants (the Jews of the Diaspora and of the Babylonian Talmud) saw the Messiah as their promised Savior, and Persians saw (or possibly saw) the fulfillment of their scriptures: a *Shaoshant*, or savior who came from a miraculous birth. Christianity was thoroughly Asian and embedded in the local contexts of present-day Syria, Iraq, and Iran . . . that is, until recently, when many of these ancient Christian churches were destroyed, closed, defaced, and retrofitted as Islamic centers. ISIS came and scattered the ancient Assyrian Christians who had survived since the second century. More refugees, more migrants: the Christian story, still bearing its dual birthmarks, continues to develop throughout the world.

Returning to third-century Persia, the church was growing rapidly until there was a change in dynasty (the Sasanians took over in 226 CE) and then a change in religion. Actually there was a change in dynasty (or religion) in

---

[8]See, for example, Elaine Padilla and Peter Phan, eds., *Theology of Migration in the Abrahamic Religions* (New York: Palgrave-Macmillan, 2014).

both the West and the East. Constantine turned to Christianity, and the Persians were conquered by the Sasanians. About the year 340 the newer Sasanian rulers in Persia became very fundamentalist Zoroastrians, and so the Persian Christians suffered. Many fled now back to the West, to the newly Christian Roman Empire. Persian religion, like the broad Persian cultures, became a religion of strong dualisms: black and white, good and evil, good god versus bad god. Christians were severely persecuted, probably worse than in the first centuries in the Roman Empire, though most Christians do not realize it. Many fled, but some went out as missionaries. They fled as exiles to the West, but they migrated as missionaries to the East. They planted churches and set up bishoprics all the way along the Old Silk Route to China. After a brief 250 years in China, there was a change in dynasty (this is a theme in Asia), and Christians were persecuted and fled back to the West. Those missionaries and Christians who returned to Persia found new rulers: Arabs. These new foreign rulers in Persia needed some Christian scholars and accountants to run their empire, and so the Christians were protected in their new *dhimmi* status. First it was the Umayyads, and then the Abbasids, both of whom tolerated Christians, but slowly the Arab rulers tightened the noose around the leadership of the church. Some defected, many were martyred, and others fled.

In Europe migration and conversion meant something very different. The conversion of tribal Europe was moving slowly indeed, mostly by Christians fleeing early persecution, and then slowly by the planting of monastic communities in each town from the Mediterranean to the North Sea. The Christianization of Europe was dramatically slowed by the constant influx of tribes from Asia; Ostrogoths, Visigoths, Huns, Vandals, and the Avars all invaded, destroyed, and slowly learned from their new neighbors to honor Jesus as Lord. They were unwanted immigrants, changing the accent and challenging the beliefs of medieval Europe. It was a long, slow process, but all of the migrant people groups were eventually Christianized by local Christian people. It is worth remembering. It didn't have to happen that way. The invading tribes could have enforced their beliefs, but instead they were Christianized. This long and slow Christianization, without printed Bibles, satellite TV, or Christian websites, lasted until the eve of the Reformation, which was also the time of the first age of globalization.

Migration in the age of exploration and colonialism. Two great transformations took place in Christianity in the half-century from 1492 to 1542: Christianity divided against itself (we call it the Reformation), and Christianity was established along with colonies in the Americas, Africa, and in South and East Asia. Both involved large movements of people. Within Europe, Christians had to relocate because of new divisions of Christian beliefs that were tied to local rulers. Luther found Wittenberg (not his home town of Eisleben) a safe place to teach and write. Calvin fled to Geneva, Strasburg, and then back to Geneva, for safety each time. Each of these moves was a type of exile, and each spread the faith to those regions. Religious persecution spread the faith of the Reformers. The migration and persecution was much more complex and violent than I have just revealed, but this gives us a glimpse as to just how important migration and exile was in the development of Christianity in early modern Europe. It was a period of great movements to the cities, along trade routes, but also to the edges of the earth.

The second great transformation was that Christianity, blocked in by Islam into the small peninsula of Eurasia called Europe, broke out and began to express itself as a missionary and a migrating faith. Small colonies were established by the Portuguese (they were sailors, after all), and large empires were built by the Spanish (they were soldiers). Latin America, with the sudden influx of Iberians, was evangelized—at least on the surface—in less than a half a century. Nothing like this had ever happened before. Part of the process of evangelization was the movement of people into villages or lands granted under the *encomienda* system. The ruler or *encomiendero* was to Christianize his village or ranch, but in fact he was also granted (*encomienda* was a trust) the free labor of the people on the land. New laws (1542) were passed to grant more rights for the indigenous people, but in fact it was a type of forced labor. Christianity grew under the harsh discipleship of a slave system that only became harsher by the importation of Africans. Africans were moved forcibly to the Americas for the purpose of digging for gold and producing sweet gold for Europeans: sugar cane. Deaths were common on the voyage across the Atlantic and in the slave plantations. However, one of the great ironies of Christian history is that most of the Afro-Brazilians, the Afro-Caribbeans, and later the African-Americans became Christians. It is one of a number of very dark chapters of forced migration and enslavement by Christian rulers.

Migration in the nineteenth and twentieth centuries. Europeans continued to move out of Europe through the early twentieth century. They established large holdings in almost all of the Asian lands and Africa.[9] Churches were planted, mostly as European cultural outposts, but others became firmly rooted in local cultures. Latin America continued to receive Iberians, who came over to rule the state and the church until early in the twentieth century. Colonists arrived in North America with the dual purposes of creating a better life (the great Irish Potato Famine: 1845–1849) and seeking freedom, both religious and political (Armenian genocide, Russian Revolution, Hitler's Germany). Most came to do better for themselves, which continues to be the ongoing cause of migration to North America (and Europe) today. Economics, missionary impulse, and political domination all were intertwined in the ages of colonization and of empire, but the result was that Christianity broke out of Europe and was no longer a European tribal religion. We could talk about the difference between Roman Catholic and Protestant missions, or between Iberian and French (Catholic) imperialism and British and Dutch, but the results were very similar. Christianity spread with, as well as in spite of, the great migration of Europeans.

It needs to be noted that the great spread of Christianity that took place at the end of the twentieth century was made possible not by empires or colonization, but by missionaries. Colonists brought their self-contained European faith and practices and had little desire to include "natives." Missionaries came for the most part for no other reason than to include local people in worship of the one true Lord of the universe. Migration made this global evangelization *possible*, but intentional missionary work made it *happen*. The missionary work was necessary, and much of the time the colonial presence was a hindrance. Thus, the movement of people during decolonialization (Europeans going home) did more for the global church than all the missionaries before, and yet the missionaries were necessary for it to happen. Some brief conclusions for our discussion may be helpful at this point.

Conclusions: Migration and the history of Christianity. The following conclusions, it is hoped, will point the way forward in the study of mission

---

[9]Most of Asia was colonized by the West, except for Arabia, Thailand, Japan, and other smaller regions. Japan became an Asian colonial power that also forced the movement of people from Manchuria and Korea to Malaya and North Borneo.

and migration. This is a study of a major theme in the *missio Dei*, but it has only been the past few decades that scholars have been working to develop migration as a major theme of missiology.

1. Christianity, from the earliest centuries, was influenced by tribes moving into the heart of Christianity, and Christians moving out because of persecution. It was a dual movement as Christians in the early church fled persecution, from pagan Rome, then from Zoroastrian Persia, then from Arab Muslims, and at times from their own Christian brothers. This two-way movement illustrates the complexity of migration that will be part of all of Christian history. In almost every case the immigrant does not just leave her home, but continues to relate to her home, often in a two- or three-way movement.

2. The Reformation was very much a matter of reforming doctrine and the movement of Christians throughout Europe. Later, Protestants (Puritans, Quakers, etc.) moved across the Atlantic, seeking "freedom" to practice their religion. In other words, some movement of Christians is self-imposed, or more accurately, self-inflicted as Christians persecute those of different convictions.

3. Empires tend toward injustice and oppression, and yet attentive Christians have used empires, such as the European movement outward, as a missionary opportunity both for proclamation and "seeking the peace of the city." The history of mission and colonization is neither a neat nor clear history, but after centuries of resistance to missionaries, Protestant colonizers and missionaries found ways of mutual synergy. Imperial powers used missionaries to help in the "civilizing" agenda. Missionaries often called on the imperial powers to "enforce" peace in local contexts. The result was that more missionaries moved out in tandem with the great European migration.

4. Before the twentieth century, most of the migration concerning Christians was European and American Christians going to encounter non-Christians. In the twentieth century this changed: non-Christians (as well as non-Western Christians) began to migrate and to come into contact with Christians in Europe and North America. Unfortunately, Christians in these migration-receiving lands have not expanded their

theology of mission to see these migrations as part of God's mission. They still see God's mission as only the sending of particular missionaries to foreign contexts. An equally strong and clear missiology that includes migration as a means of God's mission is required for the twenty-first century. Most Western Christians are missing the missionary opportunity at their doorstep because they lack an understanding of migration as mission.

5. Some of the biggest shifts in migration in the twentieth century are the distances that migration takes people, the number of non-Christians moving to Christian regions, and the number of Asians and Africans moving within their regions. These major shifts mean that there is a greater mix of global ethnicities in our major cities. But it also means that more non-Christians are brought to the doorsteps of Christians than ever before.

6. Migration is the normal Christian way of existing, requiring a mission theology that is focused on people moving away from their home region or country. The development of a mission theology that embraces both individual missionaries going out and migrants coming to us has not been done before.

A Suggested Theology of Migration and Mission

Before we talk about *what to do* regarding migration, we need to talk about *how to think* about God and migration. I would like to suggest a few basic theological statements that should be foundational in our thinking about ministry to migrants. When ministry to foreigners in our land (or in another land) becomes difficult or violent, we must be clear about our theological commitments. Some of these statements have already been suggested from what we have identified in the biblical and historical overview above.

We are all migrants; migration is the normal Christian existence. It is important to realize that on one level we are all migrants. We are all migrants from the garden of Eden (sin is the root of migration) and from foreign lands. I am a Swedish American sprinkled with Scotch-Irish flavor. My mother's family was from Scotland, and they migrated to Northern Ireland and then to New Jersey, Iowa, and Kansas. My father's family was from Sweden, and they migrated to New York and then to Kansas. I have migrated from Kansas to Ohio to Pennsylvania to North Carolina to Virginia to Massachusetts to New Jersey to Singapore, back to Pennsylvania, and now to California. It is only an accident of colonial history that my migration in the United States has all been in the same political nation-state. Most people trace their heritage to somewhere else from where they are living now. About 14 percent of the US population was born in another country today.

Some people in Sabah, Malaysia, have families from south China, or come from west Malaysia to Sabah. Some have relatives or ancestors in Indonesia or Singapore, or from Tawau, or Sandakan. Some have been settled where they now live longer than others, but all of us are guests, actually. Thus, the first humans—Adam and Eve—were migrants, and humanity has been migrating ever since. Even when we have a very strong identification with a country or region, this is all temporary. Theologically, we can say to the migrants in our neighborhood that we are all migrants or pilgrims; we are all passing through. This gives us reason to identify very closely with the migrant.

The migrant is detached from false identities and is open to finding themselves in God. When we are comfortable at home with our cultural patterns and foods, we can easily be mistaken in thinking that we are defined by our culture. I am a Batak in Batakland or an Iban in Sarawak or a Swede in Sweden. God takes great joy in cultural diversity, but cultures are ways of knowing God and ourselves; they do not define us. A Mexican in Mexico speaks Spanish and eats tamales. When a Mexican moves to Denver, Colorado, he and his children will eventually learn English, and they will learn to eat different foods. This disruption of what is comfortable can be considered a gift of God to help a person find their true identity in God. Rather than being a sedentary person, a person who becomes a pilgrim can find a shepherd for their souls: Jesus, the good shepherd.

This is a matter of pneumatology. The Holy Spirit speaks to the emptiness, loss, and the pain of the person who is displaced. Another way of looking at this is that the migrant is lost. They need to be found. The church is in the business of finding the lost in the name of Jesus, the Great Shepherd of the sheep.

Migration should be considered the search for community. Migrants, whether they be from the heights of a culture (like PhD students in London or Paris), or whether they come as refugees from natural disasters or war, are in search of community. Most migrants are looking for a better and/or a safer life. Whether they are looking for a first job, any day-laborer job, or a job as a surgeon, they seek a better life, and that includes community. There is no community more fully human than the body of Christ, and so the great opportunity of the church is to bring the beloved community of Christ into the midst of the community of migrants and refugees. Because the church is a community with the Lord of the universe in the center, the church by its very existence is the answer to the longing that the migrant has for community.

God seeks to save the lost through the church; sometimes, because the church ignores its apostolic calling, God brings the lost to us. This is a good way to see what happened in early Christian history in Europe and what has happened in the postcolonial period. The nations are coming to the Christian nations and to Christian contexts. Some of these contexts are in very non-Christian contexts: Malaysia, Algeria, and so forth. In all contexts where there are Christian communities, the arrival of migrants should be seen as a sign and opportunity from God.

More importantly, the nations are coming to the cities of the world, so a robust theology of the missional nature of the city is important for us today. Missiologically, we can say that migration can be seen as God's providential movement of people to encounter his kingdom on earth, as it is in heaven. The church's responsibility is, thus, to actually and thoroughly be the church completing God's purpose for the nations.

We can see in history and in the Bible that some types of forced migrations are God's judgments, and others are caused by human injustices. *However, all migration should be seen as the work of God's Holy Spirit to seek and save the lost.* Migrants, exiles, and asylum seekers often seem to be the objects of human injustice, and yet God is in the business of redeeming all injustices and to bring his reign in each culture, in each place. Thus, migration should cause the Christian to take notice and be ready to be the blessing God intends. Too often the migrant becomes an irritant to Christians. Christians should always see the immigrant in their neighborhood as a sign of God's presence and God's calling.

Since the church has only two purposes—worship and witness—migrants must be seen as an opportunity to fulfill the church's calling.[10] It is important to teach all Christians (from cradle to grave) that this is the calling of the church. All discipleship, education, leadership training, music, liturgy, counseling are to serve these two purposes and these only. If churches live into this calling, then the foreigner in our land, or the lost and the lonely in the neighborhood, will be recognized for what they are: opportunities to reveal God's grace and God's love. For God is love.

GLOBAL MIGRATION, GOD'S MISSION, AND THE CHURCH

It is imperative that the global church embrace the fullness of the church's calling, which understands God's mission, God's sending activity, as sending missionaries (our apostolic calling) together with sending the nations to us (our calling to love). This is the Great Commandment and the Great Commission woven together into one fabric of the *missio Dei*. Christ was the sent one and the receiving one. He received the blind, the lame, even the dead, and redeemed what was broken and bruised; and he also went to find, feed, and fulfill the lost, lonely, and unloved. Jesus' body today is the church. In the pattern of Jesus we are to fulfill the Great Commission by going into all the world. At the same time, and from the same Savior, we are to fulfill the Great Commandment of loving our neighbor by being attentive to those God brings to us. In both cases the movement of people and the dual responsibility of retranslating and embodying the message of the cross is central to what it means to be the church. Every Christian has an opportunity to be directly involved in the *missio Dei*.

Our Christology (who Jesus is) must build a strong missiology (being sent like Jesus) that reflects the life of Christ for the world. When this happens, then our missiology will shape the life and ministry of the church (our ecclesiology). If the nations are going to be reached, if Jesus' love for the nations is going to be fulfilled, if the Lord's prayer is going to be answered ("Thy kingdom come on earth"), then it will require an understanding of mission and the church that is willing to break with the more limited Reformation understanding of the church. The church is the body

---

[10]See Scott Sunquist, *Understanding Christian Mission: Participation in Suffering and Glory* (Grand Rapids: Baker Academic, 2013), 281-86.

of Christ in each country, in each neighborhood, and in and for each immigrant community. We should thank God that he is bringing the nations to our doorsteps, but then we need to prepare our churches to respond in ways that are pleasing to Jesus: by being the church migrant and missional.

Finally, we need to be attentive to this simple observation: some of those he brings to our doorsteps are Christian missionaries to us and to our neighbors. We should be thankful.

PART IV

Education

13

Moffett, Mateer, and McClure

Three Models, Two Continents, One Mission

> *Any one who succeeds to a work begun by another is interested in the history of what has already been done. He may, also, be both benefited and encouraged by it. By knowing what methods have been pursued, what experiments tried and with what measure of success, he gains in part his predecessor's experience. In days of trial and adversity, it is well sometimes to know that there have, before, been trials as hard and days as dark, but the promise has been verified that "At eventime it shall be light."*
>
> JULIA B. MATEER

The above quotation from Julia Brown Mateer of Delaware, Ohio, reveals that she combined an educator's clarity and focus on the details of a work with the love and encouragement of a mother.[1] However, Julia and Calvin Wilson Mateer had no children. Julia worked for thirty-five years in China as a translator, writer of textbooks, and founder of a school that would later

---

This address was delivered at the World Mission Conference of the PCUSA held in October 2009 in Cincinnati, Ohio, and was first published in *Pittsburgh Theological Journal* 2, no. 1 (Spring 2010): 105-19.

[1] Delaware is twenty-five miles north of Columbus. The quotation is from Hunter Corbett's *A Record of American Presbyterian Missionary Work in Shantung Province, China*, 2nd ed. (n.p., 1917), from the inside cover. I am indebted to Caroline N. Becker, who first turned me from Rev. Mateer to his wife, Julia, as a model of missionary practice.

become the first university in China,[2] and was the caring pastor for the Presbyterian missionaries in Shandong, China. Little has been written about her, but much can be learned from her life and commitments in mission.

In this brief chapter we will look at Julia Mateer, Samuel Austin Moffett, and W. Don McClure to see, as Julia has noted, "what methods have been pursued, what experiments tried." By the end of our journey we will have identified some practices and attitudes that continue to be of value for missionary work in the twenty-first century. But why have I chosen these three? Is it just because they all start with the letter *M*?

I have chosen to look at these three Presbyterian missionaries in part because they are greatly honored and respected by the people to whom they were sent. We should pay attention when the local church and even local secular scholars tell us, "We honor your dead." The body of Samuel Austin Moffett was requested by the Presbyterian Church in Korea to be moved to the seminary in Seoul. "Samuel Moffett belongs to Korea, not California," they said. And so he now rests in the center of the seminary campus in Seoul with a large bronze bust atop his grave. His grandniece has recorded the following: "Samuel A. Moffett was originally buried in Carpinteria, California but in 2006, in honor of his contribution and at the request of the Korean Presbyterian Church his remains were moved to the campus of the Presbyterian Theological Seminary, which he had founded in Pyengyang in 1901, now located in Seoul, Korea. It was a moving tribute of love on behalf of Korea's Christians."[3]

Julia and Calvin Wilson Mateer are today honored by Chinese historians in major cities of China. I have met two scholars, one from Shanghai and one from Wuhan, who have told me that the first chemistry, math, and physics terms were translated in Chinese by a Presbyterian missionary. They were so impressed that these American missionaries laid the foundation for much modern knowledge in China. They thought I would be surprised to find this out. I was not surprised, except to discover their adulation over a century after Mateer's death.

---

[2] Actually, Shangong University traces its roots back to the school for boys that Julia Mateer started in 1864. It developed into Tengchow College of Liberal Arts in 1882 and then became a university in 1901: Shandong Christian University.
[3] From the website Find a Grave, "Rev Samuel Austin Moffett," www.findagrave.com/cgi-bin/fg.cgi?page=gr&GRid=29448902.

W. Don McClure, killed by Marxist rebels in the Ogadan desert of Ethiopia in 1977, has a prominently marked grave where he was shot. Ethiopian Christians honor his life and the memory of his work on their behalf. When his grandson, Jonathan Partee, with a full shock of red hair, arrived and asked for someone to take him to his grandfather's grave, he was accompanied by a host of Christians, many Somali, who were honored to meet one of the grandsons of this red-haired man they so loved. Jonathan could not believe how much he was honored on behalf of his grandfather. Thus, there is a particular value in studying the work and lives of people honored in local contexts. Not all missionaries are so honored.

JULIA BROWN MATEER (JULY 6, 1837–FEBRUARY 16, 1898)

Julia Mateer draws us to herself with her unpretentious upbringing, frail health, and difficult life. The universal acclaim from later missionaries who were mothered by childless Julia draws us into her life further. Her self-giving, even self-sacrificial life does not set her apart from other missionaries, for this is a common theme, especially in the lives of nineteenth-century missionaries. What sets her apart, and what we want to reflect on for this essay, are two qualities both related to educational work: her understanding of the place of educational work and her crosscultural educational theory. First we will look at her understanding of the place of educational work.

Julia expressed in her journal and in her life that educational work was not an end in itself, but it was the most important means to the end. Education was foundational for the Chinese to become Christians and then, as Christians, to transform themselves and their society. Without expressing it this way, she seemed to have an intuitive understanding that the conversion of individuals is part of the path to the full conversion of cultures. Her earliest experiences in China convinced her of the need for conversion of culture, not just individuals.

She noted numerous times that the Chinese did not like the foreigner. In many ways her very presence was despised. It took years before parents would willingly send their children to Julia's school, and years later before they did so having to pay tuition fees. After ten years of the school, when clothes, board, and food were all provided for free, one could be forgiven for thinking that she was making rice Christians. Those young men who were baptized were becoming Christian for the free food and education. However, her goal was not to make converts, but to make "Chinese Christians," and to do that required education. She expressed it this way:

> I used to, as a child, drop corn and think I was doing an important work. The men who came after it, covering it with their hoes did the harder work; but the hardest of all, and certainly not the least important, was hoeing out the weeds, hilling up the corn and cutting off the suckers while the crop was growing. More are willing to preach the gospel than are willing to settle down to the persistent, steady and hard pull of educational work.[4]

It is as though from the very time she found out they were going to be appointed missionaries, the young teacher of three years determined that this was the central means that must be employed in missionary work, for a work that would last and for a church that would grow strong and healthy. It may have been an accident of fate that the only thing she was prepared for she made into the most important thing to be done. However, without judging motives, we can affirm that even today "mission schools," as separate from colleges and universities, have been one of the most important means of missionary work in Asia and Africa. Even today—over a century later—we can see how much education work, from basic literacy and health awareness to training pastors, is done in the name of mission. An argument can be made that Christian mission is basically education. We will have more on this later.

Second, the educational theory and practice that Julia and her husband developed is noteworthy. Julia ran the little temple school pretty much by herself (with some local Chinese helpers) for the first nine and half years as her husband, Calvin, tried to prove himself an itinerant evangelist. It must have irritated Julia to be working with the six and then fourteen and then twenty-four boys in the "dorm" while most of the time her husband was out "planting corn." However, as providence would have it, he was not a successful evangelist, and so he settled down to her routine and proved to be a marvelous help-meet for the gifted educationalist. Thus, the theory

---

[4] Robert McCheyne Mateer, *Character-Building in China: The Life Story of Julia Brown Mateer* (New York: Fleming H. Revell, 1910), 41. After this quotation there is a footnote put in by her brother-in-law in 1914: "In recent years it has been found easier to get men for the kind of educational work now carried on in China, than for direct evangelistic work."

and practice was put in place by Julia for nearly a decade before Calvin settled down to weed and till the plants.

This "little boarding school for boys" was highly effective. In 1895 it was considered the best educational institution in China. Of the forty-seven graduates in 1894, ten had studied for the ministry, and eleven were college professors. Others were teachers and lay leaders. When the University of Peking was started by the twenty-six-year-old Emperor Guangxu[5] and educational missionary W. A. P. Martin in 1897, twelve of the professors were Mateer graduates. The school was very effective in raising up faithful leaders for the church and for China.

But what exactly was Julia's crosscultural educational theory? Few missionaries let us in on their educational theory; Julia is an exception. In the 1914 Mission Report from Shandong, as well as in Julia's biography, we read of the following three principles: first, education must be Christian, "powerfully and effectively";[6] second, it must be thorough, because this is the first quality of character building (we might add that building character was the central concern that Julia had in her work); and third, it must be Chinese—that is, fit for Chinese in their everyday life.

The curriculum was mostly what they knew from America, but they designed it or shaped it contextually for what would be best for China and for Chinese Christians. Thus, they substituted the Chinese classics for Greek and Latin (which were being taught in the West). Imagine Western, English-speaking Christian missionaries spending years learning and then teaching Confucianism to Chinese students. They also taught every course in Chinese. What that meant was that every textbook had to be written in Chinese. They were not in China to make Chinese think and speak English, or even think as Western Christians. Thus, between the two of them, they wrote the first Chinese book on how to read and sing Western music; the first books in Chinese on chemistry, mathematics, and physics; and the first book on doing mental math, all written in Chinese. Julia's book on music—*The Laws of Western Music for Beginners with Songs Set to Music*—was the standard, written in 1872, with a third edition published in 1907. Like the school itself, the music book was to help laity sing hymns and learn music theory. It was not to train

---

[5] A year later the Empress Dowager Cixi had Guangxu deposed and placed under arrest.
[6] Mateer, *Character Building in China*, 10.

professional musicians. The Mateers had no interest in training professionals. The focus was on teaching Chinese in their context to know their language and their culture, and to follow Christ with diligence in that context.

Two notes regarding her educational theory need to be made: one on the Chinese context and one on imposing Western values. Julia learned and then either taught or had taught the Chinese classics of Confucius and Mencius for all of her students. Thus, they were learning the Chinese curriculum *and adding* much of the Western curriculum. I have not found her saying more than a few words about why she did this; she merely mentions that Greek and Latin were substituted with the more appropriate Confucian classics in the curriculum. She believed that education must include cultural awareness and appreciation. At the same time as she affirmed the culture, she resisted another element of the culture. In China, the classics had been taught by rote; students were literally to be able to repeat back the exact Chinese characters. Julia introduced understanding, debate, and oral presentations. All of this is very Western, and it came in conflict with Confucian models of learning and of ordering society. She would spend evenings visiting the boys in their rooms and asking them questions. She introduced writing compositions and debating; students would prepare debates on subjects such as the following: Which is more difficult, to rule by reason or by force? Which is better for this life, Christianity or Confucianism? Is it beneficial to be reviled? Which is better, to worship false gods or no god at all?

In short, Julia Mateer taught young Chinese boys to think, reason, and understand. Saturday mornings were times for "oration, essays and declamations"—thus, more oral practice. She even formed a literary society to encourage reading and discussion of ideas. She wanted them to be able to explain and defend their faith, and—by the way—soon the whole school was filled with Chinese Christian boys. As she expressed it, "In our school the tongue is loosed, the thoughts are trained to come quickly and to be expressed accurately."[7] With such high standards and combining some of the best of Chinese culture with the best that she knew of Western education, Julia challenges us to think carefully about what we are teaching and how we are teaching it in mission (or even in our colleges and seminaries) today.

---

[7]Mateer, *Character Building in China*, 45.

One final note on Julia Brown Mateer and her husband, Calvin. It is of interest today, with all of our wars and rumors of wars, to reflect on this fact: as the Mateers were sailing out of New York harbor on July 3, 1863, the Battle of Gettysburg was raging. In fact, they were probably passing by Gettysburg on the same train tracks that President Lincoln would pass four months later to deliver his short but famous address. By that time they were in the Indian Ocean. The Mateers spent nearly five months on the sailing ship *St. Paul* heading for China. Along the way another ship, the *Surprise*, passed them and shouted out news of the Battle of Gettysburg and the fall of Vicksburg on July 14th. The voyage was 167 days. By the time they arrived, Julia's health was permanently damaged by cholera. I think it can be argued that choosing to leave your country when it is at war could be considered unpatriotic and callous . . . even self-centered. In fact, they were almost caught in their own national war as they were traveling to the "mission field." There was much work to do at home. Why sail halfway around the world to impose your religion on people who, as they soon found out, had very little interest in the Western religion? Today we have wars—ethnic and religious conflicts in many regions. Many people do not want our religion or our values. The Chinese did not "want" Western people like the Mateers. The Boxer Rebellion "proves" it. And yet, at the height of the Battle of Gettysburg, the Mateers were passing through on their way from Delaware, Ohio, to New York to bring good news of another kingdom to the Middle Kingdom.

Samuel Austin Moffett (1864–1939)

Moffett was the pioneer missionary to Pyeong Yang, Korea. He was not only the pioneer Presbyterian missionary, and not only the pioneer Protestant missionary, but he was the pioneer *Christian* in this northern walled city. His first message of the gospel of God's love was met with absolute resistance. The foreigner was stoned and left for dead outside the city gate. A kindly elderly Korean woman took him into her home, outside the city gates, and fed him some Korean soup (and presumably some kimchi), and in three days he was back in the city again preaching. To many Koreans it seemed that the tall, thin stranger was raised from the dead. They listened and responded as he told them for the first time about Jesus, born of Mary, crucified, buried, and risen from the dead. But it is neither his near martyrdom nor his apparent resurrection that is of concern here. These are very difficult to emulate and will help us little in thinking about missionary practices or principles. I would, as with Julia Mateer, like to focus on two characteristics: Moffett's absolutely uncompromising views on education and his flexible and adaptive views on culture.

When Moffett arrived in 1890, it was just six years after the first resident missionaries were in Korea. Six months later, the young Presbyterian group of missionaries had a two-week conference to listen to the missionary theory of fellow Presbyterian John L. Nevius. Moffett was madly trying to learn his Korean (he would be one of the best in just three years), but he dropped it all and took in every idea and commitment that Nevius of Shandong, China, spoke about. The main theme (read carefully) seems to have been that churches grow and grow strong when the leaders are not taken out of their place of ministry, but are trained in short two-week courses two or three times a year. This was radical for Presbyterians, who are known for very high standards in education, especially for pastors. In fact, Presbyterians fell far behind Methodists and Baptists in Christianizing the American frontiers in the nineteenth century because they insisted on training pastors in history and theology as well as Greek and Hebrew. This took so long that after all that academic study most young pastors didn't want to go to the frontier. Presbyterians had been committed to good, deep, and long-term residential theological study. Nevius was saying their pastors should just be trained in short-term courses, sort of like distance education: do not take church workers and evangelists out of their environment, where they had relationships with local people. Moffett followed this to a T for his first ten years, and the strongest and fastest-growing church in Korea was in the north, and the training was pioneered by Moffett. He was absolutely uncompromising about this, and within about eight years he had over one thousand men coming for two-week intensives on "preaching the Gospel of Mark" or understanding Genesis. This was theological education for pastors and evangelists that was intensive, periodic, ongoing, expanding, contextual, and that kept leaders in their web of personal relationships. What Nevius could not accomplish with missionaries in China he did through Moffett in Korea.

Second, Moffett had a remarkable view of local cultures and societies, a view that was very Christian, more biblical than university education of his (and our) time, and very adaptable. I have not come across a "theory" of culture in his writings, but we can discern something of his view from what he did. Here are a few examples. Moffett arrived in Korea during a time of tremendous upheavals. After centuries of domination (empires) by China, and attempts at domination by the Russians, the Japanese were moving in to inflict their will on the dangerously exposed peninsula. This was the end of the nineteenth century when Japan was on the rise while Russia and China were caught up in internal turmoil. As the Chinese were retreating from Korea, the Japanese were advancing, and with their advance there were Korean voices crying for liberation. Cholera also came with the violence and displacement of peoples. One of the liberation movements, a movement that started as a local indigenous religious form of Neo-Confucianism, was the Donghaks (Eastern Learning). Defending Korean national determination, they moved through the countryside, and eventually Moffett ran into them in one of the newly Christianized villages. Moffett received their leader for a meeting. After the conversation, where the leader negotiated to use a Christian building for a Tonghak rally, Moffett commented, "I realized that we were very much in sympathy with the Tong Haks. I told him so and only encouraged him not to use means of violence. I then realized that these Koreans are more sinned against than sinners."[8] This is the language of the American evangelist, and it would later become the language of liberation theology. Moffett, it seems, identified with the suffering of the Korean peasants and understood their need to organize as people who were oppressed and powerless. It may be a going a little too far to say that he had an understanding of Korean *han*, but not much too far.[9]

Another window into his understanding of culture comes from his son, Samuel Hugh Moffett. Samuel Hugh says that, much to the chagrin of many Koreans, his father had a large Buddha image at the entrance to his house. When asked about it, he said simply, "I have it there to show my Korean friends that the image has no power." He could appreciate the sculpture while giving an important lesson about spiritual power: Jesus Christ is the power over all the local powers.

---

[8] Samuel A. Moffett, "The Work of the Spirit in North Korea," *Missionary Review of the World*, November 1895, 834.
[9] See one of the classic books on *minjung* theology, where the concept of *han* is explored: Kim Yong Bok, *Minjung Theology: People as the Subjects of History* (Singapore: Christian Conference of Asia, 1981).

Another story that I heard repeated two times by Samuel H. is the story of his father walking with a younger missionary up a mountain to a remote village. When they arrived at the crest, there were huts and fires and animals wandering around, but there were no people. The place seemed to have experienced the rapture and Moffett somehow missed it (which caused a quick theological hesitation on his part). As they walked to the center of the village, they saw a crowd gathered, looking up at a newly constructed stage. The head of the village was there, but there was no action. Moffett tapped the shoulder of a young man at the back and asked what they were waiting for. His response was simply, "Haven't you heard? Today a man from God is going to come and tell us how we can know God." Without missing a beat Moffett replied, "I am that man," whereupon he was quickly ushered forward and gave the message, and all of the village was later baptized. Moffett worked within the very fabric and language of the Korean culture, with all of its conflict and ambiguities. Without letting the culture dominate or redirect the message of redemption through Jesus Christ, his cultural assessment seemed to come from identification with the *han* spirit more than with academic study of cultural meaning.

W. DON MCCLURE (1906–1977)

Our third missionary did not work in Asia and was not educated in the nineteenth century. However, he is the only one of our three who bridged the colonial/postcolonial divide, and his location in Africa provides some comparison with Asia. Even though he was fully in the twentieth century, his early work was every bit as pioneering as the Mateers in mid-nineteenth-century China, but his final work was terminated in the midst of Africa's postcolonial Marxist struggle for identity.[10] Ironically, this man who dedicated his life to bring health and salvation to Ethiopians and Somalis, living in a tent in the hot Ethiopian sun in his retirement, was shot in cold blood by a "Marxist" on March 27, 1977. McClure's assignment from His Imperial Majesty, Haile Selassie I, was to help establish a settlement for Somali nomads in the Ogaden desert, but when Haile Selassie was deposed in 1974, the missionary's support and protection were gone.

---

[10]Another connection between these three is that all of our missionaries had their missionary work decimated by various Marxist movements (North Korea, China, and Ethiopia).

Once again I want to look at two characteristics of McClure's missionary work for our reflection. The two characteristics I have isolated are the following: first, his reckless love for Ethiopia and Sudan and their peoples (which got him in some trouble); and second, his ability to find humor in missionary work. First we will look at his reckless love for East Africans.

Don McClure first went to Sudan when he was twenty-three years old. "He worked as a teacher, an agriculturist, an unlicensed, and untrained, physician. . . . He was also a veterinarian, a part-time evangelist . . . and a full-time handyman."[11] His letters indicate that he saw things as they really were: dirty, hopeless, difficult, especially for women and girls. He loved it. He could make a difference in a place like that. But everywhere McClure looked there were two concerns that constantly propelled him further forward: to alleviate the suffering of the people (especially the women) and to lead them to faith in Jesus Christ. He exhaled labor to bring new crops and literacy, and inhaled prayers for faith to be engendered. "Our primary task among these people is to lead them to a saving knowledge of Jesus Christ, but hand in hand with that program we must teach them to improve their social and economic standard of living." He then went on to tell of the suffering of the Shulla children, having to eat "almost indigestible" grain, causing "a fine looking baby to turn into a little creature who is all eyes and stomach."[12] Of continual concern, because it was not only suffering from negligence, but also from injustice, was the treatment of women in the Sudan. "The plight of women especially will break your heart," he wrote to his parents. He then went on to tell of a women brought to his clinic who had been beaten, kicked, and thrown out of her house because she was too sick to prepare supper. Her husband had other wives, so he literally threw her out and shouted, "I divorce you." McClure pondered these things as he cleaned the dried blood and dirt from the gashes on her face.

McClure focused like a laser on the relationship among religious belief, justice, and welfare. His anger regarding the injustices of witchcraft and the Muslim treatment of women seldom waned. At one point his mission strategy took a turn away from anger to wisdom when he was hot to even

---

[11]Charles Partee, *Adventure in Africa: The Story of Don McClure: From Khartoum to Addis Ababa in Five Decades* (Grand Rapids: Zondervan, 1990), 21.
[12]Ibid., 64.

things up with a local witch doctor who had nearly killed a healthy young boy with red-hot coals on his chest. He was lying in wait for the witch doctor to return when a young Shulla Christian, La, said to him, "You let us take care of this. It would be better if native Shullas did it, rather than an outsider." McClure, still filled with anger, responded, "Well, La? Will you do what needs to be done?" McClure remarks that "his reply has been the guiding principle of my life in dealing with Africans ever since. 'Give us a chance!' he said." And so both missionary and Shulla proved right.

His care for people was not carefully nuanced or highly sophisticated. He just seemed to have this prodigal love for the Africans and Jesus Christ who had sent him. With the permission of His Highness, the McClures moved to far western Ethiopia to reach out to the Anuak people. Days began with 6:30 a.m. community worship and Bible teaching. After breakfast, under a tree on a table, the "clinic" opened.

> The patients come in and sat on the ground. First they must listen to a short sermon and learn a verse from the Bible, as well as sing a song or two. We want to bring healing to their souls as well as their bodies. . . . Always there are more women and children than men. Some of them are covered with terrible sores. . . . The poor little babies are the worst off, and some of them are brought in already blinded by the diseases inherited from their parents. . . . There comes no greater joy to a missionary than to see these little children begin to heal and their flesh become clear and clean as we treat them with penicillin to cure their diseases.[13]

We could go on and on about his love for the people and his anger and tears over the unnecessary suffering. But we must move on.

Equally characteristic of McClure was his joy of life and sense of humor in the midst of the most difficult situations. I don't believe enough solid scholarship has been done on missionary work and humor. It is very important, because all long-term missionaries will affirm that humor is essential to survive in foreign contexts. No joke. Except for when he met with the emperor, he always had a sense of humor and an odd angle on life. His sense of humor could be religious—as when he noted that the Ethiopian Orthodox Church has over one thousand holy days a year—and cultural—as when he

---

[13]Ibid., 249-50.

mentioned that with no public toilets in Addis Ababa, he actually saw a man greet another man with a handshake while he was relieving himself with the other hand. It is hard to hear that story and not develop a mental image. While eating a feast in a poor Sudanese home, he noted the following: "The mats on which we sat were not only filthy, but also inhabited by a number of playful creatures who were also having dinner. It is a strange experience to eat and be eaten at the same time."[14] When his Sudanese students wanted to dye their hair red to be like their teacher, McClure quickly pulled up his pants legs and told him they would have to dye their leg hairs too. Giving advice to his younger sister in a letter home, he said, "Remember, talk is cheap. I know, because I have been an expert in that expenditure." After a harrowing and nearly lethal experience cleansing an abscess on the front hump of a new camel—an experience in which the camel took a small chunk out of the young missionary—McClure was identified as "the man whose blood flows in the veins of a camel." Life was not easy for the missionary who rubbed shoulders with local people. Riding second class on a Sudanese train, he was sharing a compartment with "two Syrian men of elephantine proportions and an enormous amount of luggage." He returned to the compartment to sleep at nine at night, wondering about working out the sleeping arrangements. When he arrived, he noted "that was already settled, because those two huge, seating, stinking men were stretched out on the two seats, looking for all the world like twin hippos and sounding like twin sawmills.... I had a choice between breathing feet or garlic all night."[15]

McClure's everyday life of eating pigeons, lancing infected boils, observing Orthodox worship, and shooting crocodiles is described in all of his letters in a way that softens the edges of a hard life, but also helps us to understand how he found joy in the midst of failure and suffering. His joy of life and sense of humor I am sure turned some people off, and yet he was much loved and brought joy along with help and a message to the Shulla, Anuak, and Somalis. In one rare moment he allowed the Africans to speak about him. While McClure was still in his early twenties, one of the Muslim boys said to him, "You are a true Christian." When Don asked why, the boy replied, "You are always thinking of us, and you are always happy." Don

---
[14]Ibid., 34.
[15]Ibid., 41-42.

thought that was a good definition of a true Christian and wished the definition could be more accurately applied to him.

Conclusion

I think it is important to see that God has used these great people *with* their peculiar personalities. Their idiosyncrasies are often very trying or difficult for others. Here is a quotation from Don McClure, which those who knew him can testify is genuine McClure language: "A spear has many parts, all critical for its effective operation. However, I am only happy while riding on the point." Each of these three—Mateer in her little school made out of a temple to Guan Yin, Moffett the "looking up the road man," and McClure the pioneer in three regions of Ethiopia—each seemed happiest or most fulfilled on the point of the spear.

For our purposes and in our twenty-first century we should not imagine that we can or should imitate these people. However, we can and must realize that in their own very difficult situations, generally beyond the support of colonial powers, they found ways to remain faithful to Christ in and through local people and cultures, and are remembered today by Muslims and communists, by scholars and peasants. Each had very strong and determined personalities, and yet they were also broken and humble people. Their respect for the local cultures and confidence in the gospel message made for a winsome combination. None of them described carefully thought-out theories of mission practice. But with a little careful reading, a dash of cultural empathy, and some understanding of missionary motivation, we may begin to understand how Christian movements in Korea, Ethiopia, and China have developed through the many challenges of decolonization, communism, and globalization. These three help to open the door to understand these important Christian movements that are essential to the world Christian movement.

14

American Theological Education and Mission

Henry W. Luce, William R. Harper, and the Secularization of Christian Higher Education

> *The day schools, because of liberal financial support, have far outgrown the churches. They dominate the total mission situation and tend to draw into themselves the time and energy as administrators and teachers of all the missionaries and pastors. The large majority of pastors of churches are also teaching in schools with the result that church work is done on marginal time. A large majority of day school pupils do not attend church services or Sunday schools.*
>
> WADE C. BARCLAY

> *Purification and organization, that is Christianization . . . [wars, prisons, violence, etc.]. How did all of this come to be? Simply because of ignorance. The new Christianity will have no room for ignorance. Education will be its watchword. . . . It is a purification from ignorance and prejudice of every kind and from intellectual dishonesty. What is needed? The Gospel and education.*
>
> WILLIAM RAINEY HARPER

Of the two most important tools in the missionary toolbox—education and medicine—education has always been the primary tool. Missionaries did not have much to offer in the way of medical help in their labors until Western medicine began to understand bacteria, after the middle of the nineteenth century. But from the very beginning of Christian history, education, starting with literacy and Bible translation, has been foundational to missionary work. Missionaries indirectly bring social uplift through education. This role of education changed in the early twentieth century.

Although education was used by missionaries everywhere, there is a great difference in the amount, type, and level of education that was used. After the 1860s, "higher education," comparable to US junior colleges, began to take hold in Asia. In East Asia,[1] more schools were built for higher education earlier on than in any other region except India.[2] Just a cursory look at missionary records or seminary libraries reveals that education was a great priority in East Asia, but especially in the mother of all missionary nations: China.

---

[1] For this study we will only look at the country where American educational mission was the largest: China.

[2] The following information comes from the 1932 Laymen's Report on Missions, edited by Harvard professor William Ernest Hocking: *Re-thinking Missions: A Laymen's Inquiry After One Hundred Years* (New York: Harper and Brothers, 1932). In Japan, by 1932 there were eight Christian colleges for men: "Rikkyo (St. Paul's), Meiji and Aoyama in Tokyo; Kwanto in Yokohama; Tohaku in Sendai; Doshisha in Kyoto; Kwansai in Kobe; and Seinan in Fukuoka," with about 450 teachers and 6,400 students; about 70 percent of the teachers were Christian (six-sevenths were Japanese). There were twenty-three schools above high school for women, with approximately 500 teachers, about 80 percent of them Japanese, teaching about 4,500 students. 81 percent of the full-time and 56 percent of the part-time teachers were Christian (pp. 173-74; figures are from the 1932 Commission on Christian Education in Japan). In India, "of thirty-eight colleges, . . . nine receive their foreign support from the United States and three others are maintained by the cooperation of British and American societies. The American colleges are Judson in Rangoon (Burma), Voorhees in Vellore, the American College in Madura, Andhra in Guntur, Ewing in Allahabad, Lucknow and Isabella Thoburn (for women) in Lucknow, Forman in Lahore, and Gordon in Rawalpindi [all in India and Pakistan]. Those which are maintained by British and American cooperation are the Women's Christian College of Madras, Kinnaird College (for women) in Lahore, and St. Christopher's Training College (for women) in Madras. . . . The staffs of the nine American colleges aggregate over 300, all but about sixty of whom are Indians. Of the Indian teachers approximately 40 per cent are Christians. The total enrolment of students is in the neighborhood of 4,500, of which number about one-seventh are Christians" (pp. 165-66). In China, there were thirteen Christian colleges, "all of which are supported in part by contributions from America. Two, Yenching and Cheeloo, are in the North; six, Nanking, Ginling, St. John's, Soochow, Shanghai and Hangchow, are in the East; three, Fukien, Hwa Nan, and Lingnan, in the South; one, Hua Chung, in Central China; and one, West China Union, in the West. Seven of these colleges are union institutions, five are denominational and one, Lingnan, is non-denominational. All are coeducational except St. John's which is exclusively for men, and Ginling and Hwa Nan which are exclusively for women." Of the 700 teachers about two-thirds were Chinese, and more than half of the Chinese teachers were Christian. About one-fourth of the nearly 4,000 students were women. In India the British did more for higher education, but in China America dominated Protestant higher education. The report admits that Americans had done more for education in China than in any other country (pp. 169-70).

At the very time this great missionary educational project was taking off in China (1880s through the 1920s), education itself was being reshaped in America. At first, all education was done by pioneer missionaries themselves. As John L. Nevius and later Calvin Wilson Mateer wandered around the countryside of Shandong to make disciples, their lonely wives were back home starting some of the first schools: Julia Mateer's school eventually developed into the first university in China. Most schools started out to rear a future Christian generation (along with their parents) and then developed into residential secondary and tertiary schools. Missionaries who arrived in the 1860s were educated in the 1840s and 1850s, before the rise of the studies of sociology, anthropology, psychology, and of course social evolution and its missionary expression of social progress.[3] For Robert Morrison, Christian education in Asia was "for the purpose of training missionaries" and Chinese Christian evangelists.[4] These pioneers were trained mostly in theology, and almost none had training in education. They were not teachers. Mateer and his wife were the exception in that both had experience teaching before becoming missionaries. When the third generation of American missionaries began to arrive, education had become the major tool in a much larger program: Americanizing China.

I would like to argue here that such language is not too harsh or dramatic; in fact, it expresses the very transformation that was taking place in American missions, and it represents the internal strife in American mission boards. In short, the educational mission of Americans in China developed at the same time as the secularization of education in America and the rise of big business in universities. It was also the time of the rise of America as

---

[3]It was the three-volume work of James Dennis that put this theology in the public eye: *Christian Missions and Social Progress: A Sociological Study of Foreign Missions* (New York: Fleming H. Revell, 1897–1906).
[4]Brian Harrison, *Waiting for China: The Anglo-Chinese College at Malacca, 1818–1843, and Early Nineteenth Century Missions* (Hong Kong: Hong Kong University Press, 1979), 35. Morrison and his colleague who arrived in 1813, William Milne, had different concerns. Milne's vision captured a much larger social agenda, maybe because he was working within the context of the British company and rule. Morrison was clear: "I beg that you will (if you approve it) advocate the establishment of a College (or any other name that you may prefer) at Malacca, to train up persons for the diffusion of the gospel by itinerating and preaching. . . . We are about to erect a building at Malacca on the Society's premises, to be called the Anglo-Chinese College, for the purpose of teaching English and the principles of the Christian religion to Chinese youth, and particularly for the purpose of instructing missionaries and others in the language and literature of China" (ibid.).

a colonial power. In this essay, I will show how three themes, woven together, help to explain the shaping of Christian higher education China: education as a tool of American expansionism,[5] modern secular educational theory, and education as (and with) big business. The direct connection of these strands in Christian education can be seen in the life of one American Presbyterian missionary: Henry W. Luce.

HENRY W. LUCE AND NEWER EDUCATIONAL THOUGHT

Henry Winters Luce (1868–1941), from Scranton, Pennsylvania, studied at Yale, Union Theological Seminary in New York, and Princeton Theological Seminary. He partook of some of the best of American education at the very time that American education was going through a love affair with three new streams of thought: the idea of the research university, German higher criticism of Scripture, and the idea of social progress. These three themes are all related, and their influence on America and American missionaries sailing around the world under the wind of the Student Volunteer Movement (SVM) can easily be proven. These ideas sat uneasily with the missionary movement through the first decade of the twentieth century, but by the second decade, the three streams eroded (or carved) a great division in American Christianity. These themes also drove Chinese educational vitality through the 1920s. In this section, I will show how Luce, or "Lucifer," as his Yalies called him, was exposed and favorably disposed to these streams of thought. In the next section we will look at exactly what these ideas meant and who was teaching them. In the final section we will discover what they meant for Christian education in China.

Luce attended Yale at the very time that universities were expanding in the United States, were beginning to offer PhD degrees, and were founded on newer ideals.[6] This was the main story of education at the time, and Yale, only the

---

[5]Yu Ming Shaw, in *An American Missionary in China: John Leighton Stuart and Chinese American Relations* (Cambridge, MA: Council on East Asian Studies, Harvard University, 1992), 37, refers to an unpublished paper by Professor Akira Iriye, "The American Liberal Tradition in East Asia." In the essay he describes the "liberal expansionists" as "those who believe in America's expansive role in Asia, but not primarily for the nation's self-interest, but for Asia's sake." This is a helpful distinction, since there is no evidence that these missionaries had any concern other than for China's best interest.

[6]The most progressive of the new colleges were Cornell, Johns Hopkins, University of Chicago, and Stanford.

second US school to offer a PhD, was a pioneer in newer educational thought.[7] Luce was at Yale from 1888 to 1892. He mentioned that his two favorite—or at least most influential—professors were President Timothy Dwight V and the bright young Bible scholar and future president of the University of Chicago, William Rainey Harper.[8] Harper was a force to be reckoned with, and we will talk at greater length about him later. For now it is enough to know that Harper was a child genius who finished his PhD at age eighteen (one month short of nineteen), was gifted in languages, was a favorite speaker at the Chautauqua summer camps, and was probably the most popular professor at Yale. He edited two academic journals, ran a series of correspondence courses (with up to one thousand students), and kept up with German scholarship. The other great influences on Luce were his friends Horace Pitkin (who would later be martyred along with his family in the Boxer rebellion) and the financially independent and eclectic evangelist Sherwood Eddy. The three made commitments to missionary work by signing the SVM Pledge.[9]

The "Triumverate" all continued their preparation for missionary work by going to Union Theological Seminary in New York. Not really known as a missionary training center, Union still had a good number of students who had signed "the pledge" and were preparing to be missionaries. The SVM at this point (in the 1890s) had broad support from Bible institutes, universities, seminaries, and divinity schools. At the 1894 SVM Convention, there were forty-six delegates from Moody Bible Institute, twelve from Union Theological Seminary, fifteen from Chicago Theological Seminary, and twenty-seven from McCormick Seminary. However, the schools differed theologically, and so the three chose Union, as Eddy later remembers, because it was the more broad and liberal seminary. In fact, at the very time Luce was attending, his studies were disturbed by the heresy trial of his "theological encyclopaedia and symbolics" professor, Charles Augustus

---

[7] A second story in higher education was the reaction to the secularizing of education in the United States. Bible institutes, missionary training schools, and church colleges were being founded at the same time.

[8] B. A. (Bettis Alston) Garside, *One Increasing Purpose: The Life of Henry Winters Luce* (New York: Fleming H. Revell, 1958), 29-30.

[9] "It is my purpose, if God permit, to become a foreign missionary." The pledge was discussed extensively at the first convention of the SVM in Cleveland in 1891. *Report of the First International Convention of the Student Volunteer Movement for Foreign Missions* (Boston: Press of T. O. Metcalf), 32-36.

Briggs. Briggs brought German higher criticism and human reason to Union, and there were those who did not appreciate it. Union was broader in theological outlook, but as the three "pledgers" noted, there was little taught about the world outside Western civilization. The three rose every morning at 5:00 for an hour of prayer and a following hour of Bible study. In addition, they met daily for corporate prayer, and after two years they took on the task of being traveling secretaries for the SVM, enlisting other college students to sign the pledge. Evangelical piety and German higher-critical thinking found an uneasy home in their souls.

We get a glimpse into some of the theological tensions the three traversed in these last years of the nineteenth century in a few vignettes. When Luce was traveling in the South, he met a college president in Tennessee who, finding out that Luce attended Union Theological Seminary, reacted most unpleasantly. Luce wrote in his diary, "It was like shaking a red rag in front of him."[10] Regional variations accounted for some of this, but the gentleman also went on and spoke about each of the faculty members by name, identifying the various theological anomalies of each one. The three young scholars were also quite aware that many of the SVM recruits were motivated by an understanding similar to that of Hudson Taylor, a popular SVM speaker. Taylor's call was for young Christians to go to China because of the millions of heathen Chinese who die each year and go to a Christless grave. Eddy remarked, speaking for the three, that "ours was a gospel of love, a whole gospel which could make a new man within; and could build a new society, a new China, and a new world without."[11]

After a year of itinerating and, we might add, making valuable contacts for future fundraising for colleges in China, Eddy and Luce completed theological studies at Princeton Theological Seminary. Theologically, this was quite a change—from the broad theology and social agenda of Union to the strong Reformed theological rigor of Benjamin Breckenridge Warfield. However, the young missionaries in training were fairly well formed theologically by this time. They were picking up their last courses before a career as missionaries. What was the education they received, and how did they think about the missionary task?

---

[10] Garside, *One Increasing Purpose*, 50.
[11] Ibid., 47-48.

WILLIAM R. HARPER AND THE EVOLUTION OF AMERICAN EDUCATIONAL THEORY

One of the most influential educationalists of the age was William Rainey Harper (1856–1906), who pioneered in correspondence courses, junior colleges, and off-site course offerings, and who promoted German higher criticism. His defense of the new approaches to studying the Bible was winsome and strong. He sounded like an educational salesman. At the very time Luce was at Yale, he wrote that higher criticism "has given the world a 'fifth gospel.'" He waxed eloquently about the benefits of higher criticism for the Christian:

> Moreover, the spirit of a living criticism has breathed upon the dry bones of their prophecies, and, lo, the disjointed and scattered fragments have come together, bone to bone, form and beauty have clothed them, and again they glow and pulsate with the pristine life. . . . The service thus rendered by historical criticism in revivifying these obscure writings has been inestimable.[12]

This is Harper the biblical exegete promoting modern German approaches, to and for the church. At his new university, bankrolled by Rockefeller,[13] Harper also promoted the right of individual inquiry with as much zeal and finesse. His 1904-published *Talks to Students* focus not on the Keswick "Higher Life" theology, but on self-improvement.[14] The lectures are very practical and very American, as if to say, "You can do it if you will." Students are encouraged to develop themselves as part of "the ascent of man." As part of that progress, "religion is essential for the fullest development of these phases of the higher life."[15] As with most nineteenth-century Americans, Harper believed strongly in human progress for the individual, which would promote democracy and therefore would be good for society. The three—progress, democracy, and society—were all linked in his thought. One of his most quoted essays is called "The University and Democracy."[16] In this address he

---

[12]Editorial in *The Biblical World* 1, no. 4 (April 1893): 243.
[13]This is a very interesting relationship: brilliant scholarship with brilliant entrepreneurship. Rockefeller had complete trust in his young president. He didn't even visit the school for five years, trusting that his young scholar-president was making it a great university.
[14]William R. Harper, *Religion and the Higher Life: Talks to Students* (Chicago: University of Chicago Press, 1904).
[15]Ibid., 5.
[16]This was a 1899 address, *The Trend in Higher Education* (Chicago: University of Chicago Press, 1905). At this time (1894–1904), John Dewey was developing his Laboratory School at the University of Chicago. Although these scholars had disagreements after the turn of the century

notes that the "growing democratization in education" is "a complete revolution" that has taken place. In this revolution, the university is "the guide of the people, and an ally of humanity in its struggle for advancement." Then he notes as a contrast that in "the schools of the church there had never been an opportunity to argue." This revolution came with three birthmarks: self-government, freedom from ecclesiastical control, and the right of free utterance. He then goes on to quote Thomas Jefferson.[17] In a telling summary statement later in the book, he says, "Individualism, in education, as distinguished from collectivism, is the greatest contribution of the nineteenth century to the cause of college education."[18]

We are not saying that one person is solely responsible for the educational revolution that became part of the DNA of the later missionaries, but if we were to take time to study other major influential theorists we would not hear much different.[19] In fact it was this pragmatism, optimism, and even concern for democracy that was attractive to the reform movement in the 1890s, the late Qing reforms after 1900, and the educational movements of the 1920s. Chinese, or at least certain very influential Chinese, were making demands of what they wanted from the West, and what they wanted was "western social, political, economic institutions as well as western technology."[20] Western religion was not on their list, so Harper's analysis—that the church held back advances in education—would be well received in China. Chinese scholars who were providing direction for China's future through education were very astute. They were quite aware that, even though missionaries promoted education as coming from the Christian heritage, there was also a movement of secularization in the West that provided a critique of both the

---

that led to Dewey's exodus to Columbia University, it must be recognized that experimental and pragmatic approaches to education were the dominant concerns at the new university in the last years of the nineteenth century.

[17] All quotations are taken from Harper, *Trend in Higher Education*, viii, 4-6, 320.

[18] From *Inauguration of William Herbert Perry Faunce, President of Brown University, 1899* (Providence, RI: Remington, 1899), 20. Rainey was one of three university presidents who gave presentations. The others were the presidents of Princeton and Harvard.

[19] It would be very telling, for example, to go into further detail regarding the impact of Herbert Spencer (1820-1903) on the study of sociology, psychology, and economics. Of course, John Dewey was also a towering figure, at whom we will look briefly later.

[20] Jessie Gregory Lutz, *China and the Christian Colleges, 1850-1950* (Ithaca: Cornell University Press, 1971), 87.

missionary and Christianity.[21] Chinese officials were very interested in promoting this "new" education to develop a modern and strong China. The missionary purpose was not their purpose.

SECULARIZED CHRISTIAN HIGHER EDUCATION IN CHINA

One illustration of the transformation of mission education to secular social uplift is to look at the contrast between Calvin Wilson Mateer (1836–1907), who arrived in Shandong in 1863, and Luce, who arrived thirty-four years later. Mateer, the entrepreneur, teacher, tinkerer, linguist, and evangelist, followed his wife's lead to work through education to reach the Chinese for Christ. He began as a traveling evangelist in the Nevius pattern for over nine years, and then, giving up on the itinerant life, stayed home in the old Guanyin (goddess of mercy) temple-cum-home, cum boys' school. Julia had been quietly developing a school while he was gone. What was this type of education for, and how was it organized?

Mateer was clear: education was for evangelism and therefore must be in the local language, showing respect for the local culture. The goal was to form Christian character in the young boys.[22] In that sense, Mateer's ideas of education were more Confucian than Dewey-like. Again, like Nevius, Mateer tried to reach the common man (or boy), not the elite. Therefore all education would be in the Chinese language, for Chinese would not have to learn English to become Christian. Education was to include all (it was not exclusively for the elite). The curriculum involved some of the Chinese classics, as well as Christian doctrine, Bible, chemistry, physics, writing, music, and public speaking. The young graduates would be Chinese Christian scholars with outstanding Christian character.[23]

---

[21]Lutz notes that Alexander Michie's very critical book about missionaries—*Missionaries in China* (London: E. Stanford, 1891)—as well as Thomas Huxley's *Evolution and Ethics* (London: Macmillan, 1894) and Herbert Spencer's *Study of Sociology* (London: Henry S. King, 1873) were all translated into Chinese.

[22]According to the Mateers, one can not overestimate the goal of "Christian character." The goal and purpose was repeated over and over again. Upon Julia's sixtieth birthday, the students, teachers, and alums honored her by putting a Chinese calligraphy scroll over her door that read "Character-nourishing aged mother."

[23]"Mr. and Mrs. Mateer included in their curriculum of studies the Chinese trimetrical classics (which were explained as soon as committed), geography, mental and written arithmetic, natural philosophy, 'Peep of Day,' *Pilgrim's Progress*, *Evidences of Christianity*, and the 'Church Catechism;' later were added algebra, geometry, astronomy, chemistry, etc. They also began giving their students early

Luce's concerns were very different; in fact, although both Luce and Mateer were Pennsylvania Presbyterians, they were remarkably different. For our purposes, however, we want to focus on the differences related to education and educational theory.[24] Luce's life and approach were more elitist and purely academic. Mateer was a hands-on person who had built the first two-story house in his village and built the first "technology" museum for Shandong. In short, Mateer was an American nineteenth-century frontiersman.[25] Luce studied, traveled with the SVM, spoke, and then studied more. His concern was to bring the best of education to the Chinese and then to see Chinese society progress. Luce was an early twentieth-century progressive. Conflicts arose as the younger generation, represented by Luce, began to take over. As Luce's biographer states, "It sometimes seemed to Harry that they were too insistent upon holding to past ways of doing things and were unwilling to recognize changing conditions." The older missionaries found Luce talented, strong-willed, and "too eager to try new experiments."[26] Luce, thinking like a sociologist, worked with his friend Paul Bergen "to move the college physically and then to alter its program."[27] The physical move was to be to a larger urban area where there would be better access to services and students.[28] One of the most important curricular changes that the young missionaries promoted was teaching English and teaching other subjects in English. They were interested in opening up the riches of Western science and progress to the Chinese.

---

practice in writing compositions, a new feature of school life to them. As early as the summer of 1867, drill in debate was established as one of the regular features of the school." This quotation is taken from the aptly titled biography of Julia, written by her brother-in-law, Robert McCheyne Mateer, *Character-Building in China: The Life Story of Julia Brown Mateer* (New York: Fleming H. Revell, 1910), 50. (See chapter ten in this volume for more discussion of the Mateers and their methodology.)

[24]Mateer, farm raised near Gettysburg, Pennsylvania, studied with a lone teacher for secondary school, Mr. James Duffield, and then attended the small Jefferson College, near Pittsburgh, Pennsylvania. Upon graduation he ran a small local academy in Beaver before attending Allegheny (later Pittsburgh) Seminary. He was a farmer's son who struggled on the "frontier" to get an education. Luce came from a family of some influence in Scranton, Pennsylvania. He attended a private preparatory school and then Yale, Union, and Princeton.

[25]Irwin T. Hyatt Jr., *Our Ordered Lives Confess: Three Nineteenth-Century American Missionaries in East Shantung* (Cambridge, MA: Harvard University Press, 1976), 231.

[26]Garside, *One Increasing Purpose*, 85.

[27]Hyatt, *Our Ordered Lives Confess*, 228.

[28]Tengchow, on the sea, was bypassed as a railroad stop and therefore did not grow as rapidly and strongly as cities such as Jinan, the provincial capital.

The transition to the "new approach" can be dated fairly accurately: the 1898 Mission Meeting of the Presbyterian Church in Shandong. Luce, the thirty-year-old rookie missionary, is reported to have said to the crowd of seasoned missionaries, "The time has come when we should seriously consider both a change in location and a broader basis of cooperation for Tengchow (Dengzhou) College."[29] He explained the change of location in terms of students' access to the college. Of even greater import was his explanation of the need to cooperate with American Methodists, British Baptists, and Anglicans. Such cooperation would pave the way for a larger and more influential college, even a university. By 1902 such an agreement was made with the British Baptists, and Luce's persistence was one of the reasons for the success. The new cooperative college would begin with three "schools": the general college, a seminary, and a medical school. It sounded like a university.

By 1901 the tide had turned under the new leadership of Dr. Paul D. Bergen at the college. It was obvious to the missionaries that the move to Weihsien was going to happen, and Luce confidently wrote so to the board even before permission was granted.[30] At this point the mission had made the critical turn. Thus the rest of the story of Christian higher education in China is about how Christians could contribute to the new China. According to Luce's biographer, Luce was always doing what was right for "the Kingdom of God," not just for the denomination or the mission.[31] I think this is correct. Luce had been nurtured in what could be described as the transition between kingdom of God theology and the social gospel, which for the most part evolved into theological modernism. It was this modernism that his later colleague in Peking, John Leighton Stuart (1876–1962), taught and for which he was criticized. The emphasis was on the immanence of God's kingdom and its appearance in the structures of society. It was an attractive theology in a time of progress when much "civilizing" was being done in the world. World War I ended such theological optimism among most Europeans, but in America it continued as the dominant stream in the mainline churches until the Vietnam War.

---

[29]Garside, *One Increasing Purpose*, 100.

[30]Weihsien is located halfway between the capital of Tsintien (Jinan) and the important port city of Tsingtao (Qingdao) by train. This was the location of the Japanese internment camp for Allied civilians where missionary Eric Liddell was imprisoned and died.

[31]Garside, *One Increasing Purpose*, 107-9, 126-27, 164.

Luce's calling now was more clearly focused: he was called to lead in the total development of universities in China and in promoting teaching theology based on the life of Jesus.[32] In the former he made numerous trips to the United States to raise money, worked on the plans for campuses, negotiated "college unions,"[33] and even led in using Chinese temple design for buildings (though "with western advances"). On Luce's trips to the United States, often at great sacrifice to his family, he pioneered in raising endowments and establishing a board in the States. Luce was developing universities for China ("Cheloo" and later Yenching in Peking) based on the American business model. On his fundraising trips (over four years of his life) he met up with McCormicks[34] and Rockefellers, among others. His vision was to use American education and business to aid in the development of China. Chinese leaders were turning to American education experts for advice, and Luce reasoned that the Christian colleges and universities had an opening to serve China along this line of Chinese interest.

Luce was right about the fascination for educational things American. The well-known trip of American pragmatist philosopher John Dewey to give lectures on education in China in 1919 was one of many tours of American educational experts. Dewey's pragmatism, it has been said, so took hold in China that it survived even the Maoist liberation.[35] American

---

[32]It is not the purpose of this chapter to discuss Luce's scholarship. However, the *Harmony of the Gospels* (1901) was the first book in Chinese to aid in the study of the historical Jesus. In 1910 he published *Aids to the Study of the Life of Christ*. His concern was that people imitated Jesus in their lives. Still, Luce was an SVM man, and in 1909, in light of the declining interest in the professional ministry, he organized a type of "revival" at Wiehsien with the evangelist Rev. Ding Li-mei, who had been tortured by the Boxers. After a series of lectures and sermons, about one-third of the college (116) signed up to pursue the ministry. It was in fact like a Northfield revival, though with "no undue emotion," Luce says at least two times in his report (Garside, *One Increasing Purpose*, 128-30). This was the beginning of the SVM for Ministry in China.

[33]It is possible to say that the movement toward Union schools began with Shandong and that Luce was one of the pioneers.

[34]Cyrus McCormick had invented the "Virginia Reaper," which greatly increased farm productivity. He pioneered in providing easy credit to farmers and in advertising his product. However, he was not a friend of labor: in 1886 the famous Chicago "Haymarket Riot" started at the McCormick factory where McCormick's bosses paid factory workers eight to nine dollars per week. McCormick's son, who took over the company, married John D. Rockefeller's daughter, Edith.

[35]Nancy F. Sizer, "Dewey, China and the Philosophy of Development: A Contrast of American Progressive Educational Thought and Practice with That of Modern China" (paper presented at the Annual Meeting of the American Educational Research Association, Chicago, April 1974).

secular educationalists were invited for six months to two years to give lectures and to advise Chinese educationalists. Although Dewey was Harper's shining light for education at the University of Chicago, conflict arose for various reasons, and Dewey ended up at Columbia and the Teacher's College in New York for most of his career. As a result, there was a strong connection between Columbia and China regarding education.[36] It was Dewey's students, now returned to China, who invited him to speak.[37] At the same time that American educationalists were lecturing in China, an "Educational Commission from the United States" was sent to evaluate the Christian schools in China. This commission was fully funded by Rockefeller and was led by the broad-minded American Baptist from the University of Chicago, President Ernest DeWitte Burton.[38] It seems that such leadership (the president of the University of Chicago) would indicate that the "mission schools" were being held to the standards of American research universities.[39] With Chinese authorities developing new schools using the latest in American theory, the Christian colleges and universities could easily be left behind. Christian missionaries like Luce and his longtime friend Stuart[40] would not let that happen.

---

[36] There always was a strong connection between the University of Chicago and Chicago Theological Seminary and China. For example, N. Z. Zia, the Lingnan University professor of philosophy, studied at both Chicago and Harvard.

[37] In 1916 Dewey had written his famous book *Democracy and Education* (New York: Macmillan, 1916). It is rooted in Social Darwinism (from chapter one: "Continuity of life means continual readaptation of the environment to the needs of living organisms"), and it carries much of Dewey's overall understanding of education. "Savages" (his word) simply teach the young in the family unit, but as civilization advances, what must be communicated becomes much more complex and must be taught in schools with professional teachers. This is a matter of passing on the best of social experience as a part of the evolutionary process of societies.

[38] In 1908 Rockefeller had sent Burton to China at the request of a number of mission boards. Burton was the chair of the American Baptist Mission Board.

[39] Ernest DeWitt Burton (1856–1925) was a prodigious New Testament scholar who had written books similar to those Luce wrote in Chinese: *Harmony of the Gospels for Historical Study* (New York: Charles Scribner, 1894 and 1904), *Jesus of Nazareth* (Chicago: Chicago University Press, 1920), and (with William Arnold Stevens) *An Outline Handbook of the Life of Christ* (Boston: The Bible Study Publishing Company, 1892). Like Luce, his books apply higher criticism to the study of the New Testament, with a concern for the church.

[40] Stuart, son of missionary parents, was Southern Presbyterian, trained at Hampden-Sydney College and Union Seminary in Richmond, Virginia. In 1905 he arrived in Hangchow, but from 1909 to 1919 he was at Nanking Seminary; then from 1919 to 1941 he was the strong and visionary leader of Yenching University in Peking.

The two made a great team, although short-lived, at Yenching.[41] They shared a common vision of developing a major Chinese university that would promote the best of Chinese and Western ideas. This period from 1920 to 1926 coalesces what I call mission education as Americanizing the Chinese. Stuart's biographer notes, "As a humanistic liberal of the John Dewey school, he believed that change can evolve only out of tradition, and that the two should form a harmonious whole."[42] The academic vision more and more was shaped by this ideal to bring the best of both cultures, including religions, to advance China as a modern nation. The theologies of both men evolved with the times, becoming more accepting of truths from other religions and affirming the mission of Christianity as a socially progressive agenda, although at that time the progressive social agenda was very different from today.[43] However, we are not as concerned about the theology as we are about the three other themes mentioned at the beginning of this paper: American expansion, big business, and educational theory.

First, Luce and Stuart had become very well connected with political leaders in the United States. During the 1911 Revolution, Stuart was asked to serve as an Associated Press war correspondent. He accepted the position and ended up meeting with all of the new leaders in China, and later he became a confidant regarding information from China for people such as his good friend and fellow Presbyterian, Woodrow Wilson (president 1913–1921). Reporting on the April l, 1912, Provisional National Assembly, Stuart noted how many of the delegates were educated in mission schools and that fully 90 percent were Western educated.[44] For Stuart, the 1911 Revolution was invigorating, hopeful, and was like the American Revolution. Stuart saw his mission work in political terms and even went as far as to rally the US government and citizens to provide support for the "New China."[45] Stuart was on friendly terms

---

[41]Luce made the great sacrifice of leaving Yenching in the mid-1920s in order to serve the higher goal of making Yenching a great university. It required money to do this; therefore Luce returned to the United States to raise money and to help lead the board in New York.
[42]Shaw, *American Missionary in China*, 310.
[43]One example will suffice: John L. Stuart saw that this enlightened social agenda, promoting the best of religion, was threatened by atheistic communism. Therefore, he was from the beginning a strong supporter of a republican China and strongly opposed to the spread of communism.
[44]Shaw, *American Missionary in China*, 30.
[45]Ibid., 32-33.

with the Koumintang (Guomindang)[46] government, and as a result of his diplomatic work, the university was on good terms with the government throughout his presidency. Stuart believed that good will would lead to financial support and greater influence in China. Stuart was quite aware that greater support from Chinese political leaders could very well mean recentering the institution on a Chinese identity rather than on a Christian identity. The die was cast, however, and choosing to be a major university meant catering to political and business leaders rather than to church leaders. Unlike earlier missionaries working in education in China, Stuart and Luce were in positions of power and sought to use that power, both in politics and in business, to promote their vision of the kingdom of God for China.

In the area of business, it was Luce who took the lead and promoted the American system of big business in support of university education.[47] As we have mentioned, Luce and his family became good friends of Mrs. Cyrus McCormick of Chicago, but he also received funding from Rockefellers and from the Charles Martin Hall estate, among others.[48] The boards that he developed in New York were made up of businessmen with very few church leaders. Christian higher education in China was thus linked philosophically—mainly in pragmatism—and structurally with big business in America. Stuart made an even more direct connection between American education and business when he noted that American educational theory grew out of an "advanced economic system."[49] Chinese Christian higher education would be indebted to American big business. This was a tremendous transformation from the earlier responsibility to a mission board in New York. Luce pioneered in this transformation during his time raising support for Shantung College (Cheeloo University).

Finally, Luce accepted and promoted modern American educational theory. The schools that he helped to develop were universities more

---

[46]Chinese People's National Party, formed 1912.
[47]There are many late nineteenth- and early twentieth-century examples of the rise of big business in support of university education. The University of Chicago was Rockefeller's school, and Vanderbilt University ("a central college for Tennessee") was a result of Cornelius Vanderbilt's philanthropic investment. Many other schools were named after big business: Cornell, Duke, Stanford, Carnegie Institute, etc.
[48]Hall made his fortunes through his new process for producing aluminum.
[49]Quoted here from Shaw (*American Missionary in China*, 51), who is referring to a 1928 address by Stuart titled "Education in Applied Economics."

than Christian colleges. They developed programs to serve Chinese society (agriculture, animal husbandry, business, accounting, etc.) as well as the church. The major links with schools in the United States were with universities more than with Christian colleges. Yenching developed programs with Harvard, Princeton (where Woodrow Wilson had earlier been president), Wellesley, and the University of Missouri. Yenching and other Chinese universities were to be places of research and of the most modern approach to discipline. A higher-critical approach to the Bible was encouraged, because it fit with the most modern research and study. The best in education, it was reasoned, would do well to promote democracy in China; and thus political involvement related to the educational theory of Harper.

Chinese were not passive agents in this "Americanization of mission education." As we noted earlier, they sought out the best in Western education, even earnestly seeking relationships with American universities and their professors. But there has always been a yin and a yang to Chinese views of the West. China has always vacillated between openness and rejection of the outside. During this period of transition there was an openness to America, as long as the Chinese could choose what of America to accept. The Christian colleges tried to respond to that openness, but they did so as American businessmen competing for an important client.

I think it is best to understand this revolutionary change in mission education as an expression of the dominant theory of the period—a dominant theory that was only killed by its misuse under National Socialism in Germany: social evolution. Henry W. Luce, and those of his generation, could not help but to think of missionary work, especially in its social expressions, as evolutionary or developmental. The educational theory of Dewey is dominated by evolutionary language ("from the savage to the civilized"), and even higher criticism of the Bible was interpreted by people such as Luce and Harper as a newer and higher form of study. The assumption is that others would advance and move forward . . . "just like us." There was an assumption of evolutionary superiority in all of this, even as missionaries wrote with great respect of many things Chinese. In fact, Chinese culture was going to be "completed" (as Stuart wrote about Confucianism) by Christianity and

Western advances.[50] This evolutionary model also applied to the business model. United States educationalists were involved in a struggle of "survival of the fittest" regarding educational models (they had to "compete" with the new Chinese colleges), and they even interpreted the superiority of the Christian religion as the "fittest" religion proving itself now in China. All of life—education, society, and religion—was seen in evolutionary, competitive, and survivalist terms. These were the American progressive ideas and the creative ideas that were going to help China advance from its chaotic past.

---

[50]John Leighton Stuart, "Christianity and Confucianism," in *The Jerusalem Meeting of the International Missionary Council, March 24–April 8, 1928* (New York: International Missionary Council, 1928), 1:45-54.

15

Asian Theological Education

Earliest Trajectories, Contemporary Concerns

It may not be accurate to call earliest Persian formation for ministry "theological education," but doing so helps us to connect the most ancient formation of priests and missionaries with our present practices. As theological education in the twenty-first century rapidly adapts to the decline of Christendom, the complexification of globalization, the constantly evolving use and meaning of technologies, and the rise of new forms of Christianity, I have found it helpful to search for common themes of Christian formation: themes that are found in formation when Christianity is a minority and oppressed faith. This takes us to monastic formation in the deserts of Syria and Egypt, to the communities and the cathedral schools of Europe, and to the most basic formation of Jesus and the Twelve.

In this essay we will look at some of the earliest approaches to expressing and therefore teaching the Christian faith in Persia. Of course there is some continuity with what was happening in the Roman Empire regarding education of Christian leaders, but Persian discipleship and Persian schools did develop differently in light of the Asian context. The Asian context was not isolated from global concerns. Theological developments and divisions in the West influenced Christian education in Asia. However, the local Zoroastrian (national) religion also shaped the spirituality and theology of Persian Christians. At the end of this essay we look at a few implications that early Asian Christian education has for Asian education today.

A longer version of this paper was presented as a series of lectures at Sabah Theological Seminary in Kota Kinabalu, east Malaysia, in May 2010. In those lectures I compared nineteenth- and twentieth-century theological education with early Persian education.

Introduction to Our Approach

Asian Christianity has a much longer and enduring heritage than we usually think. In this brief overview, we will survey the development of earliest Christianity in Asia with an eye to themes and issues that might illumine the work of theological education or leadership development today. Our study is rooted in the understanding of Christianity most clearly expressed by Andrew Walls in his description of Christianity as a religion that develops with two often contrasting principles: it is a pilgrim religion and an incarnational faith.[1] On the one hand, Christians are pilgrim people who do not fully belong to the land or culture in which they sojourn. As Jesus said, "My kingdom is not from this world" (Jn 18:36). Christians, to use the expression from early detractors of Jesus people, were labeled a "third race."[2] Christians did not disagree with this name calling, but they understood it differently. Even Bardaisan, the creative, semiconverted Persian, noted that Christians do not follow local customs regarding family and sexual ethics, but all Christians, in no matter what country or nation, follow the same customs following Jesus Christ.[3]

On the other hand, Christians, like Jesus himself, are part of specific cultures and therefore do not eat different food or wear special clothes or speak a different language. Christian life and teachings enter into or "put on" local cultures, affirming the great diversity, creativity, and beauty of all cultures. There is no culture or language that is excluded from Christian life, for culture is the *imagio Dei* writ large, kingdom-like.

Thus, we will focus on the incarnational or indigenizing principle for theological education in Asian contexts. We do this largely because most discussions of theological education are situated in the Western, mostly European, tradition. Asian contexts are quite diverse, and yet there are common threads that look very different from the Western threads that have dominated much of Asian theological education in the past few centuries. It is hoped that this essay will provoke and stimulate Asian theologians to think both broadly

---

[1] Andrew Walls, "The Gospel as Prisoner and Liberator of Culture," in *The Missionary Movement in Christian History: Studies in Transformation of Faith* (Maryknoll, NY: Orbis Books, 1996), 7-9.
[2] Andrew McGowan, "A 'Third Race' or Not: A Rhetoric of Ethnic Self-Definition in Tertullian," *Patristica Bostoniensia*, November 2001.
[3] See Bardaisan's *The Book of the Laws of Countries*, trans. H. J. W. Drijvers (Piscataway, NJ: Gorgias, 2007).

(over two thousand years) and specifically (for each context) about how theological education may need to distinguish itself from the dominance of Western models. We start the discussion here by looking at how theological formation developed within early Asian societies under Zoroastrian, and later Islamic, Persia. Thus by looking at one place (Persia) under two cultural empires (Sasanian-Zoroastrian and Arab-Muslim) we will have laid a foundation for later reflections on formation in India, China, Vietnam, Japan, Indonesia, and other centers that developed schools and monastic communities for preparing Christian priests, pastors, and missionaries.

Our broader topic in which theological education in Asia is situated is a much neglected one: the development of a minority Asian religion in Asia: Christianity. Asia has stood on the periphery of Christian scholarship, since most Christian history has been written by Europeans and North Americans, whose central concern is Christian development in the West. As a result, Western Christian worship, theology, and practice have been viewed as normative, and African or Asian forms are seen as derivative. It is a strange fact, because Christianity is an Asian religion that was dominated by European empires and then European nations for about half of its life. This Asian religion found a comfortable home in the West, less so in its own home territory. From the beginning—even before the beginning of Christianity, if we start with Abraham being called out of Ur of the Chaldees—Christianity has been an Asian religion. Jesus was a west Asian. The fact that a European empire was controlling much of west Asia at the time of Jesus' life does not change the fact that Jesus was an Asian, just as the fact that the British Empire controlled much of south Asia does not make Tamils or Sinhalese Englishmen. One of Jesus' disciples is universally acclaimed as the apostle to India, and the earliest growth and the greatest number of martyrs in the first four centuries were in west and south Asia.

Although Christianity was held captive by Western culture with its own assumptions and prejudices, Christianity has recently broken out of that Western cultural captivity. Asian Christianity now has a new freedom and power to reshape and restore Asian sensibilities, if it will only seize this opportunity. However, the long-term European captivity has become so normative, even for Asians, that into the twenty-first century most seminary professors, seminary presidents, and church leaders cannot let go of the

Western standards, mistaking those Western Christendom standards for the kingdom of God. Western patterns for theological education, Western models for worship, and Western ideas of how to teach theology (I believe) are generally assumed by Asians to be Christian standards. They are not.[4]

Thus, this chapter is written as a way to open the window for fresh Asian winds to blow on the whole concept of Christian leadership training in Asia. One of the motivations for this chapter is the brain drain from Asia and the idolatry of Western education. We have all watched as good Asian Christian scholars have gone to the West, earned advanced degrees, and then began to impose Western standards, issues, and approaches on young Asian Christian leaders. Often it is inappropriate, whether it is bringing back Western postcolonialist ideologies or Western fundamentalist formulas. Both liberal and fundamentalist ideologies come out of particular contexts and issues that are mostly Western European and North American. The question that should guide the reading of this brief chapter is this: What would it mean to rethink Asian theological education in a way that is appropriate to our own historical development, that comes out of the general Asian contexts, and that is malleable to particular Asian regions? We begin with Jesus.

JESUS WAS A REFORMER OF A WEST ASIAN RELIGION

Siddhartha Gautama was a reformer of Hinduism. It was the problem of suffering, disease, aging, and death that sent him on a search to discover the causes of suffering of all types. His answer was so different from the traditional Indian answers that his followers became a new movement, named after himself: Buddhism, or the religion of the Enlightened One. Much of the Hindu view of the cosmos, of time as cyclical, and of the value of ritual over grace (or even good works), continued to be the grounding for Buddhist faith.[5] However, Buddhism developed on its own terms as a new answer to the

---

[4] Just a few years ago I was in correspondence with seminary administrators in the United States concerning a revolution that is taking place in seminary standards and curriculum in North American theological education. Asian Christian accrediting agencies were trying to keep up with the conversation, assuming (I believe) that this is an ecumenical Christian conversation rather than a North American concern.

[5] We can not really talk about Hinduism as a religion until the eighteenth century, when Europeans tried to make sense of all of the religious practices in India and came up with a common word for all Indians.

Hindu problem of endless cycles of rebirth. As Christians we have a different opinion of "rebirth," but that is another chapter at another time.

Jesus, in some ways, came as a reformer of Judaism. He came as a Jew, affirming the Jewish law, and at the same time he came to reform Jewish law and practice. "I have come not to abolish but to fulfill" the law, Jesus said (Mt 5:17). He was Jewish, but he was different. As many people quickly noticed (in the first chapters of Mark), he taught not as the scribes and Pharisees, but with authority. Jesus was a wandering teacher whose class was always in session. He went about teaching, preaching, healing, and casting out demons. Jews were concerned about the kingdom of God, and Jesus said, as he healed and taught, "The kingdom of God is among you" (Lk 17:21). Jesus was more than a teacher, but he was also a teacher sui generis. Theological education began with Jesus showing the kingdom in his works, teaching about the kingdom, and asking questions that would guide the faithful to deeper faith. His questions and answers also shut the ears of those who would not hear. He was a teacher.

EARLIEST SPREAD OF CHRISTIANITY IN ASIA

Christianity spread in the early centuries in Asia the same way it did in Africa and Europe: along trade routes, by laypeople involved in trade. Again, following the patterns elsewhere, it spread specifically along the furrows and streams of the Jewish Diaspora. In Asia, with the larger Jewish enclaves in the midst of Zoroastrian majorities, Asian Christianity developed in and with Semitic forms and patterns. In short, early Asian Christianity seems more Jewish than we are used to today. One of the earliest song books of Asia, the Odes of Solomon, was thought to be Jewish or gnostic when it was first translated.[6] However, on closer inspection it is clearly understood to be Christian. Consider how Jewish the following passage sounds from Ode 3, but then it has a clear Christian ring to it a few verses later:

> 5 I love the Beloved and I myself love Him, and where His rest is, there also am I.

---

[6]First published in 1912 by J. H. Bernard, and then reedited and published by J. Rendell Harris in 1916. Quotations are from James H. Charlesworth, ed. and trans., *The Odes of Solomon: The Syriac Texts* (Chico, CA: Scholars Press, 1977), 18-19, 34-35.

> 6 And I shall be no stranger, because there is no jealousy with the Lord Most High and Merciful.
>
> 7 I have been united to Him, because the lover has found the Beloved, because *I love Him that is the Son*, I shall become a son.
>
> 8 Indeed *he who is joined to Him, who is immortal*, truly shall be immortal.
>
> 9 And he who delights in the Life will become living.

Or, again, in a Semitic poetic form, the hymn writer tells us about the Messiah without mentioning his name, in Ode 7:

> 3 For there is a Helper for me, the Lord. He has generously shown Himself to me in His simplicity, because His kindness has diminished His dreadfulness.
>
> 4 *He became like me, that I might receive Him.* In form He was considered like me, that I might put Him on.
>
> 5 And I trembled not when I saw Him, because He was gracious to me.
>
> 6 *Like my nature He became, that I might understand Him.* And like my form, that I might not turn away from Him.
>
> 7 The Father of knowledge is the *Word of knowledge.*
>
> 8 He who created wisdom is wiser than His works.
>
> 9 And He who created me when yet I was not knew what I would do when I came into being.
>
> 10 On account of this He was gracious to me in His abundant grace, and allowed me to ask from Him and *to benefit from His sacrifice.*

Before we even get to the development of formal Christian education in Asia, we stop and note two themes here: we see the contextual nature of this early theology (for that is what it is), and we should also note that this early theology was sung. Some of the greatest theologians in early Asian Christianity were writing songs to sing theology, even in seminary. There is a strong pedagogical component to singing good theology.[7] I think it is still a good idea today.

---

[7] Ephrem the Syrian, known as the "Harp of the Spirit," wrote Christian hymns that were sung by women's choirs to combat heresies (mostly the followers of Bardaisan). Singing orthodox theology had a pedagogical power in building up the Church of the East. See, for example his *Hymns on Paradise*, ed. and trans. Sebastian Brock (Crestwood, NY: St. Vladimir's Seminary Press, 1990).

Spreading along trade routes, using local cultural forms that were available, these Christians by the third century were mostly converts from star worship or from Zoroastrianism. We are more familiar with the cultural engagement with Hellenistic thought in the West because it became so important for the theological stream that we are still very much indebted to, and that still confounds us. In the East it was more of a religious than a philosophical cultural engagement. Theology developed both within Zoroastrian culture and in resistance to that same culture. Zoroastrianism had many similarities to Christian and Jewish culture. Many modern Bible scholars, especially Old Testament scholars, have theorized that later Judaism of the prophets developed out of Zoroastrian theology, or at least from Zoroastrian concepts. Zoroastrians believe in a creator God, and they believe in a cosmic battle between God (Ahura Mazda) and an evil being similar to Satan (Ahriman). Much of the teaching about morality and purity sounds very much like Jewish law. Zoroastrianism also taught about a God who would bring about a consummation of all things through a savior figure called the *Shaoshant*. This savior would be born of a virgin and would win the final battle with the evil one. In my mind, it would be a great place to be a missionary. ("Savior . . . *Shaoshant*? Why, he has been born and he has fought the battle with Ahriman and won! Virgin birth? Yes, he was born of a virgin, and he conquered evil and even death!") It is a historic fact that the early missionaries to Persia were very successful in their preaching. Christianity grew very rapidly and extensively in Persia in the early centuries. Learning about this early Asian church and wondering about its rapid early growth was a question that drove me to write about early Asian Christianity. I asked, "How is it that early Christianity grew so rapidly in Asia, so that missionaries were already in China before the conversion of Russia and Sweden?"[8]

We don't have time to belabor the point, but a single example of how this message was communicated in a Zoroastrian context can be illustrated through a sermon on the nativity of our Lord, written in the late sixth century by Narsai. Narsai was called the "Interpreter of the School of Nisibis"; his job in leading his seminary was to preach through all of the Bible for the students to understand how to interpret Scripture. He was like a seminary president. As with

---

[8]Scott W. Sunquist, "Narsai and the Persians: A Study in Cross-cultural Contact and Conflict" (PhD diss., Princeton Theological Seminary, 1990).

most of the early Asians, he wrote sermons that sounded and looked like the Psalms: every few lines are written in parallelism. We find in the hymn-like sermons images, types, and allegories that are the vehicles used to convey the message. This type of preaching is different from what we are used to—it is heavily allegorical and extensively biblical—so let me offer some interpretive tools. The "household of Abraham" are the Jews. The "spiritual ones" are the angels. The "outsiders" are the Gentiles, which, for Narsai, are his Persian neighbors. We must remember the magi were probably Persians and therefore relatives of Narsai himself. His point in the following passage is that the Persians heard God's salvation first, and the Jews, who had all the advantages, did not understand. There are 508 lines in this long sermon; nearly one hundred of the lines of this sermon on the birth of Jesus have to do with the magi.

> To those among the Household [of Abraham],
> He sent spiritual ones and these [roused them];
> And among the outsiders,
> He sent a sign of his Will; and it gathered them.
> The members of the Household He assured by a promise,
> And those afar he encouraged by a star of light.
> With the insiders, He spoke through rational beings,
> And the outsiders He addressed by inanimate things.
> A star He sent as an envoy in search after the Gentiles,
> So that they might come and see the redemption of the universe
> To be accomplished through the Jewish people.
> ... In that very way they erred,
> He instructed them on how to learn about the truth.[9]

The Persians erred in reading the stars as a way to know truth. They were astrologers, many of them worshiping the star goddess Astarte. As they searched the stars for a sign, God condescended to their error and spoke to them through a star. As a result, they understood and worshiped by bringing gold, frankincense, and myrrh, long before the Jews worshiped Jesus. Narsai lifts up this element of his own culture and dedicates it to God in holy witness. It is a good model of contextual theology, I believe.

---

[9]From lines 261 to 271 of Narsai's "A Homily on Our Lord's Birth from the Holy Virgin." Translation by Frederick G. McLeod, SJ, in *Patrologia Orientalis*, tome XL, fascicule 1, #182 (Turnhout, Belgium: Brepols, 1979), 52-55.

A final note about this early growth of Christianity in Persia and beyond: Christian growth started among the poor and among traders, and slowly, with great persecution, Christians became people of status in the Persian Empire. The earliest church in Asia that has been found was at Dura Europus. The Jewish temple is found on a hill in the city, but the little house, converted to a church, is down near the river on what would have been a floodplain. It is clearly a church, since the artwork of the Good Shepherd and other biblical scenes are still visible on the walls. As in the West, early Christianity did not spread from a position of power, but from weakness as common people shared what they had heard and experienced. They were witnesses. Persecution was not strong in the early years because the Parthian rule was not strongly Zoroastrian. The Parthian rulers were more pluralistic, more tolerant, like the early Mongols before their conversion to Islam. However, when the Sasanians came to power (224 CE), there was a Zoroastrian revival, and the shah began to rule closely with a Zoroastrian priest or *mobed*. The land was now to be a pure and holy realm for Ahura Mazda. What this meant was that there needed to be fire temples in every town as part of the program to keep the land ritually pure. Purity was a major characteristic of Zoroastrianism, and death rituals were one way of keeping the land pure. A dead body would pollute the land, so the dead had to be exposed on towers until they dried out and the flesh was eaten by the birds. Then the dried carcass that remained would be buried in the ground.

Christians had no such customs; in fact they believed something very different. The dead must be put in the ground to await the resurrection of the dead. Because of Christians' resistance to Persian burial and other cultural practices, the Christians were severely persecuted by later Zoroastrian rulers. The catholicos moved the center of the Persian church to the Persian capital of Selucia-Ctesiphon to be near the shah and respond to requests or demands. Persecution was not consistent, so there were joyful times of toleration, but during times of persecution, bishops were rounded up, and the catholicos was called on to give names. Many bishops accepted the call to lead the church knowing it was a death sentence. At times the church would purposely choose the oldest men to be bishops, knowing that they would not live long. Christianity was shaped by this long, intermittent persecution. As a result, Christianity became austere and disciplined. A monastic theme is one of the strongest in early Asian Christianity.

Monastic Missions in Asia

It is interesting that in studying the great Asian theologian Ephrem the Syrian, many scholars have assumed that he was an ascetic monk.[10] In fact he was not. But his writings about the Christian lifestyle appear to support such an interpretation. The misunderstanding occurs because of our lack of understanding of early Persian spirituality. Persian Christians strongly emphasized the concept of *ihidaya*, from the Syriac, which means "singleminded" or "single" or "simple" or even "celibate." For them the image of Jesus as the Bridegroom of the church was a very strong image for the Christian. Both as individuals and corporately as the church, we are the bride of Christ. When a person was baptized they were returning to paradise. Baptism opened the door not to return to paradise physically, but in a spiritual sense we step into the kingdom, which is like paradise. These Syrian Christians assumed that there was no sexual intercourse in paradise, and so the idea of *ihidaya* becomes important here. The baptized is returning to a purer or holy (*qaddishe*) state of life. The baptized Christian is seen as "single," whether married or not. This may all seem strange to us today, but for the early Persian Christians this absolute identification with Jesus Christ as the bride of Christ was very strong, and from this belief came the view of singleness.

Thus, on one level the idea of singleness and holiness was a major theme for all of the laity. However, there were also people who were called out from family life to serve as monastic *qaddishe* or holy ones. Since the Christian life is seen as a marriage covenant, these people are called Sons or Daughters of the Covenant. Unlike the West, where monastics followed a rule, such as that of Benedict or Basil of Caesarea, in Persia we have to piece together some of these monastic practices. Ephrem's ascetic ideal might be called a protomonasticism. Such a lifestyle of denial and full devotion to Christ helped to give Persian Christianity its ascetic identity.

The missionary extension and development of Christianity across Asia was indebted to this monastic ethos. Persian missionaries wandered to the East, following the northern Silk Route to China (through Afghanistan, Turkmenistan, Tajikistan, etc.) and others following the southern Silk Route (through India). According to the early Persian synods—three major synods

---

[10]This discussion is indebted to Sebastian Brock's excellent introduction to Ephrem in his translation of *Hymns on Paradise*.

were held in the fifth century—bishops attended who represented places such as present-day Pakistan, Afghanistan, and Turkmenistan. This makes sense, since just a century later there would be Persian monks in western China, in the royal court of Xian.[11] The monks who arrived in China had Persian names that were inscribed in Syriac and Chinese on the Persian Monument, now found in the Forest of Steles in Xian. The leading "apostolic monk" (as he was called) was named Adam; he was identified as the pope for China. There was another Adam who was identified as the deacon, son of Jazedbuzid, vicar-bishop. Persian Christianity was so monastic that although we have a note that churches were built in every province in China (something that most historians doubt actually occurred), there is no outside indication that these were more than monastic centers for a type of monastic, Buddhist-influenced form of Christianity. The Tang emperors embraced in the early period, and then later rejected, the presence of monks. The early Christians came at a time when monks, Buddhist as well as Christian, were encouraged to translate and copy their sacred texts. This is what the Christians were famous for, according the Persian Monument: sacred texts. Later Tang rulers in the ninth and tenth centuries rejected monks as being lazy and contributing nothing to the country. Still, it is important to note that education and copying sacred texts seemed to be the main focus in earliest Chinese Christianity.

School of Nisibis

The School of Nisibis[12] is important because it became one of the largest and most influential Christian schools in all of Asian history. At its peak in the seventh century, it had about one thousand students. These students were not only preparing for ministry in local churches, but many would be part of the *peregrini*-like wandering missionaries that we have just spoken of. They were formed (theologically and spiritually) in this university-like seminary and carried this Persian form of Christianity to regions to the east, north, and south. We will focus briefly on the School of Nisibis, but first we need to look at the place of teaching and Christian education in the Persian Empire in general.

---

[11]Three major synods were held: the Synod of Isaac in 410, the Synod of Yabahallah in 420, and the Synod of Dadishu in 424. These synods established the ecclesial independence of the Church of the East, but also recognized the equality and theological agreement with the Roman Church.
[12]Nisibis is located in what would be called Kurdistan: bordering on Syria, Turkey, and Iraq.

The Syriac-speaking Christians in Persia had "a pedagogical understanding of the human being's place in the world." They understood their life in Christ as about being a student: school was always in session (and it didn't have to be a literal school). Adam Becker, author of a book on the School of Nisibis, notes that "Syriac Christians were talking about schools before they existed, and it was only later that, in a sense, the metaphor became reality."[13] At a school whose curriculum was built so closely around Scripture, this makes perfect sense. Jesus is identified as the Logos or reason of God. Jesus was called a rabbi and went around teaching "with authority." Paul turns the tables on the Greeks by saying that the foolishness of God's teaching (or wisdom) was greater than that of Greeks (1 Cor 1; 2). If others did not pick up on this important image of the Christian life, why did the Persians?[14]

One simple answer is that the Syrian Christians were working with the Peshitta rather than the Septuagint for their Old Testament. In a number of places the translator has added teaching or pedagogical examples or language. For example, in 1 Chronicles 22:13 the Masoretic text says, "the statutes and the ordinances that the LORD commanded Moses for Israel." The Peshitta says, "the statutes and the ordinances that the Lord commanded Moses to teach Israel." One more example will suffice. Exodus 18:19 in the Masoretic text says, "You should represent the people before God," but the Peshitta says, "You, be a teacher to the people of God." Those reading Syriac were predisposed to see their relationship to God as pedagogical, and therefore their life with Jesus as one of teacher to student. Ephrem, who first led a school in Syria (Edessa) that was later moved to Nisibis, also used pedagogical language concerning our relationship with God. Becker makes the comment, "The conception of God as pedagogically guiding creation to knowledge of God himself is ubiquitous in Ephrem's works." According to Ephrem, God has revealed himself to humanity through three modes:

1. types and symbols that are present in both nature and in Scripture

2. "names," or metaphors that God allows to be used of himself in Scripture

3. (above all) in the incarnation

---

[13] Adam Becker, *The Fear of God and the Beginning of Wisdom: The School of Nisibis and the Development of Scholastic Culture in Late Antique Mesopotamia* (Philadelphia: University of Pennsylvania Press, 2006), 22. All of chapter one is on the understanding of pedagogy in Syriac Christianity.

[14] The following two paragraphs are taken from Becker's first chapter on pedagogy.

For Ephrem, knowledge and learning is all about knowing God. Ephrem is one of a long line of Syriac Christian writers who play with this theme. A later Syriac father, Jacob of Sarug, writes of Jesus as the "Great Scribe" who came down from heaven and became a teacher to the world so that creation was illuminated with his teaching. A scribe is more than just one who writes things down. Following the Jewish leadership roles, the scribes were teachers who passed down the treasured teachings of the law. Jacob, in a homily on divine pedagogy, gives an invocation to God:

> Oh skilled scribe, be for me a master [*rabba*] full of wisdoms
> And I will be full of understanding for your word as a student [*talmida*].

In another homily he uses the metaphor of the cross as a teacher:

> The cross was a scribe for the world and from it [the world] learned
> To worship the Father in spirit in all places.

However, all of this learning and teaching about learning was not purely Christian or even purely Christian Persian. There were other cultural mixes here. We have already noted the strong Semitic threads in the Syriac fabric of teaching and learning. Another element was that of Hellenistic learning. In the very important history of early Persian Christianity, we learn that the Persian schools were seen as continuations and even as perfectings of the Greek academies. The title of this Syrian church history is itself telling: *Cause of the Foundation of the Schools*. Imagine writing a church history focused on schools. I think it is a great idea. Here we see the intercultural nature of Persian theology. The understanding of history (as seen through schools) was a Western borrowing, and the Persian Christians set up a major translation project to bring European (Greek) learning to Persia. Beginning in the mid- to late fourth century, an enormous amount of Greek literature was being translated into Syriac. Thus, there is no such thing as a "pure Persian theology." Persians were learning from the Greek thinkers (not the Latin thinkers), while living with Zoroastrian neighbors. However, they were shaping Greek patristic thought even as they translated it. In translating the Greek word *politeia*, from which we get the word *politics* ("a way of life"), the Syriac translator used the word *yullphana*, which means "learning" or "doctrine." When translating the word for race (*genos*), the translator used the word *talmada wihydh*, which is more properly "instruction" or "discipleship." There are many other ways that we could illustrate how Persians both borrowed and shaped early Christian thought, but this is enough to illustrate the point. One final influence in this view of teaching and learning came from the local context of Zoroastrianism. In a number of martyrdom stories in Persia, a person starts out as a student of a magi, or as one studying in a magian school. Upon conversion, they change schools; they now have a different master. Zoroastrianism was a form of learning that was substituted by Christian teaching on conversion. Religion, in fact life itself, is being a student of a master.

Regarding the important Persian School of Nisibis, I want to focus only on two elements: the curriculum and the laws. That's right, the school had a student handbook, and this handbook, called the "Laws of the School of Nisibis," tells us a lot about the school, the temptations of the students, and the standards of life with one thousand young men living in what used to be horse stalls; first the laws.

The laws indicate that seminary life was closely patterned after monastic life. The laws were written as a covenant between the school (or the main interpreter, the seminary president) and the students. The pattern looks very much like an Old Testament pattern, describing witnesses, rewards, punishments, and where the laws are placed. The concerns of the laws are obvious as we read them. The main concern is to keep the men disciplined. There are punishments for being rebellious, fighting, taking a wife, or not taking care of a sick cell mate. You could be removed from the community if you spoke out of turn (canon thirteen) or if you were caught stealing or changing books or erasing the names of deceased brothers (canon eight). There are a number of canons that proscribe students going over to the side of the Romans for trading purposes or being too involved in business. The Persian Christian's need to stay separate from the world is expressed throughout these laws. Students or "brothers" are not allowed to live with physicians, "lest books of the craft of the world be read with the books of holiness." They are not to eat at taverns and restaurants, and they are not to have picnics in the parks, "but shall endure all in their cells as is becoming for the purpose and the manner of their covenant" (canon sixteen). In short, the brothers were to be disciplined, help one another, and stay out of worldly entanglements.

The curriculum was clearly focused on Scripture and liturgy. The two were not considered completely different since the liturgy was seen as a playing out of the Scripture narrative. It is better to think not in terms of curriculum as particular courses, but as levels of learning and content areas. The school seemed to imitate the Greek schools in its tripartite division of teaching. In the Greek system, it would be elementary instructor, then grammarian, and finally rhetorician or philosopher. At this School of Nisibis the three levels are elementary instructor, reader, and then exegete. Students would learn first from the Psalms. In fact, at one time the entrance exam to the school was to prove that you had memorized all of the Psalms. Biblical exegesis was the rice diet of the school. Correct reading, correct copying, and correct interpreting of the text were all seen as one. The text was considered sacred and treated that way. Part of the education also included singing in the choirs. Poetry and singing, even singing the liturgy (and possibly some homilies), was common. Here at the school there was grammar, interpretation, liturgical studies, and singing, but unlike the Western schools there was no philosophy. The Greek-speaking schools of the West continued the tradition of Western philosophy. Persian schools never started it.

A few other items about the school will help to fill out the picture. The school calendar was built around the harvest cycle; thus the liturgical year fit it well with the school calendar. In addition, the subject areas were broadly divided up according to large portions of Scripture: in the first year the students would write the Psalms and the letters of Paul. Once again the study of liturgies was woven into the total study of the school.

> The study of scripture and the performance of liturgy are not distinct but rather two sides of the same coin, since liturgy was also an object of study (and of course consisted in part of excerpts from scripture) and the study of scripture was scheduled around and treated as part of the liturgical calendar. . . . Study itself seemed to have been a form of devotion embedded in the liturgical practice.[15]

Finally, this major institution was involved in controversies of the day. As we noted earlier, Persia was related to the churches in the Roman Empire

---

[15]Becker, *Fear of God and the Beginning of Wisdom*, 94.

even though they were not dependent on them. As is generally the case, churches have to organize around national or imperial structures. The Methodist Church split between Singapore and Malaysia when Singapore left the Federation. There is a Lutheran church in Germany and a different one in Denmark, an Anglican church in India (now part of two ecumenical churches) and an Anglican church in Sri Lanka. Also, the Church of the East (as the Persian church has been called) was related to the Byzantine Church, but it was independent. The Persian church received many immigrants from the Roman Empire as a result of persecution, and gradually Roman sins of division were visited on the Persian church. The Roman Church's divisions and arguments over Christology were exported to Persia almost as soon as the controversies broke out. Looking back over fifteen centuries later, we can see how tragic this was for the Persian church. Much of their theological development became defensive and even combative. The East Syrian Church sided with Theodore of Mopsuestia, Diodore, and Nestorius over against the Orthodox Christology of the Byzantine Church. In the fifth and sixth centuries these theological battles took center stage. Looking back at the homilies and hymns, it is hard to believe that the church had any missionary outreach at all because it became so preoccupied with internal battles. A few examples should suffice. Narsai, who was head of the School of Nisibis for about fourteen years (until 503), delivered homilies throughout the year, following the liturgical calendar. In almost every homily I have read, he waxes poetically and then suddenly stops to attack the theology of Cyril of Alexandria with lines such as, "You wicked Cyril." In a homily on the Epiphany, he tells the story of Jesus coming up to John, and John exclaiming, "Behold the Lamb who purifies the stains of sin and takes away iniquity!"[16] John then exclaims that here is one who is

> younger than me is his conception and his birth according to bodily structure,
> But older than me as regards the things that are to come and the mysteries that are awaited.

---

[16]Narsai, "Homily on the Epiphany of our Lord," lines 198, 201, 202, 213-18; in McLeod, *Patrologia Orientalis*, 82-83.

Then Narsai sets off on the issue of Christology and the two natures in Christ. His tone is sarcastic and belittling. He asks rhetorical questions and then seems to shout,

> God forbid! Let it not be that this is what we should say or think:
> that the power of Divine Essence has need of the power of lowly flesh!
> It is flesh which has been exalted and has acquired power by means of the
>   Divine Essence:
> It is not the Divine Essence that acquired assistance from a mortal being!
> A corporeal being the divine good pleasure put on;
> And he conquered and made his fellow men conquer by the power of
> his assumer.

This may seem a little pedantic and boring today, but for the Diophysites, this was a critical concern: we must protect the full divinity of Jesus and the full humanity.[17] Not once but three times during this one beautiful homily, Narsai breaks away and takes up the argument against his opponents. If I were to read you these long passages of defense, you would hardly get the subtlety and nuances of the argument. In general his approach is much less allegorical and paradoxical than Orthodox theology will allow. The Orthodox will allow that the flame of divinity existed in the wet womb of humanity, being both confined and not consuming humanity. It is a beautiful image, but Narsai will have none of it. Infinity or divine essence cannot exist in a woman. Or, as Narsai says, "The One, containing all limit, a womb of flesh can not contain." And so, poetic beauty is broken by pugnacious bantering throughout his preaching. My point here is that it is another example of how foreign or Western[18] theological arguments are taken up by Asians. We will talk later about the need to be globally or ecumenically involved, but at the same time contextually rooted. In this case the introduction of Western church divisions unnecessarily weakened Asian Christianity.

THREE TYPES OF ASIAN CHRISTIAN SCHOOLS

Before we look at what possible lessons all of this has for us today, it is important to first recognize that theological education was not done only in

---

[17]The east Syrians, as Diophysites, emphasized the two distinct natures (human and divine) in Christ, which never touch and can always be distinguished in Jesus' acts and words.

[18]From Persia, Greek theology from Constantinople is the "West."

major schools such as Nisibis. In fact theological education by the fifth century was, roughly speaking, in three forms: village schools, monastic schools, and independent schools. At the most basic level there were village schools that taught literacy and basic writing and grammar. Village schools were generally small, located in or near a church, and built around a central teacher or exegete. Some schools would have been more advanced, teaching biblical interpretation, but most concentrated on knowledge of the sacred texts and the liturgy. We read in the life of Babai of Gebilta from the *Book of Governors* that there was a time in the eighth century when much of the village school education was in disarray. It is a good guess that this situation was brought about by the Arab invasions. In the eighth century, Babai helped to reorganize the hymns, promote again their singing, and reorganize the curriculum, and then he started many new schools. Most of the new schools were freestanding, but some were attached to monasteries.

Monastic schools are the second type of school. As we might guess, these were schools that were located in monasteries and that basically served the monks. However, these schools also provided basic catechesis and elementary education for local boys. Many of the monastic schools were built by wealthy local Christians, so there was a sense of patronage about them. In historic records of the period, we read of many monasteries being built and then schools being added for famous teachers and scholars, or by wealthy Christian patrons. Monastic schools, we might add, provided the ongoing training of Christian leaders throughout the Islamic period in Persia. Schools in major cities were quickly closed, but monasteries and their schools seemed to have had greater durability.

Finally, we have the larger independent schools such as Nisibis, Edessa, Arbela, and Seleucia. As we can see, these were schools built in urban centers. They were usually built under the patronage of the catholicos (such as Seleucia) or a wealthy Christian in the region. We read that the School of Seleucia was founded by the catholicos Mar Abba after he won a public debate with a Zoroastrian priest (ca. 550). Although the account of the debate given in the *Chronicle of Seert* (or Siirt) is rather fantastic and probably mythical, the context of Zoroastrian conflict and debate is quite accurate. One might expect that with such a beginning, the curriculum was built more around apologetic concerns related to the Zoroastrian context. Until we find a curriculum or more homilies from this school, we are left to wonder and theorize. Another school in the village of Kaskar was founded by Gregory of Kaskar. The region was mostly non-Christian, so the founder and head interpreter, Gregory, encouraged his students to devote themselves to prayer and fasting while he went throughout the region preaching to the many non-Christians. Thus, both Gregory of Kaskar and Mar Abba are developing schools and theology in light of interreligious contacts. These contacts seem to be the impetus for the founding of the schools.

These independent schools also seemed to have had more money, so there was more scholarship for the larger church produced at these centers. Commentaries, books of homilies, and hymns were produced mostly from these schools. These larger schools also apparently shared or fought over faculty. We read of some faculty exchanges between Seleucia and Nisibis. As today, the larger and better endowed schools probably attracted the best teachers. Finally, we read in the famous *Chronicle of Seert* that the conflicts over Christology (Bishop Henana turned from Diophysite to Monophysite, splitting the School of Nisibis) divided seminaries and caused the founding of new schools. The School of Balad was founded (ca. 640) by scholars who left Nisibis and were supported by Marcus, the bishop of Balad. In fact at least three schools were founded to correct or compete with Nisibis.

What Hath the Eighth Century to Do with the Twenty-First Century?

I believe history always has lessons for us, but the lessons are not always clear, and they are seldom direct. We should resist direct applications and look for some of the themes of theological education in early Asian church history that may give us some perspective for today. I am not as concerned to see what this may say for Western theological education, but I would like to ask how early Asian theological education may provide some guidance for Asian theological education today. We may not think of this as at all related to Sri Lanka, China, or South Asia, but I would like to suggest that it is important to see our Christian history in Asia as in a long line of Asian Christians struggling to give a faithful witness as a minority faith. There is nothing like this in Western church history, because once seminaries and schools were being developed in Europe (in the fifth century), the empire had already become

Christian. In Asia, Christian schools have always developed in minority contexts with intermittent or (at times) extensive persecution, generally in the shadow of the West.[19] I will suggest only a few lines for future reflection. Some of what occurred in these early Asian Christian centuries is winsome and laudable. Some of it is less so!

Theological education took place in diverse forms and in diverse places. The three types of schools are general categories, not watertight education silos. There were schools that would not fit neatly in one of the three types. The ways they were initiated and how they were supported varied greatly. However, in all cases the curriculum was built on Scripture, in close interpersonal relationships, and the liturgy and the liturgical calendar sprang out of scriptural studies. I call this "diversity of sizes and structures, but unity of content and concern."

Theological education was contextual, but at the same time multicultural. There was no such thing as a purely Persian school. The schools were influenced by Greek thought, but not completely. They did not teach philosophy—something that has completely reshaped the biblical story in the West—but they did use many of the forms, and certainly they were influenced by Western church conflicts.

The schools had discipline problems. The laws of the School of Nisibis are fascinating, but not unique. They offer a window into some of the struggles that the schools had in maintaining order and focus. However, we might want to question the answer that was given in Nisibis. In this context it seems that Christian development ended up with a church (or at least a seminary) that was positioned as separated from and at times against the world. The very idea that it was bad for a seminary student to live with a low-life physician is rather odd. Today in Asia it might be good to encourage seminary students to live with teachers, lawyers, and doctors to have ongoing dialogue about Christian presence in daily life. After all, most evangelistic work of the church in Asia (as throughout Christian history) is carried out by laypeople.

Teachers seemed to be holy men or spiritual masters. When we read about Ephrem or Narsai or Babai, we often read about their holy lives. Teaching was proven by the lives of the teachers. There was a direct line of teachers from

---

[19]The one exception is the Philippines, but this is in the modern period, and it was established under the strong authority and control of New Spain (Mexico).

Jesus to the disciples to the early Asian teachers, who were rabbis of holiness. They were expected to be men (for most of them were men) of spiritual power and ascetic discipline. Today, does theological education and preparation for ministry support such a model?

Finally, I find it impressive that the way of communicating the revelation of God's redemptive love included grammar, writing, liturgy, poetic homilies, and hymns. Theology was sung and rhythmically spoken. Theology was acted out yearly through the liturgical calendar. In all of this creative exposure to the gospel message, both students in the schools and laypeople inculcated a rhythm of life that challenged the Zoroastrian rhythm of life around them. They were creating a countercultural community and ethos, presenting an alternative way of viewing the universe. I believe we can learn from such an approach, working for the complete conversion of culture.

Christianity developed across Asia from the first century, but its nerve centers, its nurturing and strengthening centers, were monasteries and theological schools; often they were the same institution. It is appropriate and even necessary to look at schools and not just churches in Asia, since the schools provide the leadership for the church: evangelistic, theological, and pastoral. We are not early Persian Christians, and therefore we are not as ascetic and monastic as they were. However, it is important for us to see that these earlier expressions of Asian Christianity are the forebearers of the Asian church. Asians in the twenty-first century are not unrelated. We may not be so ascetic, but at least in Asia we are part of a great tradition of religious ascetics and spiritual masters who helped the Asian church survive centuries of oppression and persecution.

These early Asian Christians are not really that different or distant from us. The gospel they proclaimed has not changed, and human nature—reflecting God's glory, but stained with sin—has not changed. We have seen how early Asian Christians were involved in a global or at least a multicultural world. We have seen how their theology and even their schools were developed within a persecuted minority community. Contact and conflict with the majority faiths shaped Christian teaching and life. Their faith was shaped by different languages and translation projects. Because of the incarnation principle it is expected that Jesus will eventually speak the language of each local group of people. Translation continues to be an Asian Christian concern. Early Persian Christianity was influenced by Zoroastrian cultural views and the Jewish or Semitic heritage, as well as the Hellenistic (mostly Aristotelian) philosophy and logic. Such pluralism has always been and continues to be a hallmark of Asian Christianity. Theological education in Asia should mimic these themes, as seminaries and Bible schools root themselves more deeply in Asian traditions rather than in the traditions of the West. This resistance to neocolonialism in Christian education is difficult because of the long tradition of theological education in the West, and the massive amount of literature and the money that are still available to bring in Western models as a complete and integrated whole. However, healthy partnerships that allow the local Asian contexts and leaders to set the agenda are possible. Even more so, it is necessary if Christian discipleship is really going bring about transformation of local cultures and societies.

Bibliography

Abraham, K. C., and T. K. Thomas. "Asia." In *A History of the Ecumenical Movement.* Vol. 3, *1968-2000*, ed. John Biggs, Mercy Amba Oduyoye, and Georges Tsetsis, 495-522. Geneva: World Council of Churches, 2004.

Adams, Rebekah E. *Called to China: Attie Bostick's Life and Missionary Letters from China, 1900-1943.* Huntsville, AL: Halldale, 2006.

Aland, Kurt. *A History of Christianity.* Vol. 2, *From the Reformation to the Present.* Translated by James L. Schaaf. Philadelphia: Fortress, 1986.

Allen, Roland. *Missionary Methods: St. Paul's or Ours; A Study in Four Provinces.* London: Robert Scott, 1912.

———. *Missionary Principles.* London: Robert Scott, 1913.

———. *The Spontaneous Expansion of the Church and the Causes Which Hinder It.* London: World Dominion, 1927.

Anderson, Allan. *Spreading Fires: The Missionary Nature of Early Pentecostalism.* Maryknoll, NY: Orbis Books, 2007.

Anderson, Rufus. *Foreign Missions: Their Relations and Claims.* 3rd ed. Boston: Congregational Pub. Society, 1874.

Athyal, Saphir. *Church in Asia Today: Challenges and Opportunities.* Singapore: Asia Lausanne Committee for World Evangelization, 1996.

Bardaisan. *The Book of the Laws of Countries.* Translated by H. J. W. Drijvers. Piscataway, NJ: Gorgias, 2007.

Barrett, David, George T. Kurian, and Todd Johnson. *World Christian Encyclopedia.* 2nd ed. New York: Oxford University Press, 2001.

Barth, Karl. *Church Dogmatics III/2.* Translated by Geoffrey W. Bromiley and T. F. Torrance. Edinburgh: T&T Clark, 1962.

———. *Church Dogmatics IV/3.1.* Translated by Geoffrey W. Bromiley and T. F. Torrance. Edinburgh: T&T Clark.

Baumer, Christoph. *The Church of the East: An Illustrated History of Assyrian Christianity.* London: I. B. Tauris, 2006.

Bays, Daniel H., ed. *Christianity in China: From the Eighteenth Century to the Present,* Stanford, CA: Stanford University Press, 1996.

———. "Foreign Missions and Indigenous Protestant Leaders in China, 1920–1955: Identity and Loyalty in an Age of Powerful Nationalism." In *Missions, Nationalism, and the End of Empire*, ed. Brian Stanley, 144-64. Grand Rapids: Eerdmans, 2003.

———. "The Growth of Independent Christianity in China, 1900–1937." In *Christianity in China: From the Eighteenth Century to the Present*, ed. Daniel H. Bays, 307-16. Stanford, CA: Stanford University Press, 1996.

Bays, Daniel H., and Ellen Widmer, eds. *China's Christian Colleges: Cross-Cultural Connections, 1900–1950.* Stanford, CA: Stanford University Press, 2009.

Beaver, R. Pierce. "The Legacy of Rufus Anderson." *Occasional Bulletin of Missionary Research* 3 (July 1979): 94-97.

Becker, Adam H. *Fear of God and the Beginning of Wisdom: The School of Nisibis and the Development of Scholastic Culture in Late Antique Mesopotamia.* Philadelphia: University of Pennsylvania Press, 2006.

Bergunder, Michael. *The South Indian Pentecostal Movement in the Twentieth Century.* Grand Rapids: Eerdmans, 2008.

Bohr, Paul Richard. *Famine in China and the Missionary: Timothy Richard as Relief Administrator and Advocate of National Reform, 1876–1884.* Cambridge, MA: Harvard University Press, 1972.

Brockey, Liam Matthew. *Journey to the East: The Jesuit Mission to China, 1579–1724.* Cambridge, MA: Harvard University Press, 2007.

Brown, G. Thompson. *Earthen Vessels and Transcendent Power, American Presbyterians in China, 1837–1952.* Maryknoll, NY: Orbis Books, 1997.

Bryce, James. "Responsibilities of Christian Nations Toward the Backward Races." In *Students and the Present Missionary Crisis*, 109-16. New York: Student Volunteer Movement for Foreign Missions, 1910.

Buck, Pearl S. "The Laymen's Mission Report." *Christian Century*, November 23, 1932, 1434.

Calvin, John. *Institutes of the Christian Religion.* Edited by John T. McNeill. Translated by Ford Lewis Battles. Philadelphia: Westminster, 1960.

Charbonnier, Jean-Pierre. *Christians in China, A.D. 600 to 2000.* San Francisco: Ignatius, 2008.

Charlesworth, James Hamilton, trans. *The Odes of Solomon: The Syriac Texts.* Chico, CA: Scholars Press, 1977.

Clark, Allen D. *A History of the Church in Korea.* Seoul: The Christian Literature Society of Korea, 1971.

Cliff, Norman H. "Building the Protestant Church in Shandong, China." *International Bulletin of Missionary Research* 22, no. 2 (April 1998): 62-68.

Clymer, Kenton J. *Protestant Missionaries in the Philippines, 1898–1916: An Inquiry into the Colonial American Mentality.* Chicago: University of Illinois Press, 1986.

Cooley, Frank L. *The Growing Seed: The Christian Church in Indonesia.* New York: The Division of Overseas Ministries, NCCUSA, 1981.

Corbett, Hunter. *A Record of the American Presbyterian Missionary Work in Shantung Province, China.* 2nd ed. N.p., 1914.

Crawford, Mary K. *The Shantung Revival.* Shanghai: The China Baptist Publication Society, 1933. Second printing by Revival Association Publishers, Shreveport, LA.

Cummins, J. S. *A Question of Rites: Friar Domingo Navarrete and the Jesuits in China.* Aldershot, UK: Scholar Press, 1993.

Dallet, Charles. *The History of the Catholic Church in Korea.* Vol. 1. New Haven, CT: Human Relations Area Files, 1952.

Davies, Noel, and Martin Conway. *World Christianity in the Twentieth Century.* London: SCM Press, 2008.

Deleanu, Daniel, trans. *The Doctrine of Addai the Apostle.* Toronto: LogoStar, 2012.

Dembski, William A. *The End of Christianity: Finding a Good God in an Evil World.* Nashville: B & H, 2009.

Dodgen, Randall A. *Controlling the Dragon: Confucian Engineers and the Yellow River in Late Imperial China.* Honolulu: University of Hawai'i Press, 2001.

Dong, Ting-Liang. "A Gospel Village in Shandong." *China News Update*, September 1996; translated and excerpted from *Tiang Feng*, February 1996, 18-19.

Drijvers, H. J. W. *The Book of the Laws of Countries: Dialogue on Fate of Bardaisan of Edessa.* Assen: Van Gorcum, 1965.

Dykstra, Paul Stephen. *Triumphs of His Grace in Shantung China.* Los Angeles: Angelus Temple, 1936.

Ephrem. *Hymns on Paradise.* Introduction and translated by Sebastian Brock. Crestwood, NY: St. Vladimir's Seminary Press, 1990.

Evans, E.W. Price. *Timothy Richard: A Narrative of Christian Enterprise and Statesmanship in China.* London: Carey, 1945.

Evers, Georg. *The Churches in Asia.* Delhi: ISPCK, 2005.

Fairman, Marion, ed. *Red-Headed, Rash and Religious: The Story of a Pioneer Missionary.* Pittsburgh: Board of Christian Education of the UPCNA, 1954.

Fiey, J. J. *Jalons Pour Une Histoire de L'Eglise en Iraq*. Louvain: Secrétariat du CorpusSCO, 1970.
Fisher, Daniel W. *Calvin Wilson Mateer: Forty-Five Years a Missionary in Shantung, China*. Philadelphia: Westminster, 1911. www.archive.org/stream/calvinwilson mateoofish/calvinwilsonmateoofish_djvu.txt.
Flett, John G. "God Is a Missionary God: Missio Dei, Karl Barth and the Doctrine of the Trinity." PhD diss., Princeton Theological Seminary, 2007.
Foster, John. *The Church of the T'Ang Dynasty*. London: SPCK, 1939.
Freston, Paul. *Evangelicals and Politics in Asia, Africa and Latin America*. Cambridge: Cambridge University Press, 2001.
Friesen, J. Stanley. *Missionary Responses to Tribal Religions at Edinburgh, 1910*. Frankfurt am Main: Peter Lang, 1996.
Gairdner, W. H. T. *Echoes from Edinburgh, 1910: An Account and Interpretation of the World Missionary Conference*. London: Fleming H. Revell, 1910.
Garside, Bettis A. *One Increasing Purpose: The Life of Henry Winters Luce*. New York: Fleming H. Revell, 1958.
Gillman, Ian, and Hans-Joachim Klimkeit. *Christians in Asia Before 1500*. Ann Arbor: University of Michigan Press, 1999.
Griffis, William Ellion. *Corea: The Hermit Nation*. New York: Scribner's Sons, 1894.
Grubb, Kenneth, ed. *World Christian Handbook*. London: World Dominion, 1949.
Guder, Darrell. *The Continuing Conversion of the Church*. Grand Rapids: Eerdmans, 2000.
Harper, Keith, ed. *Send the Light: Lottie Moon's Letters and Other Writings*. Macon, GA: Mercer University Press, 2002.
Harrak, Amir, trans. *Acts of Mar Mari the Apostle*. Atlanta: Society of Biblical Literature, 2005.
Harrison, Brian. *Waiting for China: The Anglo Chinese College at Malacca, 1818–1843, and Early Nineteenth-Century Missions*. Hong Kong: Hong Kong University Press, 1979.
Hattaway, Paul. *China's Christian Martyrs*. Oxford: Monarch Books, 2007.
Heeren, John J. *On the Shantung Front: A History of the Shantung Mission of the Presbyterian Church in the U.S.A., 1861–1940, in Its Historical, Economic and Political Setting*. New York: Board of Foreign Missions of the PC in the USA, 1940.
Heyler, Larry R. "Thomas, Gospel of/Acts of." In *The Oxford Encyclopaedia of South Asian Christianity*, ed. Roger E. Hedlund, 2:689. New York: Oxford University Press, 2012.

Hiebert, Paul. *Anthropological Reflections on Missiological Issues*. Grand Rapids: Baker Books, 1994.
Hood, George. *Neither Bang nor Whimper: The End of a Missionary Era in China*. Singapore: The Presbyterian Church in Singapore, 1991.
Horsley, Richard A., ed. *A People's History of Christianity*. Vol. 1, *Christian Origins*. Minneapolis: Fortress, 2005.
Hudson, D. Dennis. *Protestant Origins in India: Tamil Evangelical Christians, 1706-1835*. Grand Rapids: Eerdmans, 2000.
Hunt, Robert, Lee Kam Hing, and John Roxborogh, eds. *Christianity in Malaysia: A Denominational History*. Selangor, Malaysia: Pelanduk, 1992.
Huntley, Martha. *Caring, Growing, Changing: A History of the Protestant Mission in Korea*. New York: Friendship, 1984.
Hutchinson, William. *Errand to the World: American Protestant Thought and Foreign Mission*. Chicago: University of Chicago Press, 1987.
Hyatt, Irwin T., Jr. *Our Ordered Lives Confess: Three Nineteenth-Century American Missionaries in East Shantung*. Cambridge, MA: Harvard University Press, 1976.
Irvin, Dale T. *Christian Histories, Christian Traditioning: Rendering Accounts*. Maryknoll, NY: Orbis Books, 1998.
Irvin, Dale T., and Scott W. Sunquist. *History of the World Christian Movement*. 3 vols. Maryknoll, NY: Orbis Books, 2001-.
Jackson, Eleanor. "From Krishna Pal to Lal Behari Dey: Indian Builders of the Church in Bengal, 1800-1894." In *Converting Colonialism: Visions and Realities in Mission History, 1706-1914*, ed. Dana Robert, 166-205. Grand Rapids: Eerdmans, 2008.
Jenkins, Philip. *The Next Christendom: The Coming of Global Christianity*. Oxford: Oxford University Press, 2002.
Jongeneel, Jan A. B., Peter Tze Ming Ng, Chong Ku Paek, Scott W. Sunquist, and Yuko Watanabe, eds. *Christian Mission and Education in Modern China, Japan and Korea*. Frankfurt am Main: Peter Lang, 2009.
Kalu, Obgu U., ed. *Interpreting Contemporary Christianity: Global Processes and Local Identities*. Grand Rapids: Eerdmans, 2008.
Kim, In Soo. *Protestants and the Formation of Modern Korean Nationalism, 1885-1920*. New York: Peter Lang, 1996.
Koschorke, Klaus, Frieder Ludwig, and Mariano Delgado, eds. *A History of Christianity in Asia, Africa and Latin America, 1450-1990*. Grand Rapids: Eerdmans, 2007.
Labourt, J. *Le Christianisme dans L'Empire Perse sous la Dynastie Sassanide (224-632)*. Paris: Librairie Victor Lecoffre, 1904.

Lackner, Michael, and Natascha Vittinghoff, eds. *Mapping Meanings: The Field of New Learning in Late Qing China.* Leiden: Brill, 1985.

Latourette, Kenneth Scott. *Anno Domini: Jesus, History, and God.* New York: Harper and Brothers, 1940.

———. *Challenge and Conformity: Studies in the Interaction of Christianity and the World of Today.* New York: Harper and Brothers, 1955.

———. *The Unquenchable Light.* New York: Harper and Brothers, 1940.

Lewis, Donald M., ed. *Christianity Reborn: The Global Expansion of Evangelicalism in the Twentieth Century.* Grand Rapids: Eerdmans, 2004.

Lindell, Jonathan. *Nepal and the Gospel of God.* Kathmandu, Nepal: United Mission to Nepal, 1979.

Lineham, Peter J. *Bible and Society: A Sesquicentennial History of the Bible Society in New Zealand.* Wellington, New Zealand: The Bible Society in New Zealand, 1996.

Lumsdaine, David H. *Evangelical Christianity and Democracy in Asia.* Oxford: Oxford University Press, 2009.

Marchant, Leslie R. *British Protestant Christian Evangelists and the 1898 Reform Movement in China.* Singapore: University of Western Australia, Center for East Asian Studies, 1975.

Martel, Yann. *The Life of Pi.* New York: Alfred A. Knopf, 2001.

Martin, David. *Pentecostalism: The World Their Parish.* Malden, MA: Blackwell, 2002.

Mateer, Robert McCheyne. *Character Building in China: The Life-Story of Julia Brown Mateer.* New York: Fleming H. Revell, 1912.

McGowan, Andrew. "'A Third Race' or Not: A Rhetoric of Ethnic Self-Definition in Tertullian." *Patristica Bostoniensia*, November 2001.

McIntire, C. T., ed. *God, History, and Historians: An Anthology of Modern Christian Views of History.* New York: Oxford University Press, 1977.

McLeod, Frederick G., SJ. *Narsai's Metrical Homilies on the Nativity, Epiphany, Passion, Resurrection and Ascension.* In *Patrologia Orientalis*, tome XL, fascicule 1, no. 182. Turnhout, Belgium, 1979.

McVey, Kathleen E. *Ephrem the Syrian, Hymns.* New York: Paulist, 1989.

Mingana, A. "The Early Spread of Christianity in Central Asia and the Far East: A New Document." *Bulletin of the John Rylands Library* 9 (1925): 297-372.

Moffett, Samuel A. Letters and articles of Samuel A. Moffett as compiled by Eileen Flower Moffett: 1870–1936.

Moffett, Samuel Hugh. *A History of Christianity in Asia.* 2 vols. Maryknoll, NY: Orbis Books, 1998, 2005.

Monsen, Marie. *The Awakening: Revival in China, a Work of the Holy Spirit.* Translated by Joy Guiness. London: China Inland Mission, 1959.
Morrison, Charles Clayton. "The World Missionary Conference, 1910." *Christian Century*, July 7, 1910. www.religion-online.org/showarticle.asp?title=471.
Moule, A. C. *Christians in China Before the Year 1550.* London: SPCK, 1930.
Mullins, Mark R. "The Empire Strikes Back: Korean Pentecostal Mission to Japan." In *Charismatic Christianity as a Global Culture*, ed. Karla Poewe, 87-102. Columbia: University of South Carolina Press, 1994.
Mundadan, A. Mathias, CMI, ed. *History of Christianity in India.* 4 vols. Bangalore: Theological Publications in India, 1982-1992.
Mungello, D. E. *The Spirit and the Flesh in Shandong, 1650-1785.* New York: Rowman and Littlefield, 2001.
Murray, Robert. *Symbols of Church and Kingdom: A Study in Early Tradition.* Cambridge: Cambridge University Press, 1975.
Nevius, Helen S. Coan. *The Life of John Livingston Nevius: For Forty Years a Missionary in China.* New York: Fleming H. Revell, 1895.
Nevius, John L. *Methods of Mission Work.* New York: Foreign Missions Library, 1895.
Newbigin, J. E. Lesslie. "Can the West Be Converted?" *Princeton Seminary Bulletin* 6, no. 1 (1985): 25-37.
Ohlinger, Franklin. Editorial, *Korean Repository*, January 1892, 37.
Osgood, Cornelius. *The Koreans and Their Culture.* New York: Ronald, 1951.
Partee, Charles. *The Story of Don McClure: Adventure in Africa.* Grand Rapids: Zondervan, 1990.
Phan, Phát Huôn, CSsR. *History of the Catholic Church in Viêt Nam.* Long Beach, CA: Cúu Thê Tùng Thư, 2001.
Presbyterian Church in the USA. *A Record of American Presbyterian Mission Work in Shantung Province, China, 1861-1913.* N.p., n.d.
Rapp, Stephen H., Jr. "Georgian Christianity." In *The Blackwell Companion to Eastern Christianity*, ed. Kenneth Parry, 137-55. Malden, MA: Blackwell, 2010.
Reinink, Gerrit J. "Tradition and the Formation of the 'Nestorian' Identity in Sixth to Seventh Century Iraq." *Church History and Religious Culture* 89 (2009): 217-50.
Robert, Dana. "Changing Perceptions of Missionaries and Cultures." *Journal of Presbyterian History* 81, no. 2 (2003): 110-11.
———, ed. *Converting Colonialism: Visions and Realities in Mission History, 1706-1914.* Grand Rapids: Eerdmans, 2008.

Roxborogh, John. "The Story of Ecumenism." In *Christianity in Malaysia: A Denominational History*, ed. Robert Hunt, Lee Kam Hing, and John Roxborogh, 277-322. Petaling Jaya, Malaysia: Pelanduk, 1992.

Sanneh, Lamin. *Disciples of All Nations: Pillars of World Christianity*. Oxford: Oxford University Press, 2008.

———. *Whose Religion Is Christianity? The Gospel Beyond the West*. Grand Rapids: Eerdmans, 2003.

Scully, Jason. "The Transmission of Evagrian Theological Concepts into East Syrian Christianity: A Comparison of Evagrius and Sahdona on Contemplation and Anthropology." *Greek Orthodox Theological Review* 54 (2009): 77-96.

Shenk, Wilbert R., ed. *Enlarging the Story: Perspectives on Writing World Christian History*. Maryknoll, NY: Orbis Books, 2002.

———. "The Origins and Evolution of the Three-Selfs in Relation to China." *International Bulletin of Missionary Research* 14, no. 1 (January 1990): 28-35.

Soothill, William E. *Timothy Richard of China: Seer, Statesman, Missionary and the Most Disinterested Adviser the Chinese Ever Had*. London: Seeley, Service, 1924.

Speer, Robert E. *Missions and Modern History: A Study of the Missionary Aspects of Some Great Movements of the Nineteenth Century*. 2 vols. New York: Fleming H. Revell, 1904.

Standaert, Nicholas. *Handbook of Christianity in China*. Vol. 1, *35–1800*. Amsterdam: Brill Academic, 2000.

Stanley, Brian. *The World Missionary Conference, Edinburgh 1910*. Grand Rapids: Eerdmans, 2009.

Stanley, John R. "Missionary Education as a Community Effort in Early 20th Century North China." *Asia Pacific Perspectives* 5, no. 1 (December 2004): 27-32.

Sun, Youzhong. "The Trans-Pacific Experience of John Dewey." *The Japanese Journal of American Studies* 18 (2007): 107-35.

Sunquist, Scott W. "American Christian Mission and Education: Henry W. Luce, William R. Harper, and the Secularization of Christian Higher Education." In *Christian Mission and Education in Modern China, Japan and Korea*, 1-14. Frankfurt am Main: Peter Lang, 2009.

———. "Narsai and the Persians: A Study in Cross-cultural Contact and Conflict." PhD diss., Princeton Theological Seminary, 1990.

———. *The Unexpected Christian Century: The Reversal and Transformation of Global Christianity, 1900–2000*. Grand Rapids: Baker Academic, 2015.

Sunquist, Scott W., David Wu Chu Sing, and John Chew Hiang Chea, eds. *A Dictionary of Asian Christianity*. Grand Rapids: Eerdmans, 2001.
Tsou Mingteh. "Christian Missionary as Confucian Intellectual: Gilbert Reid (1857-1927) and the Reform Movement in the Late Qing." In *Christianity in China: From the Eighteenth Century to the Present*, ed. Daniel H. Bays, 73-90. Stanford, CA: Stanford University Press, 1996.
Van Dusen, Henry P. *World Christianity: Yesterday, Today and Tomorrow*. New York: Abingdon-Cokesbury, 1947.
Visser 't Hooft, W. A. *The Genesis and Formation of the World Council of Churches*. Geneva: World Council of Churches, 1982.
Vööbus, Arthur. *History of Asceticism in the Syrian Orient*. 2 vols. Louvain: Secrétariat du CorpusSCO, 1958, 1961.
Walker, Williston. *A History of the Christian Church*. New York: C. Scribner's Sons, 1918.
Walls, Andrew. "The Gospel as Prisoner and Liberator of Culture." In *The Missionary Movement in Christian History: Studies in Transformation of Faith*, 3-15. Maryknoll, NY: Orbis Books, 1996.
Webster, James B. *Christian Education and the National Consciousness in China*. New York: E. P. Dutton, 1923.
Wickeri, Philip. *Seeking the Common Ground: Protestant Christianity, the Three-Self Movement, and China's United Front*. Maryknoll, NY: Orbis, 1988.
Wood, John Halsey, Jr. "John Livingston Nevius and the New Missions History." *Journal of Presbyterian History* 83 (Spring/Summer 2005): 23-40.
World Missionary Conference. *The History and Records of the Conference Together with Addresses Delivered at the Evening Meetings*. Edinburgh and London: Oliphant, Anderson and Ferrier, 1910.
———. *Report of Commission I: Carrying the Gospel to All the Non-Christian World*. Edinburgh and London: Oliphant, Anderson and Ferrier, 1910.
Wu, Silas H. *Dora Yu and the Christian Revival in 20th Century China*. Boston: Pishon River, 2002.
Xi, Lian. *The Conversion of Missionaries: Liberalism in American Protestant Missions in China, 1907-1932*. University Park: The Pennsylvania State University Press, 1997.
———. *Redeemed by Fire: The Rise of Popular Christianity in Modern China*. New Haven, CT: Yale University Press, 2010.
———. "The 'Spiritual Gifts Movement' in War-Torn China." Paper presented to the American Society of Church History, January 2007.

Yao, Kevin Xiyi. *The Fundamentalist Movement Among Protestant Missionaries in China, 1920-1937.* Lanham, MD: University Press of America, 2003.

———. "The North China Theological Seminary: Evangelical Theological Education in China in the Early 1900s." In *Interpreting Contemporary Christianity: Global Processes and Local Identities*, ed. Ogbu U. Kalu, 187-204. Grand Rapids: Eerdmans, 2008.

Yap Kim Hao. "Ecumenical Movement." In *A Dictionary of Asian Christianity*, ed. Scott W. Sunquist et al., 258-65. Grand Rapids: Eerdmans, 2001.

Yates, Timothy. *Christian Mission in the Twentieth Century.* Cambridge: Cambridge University Press, 1994.

Yip, Ka-che. "China and Christianity: Perspectives on Missions, Nationalism, and the State in the Republican Period, 1912-1949." In *Missions, Nationalism, and the End of Empire*, ed. Brian Stanley, 132-43. Grand Rapids: Eerdmans, 2003.

Zürcher, Erik. *Buddhism: Its Origin and Spread in Words, Maps and Pictures.* New York: St. Martin's, 1962.

Author Index

Aland, Kurt, 95, 303
Armstrong, Herbert W., 154
Arnold, David, 183
Barclay, Wade C., 263
Barrett, David, 85, 116, 303
Barth, Karl, 99, 303, 306
Battles, Ford Lewis, 97, 304
Beaver, R. Pierce, 207, 304
Bebbington, David, 3
Becker, Adam, 292, 304
Becker, Caroline N., 249
Bergunder, Michael, 70, 304
Bernard, J. H., 285
Brock, Sebastian, 286, 290, 305
Brockey, Liam Matthew, 104, 304
Bromily, Geoffrey W., 99, 303
Brown, G. Thompson, 54, 188, 304
Bryce, James, 107, 109, 111, 304
Bühlmann, Walbert, 162
Burton, Ernest DeWitt, 275
Charlesworth, James H., 29, 285, 304
Clark, Allen D., 62, 304
Cole, Robert J., 114
Conway, Martin, 113, 305
Corbett, Hunter, 189, 195, 249, 305
Cowman, Lettie, 70
Crawford, Mary, 305
Criveller, Gianni, 186
Cummins, J. S., 187, 305
Dallet, Charles, 169, 305
Davies, Noel, 113, 305
Deleanu, Daniel, 29, 305
Dembski, William A., 121, 305
Dennis, James, 130, 132, 134, 139, 140, 265

Dodgen, Randall A., 181, 305
Drijvers, Han J. W., 29, 30, 282, 303, 305
Dusen, Henry P. Van, 162
Dykstra, Paul Stephen, 195, 305
Eerdman, Charles, 112
Eveleigh, Raymond, 212
Firth, Cyril Bruce, 74
Flett, John G., 99, 306
Garside, Bettis Alston, 267, 268, 272, 273, 274, 306
Gorman, Michael, 96
Gornik, Mark, 154
Griffis, William Ellion, 170, 306
Grubb, Kenneth, 204, 306
Guder, Darrell, 97, 306
Hancile, Jehu, 154
Harper, Keith, 199, 306
Harper, William Rainey, 263, 267, 269
Harris, J. Rendell, 285
Harrison, Brian, 265, 306
Hartch, Todd, 114
Heeren, John J., 64, 195, 306
Hiebert, Paul G., 92, 307
Horsley, Richard A., 95, 307
Hudson, Dennis, 54, 307
Huntley, Martha, 167, 169, 307
Hutchinson, William, 206, 307
Huxley, Thomas, 271
Hyatt, Irwin T., Jr., 191, 272, 307
Iriye, Akira, 266
Irvin, Dale T., 39, 57, 80, 105, 128, 143, 152, 162, 163, 307
Jaki, Stanley L., 136
Jeyaraj, Daniel, 67
Jones, E. Stanley, 81
Kalu, Ogbu, ix, xi, 157, 307, 312
Kärkkäinen, Veli-Matti, 151

Kim, In Soo, 169, 307
Kim, Yong Bok, 257
Koschorke, Klaus, ix, 147, 157, 307
Latourette, Kenneth Scott, 4, 92, 97, 134, 186, 308
Legge, James, 185
Louth, Andrew, 136, 138
Luce, Henry Winters, viii, xii, 191, 263, 266-69, 271-78, 306, 310
Lumsdaine, David H., 72, 78, 308
Lutz, Jessie Gregory, 270, 271
Maheu, Betty Ann, 186
Manchin, Robert, 113
Mandryk, Jason, 69
Marchant, Leslie R., 197, 308
Martel, Yann, 89, 308
Mateer, Robert McCheyne, 190, 272, 308
McGowan, Andrew, 282, 308
McGuckin, John, 135
McLeod, Frederick G., 288, 296, 308
McLoughlin, William, 206
McNeill, John T., 97, 304
Milne, William, 59, 140, 265
Moffett, Samuel Austin, 176, 217, 222, 250, 255, 308
Moffett, Samuel Hugh, 30, 172, 176, 218, 257, 308
Moltmann, Jurgen, 151
Monsen, Marie, 195, 200, 309
Moody, Thomas, 114
Morrison, Charles Clayton, 109, 309
Mott, John R., 42, 107-8, 111, 114, 119-20, 121, 134

Murray, Robert, 32, 309
Newbigin, J. E. Lesslie, 1, 45, 90, 137, 309
Oldham, J. H., 113
O'Neill, Michael, 146
Orr, J. Edwin, 68
Osgood, Cornelius, 168, 170, 309
Padilla, Elaine, 163, 237
Partee, Charles, 259, 309
Phan, Peter C., ix, xii, 137, 163, 237
Rapp, Stephen H., Jr., 31, 309
Richard, Timothy, 191-92, 198, 304, 305, 310
Richter, Julius, 110-11, 115
Robert, Dana L., 159, 309
Rose, Seraphim, 136
Saayman, Willem A., 160
Sanneh, Lamin, xi, 114-15, 310
Seward, Desmond, 228

Shah, Timothy Samuel, 78
Shaw, Yu Ming, 266, 276
Shenk, Wilbert, 94, 162, 310
Siew, Patricia, 82
Sizer, Nancy F., 274
Soothill, William E., 191-92, 310
Speer, Robert E., 112, 134, 217, 310
Spence, Jonathan, 82, 153
Spencer, Herbert, 270, 271
Standaert, Nicholas, 186, 310
Stanley, Brian, 108, 304, 310, 312
Stark, Rodney, 74, 228
Strahan, James, 136
Stromberg, Jean, 119
Stuart, John Leighton, 168, 266, 273, 279
Sunquist, Scott W., i, xi, xiii, 1, 39, 57, 58, 80, 82, 104, 105, 108, 116, 128, 152, 157, 163, 212, 228, 245, 287, 307, 310-12, 315

Tan, Jonathan Y., xii, 143
Taylor, James Hudson, 60-61, 111, 168, 193, 268
Tiedemann, R. Gary, 187
Torrance, T. F., 99, 303
Tran, Anh Q., xii, 143
Trimbur, Dominique, 134
Vööbus, Arthur, 31, 311
Walker, Williston, 94, 311
Walls, Andrew, ix, 90, 92, 94, 96, 147, 160-61, 163, 282, 289, 311
Ward, Kevin, 147
Whitehead, Raymond, 118
Wood, John Halsey, Jr., 205
Xi, Lian, 311
Yates, Timothy, 121, 312
Yong, Amos, xi, 1, 151, 315
Zürcher, Erik, 170, 312

Subject Index

Addai (*The Doctrine of Addai*), 29, 31, 305
Adiabene, 12
Afghanistan, 12, 76-77, 236, 290-91
Alexandria, 33, 136, 235, 296
Allah, 23
Alopen, 14, 40
Anglican, x, 20, 45, 53, 65, 67, 70, 83, 85, 116, 123-24, 208, 211, 214, 296
anthropology, 55, 110, 265, 310
Antioch, 11, 27, 28, 33
Arab, 2, 35, 37-38, 84, 172, 238, 241, 283, 298
Arabia, 13, 23, 76, 236, 240
Aramaic (language), 27, 233
Arbela, 14, 27, 298
Armenia, 2, 12, 14, 31-32, 39
asceticism, 28, 31-32, 33, 37, 290, 301, 311
Athanasius, 136, 138-39
Augustinian, 16
Azariah, Vadanayagam Samuel (bishop of Dornakal), 20, 43, 67, 213
Bangladesh, 20, 23, 25, 48, 84, 86
baptism, 24, 101, 187, 195-96, 214, 290
  unbaptized believers, 24, 149
Bardaisan, 29, 30, 33, 35, 282, 286, 303, 305
Beijing (Peking), 6, 16, 168-69, 191, 253, 273-75
Benedictine, 134
Bhutan, 24, 76
Bible, 3, 5, 18, 23-25, 28, 31, 39, 48, 50-51, 55, 57-59, 61-67, 71-74, 77-78, 82-83, 105, 119, 124, 138, 140, 144, 149, 153, 155, 160, 171-72, 175, 179, 188, 195, 204, 207, 213, 215, 219-20, 223, 225-26, 230, 231, 236, 238, 244, 260, 264, 267-69, 275, 278, 287, 302, 308
borderlands, 7, 227-30, 236
Boxer Rebellion, 77, 185, 255, 267
Buddhism, 21, 39, 69, 79-81, 92, 147, 163, 169-71, 185-86, 284, 312
Burma, v, 19, 21, 25, 49, 59, 62, 79, 80, 86, 137, 229
  See also Myanmar
Cambodia, 20, 21, 25, 49, 76, 84, 85, 117, 229
Carey, William, 18, 41, 56-58, 305
caste, 66
Chang'an. *See* Xian
charismatic, 72, 81, 114-16, 124, 151, 157, 309
China, 6-7, 11-25, 39-40, 41-54, 59-66, 71-86, 117-19, 140-50, 167-71, 179-202, 203-24, 249-55, 256-58, 263-80
China Inland Mission (CIM), 61
Christendom, 1, 53, 111-13, 119, 121, 133, 134, 146, 147, 154, 156, 228, 281, 284, 307
Christology, 28, 44, 143, 296, 297, 299
Church Mission Society (Church Missionary Society), 4, 206, 208
Church of Christ (Thailand, Japan, and USA), 20, 44, 118, 204
Church of North India (CNI), 46
Church of South India (CSI), 20, 45, 83, 158
colonialism/colonization, i, 3, 15, 43, 79, 116, 119, 148, 149, 239, 240, 241, 302, 307, 309
communism, 3, 21, 49, 70, 76, 81, 112, 117, 119, 262, 276
Confucianism, 115, 147, 168-70, 184, 185, 253, 254, 278, 279
conquistador, 17
Constantinople, 13, 14, 17, 27, 207, 297
contextualization (accommodation), 50, 63, 98, 101, 103, 130, 217
Coptic, 63, 123, 144
cosmology, 5, 136, 138
creation, 36, 93, 96, 98, 99, 136-39, 151, 163, 227, 231, 292, 293
cruciformity, 4, 93, 96, 98, 100, 102-4, 106, 130
Cultural Revolution (China), 76, 79, 118, 119
Daoism, 39, 163, 185
decolonization, 45, 76, 228, 262
Dennis, James, 130-35, 139-41, 265
Dominican, 16, 17, 40, 187
ecumenism/ecumenical movement, i, vii, xi, 3, 41, 43, 45, 49, 51, 95, 158, 160, 310
Edessa, 11, 12, 27-30, 34, 35, 292, 298, 305

Edinburgh Missionary
  Conference (1910), 42,
  107-9, 113, 115, 116, 135, 139,
  306, 309-11
education, 60, 192, 198-200,
  215, 219, 223, 229, 230, 245,
  251, 252
Egypt, 35, 157, 232, 235, 281
Enlightenment, 71, 90, 113, 135,
  136, 150, 197, 198
Ephrem (the Syrian), 33-35,
  286, 290, 293, 300, 308
ethics, 5, 104, 113, 143, 146, 147,
  150, 271, 282
Ethiopia, 13, 35, 123, 157, 251,
  260, 262
evangelicalism, xi, 3, 53, 54, 56,
  59, 62, 63, 65, 67, 70, 73, 75,
  78, 81, 83, 85, 86, 123, 308
Franciscan, 15, 16, 40, 187, 188
geography, 6, 11, 180, 190, 197,
  199, 271
Georgia, 31, 32, 39
government, 21-23, 30, 44, 45,
  183, 210, 221, 270, 276, 277
Greek (language), 27, 256, 293
Guandong (Kwantung), 6
Hinduism, 22, 58, 69, 77, 79,
  80, 137, 284
Hong Kong, xii, 6, 179, 206, 306
hymns, 26, 28, 29, 34, 35, 253,
  299, 301, 305, 308
imperialism, 3, 7, 20, 44, 65, 92,
  149, 162, 184, 204, 205, 240
incarnational, 91, 97, 98, 100,
  147, 160, 282
India, 1, 2, 12, 13, 15-17, 19-26,
  28, 32, 33, 36, 37, 41-43,
  45-46, 49, 53-59, 58, 59, 62,
  66-68, 70-72, 74-86, 89, 104,
  110, 120, 147-49, 158, 182-83,
  185, 205, 207, 210, 213, 229,
  232, 264, 283, 284, 290, 296,
  307, 309
indigenous movement, 53, 63,
  65, 67, 116, 148-51, 192, 193,
  195
Indonesia, 20, 21, 23, 25,
  43-46, 49, 69, 78, 84, 85, 148,
  204, 229, 243, 283, 305
International Missionary
  Council (IMC), 46, 115, 117

interreligious dialogue/
  relationship/cooperation,
  24, 54, 192
Iran, 13, 21, 23, 28, 77, 237
Iraq, 13, 25, 28, 237, 291, 306,
  309
Islam, Muslim, 2, 13-15, 17, 20,
  23-25, 36-37, 69, 75, 77-78,
  79-81, 84-85, 92, 101, 114, 147,
  149, 151, 158, 230, 234, 239,
  259, 261, 283, 289
Jacobite, 12
Jesuits. *See* Society of Jesus
Jews, Jewish, 28, 34, 37, 115,
  233-37, 285, 287-89, 293, 302
Kirkuk, 14, 27
Korea, v, xii, xiii, 6, 16, 19,
  21-23, 25, 42, 54, 61-63, 67,
  68, 71-72, 78, 81-82, 84-85,
  115, 149, 155, 167-72, 174, 176,
  203-4, 206, 210-11, 213-18,
  220-22, 241, 250, 255-58, 262,
  304-5, 307, 310
Laos, 20, 24, 25, 49, 76, 77, 86,
  117
Latin (language), 27, 163, 228,
  293
Lausanne Movement, 123
legend, 12, 331
liturgy, 13, 34, 50, 124, 145, 156,
  160, 162, 245, 295, 298, 300,
  301
London Missionary Society
  (LMS), 4, 18, 59, 140
Lutheran, 53, 56, 85, 94, 149,
  154, 195, 230, 296
Malabar, 11, 55, 156
Malaysia, v, 21, 23, 49, 50, 77,
  78, 84-86, 118, 203, 229, 243,
  244, 281, 296, 307, 310
Manichaeism, 35, 37
Mao Tse Tung, 47, 118
Maoist, 91, 274
marginalized, 17, 91, 96-99,
  103, 119
Marxist, 20, 90, 91, 251, 258
mass movements, 19, 22, 65,
  66, 77
Mennonite Central
  Committee (MCC), 4
Mesopotamia, 12, 28, 33, 292,
  304

Methodist, x, 20, 43, 45-46,
  49, 61, 63, 71, 81, 85, 153, 172,
  193, 195, 198, 200, 256, 273,
  296
migration, i, xii, 6, 28, 70, 148,
  154-56, 163, 182-83, 198,
  225-27, 229-45
millet (dhimmi), 2, 13, 23, 38
Mingdao, Wang, 21, 65, 196
missio Dei, xi, 89, 90, 99, 245,
  306
missiology, x-xii, 3, 5-6, 64,
  121, 125, 150, 165, 179, 197,
  212, 241-42, 245, 307, 315
missionary conferences,
  41-42, 107-9, 115, 116, 121, 135,
  175, 306, 309-11
modernism, 65, 222, 273
monasticism, 32, 290
Mongol Empire, 15
Mongolia, 25
Morrison, Robert, xi, xii, 59,
  179, 188, 265
Mott, John R., 42, 107-8, 111,
  114, 119-21, 134
Myanmar (Burma), v, 20-21,
  25, 62, 76, 79, 86, 264
nationalism, 44, 47, 76, 177,
  186, 304, 307, 312
Nepal, 20, 22-23, 25, 63, 84-85,
  123, 229, 308
Nestorian, 14, 40
Nestorius, 35, 296
Nevius, John L., 19, 61, 64, 71,
  174, 188, 206, 209-10, 213-14,
  256, 265
New Testament, 5, 17, 18, 40,
  55, 57-58, 67, 82, 105, 208,
  212, 231, 234, 236, 275
Nisibis, 12, 14, 27, 34-35, 234,
  287, 291-92, 294-95, 298-300,
  304
Nobili, Roberto de, 16
Orthodox (Church), 34, 63,
  123, 135, 159, 230, 260
Osrhoene, 12, 29, 32
Ottoman, 12, 17, 63, 108, 133
Pacific War, 20-21, 41, 43-44,
  46, 204
Pakistan, 13, 19-20, 23, 25-26,
  76-77, 84, 86, 104, 229, 232,
  264, 291

Parthian, 1, 12, 23, 27, 233, 237, 289
Pentecostal, i, 4, 20, 49, 51, 54, 70-73, 78, 83-86, 114-16, 134, 148, 151, 157-58, 193-95, 198, 206, 211-12, 304, 308-9
persecution, 4, 11-12, 14, 16, 21, 23, 28, 32-33, 35-40, 43, 48-49, 54, 56, 75-79, 86, 102, 117, 167, 169, 198, 223, 236-39, 241, 289, 296, 300-301
Persia, Persian Empire, 1-2, 7, 12-15, 27-28, 30-31, 33, 40, 76, 144, 147, 163, 198, 233-34, 236-38, 241, 282-83, 287-97, 300-302
Philippine Independent Church (Iglesia Filipina Independiente), 20
Philippines, 11, 17, 25, 41, 51, 54, 63, 78, 83, 84, 146, 204, 230, 305
Pietism, 53, 55
pilgrim, pilgrimage, 16, 26, 28, 66, 160, 168, 228, 235, 243, 282
pluralism, 1, 302
Plütschau, Henry, 18, 55
pneumatology, 150, 151, 216, 243
poetic, 29, 286, 297, 301
poetry, 35, 56, 295
poor, 19, 32, 62, 65, 66, 72, 76, 77, 85, 86, 95, 97, 133, 156, 157, 172, 174, 175, 187, 188, 190, 198, 208, 216, 260, 261, 289
postcolonial, 2, 90, 95, 244, 258, 315
poverty, 22, 48, 96, 140, 156, 172, 226
powerless, 96, 156, 216, 257
Presbyterian, v, xi, 6, 19, 20, 25, 45, 60, 61, 67, 82, 85, 127, 130, 134, 155, 156, 158, 172-76, 188, 193-96, 198, 199, 200, 206, 209, 210, 211, 214-17, 222, 250, 255, 256, 266, 273, 276, 305-7, 309, 311
Princeton Theological Seminary, xii, 99, 130, 172, 209, 266, 268, 287, 306, 310
Protestant missions, 3-4, 18, 19, 41, 54, 56, 57, 66-68, 73, 167, 206, 240, 307, 311
Qing, 77, 140, 141, 181, 186, 270, 308, 311
racism, 110, 111, 115
reconciliation, 23, 99, 106
Reformed, 20, 43, 45, 53, 56, 94, 149, 151, 153, 155, 172, 268
refugees, 11, 27, 28, 100, 225, 227, 232, 236, 237, 244
renewal, 3, 65, 85, 105, 111, 140, 196
revival, 3, 36, 37, 40, 42, 54, 56, 63, 65, 67-72, 76, 81, 116, 193, 195-97, 200, 274, 289, 305, 309, 311
Rhodes, Alexandre de, 16, 137
Ricci, Matteo, 16, 103, 168, 192, 200
Roman Catholic, 3, 18, 19, 26, 34, 46-48, 50, 53-56, 59, 63, 66, 67, 74, 80, 84, 94, 105, 119, 123, 143, 146, 154, 156, 159, 162, 169, 170, 186, 187, 240, 315
Rome, Roman Empire, 1, 12, 27, 28, 31, 33-35, 39, 91, 132, 136, 198, 228, 237, 238, 241, 281, 295, 296
royalty, 2, 11, 16, 29, 30, 33, 38, 40, 90, 167, 169, 170, 173, 291
Sabah, v, xii, 11, 230, 243, 281
Sasanian, 2, 12, 35, 36, 37, 172, 233, 237, 238, 283, 289
Saudi Arabia, 23, 76
Scandinavia, 12, 27
Scripture, i, 5, 33, 51, 57, 62, 63, 81, 82, 105, 121, 134, 148, 161, 176, 185, 191, 194, 220, 237, 266, 287, 292, 295, 300
secularization, xii, 7, 81, 117, 263, 265, 270, 310
Selucia-Ctesiphon, 11, 35, 289
Semitic, 12, 28, 285, 286, 293, 302
Seoul, v, xi, 11, 16, 22, 24, 168, 171, 173, 175, 176, 211, 250, 304
Shandong, 61, 68, 71, 72, 179-90, 192-200, 206, 265
Shanghai, 6, 41, 42, 60, 65, 91, 179, 188, 192, 194, 198, 250, 305
Shintoism, 19
Silk Road, 14, 27, 37, 39, 227
Singapore, 18, 81, 84, 85, 146, 204, 206, 227, 229, 230, 243, 296, 303, 307, 308
social evolution/progress, 115, 130, 131, 133, 134, 156, 205, 223, 265, 266, 278
Society for the Promotion of Christian Knowledge (SPCK), 56
Society for the Propagation of the Gospel in Foreign Parts (SPG), 211
Society of Jesus (Jesuits), 16, 18, 95, 104, 173, 186, 187, 210, 305
Sri Lanka, 16, 26, 45, 48, 56, 72, 84, 185, 229, 296, 299
Student Volunteer Movement (SVM), 47, 108, 109, 114, 210, 266, 267, 304
suffering, 65, 75-77, 86, 93, 96, 102, 106, 119, 120-22, 124, 125, 216, 257, 259, 260, 261, 284
Sung, John, 20, 65, 193, 196, 217
sutra, 14, 39
syncretism, 39, 81, 187
Syria, 1, 12, 13, 28, 130, 207, 237, 281, 292
Syriac (language), 12, 13, 18, 27, 28, 29, 31-34, 290, 291, 292, 293, 304
Taiping Rebellion, 82, 140, 153, 183
Taiwan, 23, 26, 81, 84, 85, 118
Tajikistan, 25, 290
Tang, 14, 38, 39, 181
Thailand, 16, 20, 21, 23, 25, 62, 76, 80, 81, 118, 204, 229
Thomas (apostle), 12, 26, 32, 33
three-self principle, 6, 189, 205, 206, 208, 209, 213, 217, 219, 221, 222
Timur (Tamerlane), 15
trade, 12, 13, 16-18, 23, 28, 32, 38, 60, 62, 75, 148, 170, 183, 186, 211, 230, 237, 239, 285, 287
trading company, 18, 27
Tranquebar, 45, 54, 55, 56, 59
transformation, 67, 98, 106, 113, 158, 197, 207, 221, 223,

239, 265, 271, 277, 302, 310
translation, 17, 18, 31, 33, 39, 41, 50, 55-59, 85, 97, 103, 105, 148, 185, 190, 207, 221, 226-29, 264, 293, 301
Trinity, trinitarian, 29, 31, 34, 35, 91, 102, 106, 150, 229, 306
Turkey, 23, 25, 291
Turkmenistan, 25, 290, 291
Underwood, Horace, 61, 211, 214
Union Theological Seminary, v, xii, 4, 64, 162, 266-68

Vietnam, 16, 20, 21, 23, 25, 49, 50, 76, 77, 80, 83-86, 117, 119, 137, 225, 229, 273, 283
vitality, 25, 26, 37, 112, 115, 196, 227, 229, 266
World Council of Churches (WCC), 46, 49, 115, 118, 123, 160
World Missionary Conference 1910. *See* Edinburgh Missionary Conference (1910)
Xavier, Francis, 16

Xiamen, 11, 60
Xian, 3, 12, 14, 27, 38, 40, 185, 234, 291
Yemen, 13, 23
YMCA, 41, 42, 67, 80, 117, 220
Ziegenbalg, Bartholomew, 18, 55, 56
Zoroastrianism, 1, 2, 12, 13, 15, 27, 36, 147, 237, 238, 241, 281, 283, 285, 287, 289, 293, 294, 298, 301, 302

MISSIOLOGICAL ENGAGEMENTS

Series Editors: Scott W. Sunquist,
Amos Yong, and John R. Franke

Missiological Engagements: Church, Theology, and Culture in Global Contexts charts interdisciplinary and innovative trajectories in the history, theology, and practice of Christian mission at the beginning of the third millennium.

Among its guiding questions are the following: What are the major opportunities and challenges for Christian mission in the twenty-first century? How does the missionary impulse of the gospel reframe theology and hermeneutics within a global and intercultural context? What kind of missiological thinking ought to be retrieved and reappropriated for a dynamic global Christianity? What innovations in the theology and practice of mission are needed for a renewed and revitalized Christian witness in a postmodern, postcolonial, postsecular, and post-Christian world?

Books in the series, both monographs and edited collections, will feature contributions by leading thinkers representing evangelical, Protestant, Roman Catholic, and Orthodox traditions, who work within or across the range of biblical, historical, theological, and social-scientific disciplines. Authors and editors will include the full spectrum from younger and emerging researchers to established and renowned scholars, from the Euro-American West and the Majority World, whose missiological scholarship will bridge church, academy, and society.

Missiological Engagements reflects cutting-edge trends, research, and innovations in the field that will be of relevance to theorists and practitioners in churches, academic domains, mission organizations, and NGOs, among other arenas.

Finding the Textbook You Need

The IVP Academic Textbook Selector
is an online tool for instantly finding the IVP books
suitable for over 250 courses across 24 disciplines.

ivpress.com/academic

www.ingramcontent.com/pod-product-compliance
Lightning Source LLC
Chambersburg PA
CBHW050857300426
44111CB00010B/1280